AMERICAN GOVERNMENT

Brief Version

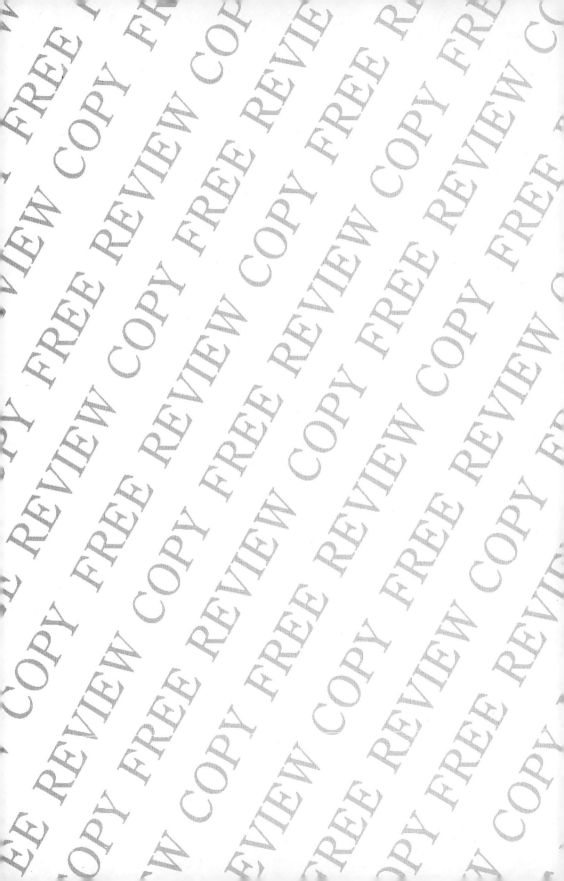

AMERICAN GOVERNMENT

BRIEF VERSION

Third Edition

James Q. Wilson
University of California,
Los Angeles

D. C. Heath and Company
Lexington, Massachusetts   Toronto

Address editorial correspondence to
D. C. Heath and Company
125 Spring Street
Lexington, MA 02173

Acquisitions Editor: Paul A. Smith
Production Editor: Karen Wise
Designer: Judith Miller
Photo Researcher: Martha Shethar
Art Editor: Gary Crespo
Production Coordinator: Charles Dutton
Permissions Editor: Margaret Roll

Published simultaneously in Canada.

Printed in the United States of America.

International Standard Book Number: 0-669-32677-1

Library of Congress Catalog Number: 93-71113

10 9 8 7 6 5 4 3 2 1

To Diane

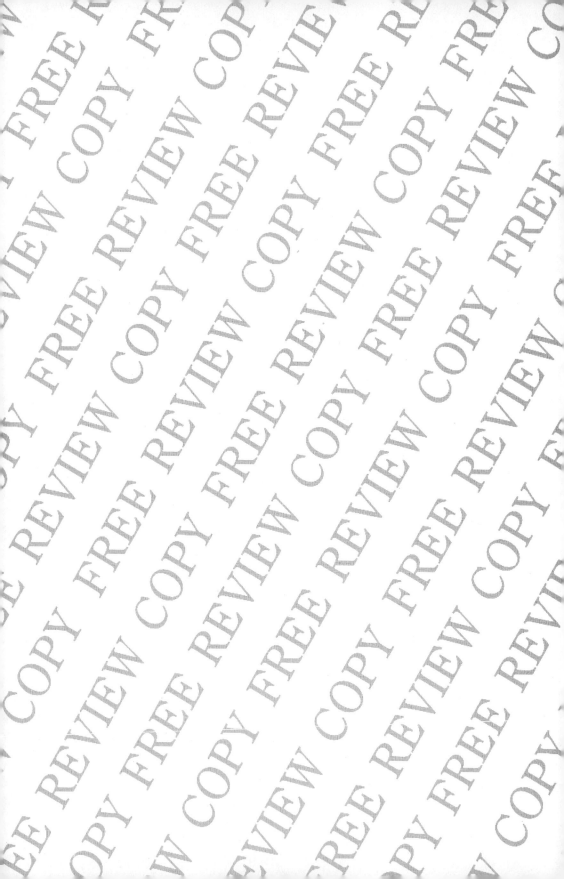

Preface

★ ★ ★

THE THIRD EDITION of *American Government,* Brief Version, was written to make it even more useful to the growing number of teachers and students who find a brief text the most convenient way to acquire an introduction to American government and politics. Based on their views, it was apparent that the single most desired change was to add a fuller discussion of the politics of public policy. In response, I have added such a chapter.

Obviously, no author can say very much about policy-making in one chapter of one short text. After much thought, I decided that the best way to introduce this subject was to put myself in the shoes of the student and ask what he or she is likely to believe about policy-making in Washington. (This was an especially interesting exercise at a time when Ross Perot was attracting 19 million voters by criticizing how Washington works!) Chapter 12 begins with a summary of what I have heard my students say about national politics in the introductory class that I teach at UCLA.

In this chapter, as in my own class, I try to put these complaints into perspective in two ways: First, I show how many of them flow, not from the personal failings of particular politicians, but from the fundamental features of our constitutional system. Since most students are disposed to like the idea of federalism, freedom of association, the separation of powers, and judicial review, they are somewhat taken aback to discover that what they most like about our system is directly implicated in what they most dislike. Second, I discuss how these features of our system affect policy-making in different policy arenas, arenas defined by the kind of issue. Within each arena, certain distinctive political coalitions tend to form. Here I borrow the typology from the hard-cover version of this text: client politics, entrepreneurial politics, interest-group politics, and majoritarian politics. To keep matters simple, I don't spend much time on the theoretical derivation of these concepts, but I describe them well enough, I hope, that the student can see how they help explain current policy controversies.

Another concern expressed by readers was to have the chapter on civil liberties and civil rights follow, rather than precede, the chapter on the judiciary so that the reader can study constitutional issues after he or she knows how the courts work. This has been done; what was once Chapter 4 is now Chapter 11. That chapter has not only been moved, it has been heavily revised. It now contains a discussion of the flag-burning cases, the use of Christmas or Chanukah displays near public buildings, the legal status of drug testing, and the most recent decisions on affirmative-action programs. There is a lengthy discussion of the evolution of abortion decisions since *Roe* v. *Wade,* ending with a box that summarizes the key elements of the landmark *Casey* decision. Another box lists the key provisions of the major civil rights laws from 1957 through 1991.

Throughout the text, there has been a complete updating. It is current through the 1992 election, depicts the allocation of electoral votes based on the 1990 census, describes the problems and ultimate defeat of the Bush administration, highlights the chronic problem of the budget deficit, refers to the fight over the confirmation of Clarence Thomas as a Supreme Court justice, portrays the changing ideological composition of the Court and the emerging voting blocs, and takes into account the breakup of the former Soviet Union.

The discussion of Congress has been deepened by explaining its individualistic focus and summarizing the debate over term limitations and congressional ethics. The chapter on public opinion now provides a fuller discussion of the various meanings of "liberal" and "conservative."

To make this a more useful book, a number of supplementary materials have been added. A glossary of key words and phrases is now included and a Study Guide has been produced, making this the only brief text with such an aid available to the students. To make it a more attractive one, the book has been redesigned, set in new type, and supplied with new photos and artwork.

In preparing this revision, I have had invaluable aid from a number of professors who commented on the previous edition. These include: Henry Carey, John Hay College; Robert R. Detlefsen, California State University — San Bernardino; Lars Hoffman, Lewis and Clark Community College; John Kearnes, Armstrong State College; Thomas Keating, Arizona State University; Kent Kirwan, University of Nebraska at Omaha; John McGowan, Villanova University; Dennis McNutt, Southern California College; Gregory S. Powell, Kilgore College; and Richard H. Reeb, Jr., Barstow College. In addition, I would like to thank reviewers who contributed to past editions of the text: Peter Bergerson, Southeast Missouri State University; John DiIulio, Princeton University; Larry Elowitz, Georgia College; William Eubank, University of Nevada at Reno; Leon Hurwitz, Cleveland State University; Willoughby Jarrell, Kennesaw College; and Sandra Thornton, Georgia Institute of Technology.

Supplements

The supplement package for this edition has been revised and expanded to provide as much help as possible to instructors and students.

The *Instructor's Guide with Test Questions* includes Chapter Outlines with new, additional information that may help in the preparation of lectures; Important Terms with definitions; new sections for each chapter on important themes, data for analysis and discussion, lists of resources (films, videos, and software); and a full bank of test questions. These test items are also available in computerized format for both Macintosh and DOS systems.

New to this edition, a *Study Guide* is now available for students who wish to drill themselves on the text's content in preparation for examinations. The Guide contains quizzes, essay questions, outlines, and conceptual applications for each chapter.

For instructors who wish to include in their course a unit on state and local politics, a chapter-length *State and Local Government* supplement is available for students at a nominal extra cost.

Last, a variety of films, videos, and software programs to help enliven classes are available free to adopters. Instructors should contact their local D. C. Heath sales representative for further information about these materials.

J. Q. W.

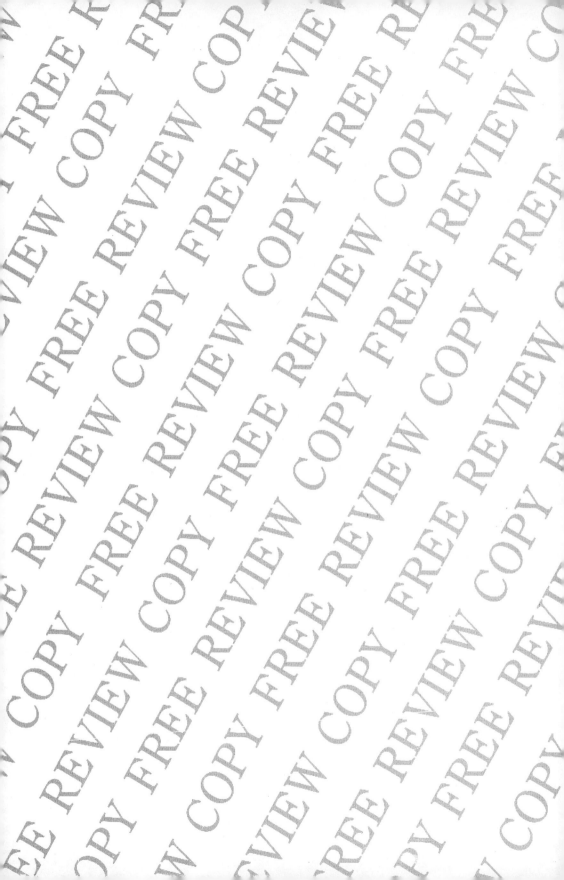

Contents

★ ★ ★

1

★ ★ ★

What Should We Know About American Government?

MOST AMERICANS THINK they know how their government works, and many don't like it. A common view goes like this:

The president gets elected because of some slick television ads, although he has ducked all the tough questions. His party's platform is a meaningless set of words that gives you no idea what he will do in office. Once in the White House, he proposes bills and then Congress decides which to pass. Congress and the president do this, not to solve problems, but to reward whichever interest groups have spent the most money getting them elected. The laws they enact are turned over to an all-powerful bureaucracy that administers them much as the bureaucrats see fit, adding a lot of needless red tape. If you don't like these laws, you can sue, but the courts will base their decisions on their own liberal or conservative preferences and not on any standards of justice or fair play. All of these people—presidents, members of Congress, bureaucrats, and judges—act without any real respect for the Constitution. No wonder our national problems don't get solved.

Almost every sentence in the paragraph above is either flatly wrong, greatly exaggerated, or seriously incomplete. If you want to find out why, read this book. By the time you are finished, you may still think our system has faults, but you will have a clearer idea of what they are and how they arose.

These criticisms contain enough truth, however, to alert us to another reason for taking a course on American government. How our government operates is quite different from how other democratic governments, such as those in Western Europe, operate. We know that the president and Congress are often at loggerheads, that neither can exercise complete control over the bureaucracy, that judges often intervene to tell government agencies what to do, and that our politicians always seem to be involved in some scandal. We are also aware that other levels of government—cities and states—seem to compete with the federal government for the right to make certain decisions.

To most Europeans, all this would be absolutely baffling. In a country such as Great Britain, the legislature automatically approves almost any policy the chief executive (the prime minister) proposes, and does so without making any changes. The bureaucracy carries out the policy without resistance, but if something should go wrong, the legislature does not investigate the agency to see what went wrong. No citizen can sue the government; if one tried, the judge would throw the case out of court. There are no governors who have to be induced to follow the national policy; the national government's policies are, for most purposes, the *only* policies. If those policies prove unpopular, there is a good chance that many members of the legislature will not be reelected.

American government is not like any other democratic government in the world. Far from taking it for granted, students here should imagine for a moment that they are not young Americans but young Swedes, Italians, or Britons and ask themselves why American politics is so different and how that difference affects the policies produced here.

Consider these differences in **politics:**

★ In the United States, the police and the public schools are controlled by towns, cities, and states. In Europe, they are usually controlled by the national government.

★ If you want to run for office in the United States, you can do so by collecting the required number of signatures on a petition to get on the ballot in a primary election; if you win the primary, you then run in the general election. In Europe, there usually aren't any primary elections; instead, party leaders decide who gets on the ballot.

★ In the United States, fewer than one worker in five belongs to a labor union. In many European nations, the majority of workers belong to unions.

SOME KEY POLITICAL CONCEPTS

★ ★ ★

GOVERNMENT

Government consists of those institutions that have the authority to make decisions binding on the whole society.

Note—Many institutions, such as colleges, corporations, and private clubs, exercise power over us. A government differs from these in two ways:

1. *Authority:* People believe that the government has the right to exercise power over all subordinate parts of society; a government can lawfully issue orders to a corporation or college, but a college or a corporation cannot lawfully issue orders to the government.

2. *Power.* A government has a monopoly over the use of legitimate force. Governments, not private organizations, control the army, the police, and the prisons.

POLITICS

Politics is the activity by which conflict is carried on over who will run the government and what decisions it will make.

Note—Politics exists wherever there is disagreement about who should hold office or what decisions he or she should make. Thus, it is no more possible to "take politics out of government" than it is to take emotion out of marriage.

★ The United States has no large socialist, communist, or Marxist political party. In France, Great Britain, Italy, and elsewhere, socialist and Marxist parties are large and powerful.

★ The United States has many politically active persons who consider themselves born-again Christians. Such persons are relatively rare in Europe and certainly not a political force there.

★ In the United States, judges decide whether abortions shall be legal, which pornographic movies can be shown, and what shall be the size of a congressional district. In Europe, the legislature decides such things.

★ When the prime minister of Great Britain signs a treaty, his nation is bound by it; when the president signs a treaty, he is making a promise only to try to get the Senate to ratify it.

Consider also these differences in **policies:**

★ The tax burden in the United States is about half what it is in Sweden and many other European nations.

The United States Capitol.

★ The United States adopted federal policies to provide benefits to the elderly and the unemployed about a quarter of a century *after* such policies were already in effect in much of Europe.

★ The United States government owns very few industries. In much of Europe, the government owns the airlines, the telephone system, the steel mills, the automobile factories, and even the oil companies. ●

★ Throughout much of the 1980s, Presidents Reagan and Bush and the Congress could not agree on a budget—on how much to spend, where to make cuts, and whether taxes should be increased; as a result, on many occasions the country had neither a budget nor the authority it needed to borrow money to keep paying its bills. In European democracies, this kind of deadlock almost never occurs.

How do we explain these differences? It is not that America is "democratic" and other nations are "undemocratic." Great Britain and the United States are both democracies—but two different *kinds* of democracies. The American kind is the product of two closely related factors: our constitutional system and the opinions and values of the people. We have the kind of constitution we do because the people who wrote it had certain beliefs about how government should be organized, and those beliefs are perpetuated and sharpened by the workings of the government created by that constitution.

In this book, we will not try to explain all the ways in which America differs from Europe. This book is not about comparative politics; it is about American politics. But keeping in mind the distinctive features of our system will, I hope, make the following chapters more interesting. You might try the following experiment. As you read this book, see how many of the differences listed above you can explain. You won't be able to explain them all, but you will be able to explain several.

THE MEANINGS OF DEMOCRACY

To explain why American democracy differs from democracy in Britain or Sweden, we must first understand what is meant by **democracy.** That word is used to describe three different political systems. In one system, found in the former Soviet Union and its satellites and in China, Cuba, and many Third World dictatorships, a government is said to be "democratic" if its decisions serve the "true interests of the people," whether or not those people had any say in making the decisions. This is called **democratic centralism.**

The term democracy is used in a second way to describe political systems in which all or most citizens participate directly in making governmental decisions. The New England town meeting, for example, comes close to fitting this definition of **direct democracy.** Once or twice a year all the adult citizens of a town come together to vote on all major issues and expenditures. In many states, such as California, a kind of direct democracy exists whenever voters are asked to approve or reject a specific policy, such as a plan to cut taxes or build a water system (a **referendum**), remove an elected official before his or her term has expired (a **recall**), or propose a new piece of legislation or a constitutional amendment (an **initiative**).

The third meaning of democracy was most concisely stated in 1942 by the economist Joseph Schumpeter: "The democratic method is that institutional arrangement for arriving at political decisions in which individuals [that is, officeholders] acquire the power to decide by means of a competitive struggle for the people's vote." This system is usually called a **representative democracy.** The Framers of the American constitution called it a **republic.**

The following arguments are made in favor of representative democracy over direct democracy. First, direct democracy is impractical because it is impossible for all the citizens to decide all the issues; they don't have the time, energy, interest, or information. It is practical, however, to expect them to choose among competing leadership groups. Second, direct democracy is undesirable because the people will often make bad decisions on the basis of fleeting desires or under the influence of unscrupulous demagogues or clever advertising. Third, direct democracy makes it difficult to negotiate compromises among contending groups; instead, one side wins and the other loses—

even when there may have been a middle ground that both sides would have accepted.

You may think that these criticisms of direct democracy are unfair. If so, ask yourself which of the following measures (especially those that you feel strongly about) you would be willing to have decided by all citizens voting in a referendum. Abortion? Gun control? Federal aid to parochial schools? The death penalty? Foreign aid? Racial integration of the public schools? The defense budget? Free trade? Most people, however "democratic" they may be, favor certain policies that they would not want decided by, in effect, a public opinion poll.

REPRESENTATIVE DEMOCRACY

In this book, we will use the word *democracy* to mean representative democracy, but we will not try to settle the argument over whether, or under what circumstances, direct democracy might be better. It is important to note, however, that representative democracy can only exist if certain conditions exist: freedom of speech and of the press (so that voters can learn about what their representatives are doing and communicate their preferences to them), freedom to organize (so that people can come forward as candidates for office), reasonably fair access to political resources (so that candidates can mount an effective campaign), a decent respect for the rights and opinions of others (so that the winners in an election are allowed to assume office and govern and the losers are not punished or banished), and a belief that the political system is legitimate (so that people will obey its laws without being coerced).

Broadly speaking, representative democracy can take one of two forms: the parliamentary system or the presidential system. The **parliamentary system,** common to almost all European democracies, vests political power in an elected legislature. The legislature, in turn, chooses the chief executive, called the prime minister. So long as the prime minister has the support of a majority of the members of parliament, he or she can carry out any policy that is not forbidden by the nation's constitution. (Some parliamentary democracies do not have a written constitution. In Great Britain, for example, the parliament can do almost anything that it believes the voters will accept.) In a parliamentary democracy, political power at the national level is centralized; the prime minister and his or her cabinet make all the important decisions. The bureaucracy works for the prime minister. The courts ordinarily do not interfere. The theory of a parliamentary system is that the government should make decisions and then be held accountable to the voters at the next election.

A **presidential system** vests political power in separately elected branches of the national government—a president and a congress. In addition, there may be an independent judiciary, as there is in the United States,

The chief executives of two different kinds of democracies: Bill Clinton heads a presidential system, John Major a parliamentary one.

that can disapprove of the actions of the president and Congress if they violate the Constitution. The president proposes legislation but has no guarantee that Congress will accept it, even if the president's party has a majority of members in Congress. The bureaucracy works for both the president and Congress; since its loyalties are divided, its actions are not always consistent with what the president or Congress wishes. Political power at the national level is decentralized and shared. The theory of a presidential system is that policies should be tested for their political acceptability at every stage of the policy-making process, and not just at election time.

Some people believe that the presidential system, based on separate branches of government sharing power, makes it very hard to enact any policies at all. So many roadblocks are built into the system that the government is biased against taking action. Moreover, when government does act, so many people are involved in making the decision that it becomes difficult for the voters to hold anyone directly accountable for the result. If you don't like the federal deficit, whom can you blame and vote against in the next election? The president? Your senator? Your representative?

To correct these features of the system, some critics have proposed that the United States change its constitution and make it more like a parliamentary democracy so that it will be easier for the government to act and easier for the voters to hold officials accountable for their actions at election time. But defenders of our constitution take a different view of the matter. The roadblocks in our constitutional system have not prevented our national government from growing about as fast, and adopting many of the same policies, as parliamentary democracies in Europe. And if the American government is not as big (measured by the taxes it levies, the money it spends, and the programs it enacts) as the governments of some European nations, maybe that is a good thing. Moreover, Americans may not be content with voting only once every four years to approve of or reject what the government is doing; they may want a chance to influence policy as it is being formulated—by writing their senator or representative, joining interest groups, marching on Washington, and bringing suit in court.

This book will not tell you whether to prefer an American-style presidential system or yearn for a British-style parliamentary one. But it will tell you how our system works and explain why it works as it does. The primary reason it functions the way it does is the Constitution of the United States, which is where we shall start.

SUGGESTED READINGS

Dionne, E. J. *Why Americans Hate Politics.* New York: Simon & Schuster, 1991. A thoughtful liberal critique of American politics since the 1960s.

King, Anthony. *The New American Political System.* Washington, D.C.: American Enterprise Institute. First edition, 1978; second edition, 1990. Two books, edited by a British scholar, that give an intelligent overview of how American national government works today.

O'Rourke, P. J. *Parliament of Whores: A Lone Humorist Attempts to Explain the Entire U.S. Government.* Boston: Atlantic Monthly Press, 1991. O'Rourke, a conservative version of Monty Python, offers a funny, outrageous, and sometimes insightful account of American politics. Caution: read only in short doses lest you hurt yourself laughing.

Schumpeter, Joseph A. *Capitalism, Socialism, and Democracy.* 3d ed. New York: Harper, 1950, Chs. 20–23. A lucid statement of the theory of representative democracy.

2

★ ★ ★

The Constitution

THE PROBLEM OF LIBERTY

FOR TWO HUNDRED YEARS the American government has derived its powers from a written constitution. Today we take that document for granted. Two centuries ago, however, the very idea of a written constitution, to say nothing of its particular contents, was a matter of great controversy.

When America was part of the British empire, Britain had no written constitution (it still doesn't). The American revolt against British rule, culminating in 1775 in the War of Independence, led many colonists to conclude that political power should never again be entrusted to rulers whose authority was based on tradition and other unwritten understandings. The central idea behind a written constitution was to limit and define political authority.

After they became independent, each of the thirteen former colonies adopted a written constitution that sharply restricted the authority of the newly chosen state governors and state legislators. But the colonies had to have some way of acting together on matters of mutual interest, such as waging the war against Britain. For this purpose, they came together in a loose alliance under the Articles of Confederation.

Many people recognized that the Confederation was too weak to manage the war effort effectively but believed that a national government that was any stronger would threaten their hard-won liberties.

When the Revolutionary War was over, many leaders decided that an even stronger national government was essential for the new nation to defend itself against foreign enemies, put down domestic insurrections, and encourage commercial activity. From May to September of 1787, fifty-five delegates from the states met in Philadelphia initially to revise the Articles of Confederation but in the end, as matters turned out, to produce an entirely new constitution. Most of the delegates had served in Congress under the Articles; few, if any, had found that experience satisfying. The chief problem faced by the Framers, as they came to be called, was that of liberty: how to devise a government strong enough to preserve order but not so strong that it would threaten liberty. In one of his most famous essays in defense of the Constitution, James Madison explained their delicate task:

> In framing a government which is to be administered by men over men, the great difficulty lies in this: you must first enable the government to control the governed; and in the next place oblige it to control itself.[1]

History has taught us, Madison and the other Framers believed, that people will seek power because they are by nature ambitious, greedy, and easily corrupted. As Madison wrote:

> But what is government itself but the greatest of all reflections on human nature? If men were angels, no government would be necessary. If angels were to govern men, neither external nor internal controls on government would be necessary.[2]

If we are to understand the institutions and policies of American government, we must first understand the historical experiences and philosophical ideas that gave birth to the Constitution on which that government rests.

THE WEAKNESSES OF THE CONFEDERATION

Turmoil, uncertainty, and fear permeated the eleven years between the Declaration of Independence in 1776 and the signing of the Constitution in 1787. General George Washington had to wage a bitter, protracted war against a world power with only the support the state governments chose to give. When peace finally came, many parts of the nation were a shambles. The British were still a powerful force in North America, with an army available in Canada (where many Americans loyal to Britain had fled) and a large navy at sea. Spain claimed the Mississippi River Valley and occupied Florida. Soldiers returning to their farms found themselves heavily in debt but with no money to pay their debts or their taxes. The paper money printed to finance the war was now virtually worthless.

The thirteen states had only a faint semblance of a national government with which to bring order and stability to the nation. The Articles of Confederation, which had gone into effect in 1781, created little more than a "league of friendship" that lacked the power to levy taxes or regulate commerce. Each state retained its sovereignty and independence; each state (regardless of size) had one vote in Congress; nine (of thirteen) votes were required to pass any measure; and the delegates who cast these votes were picked and paid by the state legislatures. Several states claimed the unsettled lands in the West and occasionally pressed those claims with guns, but there was no national judicial system to settle these or other disputes among the states. To amend the Articles of Confederation, all thirteen states had to agree.

Many leaders of the Revolution, such as George Washington and Alexander Hamilton, believed that a stronger national government was essential. A small group, conferring at Washington's home at Mount Vernon in 1785, decided to call a meeting to discuss trade regulation, one of the many seemingly insoluble problems facing Congress. That meeting, held at Annapolis, Maryland, in September 1786, was not well attended, and so another meeting was called for May 1787 in Philadelphia—this time for the more general purpose of considering ways to remedy the defects of the Confederation.

THE CONSTITUTIONAL CONVENTION

The delegates assembled in Philadelphia for what was advertised (and authorized by Congress) as a meeting to revise the Articles; they adjourned four months later having written a wholly new constitution. When they met, they were keenly aware of the problems of the confederacy but far from agreement on remedies. As in 1776, their objectives were still the protection of life, liberty, and property, but they had no accepted political theory that would tell them what kind of national government, if any, would serve that goal.

The Lessons of Experience

James Madison, who was to be one of the leading framers of the new constitution, spent a good part of 1786 studying books sent to him by Thomas Jefferson, then in Paris, in hopes of finding some model for a workable American republic—but concluded that no model existed. History showed that confederacies were too weak to govern and tended to collapse from internal dissension, whereas all stronger forms of government were so powerful

James Madison, often described as the "Father of the Constitution," prepared the Virginia Plan that formed the basis for the deliberations at the 1787 convention.

as to trample the liberties of the citizens. At home, the state governments of Pennsylvania and Massachusetts vividly illustrated the dangers of excessively weak and excessively strong governments.

The Pennsylvania constitution, adopted in 1776, created the most radically democratic of the new state regimes. All power was given to a one-house (or **unicameral**) legislature, the members of which were elected for one-year terms. No legislator could serve for more than four years. There was no real executive. The radical pamphleteer Thomas Paine and various French philosophers hailed the Pennsylvania constitution as the very embodiment of the principle of rule by the people, but it was a good deal less popular in Philadelphia. The legislature disfranchised the Quakers, persecuted conscientious objectors to the war, ignored the requirement of trial by juries, and manipulated the judiciary.[3] To Madison and his friends, the Pennsylvania constitution demonstrated how a government, though democratic, could be tyrannical by concentrating all powers in one set of hands, in this case the legislature.

The Massachusetts constitution of 1780, in contrast, was a good deal less democratic. There was a clear separation of powers among the branches of government, the directly elected governor could veto acts of the legislature, and judges served for life. But if the government of Pennsylvania was thought too strong, that of Massachusetts seemed too weak, despite its "conservative" features. In 1787 a group of ex-Revolutionary War soldiers and officers led by one Daniel Shays, plagued by debt and high taxes, forcibly prevented the courts in western Massachusetts from sitting. The governor of Massachusetts asked the Congress of the Confederation to send troops, but it could not raise the money or the manpower; the governor then discovered that he had no state militia. In desperation, private funds were collected to hire a volunteer army that, with the firing of a few shots, dispersed the rebels.

Shays's Rebellion, occurring between the aborted Annapolis convention and the upcoming Philadelphia convention, had a powerful effect on public opinion. Far away in Paris, Thomas Jefferson took a detached view: "A little rebellion now and then is a good thing," he wrote. "The tree of liberty must be refreshed from time to time with the blood of patriots and tyrants."[4] But many other leaders were aghast at the rebellion. Delegates who might otherwise have been reluctant to attend the Philadelphia meeting were galvanized by the fear that state governments were about to collapse from internal dissension. George Washington wrote to a friend despairingly: "For God's sake . . . , if they [the rebels] have *real* grievances, redress them; if they have not, employ the force of government against them at once."[5]

The Framers

The Philadelphia convention attracted fifty-five delegates, only about thirty of whom participated regularly in the proceedings. Pledged to keep their deliberations secret, the delegates had to keep an eye on the talkative, party-loving Benjamin Franklin. The delegates were not bookish intellectuals, but men of practical affairs. Most were young but experienced in politics: eight had signed the Declaration of Independence, seven had been governors, thirty-four were lawyers; a few were wealthy. Thirty-nine had served in the ineffectual Congress of the Confederation; a third were veterans of the Continental army.

The convention produced not a revision of the Articles of Confederation, as it had been authorized to do, but instead a wholly new written constitution creating a true national government unlike any that had existed before. That document is today the world's oldest written national constitution. The deliberations that produced it were not always lofty or philosophical; much hard bargaining, not a little confusion, and the accidents of time and personality helped shape the final product. But though the leading political philosophers were only rarely mentioned, the debate was profoundly influenced by philosophical beliefs, some of which were formed by the revolutionary experience and others by the eleven-year attempt at self-government.

From the debates leading up to the Revolution, the delegates had drawn a commitment to liberty, which, despite the abuses sometimes committed in its name, they continued to share. Following the seventeenth-century English philosopher John Locke, they believed that liberty was a natural right and that men created government in order to prevent the strong from oppressing the weak. And since government itself must not deprive men of their liberty, government must be limited. The chief limitation on government, Locke had said, should derive from the fact that it is created by the consent of the governed, and it governs through institutions wielding separate powers.

THE CHALLENGE

American experience since 1776, as well as the history of British government, led the Framers to doubt whether popular consent alone would be a sufficient guarantor of liberty. A popular government may prove too weak to prevent one faction from abusing another (as in Massachusetts), or a popular majority can be tyrannical (as in Pennsylvania). In fact, the tyranny of the majority can be an even greater threat than rule by the few: facing the will of the majority, the lone person cannot count on the succor of popular opinion or the possibility of popular revolt. The problem, then, was a delicate one: how to frame a government strong enough to rule effectively but not too strong to overrun the liberties of its citizens. The answer, the delegates believed, was not "democracy," as it was then understood—that is, mob rule, such as Shays's Rebellion. Aristocracy—the rule of the few—was no solution either, since the few were as likely to be corrupted by power as the many. Nor could liberty be assured, Madison believed, by simply writing a constitution that limited what government could do.

Immediately after the convention had organized itself and chosen Washington as its presiding officer, the Virginia delegation presented a comprehensive plan, largely drafted by Madison, for a wholly new national government. The plan quickly became the major item of the convention's business.

Large States Versus Small States

By agreeing to consider the **Virginia Plan,** the convention fundamentally altered its task from amending the Articles to designing a true national government. The Virginia Plan called for a strong national union organized into three governmental branches—legislative, executive, and judicial. It had two key features: (1) a national legislature would have supreme powers on all matters on which the separate states were not competent to act, as well as the power to veto any and all state laws, and (2) the people would directly elect at least one house of the legislature.

As the debate went on, the representatives of New Jersey and other small states became increasingly worried that the convention was going to write a constitution in which the states would be represented in both houses of Congress on the basis of population. If this happened, the smaller states feared they would always be outvoted by the larger states. The substitute **New Jersey Plan,** submitted to the convention by William Paterson, would have amended, not replaced, the Articles of Confederation, giving the central gov-

SOME KEY POLITICAL CONCEPTS

★ ★ ★

CONSTITUTION

The fundamental law of a nation, written or unwritten, that defines the powers of government, specifies the offices to be filled and the authority each is to exercise, and sets the limits to governmental authority.

Note—True constitutional government is limited government. Nations may have documents called "constitutions," but if they are ruled by tyrants or dictators who recognize no limits to their authority, then the "constitution" is only a piece of paper, not a fundamental law.

MAJORITY RULE

The doctrine that offices will be filled by those candidates who win the most votes and laws will be made by whichever side in a legislature has the most votes.

MINORITY RIGHTS

The limits set on the power of the majority. These limits may be of two kinds:

1. *Absolute*: There are certain things the majority, no matter how large, cannot do. For example, Congress may not pass a law that makes an individual guilty of a crime without a trial.

2. *Conditional*: There are certain things that the majority can do only if it is an "extraordinary majority"—that is, contains some percentage of the votes greater than 50 percent. For example, Congress may propose a constitutional amendment only if two-thirds of each house vote in favor of it.

ernment somewhat stronger powers than it had but retaining the Articles' one-state, one-vote system of representation. The key feature of the New Jersey Plan was a unicameral or one-house Congress in which each state would have an equal vote.

The Compromise

The small states' demand for equal representation embodied in the New Jersey Plan led to the **Great** (or **Connecticut**) **Compromise.** That compromise, hammered out by a committee headed by Benjamin Franklin, was adopted by the narrowest of margins on July 16, 1787. The structure of the national legislature was set as follows:

THE STRUCTURE OF THE NATIONAL GOVERNMENT

AS DESCRIBED IN THE CONSTITUTION OF 1787

★ ★ ★

A CONGRESS, MADE UP OF TWO HOUSES:

A HOUSE OF REPRESENTATIVES

★ Composed of members apportioned roughly in accordance with the population of each state; initially, the number varied from one (Rhode Island) to eight (Pennsylvania)

★ Representatives to be elected every two years by those people in each state eligible to vote for the members of the "most populous" (usually, the lower house) of their state legislatures

★ A House of Representatives consisting initially of sixty-five members apportioned among the states roughly on the basis of population and elected by the people.

★ A Senate consisting of two senators from each state to be chosen by the state legislatures.

The Great Compromise reconciled the interests of small and large states by allowing the former to predominate in the Senate and the latter in the House. This reconciliation was necessary to ensure support for a strong national government in small and large states alike, but it represented major concessions on both sides. In time, most of the delegates from the dissenting states accepted it.

After the Great Compromise many more issues had to be resolved, but by now a spirit of accommodation had developed, and other compromises were reached providing for the election of the president by an electoral college, establishing the president's term of office, and deciding who would select the members of the Supreme Court. Finally, on July 26, those proposals that were already accepted, together with a bundle of unresolved issues, were handed over to a "Committee of Detail"—five delegates, including James Madison and the chief draftsman of the final document, Gouverneur Morris. The committee hardly contented itself with mere "details," however. It inserted some new proposals and made changes in old ones, drawing on existing state

A SENATE

* Composed of two members from each state
* Senators to be elected by state legislatures for staggered six-year terms

A PRESIDENT

* To be elected for a four-year term by "electors" chosen in each state in such manner as the state legislature shall direct
* Each state shall have electors equal to the number of senators and representatives from that state. (No senator or representative may serve as an elector.)

THE JUDICIARY

* One Supreme Court
* Such lower courts as Congress may create
* All judges to be nominated by the president and confirmed by the Senate. The judges are to hold office during good behavior (that is, without fixed terms and without being removable except by impeachment).

constitutions and the members' beliefs as to what the other delegates might accept. On August 6, the first complete draft of the Constitution was submitted to the convention. There it was debated, item by item, revised, amended, and finally, on September 17, approved by all twelve states in attendance (Rhode Island had never sent a delegation).

THE CONSTITUTION AND DEMOCRACY

Was the Constitution intended to create a democratic government? The answer is complex. The Framers did not intend to create a "pure" or "direct" democracy—one in which the people rule directly. For one thing, the size of the country and the distances between settlements would have made that physically impossible. But for another, the Framers worried that a government in which all citizens directly participate, as in the New England town meeting, would be excessively subject to temporary popular passions and could not ensure minority rights. They intended to create a **republic**—a government in which a system of representation operates. In designing that system, the Framers chose, not without argument, to have members of the House of Representatives elected directly by the people. "No government could long subsist without the confidence of the people," argued the delegates who supported a directly elected House.

WAYS OF AMENDING THE CONSTITUTION

★ ★ ★

Under Article V, there are two ways to **propose** amendments to the Constitution and two ways to **ratify** them.

TO PROPOSE AN AMENDMENT

1. Two-thirds of both houses of Congress vote to propose an amendment, *or*

2. Two-thirds of the state legislatures ask Congress to call a national convention to propose amendments

TO RATIFY AN AMENDMENT

1. Three-fourths of the state legislatures approve it, *or*

2. Ratifying conventions in three-fourths of the states approve it

But though popular rule was one element of the new government, it was not to be the only one. State legislatures, not the people, would choose the senators; electors, not the people directly, would choose the president. As we have seen, without these arrangements, there would have been no Constitution at all, for the small states adamantly opposed any proposal that would have given undue power to the large ones. And direct popular election would clearly have made the populous states the dominant ones. In short, the Framers wished to observe the principle of majority rule, but they felt that, on the most important questions, two kinds of majorities were essential—a majority of the voters and a majority of the states.

The power of the Supreme Court to declare an act of Congress unconstitutional—or **judicial review**—is also a way of limiting the power of popular majorities. It is not clear whether the Framers intended that there be judicial review, but there is little doubt that in the Framers' minds the fundamental law, the Constitution, had to be safeguarded against popular passions. They made the process for amending the Constitution easier than it had been under the Articles but still relatively difficult (see box).

In short, the answer to the question of whether the Constitution brought about a democratic government is yes if by *democracy* is meant a system of representative government based on popular consent. The degree of that consent has changed since 1787 (for example, the people—not state legislatures—now elect the Senate).

SOME KEY FACTS

★ Only the first method of proposing an amendment has been used.

★ The second method of ratification has been used only once, to ratify the Twenty-first Amendment (repealing Prohibition).

★ Congress may limit the time within which a proposed amendment must be ratified. The usual limitation has been seven years, but the Twenty-seventh Amendment took 202 years to ratify.

★ Thousands of proposals have been made but only thirty-three have obtained the necessary two-thirds vote in Congress.

★ Twenty-seven amendments have been ratified.

★ The first ten amendments, ratified on December 15, 1791, are known as the Bill of Rights.

Two Key Principles: Separation of Powers and Federalism

The American version of representative democracy was based on two major principles, both of which distributed power—**the separation of powers** and **federalism.** In America political power was to be shared by three separate branches of government; in parliamentary democracies that power was concentrated in a single, supreme legislature. In America political authority was divided between a national government and the state governments—a division called **federalism**—whereas in most European systems authority was centralized in the national government. Neither of these principles was especially controversial at Philadelphia. The delegates began their work in broad agreement that separated powers and some measure of federalism were necessary, and both the Virginia and New Jersey Plans contained a version of each. How much of each should be written into the Constitution was quite controversial, however.

In the next chapter we shall describe how federalism developed and how it works today. Here we summarize the key features of the separation of powers system. The first point to bear in mind is that the powers of the three branches of government are not actually separated; rather they are *shared.* The checks and balances built into the constitutional system exist because three branches of government share all the powers of that system, as shown in the box on pages 20–21.

CHECKS AND BALANCES

★ ★ ★

The Constitution creates a system of *separate* institutions that *share* powers. Because the three branches of government share powers, each can (partially) check the powers of the others. This is the system of *checks and balances*. The major checks possessed by each branch are listed below.

CONGRESS

1. Can check the president in these ways:
   a. By refusing to pass a bill the president wants
   b. By passing a law over the president's veto
   c. By using the impeachment powers to remove the president from office
   d. By refusing to approve a presidential appointment (Senate only)
   e. By refusing to ratify a treaty the president has signed (Senate only)
2. Can check the federal courts in these ways:
   a. By changing the number and the jurisdiction of the lower courts
   b. By using the impeachment powers to remove a judge from office
   c. By refusing to approve a person nominated to be a judge (Senate only)

Government and Human Nature

These checks and balances were based on a theory of human nature. The Framers believed that men and women were good enough to make it possible to have a free government, but they were not good enough to make it inevitable. People will pursue their self-interest, and no "parchment barrier," like a constitution or a bill of rights, would be a sufficient check on those self-seeking tendencies. Some of the Revolutionary War leaders felt that republican government was possible only if human character were first improved, but James Madison disagreed. To him and others at the Philadelphia convention, the proper way to keep government in check while still leaving it strong enough to perform its essential tasks was to allow the self-interest of one person to check the self-interest of another. This would make republican government possible, Madison thought, "even in the absence of virtue."

Madison argued that the very self-interest that leads people toward factionalism and tyranny might, if properly harnessed by appropriate constitutional arrangements, provide a source of unity and a guarantee of liberty. This harnessing was to be accomplished by dividing the offices of the new govern-

PRESIDENT

1. Can check Congress by vetoing a bill it has passed
2. Can check the federal courts by nominating judges

COURTS

1. Can check Congress by declaring a law unconstitutional
2. Can check the president by declaring actions by him or his subordinates to be unconstitutional or not authorized by law

In addition to these checks provided for in the Constitution, each branch has informal ways of checking the others. For example, the president can try to withhold information from Congress (on the grounds of "executive privilege"), and Congress can try to get information by mounting an investigation.

The exact meaning of the various checks is explained in Chapter 7 on Congress, Chapter 8 on the president, and Chapter 10 on the courts.

ment among many people and by giving to the holder of each office the "necessary means and personal motives to resist encroachments of the others." Thus self-interest could prevent one set of officeholders from gathering all the political power into its hands. The separation of powers would work, not in spite of the imperfections of human nature, but because of them.

So also with federalism. By dividing power between the states and the national government, one level of government can be a check on the other. This should provide a "double security" to the rights of the people—especially in America, Madison thought, because it was a large country with diverse interests. Each interest would constitute a **faction*** that would seek its own advantage. One faction may come to dominate government, or part of government, in one place, and a different one may dominate it in another.

---

* Today we often think of a *faction* as a special interest group, but originally it had a broader meaning. Madison defined a faction as "a number of citizens, whether amounting to a majority or a minority of the whole, who are united and actuated by some common impulse of passion, or of interest, adverse to the rights of other citizens, or to the permanent and aggregate interests of the community" (*Federalist* Number 10).

The pulling and hauling among these factions would prevent any faction from dominating all of government. The division of powers among several governments would give to virtually every faction an opportunity to gain some—but not full—power.

THE CONSTITUTION AND LIBERTY

A more difficult question to answer is whether the Constitution created a system of government that would respect personal liberties. And that, in fact, was the question debated in the thirteen states when the document was presented for ratification by special conventions elected by the people. These conventions bypassed the existing Congress and the state legislatures, which still were operating under the Articles of Confederation.

The Antifederalist View

The great issue before the state conventions was liberty, not democracy. The opponents of the new government, who came to be called the **Antifederalists,** had a variety of objections, but they were united by the belief that liberty could only be secure in a small republic in which the rulers were physically close to—and closely checked by—the ruled. A strong national government, they felt, would be distant from the people and would use its powers to annihilate or absorb the functions that properly belonged to the states. (Many of their fears have in fact been realized: Congress taxes heavily, the Supreme Court overrules state courts, the president heads a large standing army, and so forth. Thus we cannot dismiss the Antifederalists as cranks who opposed the Framers' wise plans.) Hoping to limit the national government to a loose confederation of states, the Antifederalists wanted most of the powers of government kept firmly in the hands of state legislatures and state courts.

James Madison answered these Antifederalist objections in *Federalist* papers 10 and 51 (see Appendix for text). It was a bold answer, for it flew squarely in the face of widespread popular sentiment and of traditional political philosophy, which held that liberty was safe only in small societies governed either by direct democracy or by large legislatures with small districts and frequent turnover among members. Madison argued quite the opposite—that liberty is safest in *large* republics, where there are many opinions and interests rather than the uniformity characteristic of small communities. People with unpopular views find it easier to acquire allies in a larger, more diverse society.

By favoring a large republic, Madison was not trying to stifle democracy. Rather, he was attempting to show how democratic government really works and what can make it work better. To rule, different interests must come together and form a **coalition**—that is, an alliance. And the coalitions that formed in a larger republic would be more diverse, and hence more moderate, than those that would form in a smaller republic. He concluded that in a

Alexander Hamilton did not think that the Constitution went far enough in creating a strong national government.

nation the size of the United States, with its enormous variety of interests, "a coalition of a majority of the whole society could seldom take place on any other principles than those of justice and the general good."

The implication of Madison's argument was daring. He was suggesting that the national government should be at some distance from the people and insulated from their momentary passions, because the people did not always want to do the right thing. Liberty was threatened as much or more by public passions and popularly based factions as by strong governments. Thus the government had to be designed so as to prevent both the politicians and the people from using it for ill-considered or unjust purposes.

Arguing in 1787 against the virtues of small democracies was akin to arguing against motherhood, but the argument prevailed. Many citizens had become convinced that a reasonably strong national government was essential. The political realities of the moment and the recent bitter lessons with the Articles probably counted for more in ratifying the Constitution than did Madison's arguments. His cause was helped by the Antifederalists who, for all their legitimate concerns and their uncanny instinct for what the future might bring, could offer no agreed-upon alternative to the new Constitution. In politics, then as now, you cannot beat something with nothing.

But this does not explain why the original Constitution had no bill of rights, which was the Antifederalists' most important objection of all. If the

CONSTITUTIONAL PROTECTIONS

★ ★ ★

THE BILL OF RIGHTS

The first ten amendments to the Constitution gave American citizens important guarantees of individual liberty. But the unamended Constitution also contained such protections. Among those protections listed under Article I, sections 9 and 10, are the following:

EX POST FACTO LAW

A law that makes an act a crime that was not a crime at the time it was committed, or that increases penalties or renders conviction easier after the fact. Outlawed by the Constitution.

WRIT OF HABEAS CORPUS

Intended as a check against arbitrary arrest or imprisonment, it is a legal order requiring that a person in custody be brought to court in order that just cause by shown for the person's detention. Can be suspended only under emergency conditions.

BILL OF ATTAINDER

An act of a legislature that declares a person guilty and sets the punishment without benefit of a judicial trial. Outlawed by the Constitution.

Framers were so preoccupied with liberty, why didn't they take this most obvious step toward protecting liberty, especially since the Antifederalists were demanding it? There appear to have been several reasons.

First, the Constitution, as written, *did* contain a number of specific guarantees of individual liberty: the right of trial by jury in criminal cases, the privilege of the writ of habeas corpus (see box above for definition), prohibitions against bills of attainder and ex post facto laws, bans on religious tests for holding federal office and on laws interfering with contracts, and promises that citizens of each state would enjoy the same rights enjoyed by citizens of every other state. Second, most states in 1787 already had bills of rights, and the delegates at the convention thought that these were sufficient to guarantee individual liberties.

But third, and perhaps most important, the Framers thought they were creating a government with specific, limited powers. It could do, they thought, only what the Constitution gave it power to do, and nowhere in that document was there permission to infringe upon freedom of speech or of the press or to impose cruel and unusual punishments. Some delegates probably feared that if any serious effort were made to list the rights that were guaranteed, later officials might assume that they had the power to do anything not explicitly forbidden.

Need for a Bill of Rights

Whatever their reasons, the Framers made at least a tactical and perhaps a fundamental mistake. It quickly became clear that without at least the promise of a bill of rights, the Constitution would not be ratified. Though most small states, pleased by their equal representation in the Senate, quickly ratified, the battle in the large states was intense, and supporters of the new Constitution won only by narrow margins (often, as in Massachusetts, only after promising to add a bill of rights). Indeed, conventions in North Carolina and Rhode Island initially rejected the Constitution. By June 21, 1788, however, the ninth state—New Hampshire—had ratified and the Constitution was law.

Despite the bitterness of the ratification struggle, the new government that took office in 1789–1790, headed by President Washington, was greeted enthusiastically. By the spring of 1790, all thirteen states had ratified. There remained the task of fulfilling the promise of a bill of rights. To that end, James Madison introduced into the first session of the First Congress a set of proposals, many based on the existing Virginia bill of rights. Twelve were approved by Congress; ten of these were ratified by the states and went into effect in 1791. These amendments limited the power of the federal government over citizens. Later, the Fourteenth Amendment (1868), as interpreted by the Supreme Court, extended many of the guarantees of the Bill of Rights to limit state governmental actions.

THE CONSTITUTION AND SLAVERY

Nowhere in the Constitution can one find the words *slave* or *slavery*. Yet at the time the document was written, black slaves constituted one-third of the population of the five southern states. Everyone at the Philadelphia convention knew this, but there was little debate on the morality of slavery.

To some, the failure of the Constitution to address the question of slavery was a great betrayal of the promise of the Declaration of Independence that "all men are created equal."[6] Even though criticism of slavery mounted during the Revolutionary period—especially in the North, where most states adopted some form of emancipation—it is easy to accuse the signers of the Declaration of Independence and the Constitution of hypocrisy. They knew of slavery, many of them owned slaves, and yet they were silent. Slavery continued unabated in the South, defended by some whites because they thought it was right, by others because they found it useful. Even in the South, however, there were opponents, though rarely conspicuous ones. Washington, Madison, Jefferson, and George Mason, a large Virginia slave owner and a

THE BILL OF RIGHTS

THE FIRST TEN AMENDMENTS TO THE CONSTITUTION, GROUPED BY TOPIC AND PURPOSE

★ ★ ★

PROTECTIONS AFFORDED CITIZENS TO
PARTICIPATE IN THE POLITICAL PROCESS

AMENDMENT 1
Freedom of religion, speech, press, assembly, and of the right to petition the government.

PROTECTIONS AGAINST ARBITRARY
POLICE AND COURT ACTION

AMENDMENT 4
No unreasonable searches or seizures.

AMENDMENT 5

★ Grand jury indictment required to prosecute a person for a serious crime.

★ No "double jeopardy"—being tried twice for the same offense.

★ Cannot be forced to testify against oneself.

★ No loss of life, liberty, or property without due process.

AMENDMENT 6

Right to speedy, public, impartial trial with defense counsel and right to cross-examine witnesses.

---

delegate to the convention, were among the numerous Southerners who deplored slavery without knowing how it could safely be abolished.

The blunt fact was that any effort to use the Constitution to end slavery would have meant the end of the Constitution. The southern states would never have signed a document that seriously interfered with slavery. Without the southern states, the Articles of Confederation would have continued in effect, which would have left each state entirely sovereign and thus entirely free of any prospective challenge to slavery.

The unresolved issue of slavery was to prove the most explosive question of all and led to a great civil war. Those who opposed abolishing slavery argued that since the Constitution was silent on the subject, the federal govern-

AMENDMENT 7

Jury trials in civil suits where value exceeds $20.

AMENDMENT 8

No excessive bail or fines, no cruel and unusual punishment.

*PROTECTIONS OF STATES' RIGHTS AND
UNNAMED RIGHTS OF PEOPLE*

AMENDMENT 9

Unlisted rights are not necessarily denied.

AMENDMENT 10

Powers not delegated to the United States or denied to states
are reserved to the states.

OTHER AMENDMENTS

AMENDMENT 2

Right to bear arms.

AMENDMENT 3

Troops may not be quartered in homes in peacetime.

ment had no power to free slaves. Those who favored abolishing it argued
that the Constitution had to be interpreted in light of the Declaration of
Independence, signed eleven years earlier. The Declaration said that "all men
are created equal" and are "endowed by their Creator with certain unalienable rights." "All men," not "all white men." In the first view, the
Constitution stands alone as the charter of the nation; in the latter view, the
Constitution is a charter designed to put into effect the political and moral
principles of the Declaration.

The slaves were emancipated in 1863, but the legacy of slavery remains
with us to this day. However one interprets the relationship between the
Declaration and the Constitution, the authors of the latter clearly postponed

WERE WOMEN LEFT OUT OF THE CONSTITUTION?

★ ★ ★

In one sense, yes: Women were nowhere mentioned in the Constitution when it was written in 1787. Moreover, Article I, which set forth the provisions for electing members of the House of Representatives, granted the vote to those people who were allowed to vote for members of the lower house of the legislature in the states in which they resided. In no state could women vote in any elections or hold any offices. Furthermore, wherever the Constitution uses a pronoun, it uses the masculine form—*he* or *him*.

In another sense, no: Wherever the Constitution or the Bill of Rights defines a right that people are to have, it either grants that right to "persons" or "citizens," not to "men," or it makes no mention at all of people or gender. For example:

★ "The *citizens* of each State shall be entitled to all privileges and immunities of citizens of the several States." [Art. IV, sec. 2]

★ "No *person* shall be convicted of treason unless on the testimony of two witnesses to the same overt act, or on confession in open court." [Art. III, sec. 3]

★ "No bill of attainder or ex post facto law shall be passed." [Art. I, sec. 9]

★ "The right of the *people* to be secure in their persons, houses, papers, and effects, against unreasonable searches and seizures, shall not be violated. . . . " [Amend. IV]

★ "No *person* shall be held to answer for a capital, or otherwise infamous crime, unless on presentment or indictment of a grand jury . . . nor shall any *person* be subject for the same offense to be twice put in jeopardy of life or limb; . . . nor be deprived of life, liberty, or property, without due process of law. . . . " [Amend. V]

★ "In all criminal prosecutions the *accused* shall enjoy the right to a speedy and public trial, by an impartial jury. . . . " [Amend. VI]

Moreover, when the qualifications for elective office are stated, the word *person*, not *man*, is used:

★ "No *person* shall be a Representative who shall not have attained to the age of twenty-five years. . . . " [Art. I, sec. 2]

★ "No *person* shall be a Senator who shall not have attained to the age of thirty years. . . . " [Art. I, sec. 3]

★ "No *person* except a natural born citizen, . . . shall be eligible to the office of President; neither shall any *person* be eligible to that office who shall not have attained to the age of thirty-five years. . . . " [Art. II, sec. 1]

In places the Constitution and the Bill of Rights used the pronoun *he*, but always in the context of referring back to a *person* or *citizen*. At the time, and still today, the male pronoun was often used in legal documents to refer generically to both men and women.

Thus, though the Constitution did not give women the right to vote until the Nineteenth Amendment was ratified in 1920, it did use language that extended fundamental rights, and access to office, to women and men equally.

Of course what the Constitution permitted did not necessarily occur. State and local laws denied women many rights that men enjoyed. No women voted in state elections until 1838, and then only in school board elections in Kentucky. It was not until 1869 that women voted on an equal basis with men anywhere—in territorial elections in Wyoming.

When Amendment XIX gave women the right to vote, that document did not amend any existing language in the Constitution because nothing in the Constitution itself denied women the right to vote; the amendment simply added a new right:

★ "The right of citizens of the United States to vote shall not be denied or abridged by the United States or any state on account of sex." [Amend. XIX]

SOURCE: Adapted from Robert Goldwin, "Why Blacks, Women and Jews Are Not Mentioned in the Constitution," *Commentary* (May 1987): 28–33.

the issue of slavery in order to create a union strong enough to handle the issue when it could no longer be postponed.

POLITICAL IDEALS OR ECONOMIC INTERESTS?

In another respect as well, some modern scholars have questioned the Framers' candor. Some critics find the words and writings of the Framers an unpersuasive guide to their true intentions. To these critics, the Framers' intentions are better revealed by trying to analyze their underlying economic interests.

Scholars have debated at length whether the Constitutional Convention was made up of opposed factions that spoke and voted in ways that would protect their own economic interests. Charles A. Beard was the first and most influential historian to argue that such was the case in his widely read book, *An Economic Interpretation of the Constitution* (1913). Beard attempted to show that the convention and the subsequent ratification process were dominated by well-off urban and commercial leaders, to the disadvantage of small farmers, debtors, and the propertyless masses.

This argument has been subjected to searching analysis by many historians and, by and large, disproved. The economic interests of the Federalists and

Antifederalists were so complex and diverse as largely to offset one another, and though they played a role in the adoption of the Constitution, they did not follow any neat class lines. Creditors tended to favor the Constitution, debtors to oppose it. Urban dwellers involved in commerce, whether merchants or workers, favored the Constitution more than rural folk. But there were plenty of exceptions even among these groups. Though in some states, such as Massachusetts, economic issues were explicitly raised in the debate over ratification of the new Constitution, in most states the debate centered on *political* questions—chiefly, on whether liberty could prosper under a large national as well as under small local governments.

LIBERTY AND EQUALITY

Today some people look back at the struggle to ratify the Constitution and wonder whether the Framers, in their concern to preserve liberty from tyrannical rulers, did not end up by creating a government too weak to reduce social inequality. Even asking this question shows how much our understanding of liberty and equality has changed since the founding. To Jefferson and Madison, citizens, in the natural order of things, differed in their talents and qualities. What had to be guarded against was the use of governmental power to create *un*natural and undesirable inequalities—for example, by concentrating political power in a few people (who could then obtain special privileges) or by permitting some private parties to acquire exclusive charters and monopolies. To prevent the inequality that might result from having too strong a government, its powers must be kept strictly limited.

Today many people think of inequality quite differently. They believe that the natural social order—the marketplace and the acquisitive talents of people operating in that marketplace—leads to undesirable inequalities, especially in economic power. The government should be powerful enough to restrain these natural tendencies and produce, by law, a greater degree of equality than society allows when left alone.

To the Framers, government had to be kept limited enough to prevent it from creating the worst kind of inequality—political privilege. To some modern observers, government must be strong enough to reduce the worst kind of inequality—differences in wealth.

SUMMARY

The Framers of the Constitution sought to create a government capable of protecting both liberty for citizens and order in government. The solution they chose—one without precedent at that time—was a government based on a written constitution that combined the principles of popular consent, the separation of powers, and federalism.

Popular consent was embodied in the procedure for choosing the House of Representatives but limited by the indirect election of senators (initially) and by the electoral college system for selecting a president. Power was to be distributed by a separation of powers: political authority was to be shared by three branches of government in a manner deliberately intended to produce conflict among these branches. This conflict, motivated by the self-interest of the people occupying each branch, would, it was hoped, prevent tyranny, even by a popular majority.

Federalism came to mean a system in which both the national and state governments had independent authority. Allocating powers between the two levels of government and devising means to ensure that neither large nor small states would dominate the national government required the most delicate compromises at the Philadelphia convention. The decision to do nothing about slavery was another such compromise.

In the drafting of the Constitution and the struggle over its ratification in the states, the positions people took were not chiefly determined by their economic interests but by a variety of political opinions. Among these were profound differences of opinion over whether state governments or a national government would be the best protector of personal liberty.

Suggested Readings

Bailyn, Bernard. *The Ideological Origins of the American Revolution.* Cambridge, Mass.: Harvard University Press, 1967. A brilliant account of how the American colonists formed and justified the idea of independence.

Becker, Carl L. *The Declaration of Independence.* New York: Vintage, 1942. The classic account of the meaning of the Declaration.

Cutler, Lloyd N. "To Form a Government," *Foreign Affairs,* Fall 1980, pp. 126–143. An argument for constitutional revision to reduce the separation of powers.

Farrand, Max. *The Framing of the Constitution of the United States.* New Haven, Conn.: Yale University Press, 1913. A good, brief account of the Philadelphia convention, by the editor of Madison's notes on the convention.

Federalist Papers. By Alexander Hamilton, James Madison, and John Jay. A convenient edition was edited by Clinton Rossiter. New York: New American Library, 1961.

Goldwin, Robert A., and William A. Schambra, eds. *How Capitalistic Is the Constitution?* Washington, D.C.: American Enterprise Institute, 1982. Essays from different viewpoints discussing the relationship between the Constitution and the economic order.

Goldwin, Robert A., and William A. Schambra, eds. *How Democratic Is the Constitution?* Washington, D.C.: American Enterprise Institute, 1980. A collection of essays offering different interpretations of the political meaning of the Constitution.

Rossiter, Clinton. *1787: The Grand Convention.* New York: Macmillan, 1966. A well-written account of the Philadelphia convention and the ratification struggle.

Storing, Herbert J. *What the Anti-Federalists Were For.* Chicago: University of Chicago

Press, 1981. A close analysis of the political views of those opposed to the ratification of the Constitution.

Wood, Gordon S. *The Creation of the American Republic.* Chapel Hill, N.C.: University of North Carolina Press, 1969. A detailed study of American political thought before the Philadelphia convention.

———. *The Radicalism of the American Revolution.* New York: Knopf, 1992. A penetrating account of the nature and effects of the American Revolution, emphasizing the radical transformation that it produced.

3
★ ★ ★

Federalism

SINCE THE ADOPTION of the Constitution in 1787, the single most persistent source of political conflict has been the relations between the national and the state governments. The political conflict over slavery, for example, was intensified because some state governments condoned or supported slavery, while others took action to discourage it. The proponents and opponents of slavery thus had territorial power centers from which to carry on the dispute. Other issues, such as the regulation of business and the provision of social welfare programs, were largely fought out, for well over a century, in terms of "national interest" versus "states' rights." Even after these debates had ended—almost invariably with a decision favoring the national government—the administration and financing of the resulting programs usually involved a large role for the states. In short, federalism has long been a central feature of American politics. It continues to be even today, when many Americans think of the government in Washington as vastly powerful and state governments as weak or unimportant.

GOVERNMENTAL STRUCTURE

Federalism refers to a political system in which local (territorial, regional, provincial, state, or municipal) units of government, as well as a national government, make final decisions on at least some governmental activities and whose existence is specifically protected.[1] Almost every nation in the world has local units of government of some kind, if for no other reason than to decentralize the administrative burdens of governing. But these governments are not federal unless the local units exist independently of the preferences of the national government and can make decisions on at least some matters without regard to those preferences (see Figure 3.1). The most important federal systems today are the United States, Canada, Australia, India, Germany, and Switzerland. In the United States, highways and some welfare programs are largely state functions (though they use federal money), while education, policing, and land-use controls are primarily local functions, controlled by cities, counties, or special districts.

The special protection that local governments enjoy in a federal system derives in part from the constitution of the country but also from the habits, preferences, and dispositions of the citizens and the actual distribution of political power in society. The constitution of the former Soviet Union in theory created a federal system, but in fact none of these "socialist republics" was in the slightest degree independent of the central government in Moscow. Their lack of power was made clear when Moscow lost control: most republics demanded independence, some fought with others, and a few were convulsed by ethnic warfare. If the American Constitution were the only guarantee of the independence of the American states, the states would long since have become mere administrative subunits of the government in Washington. Their independence depends in large measure on the commitment of Americans to the idea of local self-government and on the fact that Congress consists of people who are selected by and responsive to local constituencies.

Though the national government has come to have vast powers, it exercises many of those powers through state governments. Many of us forget that "the government in Washington" spends much of its money and enforces most of its rules not on citizens directly, but on other local units of government. A large part of the welfare system, all of the interstate highway system, virtually every aspect of programs to improve cities, the largest part of the effort to supply jobs to the unemployed, the entire program to clean up our water, and even much of our military power (in the form of the National Guard) are enterprises in which the national government does not govern so much as it seeks—by regulation, grant, plan, argument, and cajolery—to get the states to govern in accordance with nationally stated (though often vaguely defined) goals.

UNITARY SYSTEM

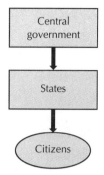

• Power centralized
• State or regional governments derive authority from central government
• Examples: United Kingdom, France

FEDERAL SYSTEM

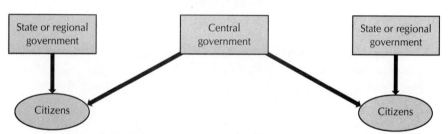

• Power divided between central and local, state, or regional governments
• Both the central government and the constituent governments act directly upon the citizens
• Both must agree to constitutional change
• Examples: Canada, United States since adoption of Constitution

CONFEDERAL SYSTEM (or CONFEDERATION)

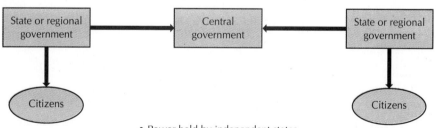

• Power held by independent states
• Central government is a creature of the constituent governments
• Examples: United States under the Articles of Confederation

FIGURE 3.1 Lines of Power in Three Systems of Government

The Complex Web of Federal, State, and Local Agencies

The Case of Oakland, California

★ ★ ★

To get an aircraft hangar and a ship terminal built in a way that would help reduce minority unemployment in Oakland, California, the following groups and agencies had to cooperate:

FEDERAL

* Economic Development Administration, U.S. Department of Commerce
* Seattle Regional Office of the EDA
* Oakland Office of the EDA
* U.S. General Accounting Office
* U.S. Department of Health, Education, and Welfare (now the Department of Health and Human Services)
* U.S. Department of Labor
* U.S. Navy

LOCAL

* Mayor of Oakland
* Oakland City Council
* Port of Oakland

FEDERALISM: GOOD OR BAD?

A measure of the importance of federalism is the controversy that surrounds it. To some critics, federalism means allowing states to block action, prevent progress, upset national plans, protect powerful local interests, and cater to the self-interest of hack politicians.[2] By contrast, others argue that the "virtue of the federal system lies in its ability to develop and maintain mechanisms vital to the perpetuation of the unique combination of governmental strength, political flexibility, and individual liberty, which has been the central concern of American politics."[3]

So diametrically opposed are these views that one wonders whether they refer to the same subject. They do, of course, but they are stressing different aspects of the same phenomenon. Whenever the opportunity to exercise po-

PRIVATE

* World Airways Company
* Oakland business leaders
* Oakland black leaders
* Conservation and environmental groups in Oakland

There were at least seventy important decisions to which some or all of these groups had to agree.

SOURCE: Jeffrey L. Pressman and Aaron B. Wildavsky, *Implementation* (Berkeley: University of California Press, 1973), pp. 95–96, 102–107.

litical power is widely available (as among the fifty states, three thousand counties, and many thousands of municipalities), invariably different people in different places will use that power for different purposes. There is no question that allowing states and cities to make autonomous, binding political decisions will allow some people in some places to maintain racial segregation, protect vested interests, and facilitate corruption. It is equally true, however, that this arrangement also enables other people in other places to pass laws that attack segregation, regulate harmful economic practices, and purify politics—often long before these ideas gain national support or become national policy. Today, many states are pioneering new policies in welfare reform, school improvement, and environmental regulation that, in time, may be copied by other states or made into federal policy.

Increased Political Activity

Federalism has many effects, but its most obvious effect has been to help mobilize political activity. Unlike Don Quixote, average citizens do not tilt at windmills. They are more likely to become involved in organized political activity if they feel there is a reasonable chance of having a practical effect. The chances of having such an effect are greater when there are many elected officials and independent governmental bodies, each with a relatively small constituency, than when there are few elected officials, most of whom have the nation as a whole for a constituency. In short, a federal system, by virtue of the decentralization of authority, lowers the cost of organized political activity; a unitary system (such as Great Britain or France), because of the centralization of authority, raises the cost of organizing protests and thus discourages local groups from challenging governmental decisions.

It is impossible to say whether the Framers, when they wrote the Constitution, planned to produce such widespread opportunities for political participation. Unfortunately, they were not very clear (at least in writing) about how the federal system was supposed to work, and thus most of the interesting questions about the jurisdiction and powers of the federal government had to be settled by a century and a half of protracted, often bitter, conflict.

THE FOUNDING

The general intention of the Framers seems clear: federalism was a device to protect personal liberty. They feared that placing final political authority in any set of hands, even in the hands of persons popularly elected, would so concentrate power as to risk tyranny. They had seen what happened, however, when independent states tried to form a confederal system, as under the Articles of Confederation. The alliance among the states that existed from 1776 to 1787 was a **confederation;** that is, a system of government in which the people create state governments that, in turn, create and operate a national government. Since the national government in a confederation derives its powers from the states, it is dependent on their continued cooperation for its survival. By 1786, that cooperation was barely forthcoming: what the states had put together, they could and did take apart.

A Bold New Plan

A **federation**—or a "federal republic," as the Framers called it—derives its powers directly from the people, as do the state governments. As the Framers envisioned it, both levels of government—the national and the state—would have certain powers, but neither would have supreme authority over the other. It was an entirely new plan, for which no historical precedent existed.

Nor did the Framers have a very clear idea of how it would work in practice, though they assumed from the outset that the national government would have only those powers granted by the Constitution. The Tenth Amendment was added to the Constitution only as an afterthought,[4] to allay fears that something else was intended. The amendment stipulates that "the powers not delegated to the United States by the Constitution, nor prohibited by it to the states, are reserved to the states respectively, or to the people."

Elastic Language

The need to reconcile the competing interests of large and small states and of northern and southern states, especially as they affected the organization of Congress, was sufficiently difficult without trying to spell out exactly what relationship ought to exist between the national and the state systems. Though some clauses bearing on federal-state relations were reasonably clear, other clauses were quite vague. The Framers knew, correctly, that they could not make an exact and exhaustive list of everything the federal government was empowered to do: circumstances would change; new exigencies would arise. Thus they added the following so-called elastic language to Article I: Congress shall have the power to "make all laws which shall be necessary and proper for carrying into execution the foregoing powers."[5]

The Framers themselves carried away from Philadelphia different views of what federalism meant. One view was championed by Alexander Hamilton. Since the people had created the national government, since the laws and treaties made pursuant to the Constitution were "the supreme law of the land" (Article VI), and since the most pressing needs were the development of a national economy and the conduct of foreign affairs, Hamilton thought that the national government was the superior and leading force in political affairs and its powers ought to be broadly defined and liberally construed.

The other view, championed by Thomas Jefferson (who had not attended the convention since he was serving abroad as minister to France), was that the federal government, though important, was the product of an agreement among the states. And though "the people" were the ultimate sovereigns, the principal threat to their liberties was likely to come from the national government. Thus Jefferson believed that the powers of the federal government should be narrowly construed and strictly limited. (James Madison, a strong supporter of national supremacy at the convention, later shifted his views and became a champion of states' rights.)

Hamilton argued for a strong federal government or **national supremacy**; Jefferson argued for **states' rights.** Though their differences were greater in theory than in practice, the differing interpretations they offered of the Constitution were to shape political debate in this country until well into the 1960s.

THE EVOLVING MEANING OF FEDERALISM

The Civil War settled one part of the argument over national supremacy versus states' rights. The war's outcome made it clear that the national government was supreme, its sovereignty derived directly from the people, and thus the states could not lawfully secede from the Union. But virtually every other aspect of the national supremacy issue was debated until the mid-twentieth century.

The Supreme Court Speaks

As arbiter of what the Constitution means, the Supreme Court became the focal point of that debate. In Chapter 10 we shall see how the Court made its decisions. For now it is enough to know that during the formative years of the new republic, the Supreme Court was led by a staunch and brilliant advocate of the Hamiltonian position, Chief Justice John Marshall. In a series of decisions, he and the Court vigorously defended the national supremacy view of the newly formed national government.

The most important decision came in 1819, in a case known as *McCulloch v. Maryland,* which arose when a branch of the Bank of the United States, created by Congress, refused to pay a state tax. The Supreme Court, in a unanimous decision, answered two questions in ways that expanded the powers of Congress and confirmed the supremacy of the federal government in the exercise of these powers.

The first question was whether Congress had the right to set up a bank, or any other corporation, since such a right is nowhere explicitly mentioned in the Constitution. Chief Justice Marshall ruled that since the Constitution empowers the national government to manage money—to lay and collect taxes, issue a currency, and borrow funds—Congress may reasonably decide that chartering a national bank is "necessary and proper" for carrying out these specified powers. Marshall's words were carefully chosen to endow the "necessary and proper" clause with the widest possible sweep:

> Let the end be legitimate, let it be within the scope of the Constitution, and all means which are appropriate, which are plainly adapted to that end, which are not prohibited, but consistent with the letter and spirit of the Constitution, are constitutional.[6]

The second question was whether a federal bank could lawfully be taxed by a state. To answer it, Marshall went back to first principles. The government of the United States was not established by the states, but by the people, and thus the federal government was supreme in the exercise of the powers conferred upon it. The federal government and its institutions must therefore be immune from destruction by the states. Since "the power to tax was the power to destroy," the states may not tax any federal instrument. Hence the Maryland law was unconstitutional.

Thus the federal government won the case. Half a century later, the Supreme Court decided that what was sauce for the goose was sauce for the gander—that the federal government, for its part, could not tax state instrumentalities. That meant that if you earned interest from a municipal bond, you did not have to pay federal income tax on it, just as you do not have to pay state income tax on interest from a United States bond. But in 1988 the Supreme Court changed its mind. Now Congress is free to tax interest on municipal bonds, although so far it hasn't.[7]

Though the Supreme Court may decide a case, it does not always settle an issue. The battle over states' rights versus national supremacy continued to rage, ultimately leading to the Civil War. Ironically, the war had an effect opposite to what the southern states had hoped for: The necessities of war led to an expansion of the powers of the Union leaders and their victory in turn brought about an enlargement of the powers of the federal government.

Nullification and War

The struggle over states' rights came to center on the doctrine of **nullification.** This word refers to the claimed ability of the states to declare a federal law null and void if, in their opinion, it violated the Constitution. The doctrine was first proposed by Jefferson and Madison as part of their opposition to a 1798 federal law that allowed newspaper editors to be punished if they published stories critical of the federal government. John C. Calhoun of South Carolina developed a more radical version of the doctrine as a way of blocking, first, a federal tariff and, later, federal efforts to restrict slavery. Calhoun argued that if Washington attempted to ban slavery, the states had the right to nullify such a law.

The issue was finally settled by the Civil War: The northern victory meant that the Union could not be dissolved and that states could not declare acts of Congress unconstitutional, a conclusion later affirmed by the Supreme Court.[8]

Dual Federalism

After the Civil War, the debate about the meaning of federalism focused on the interpretation of the commerce clause (Section 8) of the Constitution. Out of this debate emerged the doctrine of **dual federalism,** which held that though the national government was supreme in its sphere, the states were equally supreme in theirs, and that these two spheres of action could and should be kept separate.

Applied to commerce, the concept of dual federalism implied that there was such a thing as *inter*state commerce, which Congress could regulate, and *intra*state commerce, which only the states could regulate, and that the Supreme Court could define each. For a long period the Court tried to decide what was interstate commerce by the kind of business that was being conducted. But such product-based decisions were difficult to sustain. For example, was the sale of life insurance interstate or intrastate commerce? In 1869 the Court decided it was the latter, even though life insurance companies were becoming huge national businesses. In time, the effort to find some clear principles that distinguished interstate from intrastate commerce was pretty much abandoned. Commerce was like a stream flowing through the country, drawing to itself contributions from thousands of scattered enterprises and depositing its products in millions of individual homes. The Supreme Court began to permit the federal government to regulate almost anything that affected this stream, so that by the 1940s not only had farming and manufacturing been redefined as part of interstate commerce,[9] but even the janitors and window washers in buildings that housed companies engaged in interstate commerce were said to be part of that stream.[10]

The current Court interpretation of various laws pertaining to commerce is immensely complex, difficult to summarize, and impossible to explain. It would be only a mild overstatement, however, to say that the doctrine of dual federalism is virtually extinct and that, provided it has a good reason for wanting to do so, Congress can pass a law that will regulate, constitutionally, almost any kind of economic activity located anywhere in the country. In short, the principle of national supremacy has triumphed over that of states' rights.

THE DIVISION OF POWERS: FEDERAL AND STATE

Despite the growth of federal authority over economic activity, we are a long way from becoming a unitary political system. The states retain a great deal of authority for political as well as constitutional reasons. In general, the states (and within the states, the cities and towns) exercise predominant authority over at least three governmental services:

1. The police
2. The public schools
3. The use of land (zoning, housing, etc.)

Nowhere does the Constitution say that the states shall have authority over these matters; what it does say is that "the powers not delegated to the United States by the Constitution, nor prohibited by it to the states, are reserved to the states, respectively, or to the people" (Tenth Amendment). But in fact this provision has not been the effective source of much state authority. The Supreme Court did not let the Tenth Amendment stand in the way of striking down Maryland's effort to tax the Bank of the United States in 1819 or of later gradually giving Congress almost unlimited power over commerce. What, then, keeps the police, the schools, and land-use controls essentially in state and local hands?

Two things: popular beliefs and a localistic Congress. The people have made it very clear that they want local control over the police and schools (and to a lesser extent over the use of land); by contrast, they have been quite willing to allow the federal government to regulate local business activity. These popular desires become powerful ones because members of Congress act in accordance with them. Any proposal for federal regulation of local police forces would immediately be met by objections in Congress that this would create a "national police force" and reduce the degree of local self-government. Any effort to pass federal regulations regarding the content of local school curricula would confront equally strong congressional resistance.

But the police, schools, and land-use authorities have in fact been affected by federal regulations. This has happened in two ways despite the overwhelming preference for local control. First, federal courts, by their interpretations of the Constitution, have profoundly shaped these local institutions. School desegregation was ordered by the courts; in some cases, such as Boston, the implementation of these orders led federal judges to supervise countless details of local school policies—what supplies to buy, where to build schools, what teachers to hire, and the like. Police and fire departments have been ordered to alter their hiring and training policies in order to ensure that women and minorities are given access to jobs in these agencies. Judges are not elected, and so they can ignore—when in their opinion certain constitutional rights are at stake—local preferences.

The other way in which federal regulations have reduced local control over local governmental services has been by the development of federal grants-in-aid. This is often called **fiscal federalism.**

FISCAL FEDERALISM

The first federal grants to the states began even before the Constitution was adopted, in the form of land grants made by the federal government to the states in order to finance education. (State universities all over the country were built with the proceeds from the sale of these land grants; hence the name **land-grant colleges.**) Land grants were also made to support the building of wagon roads, canals, railroads, and flood-control projects. And cash grants-in-aid began almost as early.

Grant-in-aid programs remained few in number and small in cost until the twentieth century. The great growth began in the 1960s: between 1960 and 1966 federal grants to the states doubled; from 1966 to 1970 they

THE STATES AND THE CONSTITUTION

★ ★ ★

The Framers made some attempt to define the relations between the states and the federal government and how states were to relate to one another. The following points were made in the original Constitution—before the Bill of Rights was added.

RESTRICTIONS ON POWERS OF THE STATES

States may not make treaties with foreign nations, coin money, issue paper currency, grant titles of nobility, pass a bill of attainder or an ex post facto law,* or, without the consent of Congress, levy any taxes on imports or exports, keep troops and ships in time of peace, or enter into an agreement with another state or with a foreign power. [Art. I, sec. 10]

GUARANTEES BY THE FEDERAL GOVERNMENT TO THE STATES

The national government guarantees to every state a "republican form of government" and protection against foreign invasion and (provided the states request it) protection against domestic insurrection. [Art. IV, sec. 4]

---

doubled again; between 1970 and 1975 they doubled yet again. By 1985 they amounted to more than $100 billion a year and were spent through more than 400 separate programs. The five largest programs accounted for more than half the money spent and indicated the new priorities that federal policy had come to serve: housing assistance for low-income families, Medicaid, highway construction, services to the unemployed, and welfare programs for mothers with dependent children and for the disabled.

The grants-in-aid system, once under way, grew rapidly because it helped state and local officials resolve a dilemma. On the one hand, they wanted access to the superior taxing power of the federal government. On the other hand, prevailing constitutional interpretation, at least until the late 1930s, held that the federal government could not spend money for purposes not authorized by the Constitution. The solution was, obviously, to have federal money put into state hands: Washington would pay the bills; the states would run the programs.

There were four reasons why federal money seemed so attractive to state officials. For one thing, during most of the nineteenth century and the early

An existing state will not be broken up into two or more states or merged with all or part of another state without the state's consent. [Art. IV, sec. 3]

Congress may admit new states into the Union. [Art. IV, sec. 3]

Taxes levied by Congress must be uniform throughout the United States: they may not be levied on some states but not others. [Art. I, sec. 8]

The Constitution may not be amended to give states unequal representation in the Senate. [Art. V]

RULES GOVERNING HOW STATES DEAL WITH EACH OTHER

"Full faith and credit" shall be given by each state to the laws, records, and court decisions of other states. (For example, a civil case settled in the courts of one state cannot be retried in the courts of another.) [Art. IV, sec. 1]

The citizens of each state shall have the "privileges and immunities" of the citizens of every other state. (No one is quite sure what this is supposed to mean.) [Art. IV, sec. 2]

If a person charged with a crime by one state flees to another, he or she is subject to extradition—that is, the governor of the state that finds the fugitive is supposed to return the person to the governor of the state that wants him or her. [Art. IV, sec. 2]

*For the definition of bill of attainder and ex post facto law, see box on p. 24.

decades of the twentieth, the federal government was taking in more money than it was spending (the result of high-tariff policies of the Republicans). By the mid-twentieth century, when budget surpluses had pretty much become a thing of the past, a second reason for turning to Washington became evident—the income tax. Inaugurated in the 1920s, it proved to be a marvelously flexible tool of public finance, for it automatically brought in more money as economic activity (and thus personal income) grew. Third, the federal government, unlike the states, managed the currency, and thus could print more money whenever it needed it. (Technically, the government borrowed this money, and of course it paid interest on what it borrowed, but it was under no obligation to pay it all back because, as a practical matter, it had borrowed from itself.) The size of the federal public debt stayed more or less constant, or even declined, in the second half of the nineteenth century. By the mid-twentieth century, political leaders no longer worried about the national debt so much, or at least they worried about it for reasons other than the fear of being in debt. Thus the federal government came to accept, as a matter of policy, the proposition that when it needed money, it would print

In this country, unlike most others, police work is almost entirely under local control.

it. States could not do this: If they borrowed (and many could not), they had to pay it back, in full.

These three economic reasons for the attractiveness of federal grants were probably less important than a fourth reason—politics. Federal money seemed to state officials to be "free money." If Alabama could get Washington to put up the money for improving navigation on the Tombigbee River, then the citizens of the entire nation, not just Alabama, would pay for it. Of course, if Alabama gets money for such a purpose, every state will want it (and will get it). Even so, it was still an attractive political proposition: the governor of Alabama did not have to propose, collect, or take responsibility for federal taxes. Indeed, he could denounce the federal government for being profligate in its use of the people's money. Meanwhile, he would cut the ribbon opening the new dam on the Tombigbee.

Since every state had an incentive to ask for federal money to pay for local programs, it would be very difficult for one state to get money without every state getting some. The senator from Alabama who votes for the project to improve navigation on the Tombigbee will have to vote in favor of projects improving navigation on every other river in the country if he expects his Senate colleagues to support his request. Federalism as practiced in the United States means that when Washington wants to send money to one state or congressional district, it must send money to many states and districts.

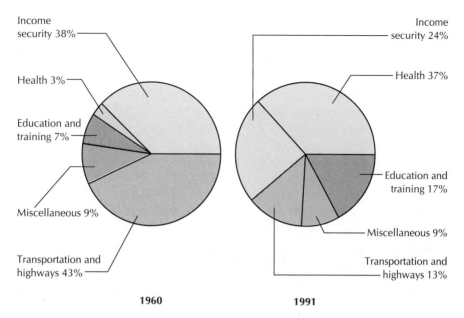

FIGURE 3.2 The Changing Purposes of Federal Grants to State and Local Governments

SOURCE: Budget of the U.S. Government, Fiscal Year 1990: *Special Analyses*, Table H-4.

Rise of Federal Activism

Until the 1960s most federal grants-in-aid were conceived by, or in cooperation with, the states and were designed to serve essentially state purposes. Large blocs of voters and a variety of organized interests would press for grants to help farmers, build highways, or support vocational education. During the 1960s, however, an important change occurred: the federal government began devising grant programs based less on what states were demanding and more on what federal officials perceived to be important *national* needs (see Figure 3.2). Federal officials, not state and local ones, were the principal proponents of grant programs to aid the urban poor, combat crime, reduce pollution, and deal with drug abuse. Some of these programs even attempted to bypass the states, providing money directly to cities or even to local citizen groups. These were worrisome developments for governors who were accustomed to being the conduit for money on its way from Washington to local communities.

The rise of federal activism in setting goals and the efforts, on occasion, to bypass state officials occurred at a time when the total amount of federal aid to states and localities had become so vast that many jurisdictions were completely dependent on the aid to support vital services. Whereas federal aid amounted to less than 2 percent of state and local spending in 1927, by 1970 it amounted to 19 percent and by 1980 to 26 percent (see Table 3.1).

TABLE **3.1** Federal Aid to State and Local Governments, 1955–1990

Year	Total federal aid (in billions)	Federal aid as percent of	
		Federal outlays	State and local outlays
1955	$3.2	4.7%	10.1%
1960	7.0	7.6	14.7
1965	10.9	9.2	15.3
1970	24.0	12.3	19.3
1975	49.8	15.0	23.0
1980	91.5	15.5	26.3
1982	88.2	11.8	21.9
1985	105.9	11.2	21.0
1990	136.9	10.9	17.9

SOURCE: *Statistical Abstract of the United States, 1992,* Table 453.

Some of the older, larger cities had become what one writer called "federal aid junkies," so dependent were they on these grants. In 1978 in Detroit, 77 percent of the revenue the city raised came from Washington.[11]

The Intergovernmental Lobby

State and local officials, both elected and appointed, began to form an important new lobby—the **intergovernmental lobby,** made up of mayors, governors, superintendents of schools, state directors of public health, county highway commissioners, local police chiefs, and others who had come to count on federal funds.[12] The five largest of these organized groups employed, in 1990, more than four hundred people and spent about $45 million, about one-sixth of which came from the federal government (see Table 3.2). The purpose of this intergovernmental lobby was the same as that of any private lobby—to get more money with fewer strings attached.

Categorical Grants Versus Block Grants

The effort to loosen the strings took the form of shifting, as much as possible, the federal aid from categorical grants to block grants or to revenue sharing. A **categorical grant** is one for a specific purpose defined by federal law: to build an airport or a college dormitory, for example, or to make welfare payments to low-income mothers. Such grants usually require that the state or locality put up money to "match" some part of the federal grant, though the amount of matching funds can be quite small. Governors and mayors complained about these categorical grants because their purposes were often so narrow that it was impossible for a state to adapt federal grants to local needs.

TABLE 3.2 State and Local Government Lobbies in Washington

Organization	Employees (1990)	Approximate budget (1990)	Percent of budget from federal government (1980)	(1990)
National Governors' Conference 55 state and territorial governors	100	$10 million	42%	33%
National Conference of State Legislatures 7,600 state legislators	140	$10 million	36%	15%
National League of Cities 14,700 cities	65	$8 million	43%	2%
U.S. Conference of Mayors 1,000 large cities	50	$7 million	60%	35%
National Association of Counties 2,000 counties	70	$10 million	30%	9%

SOURCE: Compiled by Xandra Kayden.

One response to this problem was to consolidate several categorical or project grant programs into a single **block grant** devoted to some general purpose and with fewer restrictions on its use. For example, several specific programs to improve cities were brought together into Community Development Block Grants. Block grants (sometimes called "special revenue sharing" or "broad-based aid") began in the mid-1960s. By 1989, block grants accounted for about 13 percent of all federal aid programs.

In theory, block grants were supposed to give the states and cities considerable freedom in deciding how to spend the money while helping to relieve their tax burdens. To some extent they did. However, neither the goal of "no strings" nor the one of tax relief was really attained. First, the amount of money available from federal grants did not grow as fast as the states had hoped. Second, the federal government steadily increased the number of strings attached to the spending of this supposedly "no strings" money.

The Slowdown in "Free" Money

Between 1981 and 1988, the Reagan administration made a determined effort to cut back on grants to the states, arguing that money for local projects should come from local sources. Thus any state or city official who wanted to build something would have to figure out a way to pay for it out of state or city taxes. Such an official would no longer be able to pay for things with "free" (i.e., federal) money. Moreover, the Reagan administration also believed that governments generally were doing too much and that the way to force them to do less was to cut their funds.

President Reagan had only limited success in pursuing this goal. There was no massive cutback, but there was a slowdown: grants-in-aid to the states, which had tripled between 1970 and 1980, just about stopped growing after 1981. In 1980, federal money paid for nearly 26 percent of everything the states and cities spent; by 1986, it paid for only about 20 percent. Governors and mayors complained, but they also adapted. States found new ways of raising money without raising taxes; for example, nearly two dozen started state lotteries that brought in (by 1985) nearly $4 billion a year in net revenues.[13] Moreover, they tried new ways of delivering old services. Many cities turned over trash collection and other tasks to private firms, often realizing financial savings. Many states experimented with ways of inducing welfare recipients to take jobs, thereby saving on welfare payments. During prosperous times, such as the 1980s, the cutback in federal aid was made easier to bear because the economy brought in more tax money to the states without their having to raise tax rates. In tough times, such as the early 1990s, the states struggled to make ends meet.

FEDERAL AID AND FEDERAL CONTROL

Federal aid has become so important for state and local governments that mayors and governors, along with others, began to fear that Washington was well on its way to controlling local levels of government. This would jeopardize the constitutional protection of state government (as stated in the Tenth Amendment) as a result of strings being attached to the grants-in-aid on which the states were increasingly dependent.

There are two kinds of federal controls on state government activities: **mandates** and **conditions of aid** (see box). The states and the federal government, not surprisingly, disagree about the costs and benefits of such controls. Members of Congress and federal officials feel they have an obligation to develop uniform national policies with respect to important matters and to prevent states and cities from misspending federal tax dollars. State officials, on the other hand, feel these national rules fail to take into account diverse local conditions, require the states to do things that the states must then pay for, and create serious inefficiencies. For example, in 1973 Congress passed—with little debate—a law forbidding discrimination against handicapped people in any program receiving federal aid. Under pressure from organizations representing the handicapped, federal agencies interpreted this law broadly, issuing regulations that required city transit systems receiving federal aid to equip their buses and subway cars with devices to lift wheelchairs on board. Although handicapped people were pleased, state and local officials took a

FEDERAL CONTROLS ON STATE ACTIVITIES

★ ★ ★

MANDATES

A federal law or court ruling directing states and cities to take certain actions *whether or not* they receive federal aid.

★ Most mandates concern civil rights and environmental protection.

★ States must comply with federal standards regarding clean air, pure drinking water, and sewage treatment.

CONDITIONS OF AID

Voluntary federal restrictions on state action: "if you don't want the strings, don't take the money."

★ In practice hard to refuse since the typical state depends for a quarter or more of its budget on federal grants.

★ Over the last few decades the number of conditions attached to federal aid has increased dramatically.[14]

different view. The mayor of New York, Edward Koch, argued that rebuilding existing buses and subways and buying new ones would make each trip by a wheelchair user cost $38. It would be cheaper, he said, for the city to give every handicapped person free taxicab rides, but the federal regulations would not permit that.[15] (In 1981 the Reagan administration relaxed the requirement that buses be able to lift wheelchairs aboard.)

In short, local officials discovered that "free" federal money was not quite free after all. In the 1960s federal aid seemed entirely beneficial; what mayor or governor would not want such money? But just as local officials found it attractive to do things that another level of government then paid for, in time federal officials learned the same thing. Passing laws to meet the concerns of national constituencies—and leaving the cities and states to pay the bills and manage the problems—began to seem attractive to members of Congress.

Rivalry Among the States

The more important that federal money becomes to the states, the more likely they are to compete among themselves for the largest share of it. For a century or better, the growth of the United States—in population, business,

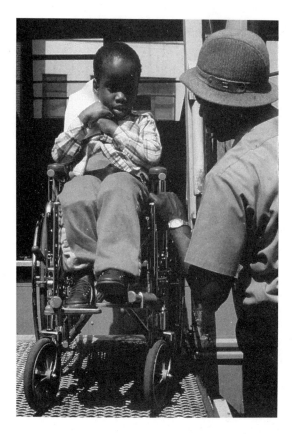

Federal control of local activities has expanded: federal regulations now require that public transit be accessible to the handicapped.

and income—was concentrated in the Northeast. In recent decades, however, that growth—at least in population and employment, if not in income—has shifted to the South, Southwest, and Far West. This change has precipitated an intense debate over whether the federal government, by the way it distributes its funds and awards its contracts, is unfairly helping some regions and states at the expense of others. Journalists and politicians have dubbed the struggle as one between "Snowbelt" and "Sunbelt" states.

Whether in fact there is anything worth arguing about is far from clear: the federal government has had great difficulty in figuring out where it ultimately spends what funds for what purposes. For example, a $1 billion defense contract may go to a company in California, but much of the money may actually be spent in Connecticut or New York, as the prime contractor in California buys from subcontractors in other states. Whether federal funds actually affect the growth rate of the regions is even less clear. The uncertainty about the facts has not prevented a debate about the issue, however. That debate focuses on the **distributional formulas** written into federal laws by which block grants and other federal funds are allocated. These formulas take into account such factors as a county's or city's population, personal income in the area, and housing quality. A slight change in a formula can shift millions of dollars in grants in ways that either favor the older, declining cities of the Northeast or the newer, still-growing cities of the Southwest.

With the advent of grants based on distributional formulas (as opposed to grants for a specific project), the results of the census, taken every ten years, assume monumental proportions. A city or state shown to be losing population may, as a result, forfeit millions of dollars in federal aid. There are more than one hundred programs (out of some five hundred federal grant programs in all) that distribute money on the basis of population. When the director of the census in 1960 announced figures showing that many big cities decreased in population, he was generally ignored. When he made the same announcement in 1980 and again in 1990, after the explosion in federal grants, he was roundly denounced by several big-city mayors.

Senators and representatives now have access to computers that can tell them instantly the effect on their states and districts of even minor changes in a formula by which federal aid is distributed. These formulas rely on objective measures, but the exact measure selected is done with an eye to its political consequences. There is nothing wrong with this in principle, since any political system must provide some benefit for everyone if it is to stay together. Given the competition among states in a federal system, however, the struggle over allocation formulas becomes especially acute. The results of these struggles are sometimes plausible, as when Congress decides to distribute money intended to help disadvantaged local school systems based largely on the proportion of poor children in each school district. But sometimes the results are a bit strange, as when the formula for determining federal aid for mass transit gives New York, a city utterly dependent on mass transit, a federal subsidy of 2 cents per transit passenger but gives Grand Rapids, a city that relies chiefly on the automobile, a subsidy of 45 cents per passenger.[16]

FEDERALISM AND PUBLIC POLICY

The growing importance of federal laws, regulations, and court orders in shaping the conduct of state and local affairs does not mean we have become a centralized, or unitary, nation. Far from it. For one thing, the people insist on maintaining local control over key policies (such as education, law enforcement, and land-use controls), and, secondly, members of Congress, as we shall see in Chapter 7, continue to think of themselves as representatives *of* localities to Washington and not the representatives *to* the localities from Washington.

As a result, local policies in the United States are more diverse than in any other industrialized democracy. One example: Though the federal government pays for most of the interstate highway program, local officials decide where those highways go. A second example: Though Washington pays most of the cost of the program providing aid to families with dependent children

(AFDC), and though it insists that states meet a large number of conditions to receive this aid, the states decide how much money each family will get. Because of this, the amount spent on each family varies enormously from state to state. The average monthly payment in Vermont is four times greater than in Mississippi. A third example: Though the unemployment compensation program operates under federal rules and with federal money, a person out of work in Ohio will receive 42 percent of his or her lost weekly wages, whereas an unemployed person in Alaska will get only 21 percent.

Not only does federalism lead to variation in public policies, it also increases the difficulty of running any program. If a tunnel is to be built under Boston harbor, an airport built in Oakland, California, or air pollution reduced in Los Angeles, local, state, and federal agencies—in some cases, dozens of them—must cooperate. Any one of them can block, or at least slow down, the actions of the others. When we complain about government dragging its feet, we should remember that much of that foot-dragging occurs because we, the people, have insisted that power be shared by many levels of government.

EVALUATING FEDERALISM

The tensions in the federal system do not arise from one level of government or another being callous or incompetent but from the kinds of political demands with which each must cope. Because of these competing demands, federal and state officials find themselves in a bargaining situation in which each side is trying to get some benefit (solving a problem, satisfying a pressure group) while passing on to the other side most of the costs (taxes, administrative problems).

The bargains struck in this process used to favor the local officials because members of Congress were essentially servants of local interests—they were elected by local political parties, they were part of local political organizations, and they supported local autonomy. Beginning in the 1960s, however, changes in American politics shifted the orientation of many members of Congress toward favoring Washington's needs over local needs.

Various presidents have tried to reverse this trend, but with little success. President Nixon proclaimed the "new federalism" and helped create revenue sharing and block grants, but federal mandates and conditions of aid *grew* rather than declined during his administration. In 1981 President Reagan asked Congress to consolidate eighty-three categorical grants into six large block grants, none of which would seriously affect how the states could spend the money. But Congress went along in name only: it consolidated fifty-seven programs into nine small block grants, each of which had many restrictions attached. The debate over this plan showed what is at stake is not simply differing views on how best to "streamline" or make "more efficient" the way in which federal money supports local programs, but rather competing philosophies of governance.

Some observers think that our federal system would work better if the endless conflict between Washington and the states over the hundreds of programs for which they are jointly responsible were reduced by sorting out in a more rational manner the functions performed by national and state governments. In this view, the federal government should pay for all programs that are truly national in scope, such as environmental protection and welfare and medical programs for the disadvantaged, while the states should pay for all programs that are primarily local in nature, such as education and community development.

In 1982 President Reagan made some proposals along these lines, but they came to nothing. In part this was because the Reagan plan envisaged making welfare a purely local matter, whereas most governors thought it should be a national responsibility. And in part the president's plan failed because any new sorting out of functions is likely to make some states pay more for some programs. No governor is likely to support a plan that will cost his or her taxpayers more.

The Framers did not write a Constitution that drew clear lines between national and state responsibilities, and two hundred years of political history have not improved matters any. For the foreseeable future, we are not likely to see any sorting out of functions; in the words of one student of the subject, American federalism will continue to look more like a marble cake than a layer cake.[17]

A federal system may be untidy, but in politics some things are more important than neatness. Federalism is a way of accommodating the differences in wants and beliefs of a diverse people without imposing an iron will on them. Americans agree on some issues and disagree on others. Federalism helps us stay together despite our ethnic, religious, and regional differences. The violent breakup of some former nations, such as Yugoslavia, shows what can happen when the central government attempts to rule without adjusting its policies to local preferences.

SUMMARY

States participate actively both in determining national policy and in administering national programs. Moreover, they reserve to themselves or the localities within them important powers over public services, such as schooling and law enforcement, and important public decisions, such as land-use control, that in a unitary system are dominated by the national government.

How one evaluates federalism depends largely on how one evaluates the competing criteria of the equal treatment of citizens and local participation in government. Federalism means that citizens living in different parts of the country will be treated differently, not only in spending programs, such as welfare, but in legal systems that assign in different places different penalties for similar offenses or that differentially enforce civil-rights laws. But federalism also means that there are more opportunities for participation in making decisions—in influencing what is taught in the schools and in deciding where to build highways and government projects. Indeed, differences in public policy—that is, unequal treatment—are in large part the result of participation in decision making. It is difficult, perhaps impossible, to have more of one of these values without having less of the other.

Politics and public policy have become decidedly more nationalized of late, with the federal government, and especially the federal courts, imposing increasingly uniform standards on the states in the form of mandates and conditions of aid. Efforts to reverse this trend by shifting to block grants have only partially succeeded.

SUGGESTED READINGS

Beer, Samuel H. *To Make a Nation: The Rediscovery of American Federalism.* Cambridge, Mass.: Harvard University Press, 1988. A profound account of the philosophical origins of American federalism.

Derthick, Martha. *The Influence of Federal Grants.* Cambridge, Mass.: Harvard University Press, 1970. Considers the extent to which federal aid leads to federal control in the area of welfare.

Diamond, Martin. *As Far As Republican Principles Will Admit: Essays by Martin Diamond.* Washington, D.C.: AEI Press, 1992. In Chapters 6–9, Diamond offers a brilliant analysis of what the Founders meant by "federalism."

Elazar, Daniel J. *American Federalism: A View from the States,* 2d ed. New York: Crowell, 1972. A sympathetic analysis of the historical development and present nature of American federalism.

Grodzins, Morton. *The American System.* Chicago: Rand McNally, 1966. Argues that American federalism has always involved extensive sharing of functions between national and state governments.

Peterson, Paul E., Barry G. Rabe, and Kenneth K. Wong. *When Federalism Works.* Washington, D.C.: Brookings Institution, 1986. An analysis of how federal grant-in-aid programs actually work.

Pressman, Jeffrey L., and Aaron B. Wildavsky. *Implementation.* Berkeley: University of California Press, 1973. An excellent case study of how federalism affected the implementation of a single economic-development project in Oakland, California.

Riker, William H. *Federalism: Origin, Operation, Significance.* Boston: Little, Brown, 1964. An explanation and critical analysis of federalism here and abroad.

4

★ ★ ★

Public Opinion and the Media

IN THE GETTYSBURG ADDRESS Abraham Lincoln said that the United States had a government "of the people, by the people, and for the people," which suggests that the government should do what the people want. If this is the case, it is puzzling that

★ The federal government has a large budget deficit, but the people want a balanced budget.

★ Courts order the busing of children to balance the schools racially, but the people oppose busing.

★ The Equal Rights Amendment to the Constitution was not ratified, but polls showed that most people supported it.

★ President Reagan sent aid to Nicaraguans fighting against their Marxist government, but Americans said they did not think our government should do this.

Some people, reflecting on the many gaps between what the government does and what the people want, may become cynical and think our system is democratic in name only. That would be a mistake. There are several very good reasons why government policy often appears to be at odds with public opinion.

First, the Framers of the Constitution did not try to create a government that would do from day to day "what the people want." They created a government for the purpose of achieving certain substantive goals. The preamble to the Constitution lists six of these: "to form a more perfect union, establish justice, ensure domestic tranquility, provide for the common defense, promote the general welfare, and secure the blessings of liberty. . . . "

One means to achieve these goals was popular rule, as provided by the right of the people to vote for members of the House of Representatives (and later for senators and presidential electors). But other means were provided as well: representative government, federalism, the separation of powers, a Bill of Rights, and an independent judiciary. These were all intended to be *checks* on public opinion. In addition the Framers knew that in a nation as large and diverse as the United States, there would rarely be any such thing as "public opinion"; rather there would be many "publics" (that is, factions) holding many opinions. The Framers hoped that the struggle among these many publics would protect liberty (no one "public" would dominate) while at the same time permitting the adoption of reasonable policies that commanded the support of many factions.

Second, it is more difficult than one may suppose to know what the public thinks. We are so inundated these days with public-opinion polls that we may imagine that they tell us what the public believes. That may be true on a few rather simple, clear-cut, and widely discussed issues, but it is not true for most matters on which government must act. The best pollsters know the limits of their methods, and the citizen should know them as well.

Third, the more people are active in and knowledgeable about politics, the more weight their opinions carry in governmental affairs. For most of us, politics ranks way down on the list of things to think about, well below families, jobs, health, sweethearts, entertainment, and sports. Some people, however, are political activists, and so come to know as much about politics as the rest of us know about batting averages, soap operas, and car repair. Not only do these activists, or political elites, *know more* about politics than the rest of us, they *think differently* about it—they have different views and beliefs. The government attends more to the elite views than to the popular views, at least on many matters.

An important kind of elite consists of the mass-communications media. The media—especially the national television networks, the news magazines, and the New York and Washington, D.C., newspapers—are shaped in part by the attitudes of the people who have been attracted into leading positions in journalism. There has always been an adversary relationship between those who govern and those who write, but events of recent decades have, as we shall see, made that conflict especially keen.

In the United States, the media are accorded a degree of freedom greater than that found in almost any other nation, including other democracies. In

England, for example, the laws governing libel are so strict that public figures frequently sue newspapers for defaming or ridiculing them—and they collect. But the law of libel in the United States is loose enough to permit intense and even inaccurate criticism of anybody who is in the public eye. And the Freedom of Information Act (1966), together with a long tradition of leaking inside stories and writing memoirs about one's public service, virtually guarantees that in the United States very little can be kept very secret for very long. Again in sharp contrast, in England any past or present government official can be punished for divulging to the press private government business.[1]

In America, radio and television stations are privately owned, and although the federal government licenses them, it does not have the power to censor or dictate the contents of routine stories. Until recently, the French government could censor or dictate to the broadcasting agencies, many of which are state owned.[2] (We shall see, however, that the federal government's power to license broadcasters has been used, on occasion, to harass station owners who are out of favor with the White House.)

Some people worry that newspapers and television have too much influence on politics and political opinions; others worry that journalists are tame mouthpieces for manipulative politicians or cater to the prejudices of readers and viewers. To untangle these questions, it is first necessary to know how public opinion is formed and why different people have different opinions. Then we must understand how the media are organized and the legal rules under which they operate. Finally, we shall describe the relations between the media and the government and the extent to which news stories are slanted or biased. The purpose of this chapter is to help the reader understand the complex role that public opinion plays in shaping—or being shaped by—American politics.

WHAT IS PUBLIC OPINION?

A few years ago some researchers at the University of Cincinnati asked twelve hundred local residents whether they favored passage of the Monetary Control Bill of 1983. About 21 percent said that they favored the bill, 25 percent said that they opposed it, and the rest said that they hadn't thought much about the matter or didn't know.

The members of Congress from Cincinnati would have been surprised to learn of this expression of "public opinion" from their constituents, for there was no such thing as the Monetary Control Bill. The researchers had made it up. Nor is there anything unusual about people in Cincinnati. A few years earlier, about 26 percent of the people questioned in a national survey also expressed opinions on the same piece of "legislation."

Ignorance (or an inclination to pretend that one is informed) is not limited to arcane bits of legislation. In 1986 a national survey found that only a

TABLE 4.1 The Effects of Question Wording: The Issue of Public Housing

One-sided

Do you agree or disagree with the following statement: The federal government should see to it that all people have adequate housing.	Agree: government responsible	55%
	Disagree: government not responsible	45%

Two-sided, government option first

Some people feel that the federal government should see to it that all people have adequate housing, while others feel each person should provide for his own housing. Which comes *closest* to how you feel about this?	Government responsible	44.6%
	Government not responsible	55.4%

Two-sided, government option second

Some people feel that each person should provide for his own housing, while others feel the federal government should see to it that all people have adequate housing. Which comes *closest* to how you feel about this?	Government responsible	29.5%
	Government not responsible	70.5%

SOURCE: Howard Schuman and Stanley Presser, *Questions and Answers in Attitude Surveys* (New York: Academic Press, 1981), 70–71.

third of the people could identify Caspar Weinberger (he was then the secretary of defense) and only 14 percent knew who William Rehnquist was (the chief justice of the United States). Robert Dole was running for president (and according to some polls, doing reasonably well), but only 12 percent of the people could identify him accurately. Given this low level of name recognition, how much confidence should we place in the polls that presumably tell us what "the American people" think about our defense policy, the posture of the Supreme Court, and presidential candidates?

Even if people have heard of the matter, how we word the question can dramatically affect the answer we get. Suppose we want to know whether the public believes that the federal government should provide housing for people. In Table 4.1 we see the results obtained from asking that question in three different ways. In the first example people are asked whether they agree or disagree with a one-sided statement ("The federal government should see to it that all people have adequate housing"). A majority agree. In the second example we give people a choice between two statements, one favoring a

federal housing policy (mentioned first) and the other favoring individual responsibility ("each person should provide for his own housing"). Given this
choice, a majority now opposes federal housing programs. In the third example the question is repeated, but this time with the individual-responsibility
option mentioned first. Now more than 70 percent of the respondents oppose federal housing programs. Obviously just altering the *order* in which
people are presented with options affects which option they choose and thus
what is "public opinion" on housing programs.

Moreover, opinions on public issues may not be stable—that is, firmly
held. In January 1980 and again in June of the same year, the same people
were asked the same questions. The first had to do with how tough we
should be in dealing with Russia, the second with whether spending should
be cut on things like health and education programs. Many people gave one
opinion in January and then a different one in June. Of those who said in
January that we should cooperate more with Russia, one-quarter said in June
that we should get tougher with Russia. Of those who said in January that
the government should cut the services it provides, more than one-quarter
said in June that they wanted to keep those services at the same level or expressed a middle-of-the-road position.

In sum, public opinion on many matters suffers from ignorance, instability, and sensitivity to the way the question is worded. This does not mean that
the American people are ignorant, unstable, or gullible, only that most
Americans do not find it worth their while to spend the amount of time
thinking about politics that they spend on their jobs, families, and friends.
Moreover, just because people do not think much about politics does not
mean that democracy is impossible, only that it can work best when people
are given relatively simple, clear-cut choices—like between Democrats and
Republicans, or between one presidential candidate and another.

THE ORIGINS OF POLITICAL ATTITUDES

People take pride in having their own opinions—about politics as well as
about music and movies. "Nobody tells me what to think," they say. But
these same people lament the power of television and advertising: "the media
manipulate the public," they argue, or "television sells candidates the same
way it sells soap." These views are a bit contradictory: if we all believe that we
decide for ourselves what to think, then we can't all be the puppets of
Madison Avenue.

The facts are a bit different from these popular conceptions. The beliefs
we have about politics are not entirely the result of independent thought and
study; they reflect a variety of forces, some of which we may not even be
aware of. But neither is it the case that television seduces us into voting for a

THE ART OF
PUBLIC-OPINION POLLING

★ ★ ★

A survey of public opinion—popularly called a poll—can provide us with a reasonably accurate measure of how people think, provided certain conditions are met. First, **the persons interviewed must be a random sample** of the entire population. (By *random* is meant that any given person, or any given voter or adult, must have an equal chance of being interviewed.) Most national surveys draw a sample of between a thousand and fifteen hundred persons by a process called stratified or multistage area sampling. The pollster makes a list of all geographical units in the country (say, all counties) and groups (or "stratifies") them by the sizes of their populations. The pollster then randomly selects units from each group or stratum in proportion to their total population. For example, if one stratum contains counties whose total population is 10 percent of the national population, then in the sample 10 percent of the counties will be drawn from this stratum. Within each selected county, smaller and smaller geographical units (cities, towns, census tracts, blocks) are chosen and then, within the smallest unit, individuals are selected at random (by, for example, choosing the occupant of every fifth house). The key is to stick to the sample and not let people volunteer to be interviewed—volunteers often have views different from those who do not volunteer.

Second, **the questions must be comprehensible,** asking people about subjects of which they have some knowledge and some basis on which to form an opinion. Most people know, at least at election time, whom they would prefer as president; most people also have views about what they think the most important national problems are. But relatively few voters will have any opinion about our policy toward El Salvador (if indeed they have even heard of it) or about the investment tax credit. If everybody refused to answer questions about which they are poorly informed, no problem would arise, but unfortunately many of us like to pretend we know things that in fact we don't, or to be helpful to interviewers by inventing opinions on the spur of the moment.

Third, **the questions must be asked fairly**—in clear language, without the use of "loaded" or "emotional" words. They must give no indication of what the "right" answer is, but offer a reasonable explanation, where necessary, of the consequences of each possible answer. For example, in 1971 the Gallup poll asked people whether they favored a proposal "to bring home all U.S. troops [from Vietnam] before the end of the year." Two-thirds of the public agreed with that. Then the question was asked in a different way: Do you agree or disagree with a proposal to withdraw all U.S. troops by the end of the year "regardless of what happens there [in Vietnam] after U.S. troops leave"? In this form substantially less than half the public agreed.

Fourth, **the answer categories offered to a person must be carefully considered.** This is no problem when there are only two candidates for office—say George Bush and Bill Clinton—and you want only to know which one the voters prefer. But it can be a big problem when you want more complex information. For example, if you ask people (as does George Gallup) whether they "approve" or "disapprove" of how the president is handling his job, you will get one kind of answer—let us say that 55 percent approve and 45 percent disapprove. On the other hand if you ask them (as does Louis Harris) how they rate the job the president is doing, "excellent, pretty good, only fair, or poor," you will get very different results. It is quite possible that only 46 percent will pick such positive answers as "excellent" or "pretty good," and the rest will pick the negative answers, "only fair" and "poor." If you are president, you can choose to believe Mr. Gallup (and feel pleased) or Mr. Harris (and be worried). The differences in the two polls do not arise from the competence of the two pollsters, but entirely from the choice of answers that they include with their questions.

Finally, remember that not every difference in answers is a significant difference. A survey is based on a sample of people. Select another sample, by equally randomized methods, and you might get slightly different results. This difference is called a **sampling error,** and its likely size can be computed mathematically. In general, the bigger the sample and the bigger the difference between the percentage of people giving one answer and the percentage giving another, the smaller the sampling error. If a poll of fifteen hundred voters reveals that 47 percent favor Bill Clinton, we can be 95 percent certain that the *actual* proportion of *all* voters favoring Clinton is within three percentage points of this figure—that is, it lies somewhere between 44 and 50 percent. In a close race an error of this size could be quite important. It could be reduced by using a bigger sample, but the cost of interviewing a sample big enough to make the error much smaller is huge.

As a result of sampling error and for other reasons, it is very hard for pollsters to predict the winner in a close election. Since 1952 every major national poll has in fact picked the winner of the presidential election, but there may have been some luck involved in such close races as the 1960 Kennedy-Nixon and the 1976 Carter-Ford contests. In 1980 the polls greatly underestimated the Reagan vote, partly because many voters made up their minds at the last minute and partly because a bigger percentage of Carter supporters decided not to vote at all.

politician the way it may lure us into buying a bar of soap. To understand how we see the political world, we must look at what has been learned about the origin of political attitudes.

The Role of the Family

The best-studied (though not necessarily the most important) case of opinion formation is that of party identification. Young people whose parents were Democrats tend to become Democrats themselves; those whose parents were Republicans tend to become Republicans.[3] Naturally, as people grow older, they become more independent of their parents in many ways, including politically, but there nonetheless remains a great deal of continuity between youthful partisanship, learned from one's parents, and adult partisanship.[4]

The ability of the family to inculcate a strong sense of party identification has declined in recent years. The proportion of citizens who say they consider themselves to be Democrats or Republicans has become steadily smaller since the early 1950s. This drop has been greatest among those who strongly identify with one party or another. In 1952, 22 percent of the voters said they were strong Democrats, and 13 percent said they were strong Republicans; by 1976, only 15 percent claimed to be strong Democrats and 9 percent to be strong Republicans. Accompanying this decline in partisanship has been a sharp rise in the proportion of citizens describing themselves as independents. By 1985 there had been some increase in the percentage of people who identified with a political party; the Republican party showed the largest gains.

Part of the decline in party identification results from the fact that young voters have always had a weaker sense of partisanship than older ones, and today there are, proportionally, a larger number of young voters than thirty or forty years ago. But the youthfulness of the population cannot explain all of the changes, for the decline in partisanship has occurred at all age levels. Moreover, those who reached voting age in the 1960s were less likely than those who came of age in the 1950s to acquire or maintain the party identification of their parents.[5] The decline in partisanship is real.

Children are more independent of their parents in policy preferences than in party identification. The correlation of children's attitudes with parental attitudes on issues involving civil liberties and racial questions is much lower than the correlation of party identification.[6] This may be because the issues change from one generation to the next, because children are more idealistic than their parents, or because most parents do not communicate to their children clear, consistent positions on a range of political issues.

However, in that small proportion of families where politics is the dominant topic of conversation and where political views are strongly held, fairly clear political ideologies (a term we shall define in a later section) do seem to be communicated to children. Apparently the college radicals of the 1960s were often the sons and daughters of people who had themselves been young

radicals. Presumably, deeply conservative young people come disproportion-
ately from families that were also deeply conservative. This transfer of political beliefs from one generation to another does not appear in large national
studies because the proportion of the population at either the far left or the
far right of the political spectrum is so small.

Effects of Religion

How the family forms and transmits political attitudes is not well understood,
but one important factor seems to be its religious traditions. In general,
Catholic families are somewhat more liberal, especially on economic issues,
than white Protestant ones, while Jewish families are decidedly more liberal
on both economic and noneconomic issues than either.[7] Among northern
whites, Protestants are likely to be Republican, Catholics are likely to be
Democratic, and Jews are overwhelmingly Democratic.[8] This may strike
some readers as strange, since in most elections and political debates no explicitly religious questions are at stake. But religion in the United States, and
probably elsewhere, conveys to its adherents not simply a set of beliefs about
God and morality but also a way of looking at human nature and human affairs. A religious tradition that emphasizes salvation through faith alone and
the need to avoid personal dissipation and worldly sin is likely to imbue a different way of looking at politics than one that has an optimistic view of
human nature, stresses the obligation to do good works, and is concerned as
much about social justice as personal rectitude.

In the 1980 election, America became aware of the political views of one
important religious tradition—that of evangelical Christians. The Moral
Majority and such ministers as Jerry Falwell campaigned on behalf of nearly
thirty million "born-again" people, nearly 20 percent of American adults.
Most of them live in the South, and almost all are Protestants (mainly
Baptists). Though their leaders endorse various causes, whether these endorsements have a large effect on voting, at least in general elections, is unclear. Pat Robertson, a fundamentalist minister, was unable to get all of his
co-religionists to vote for him in the 1988 presidential primaries. Moreover,
it would be a mistake to assume that the evangelical Protestants have distinctive attitudes toward all political issues.

Since religious involvement is essentially a moral commitment, it is not
surprising that born-again Christians are likely to differ from other people
mainly with respect to those moral or ethical issues that are on the political
agenda. Evangelicals are much more likely than nonevangelicals to oppose
abortions and the Equal Rights Amendment and to favor prayer in the public
schools. But on economic and defense issues, their views are much like those
of other people. They are culturally but not economically conservative; their
recent activity and prominence may reflect their strong reaction against the
"counterculture" of the 1960s and the prevalence of crime and drugs.[9]

The Gender Gap

During the 1984 and 1988 elections, much was made of the gender gap—that is, the differences in political views between women and men. In fact, such differences have existed for as long as we have records, though they have not always been big enough to make much difference in elections. What has changed about the gender gap is which party benefits from it.

During the 1950s, women were more likely than men to be Republicans; since the late 1960s, they have been more likely to be Democrats. The reason for the shift is that the political parties have changed their positions on the kinds of issues to which women respond differently from men—particularly certain social questions (such as prohibition and gun control) and foreign policy (especially the threat of war). For example, in the 1930s and 1940s more women than men wanted to ban the sale of liquor and keep the country out of war; this helped Republicans, who were then more sympathetic to such policies than were Democrats. In 1980 the aversion women felt to any policy that might increase the risk of war hurt the Republicans, whom they saw being led by a president (Reagan) ready to send troops into combat.[10]

The gender gap tends to disappear when gender-sensitive policies (such as war, gun control, or pornography) are not in the limelight and to reemerge when these topics become hotly partisan. Today the biggest male-female differences are over the use of force and confidence in the future.[11] Interestingly there are not great differences between men and women in their attitudes toward abortion or the Equal Rights Amendment (see Table 4.2).

Effects of Education

Studies going back more than half a century seem to show that attending college affects political attitudes, usually in a liberal direction. And these changes in political attitude tend to persist past college.[12] No one is entirely certain why college has this effect, but the attitudes and role of the faculty are surely an important part of the explanation. Professors are more liberal than members of other occupations, professors at the most prestigious schools are more liberal than those at less celebrated ones, professors in the social studies are more liberal than those in engineering or business, and younger faculty members are more liberal than older ones.[13]

At one time, the liberalizing effect of college had only a small impact on national policies because so few people were college graduates. In 1900 only 6 percent of Americans seventeen years of age had even graduated from high school, and less than 1 percent of twenty-three-year-olds were college graduates. By 1990, 78 percent of all Americans aged twenty-five and over were high school graduates, and 21 percent of those twenty-five and over were college graduates.[14] College has become, along with the family, an important source of political opinion for the American electorate.

TABLE 4.2 The Gender Gap: Differences in Political Views of Women and Men

Issue	Women	Men
The United States should keep out of world affairs. (1981)	43%	31%
I favor increased spending on the military. (1981)	67	80
Law should forbid anyone except police from possessing handguns. (1981)	51	35
We should return to a military draft. (1981)	39	52
I have a lot of confidence the country in a few years will be strong and prosperous. (1981)	27	39
I favor passage of the Equal Rights Amendment.	67	68
I favor making abortions legal. (1977)	45	49
I voted for George Bush in 1992.	37	38

SOURCE: Polls by Gallup, ABC News/*Washington Post*, and *TIME*/Yankelovich, Skelly and White, as summarized in *Public Opinion*, April/May 1982, pp. 30–32. Bush vote from *New York Times*, Nov. 5, 1992, p. B9.

CLEAVAGES IN PUBLIC OPINION

The way in which political opinions are formed helps explain the cleavages that exist among these opinions and why these cleavages do not follow any single political principle, but instead overlap and crosscut in bewildering complexity. If, for example, the United States were composed almost entirely of white Protestants, the great majority of whom did not attend college, and all of whom lived in the North, there would still be plenty of political conflict—the rich would have different views from the poor, the workers different views from the farmers—but that conflict would be much simpler to describe and explain. It might even lead to political parties that were more clearly aligned with competing political philosophies than those we now have. In fact, some democratic nations in the world today do have a population very much like the one I have just described, and the United States itself, during the first half of the nineteenth century, was overwhelmingly white, Protestant, and without much formal schooling.

Today, however, there are crosscutting cleavages based on race, ethnicity, religion, region, and education, in addition to those created by income and occupation. To the extent politics is sensitive to public opinion, it is sensitive to a variety of different and even competing publics. Not all of these publics have influence proportionate to their numbers or even to their numbers adjusted for the intensity of their feelings. A filtering process occurs that makes the opinions of some publics more influential than those of others.

Whatever this state of affairs may mean for democracy, it creates a messy situation for social scientists. It would be so much easier if everybody's opinion on political affairs reflected some single feature of one's life—one's income, occupation, age, race, or sex. Of course, some writers have argued that political opinion *is* a reflection of one such feature, social class, usually defined in terms of income or occupation. But that view, though containing some truth, is beset with inconsistencies: many groups with similar incomes or social positions are deeply divided over important political issues. For example, plumbers and professors have similar incomes, but they rarely have similar views.

In some other democracies, a single factor such as class may explain more of the differences in political attitudes than it does in the more socially heterogeneous United States. Most American blue-collar workers think of themselves as being "middle class," whereas most such workers in Britain or France describe themselves as "working class."[15] In Britain, the working class prefers the Labour party by a margin of three to one, while in the United States workers prefer the Democratic party by less than two to one (and in 1984 they gave most of their votes to Republican Ronald Reagan).[16]

Occupation

Indeed, some evidence indicates that occupation is becoming less important as an explanation of political opinions in this country than it once was. In the 1950s, differences in opinion on current political issues tended to be closely associated with occupations: those holding managerial or professional jobs had distinctly more conservative views on social-welfare policy and more internationalist views on foreign policy than did manual workers. During the next decade this pattern changed greatly.[17] Although some differences remain, over a long period of time—the data go back to the 1930s—the correlation between occupation (and income) and policy preferences has become steadily weaker. No one is quite certain why this has happened, but it is probably due in part to the changing effects of education on all levels of society but especially on people entering higher status occupations.

Race

If occupation has become less important in explaining political attitudes, race has become more so. Whites and blacks differ profoundly over busing to achieve racially balanced schools and the right of individuals to discriminate in housing sales, as well as over such nonracial matters as the death penalty (whites tend to favor), increased spending for national defense (whites tend to favor), and national health insurance (blacks tend to favor). In the 1960s, blacks were more opposed than whites to the war in Vietnam. The races feel pretty much the same, however, about such issues as wanting the courts to

TABLE 4.3 White Versus Black Opinions

Issue	Whites	Blacks
Favor busing children to achieve better racial balance in schools[a]	18%	67%
Favor homeowner's right to refuse to sell to black[a]	55	26
Favor spending more on national defense[b]	52	29
Favor national health insurance by government[c]	47	75
Oppose the death penalty[c]	26	57
Favor registration of young men for draft[b]	85	68
Favor harsher treatment of criminals by the courts[a]	86	76
Favor legalization of marijuana use[a]	25	29

SOURCE: (a) *Public Opinion* (April/May 1981), pp. 32–40, citing polls by Gallup, NORC, and ABC News/*Washington Post.* (b) Philip E. Converse et al., *American Social Attitudes, 1947–1978* (Cambridge, Mass.: Harvard University Press, 1980), p. 109. (c) Robert S. Erikson, Norman R. Luttbeg, and Kent L. Tedin, *American Public Opinion*, 2d ed. (New York: John Wiley & Sons, 1980), p. 169, citing polls by University of Michigan and Gallup.

deal more harshly with criminals, favoring draft registration, and opposing the legalization of marijuana.[18] (See Table 4.3.)

Blacks have become the single most consistently liberal group within the Democratic party.[19] A majority of blacks believe they are as a group better off today than they were ten years ago and that their children's opportunities will be better yet.[20] Curiously—and perhaps ominously—it is among *better-off* blacks that one finds the greatest skepticism about American society. Blacks holding professional jobs are much more likely than black manual laborers to believe that whites get unfair advantages and to say they have experienced discrimination.[21] Continued economic progress by blacks is no guarantee that black attitudes toward American society will change.

Other ethnic groups, such as Latinos and Asian-Americans, also have distinctive views (see Table 4.4). In general, Asians tend to be rather close to Anglo-whites in their opinions, while Latinos (except for Cuban-Americans) are somewhat closer to blacks in their views.

Region

It is widely believed that geographic region affects political attitudes and in particular that southerners and northerners disagree strongly on many policy questions. Southern members of Congress tend to vote more conservatively than northern ones,[22] and it stands to reason that this is because southern voters expect them to vote differently. The available evidence suggests that this difference among regions is greatest for noneconomic issues.[23] (See Table 4.5)

The family remains an important source of political beliefs even though families now take many forms, from single parents to this extended Hispanic family.

This helps explain why the South was so long a part of the Democratic party coalition: on national economic and social welfare policies (and on foreign policy), southerners express views not very different from northerners. That coalition is threatened, however, by the divisiveness produced by issues of race and liberty.

Anyone who has lived in both regions knows that the southern lifestyle differs from that of the Northeast. The South has, on the whole, been more accommodating to business enterprise and less accommodating to organized labor than the Northeast. It gave greater support to the third-party candidacy of George Wallace in 1968, which was a protest against big government and the growth of national power as well as against the extension of civil rights. Moreover, there is some evidence that by the 1970s, white southerners became more conservative than they had been in the 1950s, at least when compared to white northerners.[24] Finally, white southerners have become less attached to the Democratic party: whereas more than three-fourths described themselves as Democrats in 1952, only one-third did in 1986.[25] In 1980, 1984, 1988, and 1992, the South voted for the Republican presidential candidate by a large margin. These southern views are important. From 1940 to 1976, no Democrat except Lyndon Johnson in 1964 was able to win the presidency unless he carried the South.[26] In 1992, Bill Clinton carried only four southern states but still won the presidency.

TABLE 4.4 Party Identification and Political Attitudes of Ethnic Groups in California (1984)

	Anglo-white (*n* = 409)	Black (*n* = 335)	Latino (*n* = 593)	Asian-American (*n* = 305)
Party identification:				
Democrat	37%	78%	54%	35%
Republican	35	3	20	38
In between, other	28	18	26	27
Favor increased military spending	32	18	28	38
Favor increased welfare spending	59	84	73	66
Favor prayer in public schools	50	62	53	46
Favor death penalty for murder	75	47	57	73
Favor abortion on demand	60	47	40	53
Favor bilingual education programs	41	63	69	51

SOURCE: Bruce Cain and Roderick Kiewit, "California's Coming Minority Majority," *Public Opinion* (February-March 1986): 50–52. Reprinted with permission of American Enterprise Institute for Public Policy Research.

POLITICAL IDEOLOGY

Up to now, we have used the words *liberal* and *conservative* as if everyone agreed on what they meant and as if they accurately described general sets of political beliefs held by large segments of the population. Neither of these assumptions is correct. Like many useful words—love, peace, happiness—they are as vague as they are indispensable.

When we refer to people as liberals, conservatives, socialists, or radicals, we are implying that they have a political **ideology**—a coherent and consistent set of beliefs about who ought to rule, what principles rulers ought to obey, and what policies rulers ought to pursue.

Most studies of public opinion suggest that the great majority of citizens display relatively little ideology in their thinking, however that term is defined or measured. According to a leading study, people do not usually employ words like *liberal* or *conservative* in explaining or justifying their preferences for candidates or policies; not many more than half can define these terms; and there are relatively low correlations among the opinions people have on various political issues. From this, many scholars have concluded that the great

TABLE 4.5 Whites in the South Turning Republican

Percentage of southern white registered voters who identified with each party

1980	Republican	19%
	Democrat	52%
1982	Republican	27%
	Democrat	46%
1984	Republican	38%
	Democrat	37%
1986	Republican	36%
	Democrat	33%

SOURCE: *New York Times*–CBS News polls, as reported in *New York Times* (October 16, 1986), B16. Copyright © 1986 by the New York Times Company. Reprinted by permission.

NOTE: Surveys taken in September of each year.

majority of Americans do not think about politics in an ideological or even a very coherent manner and make little use of such concepts—so dear to political commentators and professors—as "liberal" or "conservative."[27]

Consistent Attitudes

This does not settle the question of ideology entirely, however. Critics who view Americans as ideological have argued that people can have general, and strongly felt, political dispositions even though they are not able to use such terms as *liberal* correctly. Moreover, public-opinion polls must, of necessity, ask rather simple questions, and so the apparent inconsistency in the answers people give at different times may only mean that the nature of the problem or the wording of the question has changed in ways not obvious to people analyzing the surveys.[28]

What constitutes consistency is very much in the mind of the observer. A voter might well believe that he or she is being quite consistent by, for example, favoring both strong government efforts on behalf of various social programs and the use of military force to protect oil supplies in the Middle East—yet to others such a mixture of "liberal" and "conservative" views would be considered ideologically "inconsistent."

Finally, some scholars argue that the dramatic events of the 1960s—the civil-rights revolution, the war in Vietnam, and the riots and protest demonstrations—increased the extent to which voters followed coherent ideological lines. The big increase in ideological thinking apparently occurred in 1964 when the election for president offered about as clear a choice as one could imagine between a defender of a large, activist federal government (Lyndon Johnson) and a staunch critic of such a government (Barry Goldwater).[29]

Other scholars disagree with this interpretation, arguing that changes in the way the questions were worded on opinion polls taken during the 1950s and 1960s make any comparison invalid.[30] Still others point out that voters may think more ideologically when one or both presidential candidates take sharply ideological positions (as happened in 1964, 1972, and 1980) and think less ideologically when both candidates are centrists (as was the case in 1952, 1956, 1960, and 1976).

Activists

Political activists, however, are much more likely than the average citizen to think in ideological terms and to take "consistent" positions on various issues.[31] In part, this may simply be the result of better information: activists spend all or most of their time on political affairs, and they may see relationships among issues that others do not. It may also reflect the kinds of people with whom activists associate: politics does not ordinarily make strange bedfellows; rather it brings like-minded people together. And activists have more structured opinions because, in part, the motives that lead them to engage in politics arise in many cases out of strong convictions about how the country ought to be run—that is to say, out of having a political ideology to begin with.

Various Categories of Opinion

It is useful to divide into three broad categories the opinions to which different people subscribe. The first involves questions about government policy toward the **economy.** We will describe as liberal those people who favor government efforts to ensure that everyone has a job, to spend more money on educational and social programs, and to increase rates of taxation for well-to-do persons.

The second category involves questions about **civil rights** and race relations. Here, liberals favor strong federal action to increase hiring opportunities for minorities, to provide compensatory programs for minorities, and to enforce civil-rights laws strictly.

The third involves questions about **personal conduct**. Liberals are tolerant of protest demonstrations, favor decriminalizing marijuana use and other "victimless crimes," emphasize protecting the rights of the accused over punishing criminals, and see the solution to crime in eliminating its causes rather than in getting tough with offenders.

Analyzing Consistency

Obviously a person can take a liberal position on one of these issues and take a conservative position on another without feeling the slightest degree "inconsistent"; several studies suggest that this is exactly what most people do.[32]

But some people have fairly consistent views. To simplify a complex picture, consider four ideological groups:

1. **Pure liberals**: These people are liberal on both economic and social issues. They want the government to reduce economic inequality, regulate business, tax the rich heavily, deal with crime by addressing its (allegedly) economic causes, protect the rights of accused criminals, allow abortion on demand, and guarantee the broadest possible freedoms of speech and press.

2. **Pure conservatives**: These people are conservative on both economic and social issues. They want less government regulation of business, lower taxes, and a greater reliance on markets, and they advocate getting tough on criminals, punishing pornographers, and cutting back on welfare payments.

3. **Libertarians**: These people are advocates of free markets, low taxes, and a small government (which makes them economic conservatives), but they also support the greatest amount of personal freedom in social matters, such as speech, drug use, and abortion (which makes them social liberals).

4. **Populists**: These people are liberal on economic matters, desiring government regulation of business and heavy federal spending on public programs, but conservative on social matters, opposing abortion on demand and favoring a crackdown on crime, drug use, and pornography. Many also favor legalizing prayers in school.

There are many exceptions and mixed cases, of course, but in general certain kinds of people are more likely than others to fit into one or another category. Pure liberals are usually in professional occupations, live in big cities, and have postgraduate educations. Pure conservatives are more likely to have come from small towns, to live in the Midwest or South, and to be in business. Libertarians are a small group, mostly found in big cities, and have had college educations and business employment, especially in high-tech industries. Populists are often blue-collar workers who have not been to college.

Many individuals do not fit into any of these categories. Moreover, the classification scheme would become even more complicated if additional issues were added—foreign policy, for example. Nevertheless, the complicated nature in which these categories of opinion are packaged together can help us understand the diversity of political opinion in the United States and the difficulty of putting together—and keeping united—a winning coalition of groups.

Though the average citizen cannot be described as being purely liberal or purely conservative, bear in mind that political activists often do display a great deal of attitude consistency. In other words, if they are liberal on one set of issues, they are likely to be liberal on all others. This applies both to congressional candidates and to voters who have the highest levels of education and the most information about politics and government.[33] Since such informed, educated people are more likely to vote and otherwise participate in politics than uninformed, uneducated people, the activists' ideology is more important than their numbers might indicate. Candidates, activists, and knowledgeable followers of politics may thus impart to political decision making a greater degree of ideological consistency than the average voter cares to see. This is one reason (though surely not the only one) why some policies preferred by the voters get filtered out by the process of political representation.

POLITICAL ELITES AND THE "NEW CLASS"

Since the views of political activists differ from those of the average citizen, it is important to give special attention to the opinions of political elites. By **elite** we do not mean people who are "better" than other people, but rather those who have a disproportionate amount of some valued social resource—money, schooling, prestige, political power, or whatever. Every society, capitalist or socialist, has an elite because in every society government officials will have more power than ordinary citizens, some people will earn more money than others, and some people will have more prestige than others because of popularity, beauty, wealth, athletic prowess, artistic talents, or political power.

Shift to Liberalism

American elites once were overwhelmingly conservative and Republican, but by the mid-1960s this had begun to change. Certain elite groups were becoming much more liberal, and one could no longer assume that anybody with a high income or a professional occupation was a conservative.[34] This change should not be overstated. During economic recessions, college-educated persons are less likely to vote Democratic than are people without a college degree. But in good times, the differences have almost disappeared: in 1984, for example, 40 percent of college graduates, compared to 39 percent of high school graduates, voted for Democratic candidates, an insignificant difference. A clear majority of one group of educated persons—those with post-graduate degrees—now supports the Democrats.[35]

The New Class

Some writers have described the split that has occurred among middle-class voters as one pitting the *traditional middle class* against the *new class*. The former lives in the suburbs, attends religious services, is friendly toward business, has conservative views on economic issues and most social questions, and tends to vote Republican. Members of the so-called new class may earn roughly the same amount of money as those in the traditional middle class, but they are younger, live in cities, rarely attend religious services, have liberal views on economic and social issues, include many people with post-graduate degrees, and vote Democratic.[36] (The term *Yuppies*, from *Young Urban Professionals*, which reporters began using in the mid-1980s, covers too broad a collection of people to have much meaning. The serious student of politics is well advised to be skeptical of the latest fads in pop sociology.) Because the middle class is split between these two groups, the historical link between economic status and political attitudes has weakened: both groups are affluent, but they disagree politically.

The key to this split is education and, to a lesser degree, occupation. Members of the new class tend to have more post-graduate education and to work in the professions, not business. Their privileges arise from their command of technical skills more than their business acumen. This is why they are called a "new" class. The old class distinctions, of the sort Karl Marx made famous, were based simply on wealth or ownership of the means of production. The new class distinctions are based in part on education and talent at managing words. Such people are found employed by universities, government, voluntary associations, and the mass media, or as technicians, researchers, and writers. They often live in or near cities with large universities or major research firms.[37]

This split in the American middle class has created great strains within the political parties. As we shall see in Chapter 5, both parties have been deeply divided by the conflict between their ideological and nonideological wings, with enormous differences over such questions as divorce, abortion, homosexuality, environmental protection, and civil rights. (On economic issues, the differences are much less.)

The conflict between the liberal new class and the more conservative traditional middle class has often been so intense that it has dominated politics. Some have even described it as a **culture war**. One side favors abortion on demand and quotas in hiring and school admissions in order to help minorities; believes that society is largely responsible for poverty, crime, drug abuse, and growing welfare rolls; and laughs when Vice President Quayle supports "traditional family values" by attacking the television character, Murphy Brown, who conceived a child out of wedlock. The other side opposes abortion and quotas; thinks individual irresponsibility explains much poverty, crime, drug use, and welfare dependency; and may enjoy Murphy Brown on television but thinks children should be born and raised in two-parent families.

In good times, this culture war may dominate political campaigns, as it did in 1972, 1984, and 1988. In bad times, economic problems push the culture war into the background, as happened in 1980 and 1992. But between elections, the war continues in magazines, newspapers, and popular discourse.

THE IMPACT OF THE MEDIA

Many of the changes in the nature of American politics have gone hand in hand with major changes in the organization and technology of the press. This is not to say that the nature of journalism dictates the nature of politics, but that politics, being essentially a form of communication, responds to changes in how communications are carried on.

Journalism in American Political History

We can trace four important periods in journalistic history. In the early years of the Republic, politicians of various factions and parties created, sponsored, and controlled newspapers to further their interests. The newspapers themselves were small and expensive (the type was set by hand); they had few large advertisers to pay their bills (hence their dependence on politicians); and they circulated chiefly among the political and cultural elites who could afford them.

In the mid-nineteenth century, however, the rise of self-supporting, mass-readership daily newspapers became possible because of changes in technology and society: the development of the high-speed rotary press, the invention of the telegraph, the creation in 1848 of the Associated Press, and the emergence of large urban centers that could support cheap daily newspapers and patronize the merchants who paid for advertising. Consequently newspapers no longer needed political patronage to prosper. The partisanship they displayed arose from the convictions of editors and publishers rather than party sponsors. Sensationalism attracted large readerships. Strong-willed journalists like Joseph Pulitzer and William Randolph Hearst, whose newspapers appealed to the average citizen and especially the immigrants flooding into the large cities, often became powerful political forces. For all their excesses, the mass newspapers began to create a common national culture, to free the press from government control, and to demonstrate how exciting (and profitable) the criticism of public policy and the revelation of public scandal could be.

The growing middle class was often repelled by what it called "yellow journalism" and, around the turn of the century, developed a taste for political reform. To meet this market, a variety of national magazines appeared that, unlike the existing ones devoted to manners and literature, discussed issues of public policy. The new national opinion magazines provided an opportunity for individual writers, including the so-called muckrakers who set the pattern for what we now call investigative reporting, to gain a national

The media have always been important in American politics, as when newspapers flamboyantly covered—and perhaps helped cause—the Spanish-American war.

following. Meanwhile, the great circulation wars among the big-city daily newspapers started to wane as the more successful papers bought up or otherwise eliminated their competition. This, combined with the growing education and sophistication of readers, reduced the need for sensationalism. And the founding publishers were gradually replaced by less flamboyant managers. Taken together, these changes helped increase the power of editors and reporters and made them a force to be reckoned with, along with advertisers, readers, and other interest groups.

Radio came on the national scene in the 1920s; television appeared in the late 1940s. They represented a major change in the way news was gathered and disseminated, though few politicians at first understood the importance of this change. A broadcast permits public officials to speak directly to audiences without their remarks being filtered through editors and reporters. But this obvious advantage to politicians was offset by a disadvantage: people could easily ignore a speech broadcast on radio or television either by not listening at all or by tuning in a different station. And space in a newspaper is cheap compared with time on a broadcast. As a result, far fewer political personalities can be covered by radio and television news than by newspapers, and each news segment must be quite brief to hold the audience's attention.

Thus, to obtain the advantages of electronic media coverage, public officials must do something sufficiently bold or colorful to gain free access to radio and television news broadcasts, or else they must find the money to purchase radio and television time. Except for the president (who is routinely covered by the media and ordinarily can get free time to speak to the nation on important matters), politicians must struggle for access to the media by making controversial statements, acquiring a national name, or purchasing expensive time. In short, broadcast journalism has made it possible for politicians to develop personal followings independent of party structure, perhaps contributing to the decline of party loyalties and organization that will be discussed in Chapter 5.

THE STRUCTURE OF THE MEDIA

The relationship between journalism and politics is a two-way street: though politicians take advantage, as best they can, of the media available to them, these media, in turn, attempt to use politics and politicians as a way of both entertaining and informing their audiences. The mass media, whatever they may say to the contrary, are not simply a mirror held up to reality. There is inevitably a process of selection, of editing, and of emphasis; this process reflects, to some degree, the way in which the media are organized, the kinds of audiences they hope to attract, and the preferences and opinions of the members of the media.

Degree of Competition

Contrary to popular belief, the number of daily newspapers in this country has not significantly declined. There has been a decline, however, in the number of cities that have competing daily newspapers. Many of the largest cities—New York, Chicago, Los Angeles—have at least two central-city newspapers, but most smaller cities have only one. This is partially offset by the fact that many metropolitan areas have two or more neighboring cities that each have a newspaper with overlapping readership.

Radio and television, by contrast, are intensely competitive and becoming more so. Almost every American home has a radio and a television set. Though there are only four national television networks, there are more than seven hundred television stations, each of which has its own news program. Local stations affiliated with a network are free to accept or reject network programs. There are also more than eight thousand cable-TV systems serving more than 48 million people, and more than nine thousand radio stations, some of which broadcast nothing but the news whereas others develop a specialized following among blacks, Hispanics, or other minorities. Magazines exist for every conceivable interest. The number of news sources available to an American is vast.

In most other democratic nations (Britain, France, Sweden, Japan, and elsewhere), the media are owned and operated with a national audience in mind. But to a degree that would astonish most foreigners, the American press—radio, television, and newspapers—is made up of locally owned and managed enterprises, and it is primarily oriented to its local market and local audience. Government regulations developed by the Federal Communications Commission prevent anyone (including the networks) from owning and operating more than one AM radio, one FM radio, or one television station in a given market. Nationally (with some exceptions), no one may own more than twelve television stations and twelve AM and FM radio stations, and the networks may not compel any local affiliate to accept any particular broadcast. (In fact, almost all network news programs are carried by the affiliates.) The result has been the development of a decentralized broadcasting industry that offers more local than national news.

The National Media

The local orientation of much of the American communications media is partially offset, however, by the emergence of certain publications and broadcast services that constitute a kind of national press. The wire services—the Associated Press (AP) and United Press International (UPI)—supply most of the national news that local papers publish. Certain news magazines—*Time, Newsweek, U.S. News & World Report*—have a national readership. The network evening news broadcasts produced by ABC, CBS, and NBC are carried by most television stations with a network affiliation. Many people in government—including the CIA—closely watch CNN, the all-news television network, in order to keep abreast of world developments. There are only two large, truly national newspapers, the *Wall Street Journal* and *USA Today*, but the *New York Times* and the *Washington Post* have acquired national influence because they are read daily by virtually every important official in Washington and because the television networks and many local newspapers use the stories that the *Times* and the *Post* print.[38]

The existence of a national press is important for two reasons: First, government officials in Washington pay great attention to what these media say about them—and much less, if any, attention to what local papers and broadcasters say. Second, reporters and editors for the national press tend to differ from local journalists: they are usually better paid, often graduates of more prestigious universities, and generally more liberal.[39] Above all, they seek—and frequently obtain—the opportunity to write "background," "investigative," or interpretive stories about issues and policies.[40]

The national press plays a role of gatekeeper, scorekeeper, and watchdog for the federal government. As **gatekeeper**, it can influence what subjects become national political issues, and for how long. Automobile safety, water pollution, and the quality of prescription drugs were not major political issues before the national press began giving substantial attention to them. Elite opinion about the war in Vietnam also changed significantly as the attitude toward the war expressed by the national media changed. And media attention to crime varied considerably between the late 1960s and the early 1980s, although the reality was that crime rates increased steadily.

As **scorekeeper**, the national media help make political reputations, note who is being "mentioned" as a presidential candidate, and help decide who wins and who loses in Washington politics. The media's attention can be very useful in launching a presidential campaign. As a virtually unknown former Georgia governor planning his presidential campaign in 1975, Jimmy Carter successfully cultivated the national press and, before the primary elections, was getting as much national news coverage as his better-known rivals. And media attention to Gary Hart increased enormously after he managed to come in second in the Iowa caucuses in February 1984, probably aiding this little-known candidate in his big victory in the subsequent New Hampshire primary (to which, as the first primary election, the press always accords far more coverage than is warranted by the state's small size).

Finally, the media has a **watchdog** role. For example, Hart's background and record were closely examined only after his New Hampshire victory, when the press decided he was the "man to beat." This close scrutiny is perfectly natural. The media have an instinctive—and profitable—desire to expose scandals and investigate personalities, to be tolerant of underdogs and tough on frontrunners.

Newspapers and television stations play these three roles in somewhat different ways. A newspaper can cover more stories in greater depth than a TV station and faces less competition from other papers. A TV station faces brutal competition, must select its programs in part for their visual impact, and has to keep its stories short and punchy. As a result, newspaper reporters have more freedom but earn less money than television news broadcasters, who have little freedom (the fear of losing audiences is keen) but can make a lot of money if they are attractive personalities who photograph well. Because of these organizational differences, it is newspapers and magazines, much more than television, that perform the gatekeeper, scorekeeper, and watchdog functions.

RULES GOVERNING THE MEDIA

Ironically the most competitive part of the media—radio and television broadcasting—must have a governmental license to operate and must conform to a variety of government regulations whereas the least competitive part—the big-city newspapers—is almost entirely free from government regulation.

ON BACKGROUND

★ ★ ★

When politicians talk to the press, they set certain ground rules that the press (usually) observes. These rules specify who, if anyone, is quoted as the source of the story.

ON THE RECORD

The official is quoted by name. For example: "I say that water runs downhill, and you can quote me on that."

OFF THE RECORD

What the official says cannot be printed. For example: "Off the record, the head of my party is a complete whacko."

ON BACKGROUND

What the official says can be printed, but it may not be attributed to him or her by name. For example: "A well-placed source said today that the sun will continue to rise in the East."

ON DEEP BACKGROUND

What the official says can be printed, but it cannot be attributed to anybody. The reporter must say it on his or her own authority. For example: "In my opinion this administration secretly believes that two plus two equals five."

Freedom of the Press

Newspapers and magazines need no license to publish. The First Amendment to the Constitution has been interpreted to mean that no federal or state government can place "prior restraints" (that is, censorship) on the press except in very narrowly defined circumstances. (For example, the Supreme Court refused to allow the federal government to stop the *New York Times* from publishing the Pentagon Papers, a set of secret documents that had been stolen by an antiwar activist.[41]) And once something is published—including attacks on public figures or private persons—the courts have so narrowly defined "libelous," "obscene," and "incitement to commit an illegal act" as to make it more difficult in the United States than in any other nation for the press to be found guilty of misconduct.[42]

Reporters believe they should have the right to keep confidential the sources of their stories. Although some states have passed laws to that effect, most states and the federal government have not. Thus the courts must decide, in each case, whether a journalist's need to protect confidentiality outweighs the government's need to gather evidence in a criminal investigation or an accused person's need to be informed of the evidence against him. In 1978 a *New York Times* reporter was jailed for contempt of court for refusing to reveal confidential sources that the court determined should be given to the defense attorney in a murder trial. On appeal, the Supreme Court decided against the reporter, holding that the accused person's right to a fair trial includes the right to compel the production of evidence, even from reporters.

Regulation and Deregulation

No one may operate a radio or television station without a license from the Federal Communications Commission (FCC), renewable every seven years for radio and every five for television. An application for renewal is rarely refused, but in order to get a renewal the FCC until recently required the broadcaster to provide detailed information about its programming and on how it planned to serve "community needs." Thereby the FCC could influence the station, for example, to reduce the amount of violence or to alter the way it portrayed ethnic groups. But of late, a movement has arisen to deregulate broadcasting on the grounds that competition should be allowed to determine how each station defines and serves a community's needs. Since the 1980s, licenses are automatically renewed unless some community group formally objects, in which case the FCC holds a hearing. As a result, some of the old rules—for instance, that each hour on TV could contain only sixteen minutes of commercials—are no longer strictly enforced.

Political broadcasts on radio and TV are regulated in ways that stories and advertisements in newspapers are not. The **personal-attack rule** gives a person whose character is attacked on the air a chance to respond. The **equal-time rule** requires broadcasters who give or sell advertising to one political candidate to make available equal time to that candidate's opponent. (The equal-time rule has been modified to allow televised debates between major-party candidates without requiring that minor-party candidates also be invited to participate.) At one time there was also a rule, called the **fairness doctrine**, that required broadcasters to present both sides of a controversial issue, but in 1988 the FCC abolished it on the grounds that it violated the right to free speech. Even so, many stations that broadcast editorials will invite a responsible spokesperson to present an opposed point of view.

GOVERNMENT AND THE NEWS

Every government agency, every public official, spends a great deal of time trying to shape public opinion. In a government of separated powers, any government agency that fails to cultivate public opinion will sooner or later find itself weak, without allies, and in trouble.

Prominence of the President

Theodore Roosevelt was the first president to raise to an art form the systematic cultivation of the press; Teddy's nephew, Franklin Roosevelt, institutionalized the relationship between reporters and the president by making his press secretary a major instrument for cultivating and managing, as well as informing, the press.[43]

Today the press secretary heads a large staff that meets with reporters, briefs the president on questions the president is likely to be asked, attempts to control the flow of news from cabinet departments to the press, and arranges briefings for out-of-town editors. All this effort is directed toward influencing (or bypassing) the White House press corps, a group of journalists who have a lounge in the White House itself. No other nation in the world has brought the press into such close physical proximity to the head of its government: the press is on hand if the president goes jogging, has any sort of medical problem, greets a boy scout, or takes a trip to his country retreat at Camp David.

Coverage of Congress

Congress has watched all this with irritation and envy, resenting the attention given the president but uncertain how it can compete. The 435 members of the House are so numerous and play such specialized roles that they do not get much individualized press coverage. And until the 1974 Nixon impeachment hearings, House committees generally refused to permit electronic coverage. In 1979 cable TV began carrying House sessions gavel-to-gavel, though not many people watch.[44]

No other nation exposes the private lives of its chief executives to such close media attention.

The Senate has used television much more fully, heightening the already substantial advantage senators have over representatives in getting into the public eye. Although televised debates on the Senate floor were not permitted until 1978, Senate committee hearings have been frequently televised ever since Senator Estes Kefauver demonstrated the power of the medium in 1950. In June 1986, regular television coverage of Senate floor debates began. Now you can see every meeting of the House and Senate, unedited and without commercials, on C-SPAN.

Senatorial use of television has helped turn the Senate into the incubator of presidential candidates, for Washington is a city full of cameras, and an investigation, a scandal, a major political conflict, or an articulate and telegenic personality can usually get a senator on the air.

INTERPRETING POLITICAL NEWS

We are inclined to accept news stories—especially those about events of which we have no firsthand knowledge—without question. This may be particularly true of television stories since they enable us to judge both what is said and how it is said. Because of this, Americans say that they are more likely to rely on and believe television than newspaper stories. This claim should be taken with a grain of salt, however, for careful audience surveys suggest that far more people read some part of a newspaper every day than watch a daily TV news program (see Table 4.6).

One reason for questioning news stories is that members of the national media have political views very different from those of the average citizen (see

TABLE 4.6 The Sources and Creditability of News

Source of Most News*	1959	1986
Television	51%	66%
Newspapers	57	36
Radio	34	14
Magazines	8	4
Other	4	5
Most Believable Source of News	**1959**	**1986**
Television	29%	55%
Newspapers	32	21
Radio	12	6
Magazines	10	7

*Percentages add to more than 100 because people mentioned more than one source.

SOURCE: The Roper Organization, Inc. Reprinted by permission.

Table 4.7). Several studies show that editors, reporters, TV producers, and commentators are far more liberal than voters in general.[45] In 1980, for example, members of the national media voted overwhelmingly against Reagan.

ARE NEWS STORIES SLANTED?

One should not assume that the political opinions of journalists automatically lead them to slant their stories in certain ways. Other factors influence how these stories are written, including the need to meet an urgent deadline, the desire to attract an audience, a professional obligation to be fair and tell the truth, and the need to develop sources among people holding different views. For example, whatever their views, the national media gave, according to a careful study, quite evenhanded treatment to the opposing candidates during the 1980 presidential campaign.[46] In the 1984 campaign, on the other hand, Mondale received more favorable coverage than Reagan, and in the 1988 primaries, both leading Democratic candidates, Dukakis and Jackson, got kinder treatment than George Bush, the Republican nominee.

Still, it would be astonishing if strongly held beliefs had *no* effect on what is written or broadcast. To understand the circumstances under which a reporter's or editor's opinion can affect a story, and thus to interpret intelligently what we read and hear, we must distinguish among three *kinds* of stories:

TABLE 4.7 Journalist Opinion versus Public Opinion

	Journalists	The public
Self-described ideology:		
Liberal	55%	23%
Conservative	17	29
Favor government regulation of business	49	22
U.S. should withdraw investments from South Africa	62	31
Allow women to have abortions	82	49
Allow prayer in public schools	25	74
Favor "affirmative action"	81	56
Favor death penalty for murder	47	75
Want stricter controls on handguns	78	50
Increase defense budget	15	38
Favor hiring homosexuals	89	55

SOURCE: *Los Angeles Times* poll of about 3,000 citizens and 2,700 journalists nationwide, as reported in William Schneider and I. A. Lewis, "Views on the News," *Public Opinion* (August–September 1985), 7. Reprinted with permission of American Enterprise Institute for Public Policy Research.

1. **Routine Stories**: These are public events, routinely covered by re-porters, involving relatively simple, easily described acts or statements.
2. **Selected Stories**: These are public events knowable to any reporter who cares to inquire, but involving acts and statements not routinely covered by a group of reporters, such as an obscure agency issuing a controversial ruling, an unknown member of Congress conducting an investigation, or an interest group working for the passage of a bill.
3. **Insider Stories**: Events not usually made public become public because someone with inside knowledge about them tells a reporter. The reporter may have worked hard to learn these facts, in which case we say it is "in-vestigative reporting," or some official may have wanted a story to get out, in which case we call it a "leak."

Routine stories are covered in virtually the same way by almost all the media, differing only in their length, their headlines, and the position the story occupies on the pages or in the evening news broadcast. The wire ser-vices—AP and UPI—supply routine stories immediately to practically every daily newspaper in America. (The headlines and placement, however, can make a big difference in how the same story is perceived.) The political opin-ions of journalists have the least effect on these stories, especially if several competing journalists are covering the same story over a protracted period of time. That is why coverage of a presidential campaign tends to be even-handed.

Even a routine news story can be incorrectly reported, however, if something dramatic or unique occurs. An important example was the reporting of the Tet Offensive toward the end of the Vietnam War—an all-out North Vietnamese attack on cities held by the South Vietnamese and their American allies. The attack failed—repulsed with heavy North Vietnamese casualties—but the news stories reported exactly the opposite, that the North Vietnamese could move and fight at will and that the Americans were help-less to oppose them. A painstaking analysis of the offensive later revealed the errors and omissions that led to the misleading versions published. Although the reporters' political views were not the whole explanation of these mis-takes—it is always difficult for reporters, however fair, to grasp quickly and accurately a major military struggle—the antiwar views of most reporters probably did reinforce their interpretations of Tet.[47]

Nonroutine stories must be selected, and thus someone must do the se-lecting. The grounds on which the selections are made include the intrinsic interest of a story as well as the reporter's or editor's beliefs about what *ought* to be interesting. Among these beliefs are the political ideologies of the jour-nalists. A liberal paper may choose to cover stories about white-collar crime, consumerism, the problems of minorities, and the arms race; a conservative paper might instead select stories about street crime, the decline of the central business district, and the problems of drug abuse and welfare fraud.

Nor are selected stories rare. In order to compete with television, news-papers increasingly print feature stories, thereby becoming more like a maga-zine with something for everybody. As a result, a large part of a newspaper consists of precisely the kind of stories that are most likely to be influenced by the attitudes of reporters.

Every reader should examine such stories by asking: What beliefs or ideas led the editors to print this story rather than a quite different one? Sometimes the answer is simple—human interest or a desire to attract certain readers. At other times the answer is more complex—a belief in the goodness or badness of some cause or special interest.

News Leaks

Insider stories raise the most difficult questions of all, those of motive. When somebody in government with private or confidential information gives a story to a reporter, that somebody must have a reason for doing so. But the motives of those who leak information are almost never reported. Sometimes the reporter does not know the motives. More often, one suspects, the re-porter is dependent on "highly placed sources" and is reluctant to compro-mise them.

The reliance on the insider leak is as old as the Republic. At one time reporters were grateful for "background briefings" at which top government officials tried to put themselves in the best possible light while explaining the inner meaning of American policy. In the aftermath of Vietnam and Watergate, both of which weakened the credibility of "the Establishment," many reporters became more interested in the leaks from insiders critical of top officials. In neither case were the motives of the sources discussed, leaving the reader or viewer to accept at face value whatever remarks are attributed to unnamed "highly placed sources" or "well-informed observers."

American government is the leakiest of the world. The bureaucracy, members of Congress, and the White House staff regularly leak stories favorable to their interests. Of late, the leaks have become geysers, gushing forth torrents of insider stories. Many people in and out of government find it distressing that our government seems unable to keep anything secret for long. Others think that the public has a right to know even more information and that there are still too many secrets.

However you evaluate leaks, you should understand why we have so many. The answer can be found in the Constitution of the United States. Because we have separate institutions sharing powers, each branch of government competes with the other branches to get power. One way to compete is to try to use the press to advance your pet projects and to make someone else look bad. There are far fewer leaks in other democratic nations, mainly because power is centralized in the hands of a prime minister who does not need to leak information in order to get the upper hand over the legislature and because the legislature has too little information to be a good source of leaks. In addition, we have no Official Secrets Act of the kind that exists in England; except for a few matters, it is not against the law for the press to receive and print government secrets.

The Influence of Media Opinions on Opinion and Politics

For the opinions of journalists to influence the opinions of the public, two things must happen. First, the views of journalists must affect what they write or televise. Second, what they write or televise must change what citizens think.

As we saw, the beliefs of journalists probably have the least effect on routine stories and the greatest effect on selected and insider stories. But even if we assume that the selection of these nonroutine stories is affected by the media's political beliefs, what effect do such stories have on readers and viewers? We cannot be certain, but in general the evidence seems to be this: If the citizenry has personal knowledge of the facts, the media are not likely to have much influence at all. Thus it makes little difference whether the media give much or little coverage to crime, interest rates, gasoline prices, or the quality of the public schools. Most people already have some knowledge and strong beliefs about these matters. Similarly the media are not likely to affect the outcome of important elections—say, presidential races—because people have lots of sources of information about presidential candidates: friends, neighbors, magazines, business and labor union associates, and the like.

But the media are likely to have significant influence on how we think about matters on which we are not well informed. For example, most of us have no direct knowledge of Central America, Russia, military technology, or space exploration. We don't even have much firsthand experience with environmental issues (unless there is a major and obvious smog or pollution problem where we live). What the media choose to say about these things may well have a major effect on what we think. Even if such stories don't tell us *what* to think about these problems, they at least tell us that such matters are problems; in that way, these issues get on the public agenda. By the same token, most of us have little information about candidates for lesser offices (members of Congress or state legislators), and so we may rely on media accounts of the candidates for cues as to how to vote. But even in these cases, many of us read or view the news selectively: we filter stories through our own prior beliefs about how the world works, what policies make sense, how much the government should spend, and whether we think we can trust the Russians (or the Nicaraguans, or the South Africans).

The most important effect television has had on politics has been its ability to give candidates and officeholders access to tens of millions of people—provided these politicians supply stories that are profitable to produce. These are:

1. *Scandals*: Attacking your opponent has been part of American politics since the time of John Adams and Thomas Jefferson, but a juicy scandal or personal criticism gets more attention more quickly today than ever before. People may lament "negative advertising" and "attack journalism," but the blunt and sad truth is, they work.

2. *Visuals*: Rather than being interested in long speeches or policy papers, television wants to show action. Politicians, therefore, spend a lot of time finding opportunities to pose in front of dramatic backdrops (such as the scene of a hurricane) or with people who symbolize some message (such as police officers, factory workers, or senior citizens).

3. *Sound bites*: Radio and television don't want to broadcast an entire speech, or even one paragraph from a speech, nor do they want to dissect a complex argument; they prefer a ten-second phrase, called a sound bite, that they can air to let people think that the bite conveys the whole message.

4. *Prettiness*: Television favors attractive faces and, among men, deep voices. It flatters youthfulness and penalizes old age; it makes chubby people look obese and causes high-pitched voices to sound shrill.

Politicians know this, and they play to it. Candidates who are young and attractive and who can pose in interesting settings have an advantage over those who are old and ugly or who spend their time in an office. Officials who can make their point in a dramatic ten-second phrase, especially one that attacks their rivals, have an advantage over those who think that clarifying an issue requires five or ten minutes and who feel that discussing a problem should not involve personalities.

The most important political debates in American history occurred between two candidates for the Senate who were campaigning in Illinois. At the time (1858), every word they said was reported and widely discussed. If television had been around, these debates wouldn't have been covered. Here was a tall, skinny man with a high-pitched voice, followed by a short, fat man, each talking for an hour or so while standing motionless on a platform. Moreover, a Senate race in one state was hardly as important as other events with more visual appeal that happened in 1858, such as a new stagecoach line completing its first trip to San Francisco. And so we would not have been aware of the debate between Abraham Lincoln and Stephen A. Douglas over the morality of slavery, the meaning of popular sovereignty, and the future of the republic. But we would have seen some great shots of that stagecoach pulling into San Francisco.

The Influence of Politicians on the Media

The media may, within limits, shape opinion and politics, but politicians can shape the media. They cannot regulate or control it, but they can influence it. Among the most effective techniques are these:

1. *Press officers*: Every agency and high-ranking official has one or several (sometimes scores) of press officers who not only release information but try to shape the news so that it gets the most favorable attention.

2. *Targeting the 6 P.M. news*: The White House especially, but many other government institutions as well, organize their daily business and speech making with one thought in mind: How will this look on the 6 P.M. news?

3. *Spin control*: When a political event occurs, presidents and presidential candidates rally key aides to contact reporters and go on talk shows to shape, as best they can, the way the event is interpreted. This is called spin control, and people who are good at it are called spin doctors.

4. *Leaks, flattery, and ideology*: Politicians can win the goodwill of reporters, up to a point, by (a) giving them off-the-record information and insider stories that will enable the reporter to publish or broadcast an attention-getting story, (b) flattering reporters and editors by asking their advice or appearing to take them seriously, and (c) expressing the same ideological or political convictions the journalists may have.

5. *Rewards and penalties*: The ultimate weapon a president has in his love-hate relationship with the press is to give special access to favored reporters and deny it to those who are disliked. Presidents Kennedy and Johnson regularly gave brutal but private tongue-lashings to journalists they didn't like and exclusive interviews to those they did. President Nixon made the mistake of making his complaints publicly, thus earning him enduring hostility from the press.

These techniques have their limitations. The most important one is that running a good story, especially if it involves a scandal, will almost always be more important to a reporter or editor than maintaining good relations with political sources. Lyndon Johnson knew and practiced every trick in the book to win journalistic support, but after the Vietnam War became unpopular, it was all for naught. Richard Nixon was brought down by press exposés of Watergate, and Jimmy Carter was never popular with most journalists while in office. (He became more popular as an ex-president.) The press and the president need but do not trust one another; theirs is inevitably a stormy relationship.

SUMMARY

Political opinions are shaped by sex, by family, religious, and ethnic traditions, by occupational experiences, and by higher education. Though still important, economic and occupational sources of opinion have become less significant with the increase in the number of people attending college and holding high-paying but nonbusiness jobs (the new class).

Most Americans do not have highly ideological (that is, systematic and "consistent") political views, but a substantial proportion of those active in political life—the political elite—can be described as liberals or conservatives. Among citizens at large, many people are likely to have mixed ideologies—for example, to be liberal on economic issues but conservative on social ones, or vice versa. A sense of party identification remains important even though it has been growing weaker among many voters. Though parental influence is strong in shaping one's party identification, it is not decisive.

Changes in the nature of American politics have been accompanied by and influenced by changes in the nature of the mass media. The recent weakening of political parties has been accelerated by the ability of candidates to speak directly to their constituents by radio and television.

The role of journalists in a democratic society poses an inevitable dilemma: if they are to serve well, their functions as information gatherer, gatekeeper, scorekeeper, and watchdog, they must be free of government control. But to the extent they are free of such controls, they are also free to act in their own interests, whether political or economic. In the United States a competitive press largely free of government controls (except in the area of broadcast licenses) has produced a substantial diversity of opinion and a general (though not unanimous) commitment to the goal of fairness in news reporting. The national media are in general more liberal than the local media, but the extent to which a reporter's opinion affects a story varies greatly with the kind of story—routine, selective, or insider.

SUGGESTED READINGS

Braestrup, Peter. *Big Story: How the American Press and Television Reported and Interpreted the Crisis of Tet 1968 in Vietnam and Washington*. Boulder, Col.: Westview, 1977, 2 volumes. A massive, detailed account on how the press reported one critical event; the factual accuracy or inaccuracy of each story is carefully checked.

Crouse, Timothy. *The Boys on the Bus*. New York: Random House, 1973. A lively, irreverent account by a reporter of how reporters cover a presidential campaign.

Epstein, Edward J. *Between Fact and Fiction: The Problem of Journalism*. New York: Random House, 1975. Essays by a perceptive student of the press on media coverage of Watergate, the Pentagon Papers, the deaths of Black Panthers, and other major stories.

———.*News from Nowhere*. New York: Random House, 1973. Analysis of how television network news programs are produced and shaped.

Garment, Suzanne. *Scandal: The Culture of Mistrust in American Government*. New York: Random House, 1991. A penetrating analysis of our growing fascination with political scandal and the journalistic and governmental forces that pander to this obsession.

Graber, Doris A. *Mass Media and American Politics*, 3d ed. Washington, D.C.: Congressional Quarterly Press, 1988. A good summary of what we know about the press and politics.

Grossman, Michael Baruch, and Martha Joynt Kumar. *Portraying the President: The White House and the News Media*. Baltimore: Johns Hopkins University Press, 1981. How the White House is organized to handle the press and how the press is organized to cover the president.

Iyengar, Shanto, and Donald R. Kinder. *News That Matters*. Chicago: University of Chicago Press, 1987. Reports on experiments that test the effect of television news on how we think about politics.

Jennings, M. Kent, and Richard G. Niemi. *The Political Character of Adolescence: The Influence of Families and Schools*. Princeton, N.J.: Princeton University Press, 1974. A study of political attitudes among high-school students.

Lichter, S. Robert, Stanley Rothman, and Linda S. Lichter. *The Media Elite*. Bethesda, Md.: Adler & Adler, 1986. A study of the political beliefs of "elite" journalists and how those beliefs influence what we read and hear.

McCloskey, Herbert, and John Zaller. *The American Ethos*. Cambridge, Mass.: Harvard University Press, 1984. A study of how Americans evaluate their political and economic arrangements.

Patterson, Thomas W. *The Mass Media Election*. New York: Praeger, 1980. An analysis of what effect, if any, the media had on the 1976 election.

Robinson, Michael J., and Margaret A. Sheehan. *Over the Wire and on TV.* New York: Russell Sage Foundation, 1983. Analyzes how CBS News and United Press International covered the 1980 election.

Sabato, Larry J. *Feeding Frenzy: How Journalism Has Transformed American Politics.* New York: Free Press, 1991. Explains why the press has become more concerned with the real or alleged misconduct of politicians and how this preoccupation has changed the character of political journalism.

5

★ ★ ★

Political Parties and Interest Groups

THE POLITICAL PARTIES of the United States are the oldest in the world; among democratic nations, they may also be the weakest. It is not their age that has enfeebled them, however; when they were a hundred years old, they were still vigorous and played a dominant role in national politics. Rather, they have declined in significance as a result of changes in the legal rules under which they operate and in the attitudes of the citizens whom they seek to organize. All of this has occurred—and still is occurring—in a constitutional system that has caused the parties, even in their heyday, to be decentralized and fragmented.

As parties have declined, the relative importance of organized interest groups—or, if you prefer, lobbies—has probably risen. Interest groups have always been part of American political life: they existed before parties, and the Framers hoped that the constitutional machinery they were designing, as well as the federal republic's size and diversity, would keep interest groups (or **factions** as they were then called) so divided among themselves that none would dominate. Some scholars believe that the decline of political parties has made it easier for interest groups

95

to exercise influence—the lobbyists have rushed in to fill the vacuum created by the absence of strong party leaders.

PARTIES—HERE AND ABROAD

A **political party** is a group that seeks to elect candidates to public office by supplying them with labels—a party identification—by which they are known to the electorate.[1] This broad definition suggests the three political arenas within which parties operate. A party exists as a **label** in the minds of the voters, as an **organization** that recruits and campaigns for candidates, and as a **set of leaders** who try to organize and control the legislative and executive branches of government.

In the United States the labels of the two major parties have always had sufficient appeal for the voters so that third parties and independent candidates have rarely had much success at the national or even the state level. Even the party label, however, has of late begun to lose its hold on the voters' minds. There has never been a strong national party organization in this country, though there have been long periods in which certain state, city, or county components of the Democratic or Republican parties have been organizationally powerful. And only occasionally have the political parties been able to dominate Congress, though parties have always been able to influence the choice of congressional leaders and the votes of many members of Congress on at least certain matters.

Parties are very different in Europe, where party leaders select candidates. Parties—not candidates—run election campaigns; elected officials are expected to vote a party line; and the principal criterion by which voters choose among candidates is their party identification or label. (This has been changing somewhat of late: European parties, like American ones, have not been able to rely as heavily as in the past on voters' party loyalty.)

Decentralization

Several factors explain the striking differences between American and European political parties. First, the American federal system decentralizes political authority and thus decentralizes party organizations. Even the recent trend toward governmental centralization in the United States has not made the parties more centralized. If anything, parties have grown weaker and more decentralized—in part, because American parties are closely regulated by federal and state laws that have had the effect of weakening them substantially. Perhaps the most important regulations are those that prescribe how a party's candidates are chosen.

In almost all states, candidates are selected not by party leaders but by the voters in primary elections, which are unknown in Europe. Furthermore, if an American political party wins control of Congress, it does not also win the right to select the chief executive of government—as it does in European countries. Elected independently of Congress, the president chooses his principal subordinates from outside Congress (if he chooses a member of Congress, that person must resign from Congress). All this weakens the significance and power of the party as a means of organizing and running the government.

Political Culture

The attitudes and traditions of American voters reinforce the institutional and legal factors that make American parties relatively weak. Unlike Europeans— who formally join political parties, pay dues, attend meetings, and often participate in the many party-organized social activities—Americans do not usually "join" parties except by voting for their candidates, and they tend to keep their social, business, working, and cultural lives almost entirely nonpartisan. Thus American parties play a limited, rather than comprehensive, role in citizens' lives, and even this role diminishes as more and more Americans proclaim themselves to be independents.

The Rise and Decline of American Political Parties

Our nation began without parties; today parties, though far from extinct, are about as weak as at any time in our history. In between the Founding and the present, however, parties arose and became powerful. We can see this process in four broad periods of party history (see Figure 5.1).

The Founders feared parties, thinking of them as "factions" motivated by ambition and self-interest. Their concerns were understandable, for the legitimacy and stability of the newly created federal government were still very much in doubt. When Thomas Jefferson organized his followers, called the Democratic-Republicans, to oppose Hamilton's policies, Hamilton and *his* followers (who kept the name of Federalists) thought the Jeffersonians were out to subvert the government, and vice versa. But in 1800 the Democratic-Republicans came to power peacefully, and Jefferson adopted a relatively conciliatory posture. So successful were Jefferson's followers that by 1820 the Federalists virtually ceased to exist as a party, and the Democratic-Republicans themselves were dissolving. Parties seemed to be vanishing, just as Jefferson had hoped. This "first" party system was weak *because* it was the first: there was no ancestral party loyalty to defend, and the early parties were essentially small groups of local notables.

What is often called the "second party system" emerged around 1824 with Andrew Jackson's first run for the presidency and lasted until the eve of

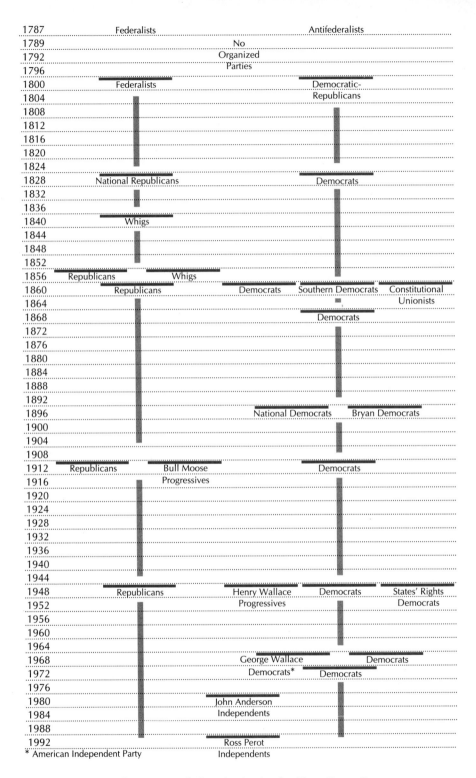

1787	Federalists			Antifederalists		
1789			No			
1792			Organized			
1796			Parties			
1800	Federalists			Democratic-		
1804				Republicans		
1808						
1812						
1816						
1820						
1824						
1828	National Republicans			Democrats		
1832						
1836						
1840	Whigs					
1844						
1848						
1852						
1856	Republicans	Whigs				
1860	Republicans		Democrats	Southern Democrats	Constitutional	
1864					Unionists	
1868			Democrats			
1872						
1876						
1880						
1884						
1888						
1892						
1896			National Democrats	Bryan Democrats		
1900						
1904						
1908						
1912	Republicans	Bull Moose	Democrats			
1916		Progressives				
1920						
1924						
1928						
1932						
1936						
1940						
1944						
1948	Republicans		Henry Wallace	Democrats	States' Rights	
1952			Progressives		Democrats	
1956						
1960						
1964						
1968			George Wallace	Democrats		
1972			Democrats*	Democrats		
1976						
1980			John Anderson			
1984			Independents			
1988						
1992			Ross Perot			

*American Independent Party   Independents

FIGURE 5.1 Cleavages and Continuity in the Two-Party System

the Civil War. Its distinctive feature was that political participation became a mass phenomenon, with an enormous increase in the number of men eligible to vote and (by 1832) with presidential electors selected by popular vote in almost every state. The Jacksonian party system was built from the bottom up rather than, as in the period of the Founding, from the top down. And it was during this period that the political convention emerged as a way of allowing for some measure of local control over the nominating process.

Though the Jacksonian party system was the first truly national system, with the Democrats (followers of Jackson) and Whigs (opponents of Jackson) fairly evenly balanced in most regions, it could not withstand the deep split in opinion created by the agitation over slavery. Because the issues of slavery and sectionalism could not be straddled, both parties split and new ones emerged. The modern Republican party (not the Democratic-Republican party of Thomas Jefferson) began as a third party, but as a result of the Civil War, it became a major party that dominated national politics with only occasional interruptions until the 1930s. The fact that the post-Civil War Republicans solidly controlled the northern states and the Democrats the southern ones profoundly affected the organization of political parties, for it meant that most states were now one-party states. Because competition for office had to take place *within* a single dominant party, both parties were split into two factions—those in power and those wanting to be in power. Often this split between "ins" and "outs" was magnified by differences in political philosophy and by clashing opinions on whether the election system should be reformed.

In the late nineteenth century, one group of outsiders, known as Progressives, were generally losing their struggle against machine politics. If they were to have any power, they would have to attack the very concept of partisanship itself. Thus they began to espouse measures to curtail or even abolish political parties: primary elections to replace boss-manipulated nominating conventions, nonpartisan local elections, strict voter registration requirements (which, in fact, kept many ordinary citizens from voting), and civil-service reform to eliminate patronage. They were most successful in such states as California and Wisconsin.

Progressive reforms substantially reduced the worst forms of political corruption and ultimately made boss rule difficult if not impossible, but they also made political parties, no matter who led them, weaker, less able to make officeholders accountable, and less able to assemble the power necessary for governing the fragmented political institutions created by the Constitution. Above all, the Progressives failed to solve the problem of how to select candidates. Political candidacies, like people, are not products of virgin births. They must be arranged, if not by a party, then by another type of interest group, the mass media, or the candidates' families and personal supporters. These alternatives are best examined by looking at the forms of party structure now operating.

THE NATIONAL PARTY STRUCTURE
TODAY

Since political parties exist at the national, state, and local level, you might suppose that they are arranged like a big corporation, with a national board of directors giving orders to state managers, who in turn direct the activities of rank-and-file workers at the county and city level.

Nothing could be further from the truth. At each level a separate and almost entirely independent organization exists that does pretty much what it wants, and in many counties and cities there is virtually no organization at all.

On paper the national Democratic and Republican parties look quite similar. In both parties ultimate authority is in the hands of the **national convention** that meets every four years to nominate a presidential candidate. Between these conventions party affairs are managed by a **national committee,** made up of delegates from each state and territory. In the Congress each party has a **congressional campaign committee** that helps members who are running for reelection or would-be members running for an open seat or challenging a candidate from the opposition party. The day-to-day work of the party is managed by a full-time, paid **national chairman** who is elected by the committee.

For a long time the two national parties were alike in behavior as well as description. The national chairman, if his party held the White House, would help decide who among the party faithful would get federal jobs. Otherwise the parties did very little.

But beginning in the late 1960s and early 1970s, the Republicans began to convert their national party into a well-financed, highly staffed organization devoted to finding and electing Republican candidates, especially to Congress. At about the same time, the Democrats began changing the rules governing how presidential candidates are nominated in ways that profoundly altered the distribution of power within the party. As a consequence the Republicans became a bureaucratized party and the Democrats became a factionalized one. After the Republicans won four out of five presidential elections from 1968 to 1984 and briefly took control of the Senate, the Democrats began to suspect that maybe an efficient bureaucracy was better than a collection of warring factions, and so they made an effort to emulate the Republicans.

What the Republicans had done was take advantage of a new bit of technology—computerized mailings. They built up a huge file of people who had given or might give money to the party, usually in small amounts, and used that list to raise a big budget for the national party. In 1983 the Republican National Committee (RNC) raised $35 million from over 1.7 million individual donors; by the 1986 election, the RNC was able to raise $75 million from 1.8 million donors. In presidential election years it raised even more.

The RNC used this money to run, in effect, a national political consulting firm. Money went to recruit and train Republican candidates, give them legal and financial advice, study issues and analyze voting trends, and conduct national advertising campaigns on behalf of the party as a whole. No one can be sure how much political success this money bought (after all, the Republicans lost control of the Senate in 1986), but many observers believed that Republican losses in Congress in 1982 and 1986 would have been even greater if the RNC had not worked so vigorously on behalf of its candidates.

When the Democratic National Committee (DNC) decided to play catch-up, it followed the RNC strategy. Using the same computerized direct-mail techniques, the DNC managed to raise $15 million in the 1989–1990 election period, only one-fourth of what the Republicans raised, but still a lot better than what it had done in the 1970s.

A lot of RNC money goes to commission public-opinion polls, not only to find out which candidate is likely to win an election, but more important, to find out what issues are troubling the voters, how different segments of the population respond to different kinds of issues and news stories, and how people react to the campaign efforts of specific candidates. During the Reagan administration the RNC's principal pollster, Richard Wirthlin, was doing polls at least monthly, and sometimes daily. For reasons explained in Chapter 4, these polls can take you just so far; they are helpful, but they are not a surefire guide to public opinion or how to change it.

The Democrats still have a long way to go to catch up with the Republicans organizationally. Though the RNC began the new era in national politics by backing individual candidates, it now tries to help state and local party organizations as well. In 1986 it spent about $2.5 million on state Republican parties (the DNC, by contrast, spent $160,000). But the differences are not just monetary. Whereas the RNC has been able to develop a smooth-running organization that often has good relations with state and local parties, the DNC is still to some degree a collection of feuding factions. To see why this should be, we must look closely at how the parties nominate their presidential candidates.

National Conventions

The national committee selects the time and place of the national convention, sets the number of delegates each state and territory is to have, and indicates the rules under which delegates must be chosen. The number of delegates, and the manner of their selection, can significantly influence the chances of various presidential candidates, and considerable attention is thus devoted to working out extremely complex delegate allocation formulas. In recent years, voting strength in the Democratic convention has shifted away from the conservative South and toward the North and West; in the Republican convention, it has shifted away from the more liberal East and toward the South and Southwest. This is but one sign—others will be mentioned later in this chapter—of the tendency of the two parties' conventions to move in opposite directions, the Democrats to the left and the Republicans to the right.

Even in the age of television, there is still plenty of old-fashioned hoopla at national political conventions.

The exact formula for apportioning delegates to the conventions is complex. The Democrats, beginning in 1972, have developed an elaborate set of rules designed to weaken the control of local party leaders over delegates and to increase the proportion of women, young people, and minorities attending the convention. These rules were first drafted by a party commission headed by Senator George McGovern (who was later to make skillful use of them in his successful bid for the presidential nomination) and have been revised every few years thereafter. The general thrust of these rules commissions during the 1970s was to broaden the antiparty changes begun by the Progressives at the beginning of this century. But whereas the earlier reformers had sought to minimize the role of parties in the election process, those of the 1970s sought to weaken the influence of leaders within the party—to create *intra*party democracy as well as *inter*party democracy. In 1981, however, yet another party commission changed some of these rules in order to increase the influence of elected officials and to make the convention more of a deliberative body, and in 1986 the Democrats increased the role of senators and representatives still further.

Rules have consequences. In the 1988 presidential primaries, Michael Dukakis was the chief beneficiary of the delegate selection rules. He won the support of the overwhelming majority of elected officials (to whom were reserved 15 percent of the delegate seats) and did especially well in those states that had winner-take-all primaries. New rules, adopted for 1992, abolished winner-take-all primaries. Delegates to the Democratic convention were assigned to candidates in proportion to their primary or caucus vote, provided the candidate won at least 15 percent of those votes.

But the "reform" of the parties, especially of the Democrats, has had far more profound consequences than merely helping one candidate or another. Before 1968, the Republican party represented essentially white-collar voters, and the Democratic party represented blue-collar ones. After a decade of reform, the Republican and Democratic parties each represented two ideologically different sets of white-collar voters.[2] Democratic delegates are usually very liberal, Republican delegates very conservative.

Moreover, the reforms have changed the nature of national political conventions. Before 1972, the Democratic convention was a place where party leaders met to bargain over who their presidential candidate would be; after 1972, it became a place where delegates met to ratify decisions made by voters in primary elections and local caucuses. Party leaders gathering in a smoke-filled room were replaced by ideologically motivated activists assembling before television cameras.

Most Americans dislike bosses, deals, and manipulation and prefer democracy, reform, and openness. But we may make the mistake of assuming that anything carried out in the name of reform is a good idea. Rules must be judged both by their practical results as well as by their conformity to some principle of fairness. Rules affect the distribution of power: they help some people win and others lose. Later in this chapter we shall try to assess delegate selection rules by looking more closely at how they affect who attends conventions and which presidential candidates are chosen.

STATE AND LOCAL PARTIES

To the extent that there is anything like regular, ongoing party organizations, they are found at the city, county, and state levels. In their day-to-day affairs, they are autonomous, independent units, affiliated with—but not controlled by—the national Democratic or Republican parties.

Formally these party units are organized under state law. Occasionally the power structure follows the formal structure: a hierarchy of committees from the state level down to the county, sometimes city or town, and sometimes even precinct level. But more often the party can be understood only in terms of the informal processes whereby workers are recruited and leaders selected. There is no single kind of local party organization but rather five kinds, each of which operates within a party structure defined by law: legally they are all precinct, city, or county organizations.

When Tammany Hall had this imposing headquarters in New York City, political parties were powerful institutions in many big cities.

The Machine

The political **machine** is a party organization that recruits its members by the use of tangible incentives—money, political jobs, an opportunity to get favors from government—and that is characterized by a high degree of leadership control over member activity. At one time, many local party organizations were machines. Chicago still has one, though it is far less powerful than when it was led by Richard Daley. In the nineteenth century, well before the arrival of vast numbers of immigrants, old-stock Americans had perfected the machine, run up the cost of government, and systematized vote fraud and corruption. When the immigrants began flooding the eastern cities, the machines provided them with all manner of services—akin to an informal welfare system—in exchange for their support at the polls.

The abuses of the machine gradually diminished through stricter voter registration, civil-service reform, competitive bidding laws, and the Hatch Act of 1939, which took federal employees out of machine politics. But far more important than the various progressive reforms that weakened the machines were changes among voters. As voters grew in education, income, and sophistication, they depended less on the advice and leadership of local party officials. And as the federal government created a bureaucratic welfare state, the party's welfare system declined in value.

In its heyday, the machine was both a self-serving organization and an informal social-welfare system—but above all, it was a frank recognition that politics requires organization. Even allowing for vote fraud, these organizations turned out huge votes: more people participated in politics when mobilized by a machine than when appealed to by television or good government associations.[3] And because the machines were interested in winning, they were willing to support the presidential candidate with the best chance of winning, regardless of his policy views (provided, of course, that he was not determined to wreck the machine once in office). Republican machines helped elect Abraham Lincoln as well as Warren G. Harding; Democratic machines were of crucial importance in electing Franklin D. Roosevelt and John F. Kennedy.

The old-style machine is almost extinct, though important examples still can be found in the Democratic organization in Cook County (Chicago) and the Republican organization in Nassau County (New York). But a new-style machine has emerged in a few places. It is a machine in the sense that it uses money to knit together many politicians, but it is new-style in that the money comes not from patronage and contracts, but from campaign contributions supplied by wealthy individuals and the proceeds of direct-mail campaigns.

The political organization headed by Democratic congressmen Henry A. Waxman and Howard L. Berman on the west side of Los Angeles is one such new-style machine. By the astute use of campaign funds, the "Waxman-Berman organization" builds loyalties among a variety of elected officials at all levels of government. Moreover this new-style machine, unlike the old ones, has a strong interest in issues, especially at the national level. In this sense it is not a pure machine, but a cross between a machine and an ideological party.

Ideological Parties

At the opposite extreme from the machine is the **ideological party.** Where the machine values winning above all else, the ideological party values principle above all else. Where the former depends on money incentives, the latter spurns them. And whereas the former is strongly hierarchical and disciplined, the latter is usually contentious and riddled by factions.

The typical ideological party is a "third party," such as the Socialist, Socialist Workers, Prohibition, and Libertarian parties. But even within the mainstream Democratic and Republican parties, local units can be found that are, if not rigidly ideological, then certainly more devoted to issues and principles than to party loyalty.

Important examples of issue-oriented groups within the two main parties are the "reform" or "amateur" clubs that sprang up in the late 1950s and early 1960s in such cities as New York, Los Angeles, and San Francisco and in many parts of Wisconsin and Minnesota. The New York clubs successfully challenged the Democratic machine and became a dominant force in

Manhattan. In California where there was no machine to attack, the clubs moved to fill a vacuum created by the absence of any other kind of organization. From time to time they have been the major locus of power in the state.[4] Similarly, in California, the Republican Assembly—a collection of conservative clubs—was for a long time more important than the formal party machinery in promoting candidates.

Members of these clubs became active in politics because of their strong interest in issues, and they expected that decisions within the party would be as participatory and democratic as possible. Thus such clubs were subject to intense internal conflict and, unlike the machines, their leaders had much less room to maneuver without being accused of "selling out." Since politics, especially in a two-party system, requires that coalitions be built among groups and people who do not always agree on issues, this constraint on the ability of a club leader to make useful alliances can be a weakness.

Democratic club members tend to be much more left-liberal than the average Democratic voter; Republican members, much more right-conservative than the typical Republican voter.[5] And recently, a new group of issue-oriented activists—conservative, fundamentalist Christians—have become an important force in some local parties.

Solidary Groups

The most common types of party organizations are not machines or issue-oriented clubs, but groups of people who participate in politics because they enjoy the game, or because it is a way of meeting and being with people. These groups are called "sociability" or **solidary** associations.

Some of these associations were once machines that have lost their patronage but whose members—especially the older ones—continue to serve in the organization out of a desire for camaraderie. In other cases, precinct, ward, and district committees are built up in the same way as bowling leagues and bridge clubs—on the basis of friendship networks.[6]

The advantage of such groups is that they are neither corrupt nor inflexible; the disadvantage is that they often do not work very hard. Knocking on doors on rainy November evenings to talk people into voting for your candidate is not especially appealing if you joined the party primarily because you like to attend meetings or drink coffee with your friends.[7]

Sponsored Parties

Sometimes a relatively strong party organization can be created among volunteers without heavy reliance on money or ideology and without depending entirely on people finding the work fun. This occurs when another organization exists in the community that can create, or at least sponsor, a local party structure. The clearest example of this is the Democratic party in and around Detroit, which has been developed, led, and to some extent financed by the political arm of the United Auto Workers union. The UAW has had a long tradition of rank-and-file activism, and since the city is virtually a one-industry town, it was not hard to transfer some of this activism from union organizing to voter organizing.[8]

Few locations have organizations as effective or as dominant as the UAW that can bolster, sponsor, or even take over the weak formal party structure. Thus sponsored local parties are not common in the United States.

Personal Followings

Because in most areas candidates can no longer count on the backing of a machine, because issue-oriented clubs are limited to upper-middle-class members and sponsored parties to a few unionized areas, and because solidary groups are not always very productive, a person wanting to win an election will usually try to form a **personal following,** a group that will work for him or her without pay during a specific election campaign and then disband until the next election rolls around.

For this approach to succeed, a candidate must have an appealing personality, a lot of friends, or a big bank account. The Kennedy family has had all three, and the electoral successes of John F. and Edward M. Kennedy in Massachusetts and of Robert Kennedy in New York became legendary. Other powerful politicians who have relied on personal followings have included Mayor James Michael Curley of Boston (often erroneously described as a "boss") and such southerners as Eugene and Herman Talmadge in Georgia; Huey, Earl, and Russell Long in Louisiana; and Harry F. Byrd and his son in Virginia.

Before radio and television, many politicians wishing to build a personal following had to content themselves with running in small constituencies where they could easily become known. Radio and television changed all this, permitting a candidate to speak directly to large numbers of voters, without editing, and thus to build statewide and even national followings completely outside the party structure.

Some readers may take it for granted that a personal following is a good thing, since it makes it easier to vote for the person rather than the party and to keep party "bosses" from interfering with the popular will. But there is another side to the story. With so many offices to be filled and so many personalities offering to fill them, the average voter will be lucky to form a reasonable judgment about even two or three of the candidates in the course of a year.

Though all of these kinds of local parties are important, political activists on the national scene increasingly do not work their way up from the local parties but enter the national party directly via various interest groups, such as those concerned with abortion, civil rights, or union affairs. At the 1984 Democratic national convention, for example, more than 60 percent of the delegates pledged to Walter Mondale were members of three organizations— the AFL-CIO, the National Education Association, and the National Organization for Women.[9] Increasingly, political elites come not from the parties but from social movements concerned with abortion, feminism, civil rights, or evangelical religions.

THE TWO-PARTY SYSTEM

With so many different varieties of local party organizations (or non-organizations) and with such a great range of opinion found within each party, it is remarkable that we have had only two major political parties for most of our history. In the world at large a two-party system is a rarity; most European democracies are multiparty systems.[10] Not only do we have but two parties with any chance of winning nationally, these parties have been, over time, rather evenly balanced. And whenever one party has achieved a temporary ascendancy and the other has been pronounced dead, the "dead" party has displayed remarkable powers of recuperation, coming back with important victories.

At the state or congressional district level, however, the parties are not evenly balanced. Though all regions are now more competitive than they once were—the South is no longer exclusively Democratic and much of New England is no longer unshakably Republican—one party or the other tends to enjoy a substantial advantage in at least half the states and in perhaps two-thirds of the congressional districts.

Scholars do not entirely agree as to why the two-party system should be so permanent a feature of American political life, but two kinds of explanations are of major importance—electoral laws and public opinion.

The Two-Party System and Electoral Laws

In several ways the laws governing elections make it hard for a third-party candidate to win. First, members of the House of Representatives are elected from **single-member districts.** Since the candidate of only one party can win a seat in a given district, only two parties are likely to put up candidates. Third and fourth parties would have no chance to win anything. By contrast, in France the members of the national legislature are chosen by **proportional representation,** which means that several members are elected from each district and are divided among the parties in proportion to the number of votes each party receives. For example, if a party wins 37 percent of the votes, it gets 37 percent of the seats; if it gets 5 percent of the votes, it gets 5 percent of the seats. Thus even the smallest parties have a chance to win something, and so many third parties form and run candidates.

Second, the winner in a race for the Senate or the House of Representatives is determined by a candidate's ability to win a **plurality** of votes cast. (Winning a plurality means simply getting more votes than any other candidate, even if the winner does not get a majority—over half—of all the votes cast.) In most states there are no runoff elections between the two candidates with the most votes. If there were runoff elections, then many parties might enter the first election hoping to do well enough to get into the runoff, at which time they would form alliances with the other minor parties in an effort to win a majority. Just this sort of thing happens in some European nations. It also occurs in some American states in primary elections held to choose party candidates (see Chapter 6).

The most dramatic example of the plurality principle is the American electoral college. The presidential candidate who carries a state—even with a minority of the popular vote—gets all that state's electoral votes (except in Maine and Nebraska). Minor parties cannot compete under this system. Voters know this and are often reluctant to "waste" their votes on a minor-party candidate who cannot win. Since the presidency is the greatest prize of American politics, parties that hope to win must be as broadly based as possible. As a practical matter, there will thus be only two parties—one made up of the supporters of the party in power and the other encompassing everyone else. In 1992 Ross Perot learned that lesson. Though he received 19 percent of the popular vote, he received no electoral votes.

The Two-Party System and Public Opinion

The other kind of explanation for the persistence of the two-party system is found in the opinions of the voters. Though there have been periods of bitter dissent, most citizens have agreed often enough to permit them to come together into two broad coalitions. In some European countries, such major issues as the nature of the economic system, the prerogatives of the monarchy, and the role of the church in government have been so divisive that they have helped prevent the formation of broad coalition parties.

Americans have had other deep divisions—between black and white or between North and South—and yet the two-party system has endured. This suggests that electoral procedures are of great importance, making it impossible to form an all-white or all-black party except as an act of momentary defiance or as a ploy (perhaps used by George Wallace in 1968) to take enough votes away from the two major parties to force the presidential election into the House of Representatives. Both Democratic and Republican parties have changed their procedures and policies enough to keep most would-be dissidents inside the major parties and away from third parties.

TYPES OF MINOR PARTIES

★ ★ ★

1. IDEOLOGICAL PARTIES

Parties professing a comprehensive view of American society and government radically different from that of the established parties. Most have been Marxist in outlook, but some are quite the opposite, such as the Libertarian party.

EXAMPLES:

Socialist party (1901 to 1960s)

Socialist Labor party (1888 to present)

Socialist Workers party (1938 to present)

Communist party (1920s to present)

Libertarian party (1972 to present)

2. ONE-ISSUE PARTIES

Parties seeking a single policy, usually revealed by their names, and avoiding other issues.

EXAMPLES:

Free Soil party—to prevent spread of slavery (1848–1852)

American or "Know-Nothing" party—to oppose immigration and Catholics (1856)

Prohibition party—to ban the sale of liquor (1869 to present)

Women's party—to obtain the right to vote for women (1913–1920)

The minor (or "third") parties that have had the greatest influence on public policy were those formed as factional offshoots of the major parties—the Liberal Republicans of the post–Civil War era, Theodore Roosevelt's Bull Moose Progressives of 1912, Robert LaFollette's Progressives of 1924, and the Dixiecrat and Wallace movements of more recent times (see box). The formation of all these groups probably encouraged the major parties to pay more attention to the issues the groups raised: civil-service reform, business regulation, and the slowing pace of desegregation. The threat of a factional split is a risk both major parties must face. In their efforts to avoid such splits, each party tends to accommodate the views of minority factions in ways that usually keep these factions from forming third parties.

3. ECONOMIC-PROTEST PARTIES

Parties, usually based in a particular region, especially involving farmers, that protest against depressed economic conditions. These tend to disappear as conditions improve.

EXAMPLES:

Greenback party (1876–1884)

Populist party (1892–1908)

4. FACTIONAL PARTIES

Parties that are created by a split in a major party, usually over the identity and philosophy of the major party's presidential candidate.

EXAMPLES:

Split off from the Republican party—
   "Bull Moose" Progressive party (1912)
   LaFollette Progressive party (1924)

Split off from the Democratic party—
   States' Rights ("Dixiecrat") party (1948)
   Henry Wallace Progressive party (1948)
   American Independent (George Wallace) party (1968)

Split off from both parties—
   Ross Perot ("United We Stand America") party (1992)

NOMINATING A PRESIDENT

As we have seen, the major parties are pulled by two contrary pressures. One, generated by a desire to win the presidency, pushes them in the direction of nominating a candidate who can appeal to the majority of voters and who will thus have essentially middle-of-the-road views. The other, produced by the need to keep dissident elements in the party from bolting and forming a third party, leads them to compromise with dissidents or extremists in ways that may damage the party's standing with the voters.

The Democrats and Republicans have always faced such conflicting pressures, but of late the strains have become especially acute. Conventions are no longer dominated by party leaders and elected officials who, in order to win, usually ignore dissident factions. Today, with most delegates selected in primary elections and with the power of party leaders greatly diminished, a larger proportion of the delegates is likely to be more actively interested in issues and less amenable to compromise.[11]

Are the Delegates Representative of the Voters?

There would be no conflict between the party's desire to win and its desire to uphold principles if the delegates to nominating conventions had the same policy views as most voters, or at least as most party supporters. But they do not. In recent years, the difference between the views of party activists and the rank-and-file has become very great.

At every Democratic national convention since 1972, the delegates had views on a variety of important issues—welfare, military policy, school desegregation, crime, and abortion—that were vastly different from those of rank-and-file Democrats. Likewise the delegates to most recent Republican conventions were ideologically different from the voters at large. The Democratic delegates have been more liberal; the Republicans, more conservative.[12] (See Table 5.1)

What accounts for the sharp disparity between delegate opinion (and often delegate candidate preference) and rank-and-file voter attitude? Some have blamed the discrepancy on the revised rules (described earlier in this chapter) by which delegates are chosen, especially those rules that require increased representation for women, minorities, and the young. But this does not explain why the Republicans nominated Barry Goldwater in 1964 and almost nominated Ronald Reagan instead of Gerald Ford in 1976. Moreover, women, minorities, and youth have among them all shades of opinion. Why are only *certain* elements in these groups heavily represented at the conventions?

Who Votes in Primaries and Caucuses?

A second explanation is the growth in the number and importance of primaries and caucuses. Between 1952 and 1968, fewer than half of each party's delegates were selected in primaries, and some presidential nominees—Adlai Stevenson in 1952, Hubert Humphrey in 1968—won the nomination without even *entering* a primary. But beginning in 1972, the number of primaries increased, and from then on, no candidate could win the presidential nomination without first winning the largest share of primary votes.[13] In 1984 twenty-six states had primary elections in which 63 percent of the delegates to the Democratic convention were chosen. Primaries were no longer, as Harry Truman once called them, "eyewash."

Primaries affect the kind of delegates chosen to the convention because people who vote in such primary elections tend to differ from those who

TABLE 5.1 Party Delegates and Party Voters Differ in Ideology (1992)

Ideology	Democrats		Republicans	
	Delegates	Voters	Delegates	Voters
Liberal	48%	29%	1%	12%
Conservative	5	23	63	43

SOURCE: CBS News Poll and *New York Times* Poll, August 3 and June 18, 1992.

vote in the general elections. Only about half as many people vote in a primary as in general elections, and those who do tend to be more affluent and better educated than the average voter.[14] Since upper-status voters are more likely to have a consistent ideology, it stands to reason that Democratic primary voters will support more liberal candidates, and Republicans more conservative ones, than would the average voter.

Caucuses overrepresent activist opinion even more than do primaries. This is because going to a caucus—a meeting of party members, often lasting for hours and held in the dead of winter in a schoolhouse miles from home— is far more arduous than voting in a primary. Hence, only the most dedicated partisans attend. For the Democrats, these have tended to be the most liberal Democrats. In 1988 Jesse Jackson, the most liberal Democratic candidate, made his best showing among white voters in those states that held caucuses—he beat Michael Dukakis, the more moderate candidate, in Alaska, Delaware, Michigan, and Vermont, all caucus states. By contrast, Dukakis beat Jackson among white voters in those states that held primaries. On the Republican side, Pat Robertson, the conservative television evangelist, could not win a single primary, but he won the caucuses in Alaska, Hawaii, and Washington.

Who Are the New Delegates?

A third explanation is that, no matter how delegates are chosen, they are a different breed today than they once were. Far more Republican and Democratic delegates are now issue-oriented activists with a "purist" attitude toward politics than was formerly the case when conventions were dominated by professional politicians. And the activists have generally favored the more ideological candidate.[15]

In sum, the changing incentives for participation in party work, in addition to the rise of primary elections, have contributed to the development of a presidential nominating system different from that which once existed. The advantage of the new system is that it increases the opportunity for those with strong policy preferences to play a role in the party and thus reduces the chance that they will form a factional minor party. The disadvantage is that it

TABLE 5.2 Policy Preferences of Democratic and
Republican Voters (1988)

	Preferences of	
Issue	**Democratic Voters**	**Republican Voters**
Prefer bigger government providing more services	56%	30%
Favor more federal spending on day care for children	56	44
Think abortion should be legal	43	39
Think government pays too little attention to needs of blacks	45	19
Favor military spending at least at current level	59	73
Worry more about communist takeover in Central America than about U.S. involvement in a war there	25	55

SOURCE: *New York Times*/CBS News Poll, as reported in *New York Times,* August 14, 1988, p. 14.

increases the chances that one or both parties may nominate presidential candidates who are not appealing to the average voter or even to a party's rank and file.

DO THE PARTIES DIFFER?

Many people think that there are no real differences between the Democratic and the Republican parties. They may agree with George Wallace (Alabama governor and third-party candidate for president in 1968), who liked to say that there was not "a dime's worth of difference" between the two parties.

It is true that the need to win elections pulls each party to the political center as it tries to attract the uncommitted voter. But there is still a significant difference in the general policy attitudes of the two parties, especially among leaders and activists. And some differences in preference are evident between rank-and-file voters who identify with one party or another (see Table 5.2). In 1988, for example, voters who identified with the Democratic party were slightly more liberal on a number of policy questions—in favor of federal spending on day care, paying more attention to the needs of blacks, and reducing military spending—than were voters who identified with the Republican party.[16] But if these were the only differences between the parties, one might be justified in concluding that they are but two slightly different versions of the same political creed.

Among party activists, leaders, and officeholders, however, the differences between the two parties are very large. The delegates to the Democratic and Republican presidential nominating conventions usually have almost totally opposed views on such broad and basic questions as welfare, busing, crime, and the military. Studies of party activists from 1972 to the present confirm this.[17] And among people elected to office, the same partisan differences are apparent.

It seems that the differences between the two parties grew in the 1960s and 1970s. As we saw in Chapter 4, there is some evidence, though not yet clear proof, that more people consider themselves liberals or conservatives than formerly. This change has especially affected activists in the Democratic party. In 1968 and again in 1972, the proportion of Democratic activists who had distinctly liberal views was more than twice that in 1956 or 1960.[18]

These facts suggest the central problem faced by a political party today. In most elections, voters cluster in the middle of the political spectrum. But the activists, leaders, convention delegates, and officeholders within each party tend to be closer to the political extremes than to the middle. Thus a person seeking to obtain power in a party, to become a convention delegate, or to win a party's nomination for office must often move closer to the extremes than to the center. This creates a potential dilemma: the stance one takes to obtain the support of party activists will often be quite different from the stance one must take to win a general election. In Chapter 6 we shall look closely at how politicians try to cope with that dilemma.

INTEREST GROUPS AND POLITICAL PARTIES

Almost every tourist arriving in Washington will visit the White House and the Capitol. Many will look at the Supreme Court building. But hardly any will walk down K Street where much of the political life of the country occurs. For in these ordinary-looking office buildings, and in similar ones lining nearby streets, are the offices of the nearly seven thousand organizations that are represented in Washington and that participate in politics. It is doubtful whether any other nation in the world has so many interest groups—that is, lobbies—represented in its capital.

The Proliferation of Interest Groups

There are several reasons that these organizations play so important a role in American politics. First, the more cleavages in a society, the greater the variety of interests that will exist. In addition to divisions along lines of income and occupation found in any society, America is a nation of countless immigrants and many races. As James Madison said in *Federalist* No. 10, "The la-

TABLE 5.3 Founding Dates of Organizations with Washington Offices

Organization	Percentage founded	
	After 1960	After 1970
Corporations	14%	6%
Unions	21	14
Professional	30	14
Trade	38	23
Civil rights	56	46
Women/elderly/handicapped	56	43
"Public interest"	76	57
Social welfare	79	51

SOURCE: Kay Lehman Schlozman and John T. Tierney, *Organized Interests and American Democracy* (New York: Harper & Row, 1985), 76.

tent causes of factions are thus sown in the nature of man." Second, the decentralized American constitutional system contributes to the number of interest groups by multiplying the points at which groups can gain access to the government, and the more chances there are to influence policy the more interest groups there will be that seek to influence policy.

Third, the weakness of political parties in this country may help explain the number and strength of interest groups. Where parties are strong, interest groups work through the parties; where parties are weak, interests operate directly on the government. Thus in Chicago, where the Democratic party has been very strong, labor unions, business associations, and citizens' groups have had to work with the party and on its terms. But in Boston or Los Angeles, where the parties are very weak, interest groups proliferate and play a large role in making policy.[19] The difference is even more striking when one contrasts the United States with Europe.[20] In Europe, parties are still very strong; interest groups are much less powerful.

The Birth of Interest Groups

American interest groups are not only numerous but have proliferated rapidly in the last two decades. Roughly 70 percent of all groups now represented in Washington located there after 1960, and nearly half opened their doors just since 1970.[21] (See Table 5.3.) These have included numerous environmental, consumer, and political-reform organizations, such as those sponsored by Ralph Nader.

There have been other periods in our history when political associations were created in especially large numbers: in the 1770s, groups agitated for American independence; in the 1830s and 1840s, religious associations and antislavery groups organized; in the 1860s, craft-based trade unions, the Grange (a farmers' group), and various fraternal organizations emerged; in the 1880s and 1890s, business associations proliferated. The great era of organization building, however, was in the first two decades of the twentieth century, which saw the formation of such groups as the Chamber of Commerce, the National Association of Manufacturers, the American Medical Association, the NAACP, the Urban League, the American Farm Bureau, the Farmers' Union, the National Catholic Welfare Conference, the American Jewish Committee, and the Anti-Defamation League.

The fact that associations in general, and political interest groups in particular, are created more rapidly in some periods than in others suggests that these groups do not arise inevitably out of natural social processes. At least four factors help explain the episodic rise of interest groups.

First, broad economic developments create new interests and redefine old ones. Farmers began organizing when market forces changed; large mass-membership labor unions did not exist until there arose mass-production industry operated by large corporations.

Second, government policy itself helped create interest groups. Wars create veterans who in turn demand pensions and other benefits from the government. The first large veterans' organization was made up of Union soldiers after the Civil War. The federal government indirectly encouraged the formation of the American Farm Bureau Federation. The Chamber of Commerce was launched at a conference attended by President William Howard Taft. Medical and legal societies became important in part because state governments gave such groups the power to decide who was qualified to become a doctor or lawyer. And unions, especially those in mass-production industries, began to flourish in the 1930s after Congress outlawed many unfair labor practices.[22]

Third, political organizations do not emerge automatically even when economic conditions and government policy seem to encourage them: somebody must exercise leadership, often at substantial personal cost. At certain times leaders—frequently young people caught up in social change—appear in greater numbers. In the 1830s and 1840s, young people, affected by a great religious revival, created antislavery and other moral-reform organizations. Between 1890 and 1920, the rapidly growing college-educated middle class established numerous reform and professional organizations. And in the 1960s, when college enrollments more than doubled, many new organizations appealed to young people powerfully influenced by the civil-rights and anti-Vietnam War movements.

Finally, the expansion of government into a given area stimulates the expansion of groups and lobbies interested in that area. Most Washington offices representing corporations, labor unions, and trade and professional associations were established before 1960, in a period when government began to make policies important to business and labor. The great majority of environmental and consumer-protection lobbies, social welfare associations, and groups concerned with civil rights, the elderly, and the handicapped came to Washington after 1960, when policies of interest to these causes were being adopted.[23]

KINDS OF ORGANIZATION

When we think of an organization, we usually think of something like the Boy Scouts or the League of Women Voters—a group consisting of individual members. In Washington, however, many organizations do not have individual members at all, but are offices operated by a staff or "letterhead" organizations that get most of their money from foundations or from the government. It is a bit misleading to call such organizations "interest groups" since that name implies a group (or association) of interested members. But the term **interest group** has become too common to abandon its use now. So instead we shall speak of two kinds of interest groups—**institutional interests** and **membership interests**.[24]

Institutional Interests

Institutional interests are individuals or organizations representing other usually major organizations—business firms, local governments, foundations, and universities. Over five hundred firms have representatives in Washington, most of whom have opened their offices since 1970. Business firms that do not want to maintain a full-time representative in Washington can hire a Washington lawyer or public relations expert on a part-time basis (often at $250 or more an hour). Between 1970 and 1980, the number of lawyers in Washington more than tripled; Washington now has more than 38,000 lawyers—more than Los Angeles, a city three times its size.[25] Another kind of institutional interest is the trade or governmental associations, such as the National Independent Retail Jewelers or the National Association of Counties.

Institutions that represent other organizations tend to be interested in bread-and-butter issues of vital concern to their clients; their leaders often earn a lot, and they are expected to deliver a lot. Just what they are expected to deliver, however, varies with the diversity of the groups making up the organization. Those that represent a limited number of firms with a similar outlook can formulate and carry out clear policies squarely based on their business interests. By contrast, the United States Chamber of Commerce represents thousands of different businesses in hundreds of different communities. Its membership is so large and diverse that it can take clear positions on only certain issues (like lower taxes), while ignoring others (like tariffs) over which business leaders are divided.

Membership Interests

Although Americans claim to be a nation of joiners, they are distinctive only for their readiness to join religious and civic or political associations.[26] This proclivity to get together with other citizens to engage in civic or political action reflects, apparently, a greater sense of political **efficacy** (a citizen's sense that he or she can understand and influence politics) and civic duty in this country. Asked in a survey what they would do to protest an unjust local regulation, 56 percent of the Americans—but only 34 percent of the British and 13 percent of the Germans—said they would try to organize their neighbors to write letters, sign petitions, or otherwise act together.[27] In the same spirit, Americans are also more likely than Europeans to think that organized activity is an effective way to influence the national government, remote as that institution may seem. And this American willingness to form civic or political groups is not only a product of higher levels of education; at every level of schooling Americans are political joiners.[28]

We take for granted that Americans join a lot of organizations. But when you think about it, it is a puzzle. No matter how dutiful a citizen may be, no matter how much that citizen understands and worries about an issue, why should that person pay dues to an organization when those dues—maybe $15 or $25 a year—will have little effect on the power of the organization? Why should that person attend a meeting when, chances are, his or her presence will scarcely be noticed? Why do *anything* for an organization if you can't make a difference and you will benefit anyway from whatever success the organization has in influencing policy?

To get people to join large membership organizations like the Sierra Club, the NAACP, or the National Rifle Association, organizations must offer would-be members some kind of incentive. There are three kinds.

Solidary incentives are the sense of pleasure, status, or companionship that arises out of meeting together in small groups. Since such rewards require face-to-face contact, national interest groups offering them often have to organize themselves as coalitions of small, local units—something more easily done in the United States than in Europe because of the great importance of local government in our federal system. Examples include the League of Women Voters, the Parent-Teachers Association, the NAACP, the Rotary Club, and the American Legion, all of which have local chapters that keep busy with local affairs while the national staff pursues larger goals.

Ralph Nader uses publicity and lawsuits to enhance the power of various public-interest lobbies he has helped found.

Material incentives are offered by some groups to make it financially attractive to join. Farm organizations offer members supplies at discount prices, marketing through cooperatives, and low-cost insurance; the American Association of Retired Persons has recruited more than 25 million members by supplying them with everything from low-cost life insurance to group travel plans. Although such organizations get most of their money from members who join for their own material benefit, they claim to represent these members and lobby accordingly.

The third—and most difficult—kind of incentive to use is the **purpose** of the organization. Many such associations rely chiefly on the appeal of their stated goals to recruit members, who obviously must feel passionately about the goal, have a strong sense of duty, or be unable to say no to a friend. Organizations that rely wholly on a sense of purpose tend to be small. The American Civil Liberties Union and United We Stand America rely chiefly on purpose as incentives.

When the purpose of the organization, if attained, will principally benefit nonmembers, it is customary to call the group a **public-interest lobby.** (Whether the public at large will benefit is, of course, a matter of opinion, but at least the group members think they are working selflessly for the common good.) Many such organizations are highly controversial: it is precisely the controversy that attracts members, or at least those members who support one side of the issue. Most of these groups are either markedly liberal or markedly conservative in outlook.

Perhaps the best known of the liberal public-interest groups are those founded by or associated with Ralph Nader, who first won fame in the mid-1960s as a critic of unsafe automobiles. Nader created various organizations dealing with matters of interest to consumers and turned over to them the money he had made from an out-of-court settlement with General Motors (which had clumsily attempted to discredit him), from the sale of his books, and from lecture fees. He also founded Public Citizen, which raised money by direct-mail solicitation from thousands of small contributors and sought foundation grants. Finally, he helped create Public Interest Research Groups (PIRGs) in a number of states, supported by donations from college students and concerned with organizing student activists to work on local projects.

Conservatives, though slow to get started, have also adopted the public-interest organizational strategy. James G. Watt was the head of the Mountain States Legal Foundation in Denver just before he became the first secretary of the interior in the Reagan administration.

Membership organizations relying on their stated purpose as incentive, especially deeply controversial purposes, tend to be shaped by the mood of the times. To stay in the public eye, the issues they espouse must be hot. Thus they devote a lot of attention to getting publicity, especially by developing good contacts with the media. And they often do best at getting members and attention when the national administration is hostile, not sympathetic, to their views. That is because it is easier to raise money from small donors by calling their attention to the "enemies" the organization faces.

The Influence of the Staff

When all members have a clear and similar stake in an issue, an interest group simply exerts influence politically on behalf of its members. But if the members have joined mainly to obtain solidary or material benefits, they may not care very much about many of the issues in which the organization gets involved. Thus what the interest group does may reflect more what the staff wants than what the members believe. A good example is the aggressive lobbying that a large labor union did on behalf of tougher civil-rights laws, even though most of the union's members did not think they were needed.[29] Likewise the National Council of the Churches of Christ, an organization of various Protestant denominations with several million members, has taken a strongly liberal position on many political issues, almost certainly unrepresentative of the conservative views of most white Protestants, especially southern ones.[30] These organizations can do this because people generally join unions or churches for reasons other than how staff members in New York or Washington think.

FUNDS FOR INTEREST GROUPS

All interest groups have some trouble raising money, but membership organizations have more trouble than most, and membership organizations relying on appeals to purpose have the most difficulty.

To raise more money than members supply in dues, lobbying organizations have turned to three sources that have become important in recent years: foundation grants, government grants, and direct-mail solicitation.

Foundation Grants

One study of eighty-three (primarily liberal) public-interest lobbying groups found that one-third of them received half or more of all their funds from foundation grants; one-tenth received more than 90 percent from such sources.[31] Between 1970 and 1980, the Ford Foundation alone contributed about $21 million to liberal public-interest groups.[32]

Federal Grants and Contracts

The expansion of federal grants during the 1960s and 1970s benefited interest groups as well as cities and states; the cutbacks in those grants during the early 1980s hurt those groups even more than it hurt local governments.[33] Of course, the federal government usually does not give the money directly to support lobbying itself; instead funds are given to support some project the organization has undertaken. But money for a project helps support the organization as a whole and thus enables it to press Congress for more money and for favorable policies. Beneficiaries of such grants have ranged from the National Alliance of Business for summer youth job projects to the Reverend Jesse Jackson for his community-development organization, PUSH.

Since most public-interest groups pursued liberal policies, the Reagan administration was not only interested in saving federal money by reducing grants to interest groups but particularly wanted to cut back on money spent to lobby for liberal causes. But complaints by conservative activists as late as mid-1984 that federal money was still "funding the left" show how difficult it is to make sweeping changes in anything the federal government does.

Direct Mail

If one technique is unique to the modern membership group, it is the sophistication with which computerized mailings are used both to raise money and mobilize supporters. Mailing lists themselves are frequently sold to other groups with similar views, and letters can be tailor-made to target the most likely contributors. But raising money by mail is expensive. To bring in more money than it spends, an organization must write a letter that will galvanize at least 2 or 3 percent of the names on the list to send in a check. Some organizations that use direct mail spend 80 or 90 cents out of every dollar received to pay for fund-raising and administrative costs.

THE PROBLEM OF BIAS

The interest groups active in Washington certainly reflect an upper-class bias: well-off people are more likely than poor people to join and be active in interest groups, and interest groups representing business and the professions are much more numerous and better financed than those representing minorities, consumers, or the disadvantaged.[34] More than half the nearly seven thousand groups represented in Washington are corporations, and another third are professional and trade associations. Only 4 percent are public-interest groups; fewer than 2 percent are civil-rights or minority groups.[35]

But these facts alone say nothing about who wins and who loses on particular issues. Moreover, business-oriented interest groups are often divided among themselves. This divisiveness is even more characteristic of agricultural organizations, representing many different commodities and regions. Thus, although farmers still have great influence in *blocking* a bill they oppose, they encounter increasing difficulty in getting Congress to *pass* a bill they want.[36]

Whenever American politics is described as having an "upper-class bias," it is important to ask exactly what this bias is. Most of the major conflicts in American politics—over foreign policy, economic affairs, environmental protection, or equal rights for women—are conflicts *within* the upper-middle classes; they are conflicts, that is, among politically active elites. As we saw in Chapter 4, there are profound cleavages of opinion among these elites. Interest-group activity reflects these cleavages.

At one time scholars liked to describe the American political system as **pluralistic,** representing the free, complete, and effective competition of interest groups. But when these accounts were written in the 1950s, they were probably wrong, or at least incomplete. Blacks, women, consumers, and environmentalists were largely unorganized and thus underrepresented in the world of pressure politics. Today all these groups are represented by a variety of organizations that win a significant number of political victories, so that American politics is now more pluralistic than it used to be despite the fact that interest-group leaders tend to be upper-middle-class.

THE ACTIVITIES OF INTEREST GROUPS

The size and wealth of an interest group are no longer very accurate measures of its influence—if, indeed, they ever were. Depending on the issue, the key to political influence may be the ability to generate a dramatic newspaper headline, mobilize a big letter-writing campaign, stage a protest demonstration, file suit in a federal court to block (or compel) some government action, or supply information quietly to key legislators. All of these actions require organization, but only some require big or expensive organizations.

Information

Of all these tactics open to interest groups, the single most important one is the ability to supply credible information to the right person. To busy members of Congress and bureaucrats, information is in short supply. Legislators in particular must take positions on a staggering number of issues about which they cannot possibly be fully informed. And the kind of detailed, up-to-the-minute information that politicians need is ordinarily unavailable in encyclopedias and other standard reference sources: it can be gathered only by a group that has a strong interest in some issue. Most lobbyists are not flamboyant arm-twisters, but specialists who collect information (favorable to their client, naturally) and present it in as organized, persuasive, and factual manner as possible. Information provided by lobbyists is often most valuable when it concerns a fairly narrow, technical issue rather than broad and highly visible national policy. But lobbyists must maintain the trust of those they deal with: misrepresenting an issue or giving bad advice can seriously damage their long-term credibility with legislators.

Public officials not only want technical information but also political cues. A **cue** is a signal telling the official what values are at stake in an issue—who is for and who against a proposal—and how that issue fits into the official's own political beliefs. Often all a legislator needs to know is how the AFL-CIO, the NAACP, the Americans for Democratic Action, the Farmers' Union, and various Naderite organizations—or corresponding conversative groups—stand on an issue. (A legislator will worry and try to look more closely, however, if such organizations are split.) As a result of this process, lobbyists often work together in informal coalitions based on general political ideology.

Public Support

Considering that conflict is the essence of politics, it may seem strange that politicians dislike controversy. But being human, they do: no one enjoys dealing with people who are upset or find you objectionable or unworthy. Thus most legislators tend to hear what they want to hear and to deal with those interest groups that agree with them.[37] Members of an interest group, in turn, tend to work primarily with legislators with whom they agree.

For the lobbyist, the key target is the undecided or wavering legislator or bureaucrat. Sometimes the lobbyist will make a major effort to persuade the undecided legislator that public opinion is strongly inclined in one direction or another. The lobbyist will do this by commissioning public-opinion polls, by stimulating local citizens to write letters or make phone calls, by arranging for constituents to pay personal visits to the legislator, or getting newspapers to run editorials supporting the lobbyist's position.

But there are important exceptions to these low-keyed approaches. Some groups, especially those that use an ideological appeal to attract supporters or that depend on publicity, will deliberately attack not only their political enemies but also potential allies in government to embarrass them. Ralph Nader, who acquired substantial political power by his skill at attacking public officials who he felt did not serve consumer interests, is as likely to denounce as to praise those officials who agree with him if their agreement is not sufficiently close or public.

It is not clear how often the tactics of interest groups work. Members of Congress are skilled at recognizing and discounting organized mail campaigns and are usually satisfied that they can occasionally afford to go against expressions of hostile opinion. Only a few issues of great symbolic significance and high visibility are so important that a member of Congress believes that ignoring public opinion would be courting defeat in the next election. Being for or against the Panama Canal treaties or for or against abortion have created serious electoral problems for several members of Congress.

Of late, interest groups have placed great emphasis on developing "grass-roots" support. Sometimes that is impossible, as when a complicated tax regulation affecting only a few firms is being changed. But sometimes a proposed bill touches a public nerve such that even businesses can help generate an outpouring of mail. When the Food and Drug Administration announced plans to ban saccharin on the grounds that it caused cancer in laboratory animals, the Calorie Control Council (closely tied to the Coca-Cola Company, a big user of saccharin in such soft drinks as Tab) ran newspaper ads denouncing the policy. The public, worried about losing access to an artificial sweetener important to dieters, responded with an avalanche of mail to Congress, which promptly passed a law reversing the ban.

Usually, however, the public at large doesn't care that much about an issue, and so interest groups will try by direct-mail campaigns to arouse a small but passionate group to write letters or vote for favored candidates. For example, Environmental Action, Inc., has from time to time designated certain members of the House of Representatives as the "Dirty Dozen" on account of their allegedly antienvironmental votes. Of the thirty-one members of Congress so designated, only seven survived in office. Many legislators believe that the "Dirty Dozen" label, even when unfairly applied, hurts them with proenvironmentalists in their districts, and they strive to avoid it if possible.

Money and PACs

Interest groups have always given money to politicians, usually for campaigns, sometimes as favors, occasionally as bribes. But the scope of giving reached gargantuan proportions only after laws were passed to regulate how the

TABLE 5.4 Spending by Political-Action Committees (PACs), 1990

The ten largest PAC contributors to congressional candidates during the 1990 election were:

Committee	Contribution
1. Realtors	$3,094,228
2. American Medical Association	2,375,537
3. Independent Voter Education Committee	2,339,575
4. National Education Association	2,318,655
5. United Auto Workers	1,790,912
6. Letter Carriers Union	1,730,050
7. State, County, and Municipal Employees	1,548,970
8. Retired Federal Employees	1,533,000
9. Trial Lawyers Association	1,526,600
10. Carpenters Union	1,489,520

SOURCE: Federal Election Commission (December 1991).

money was given. The effect of trying to reform the process of making campaign contributions, as we shall see in Chapter 6, unleashed a torrent of fresh cash by means of legally regulated **political-action committees** (PACs).

Between 1975 and 1982, the number of PACs more than quadrupled—to a total of around three thousand. Today there are well over four thousand. In the 1982 elections, these organizations gave more than $83 million to congressional candidates.[38] In the 1990 elections, they gave nearly $160 million to congressional candidates (see Table 5.4).

Almost any kind of organization can form a PAC. More than half of all PACs are sponsored by corporations, about a tenth by labor unions, and the rest by a variety of groups, including ideological ones.

The most remarkable development in interest-group activity in recent years has been the rise of ideological PACs. They have increased in number faster than business or labor PACs, and in the 1980 and 1982 elections they raised more money than either business or labor. In the 1990 election, there were more than one thousand ideological PACs; about one-third were liberal, about two-thirds conservative.[39]

But though the ideological PACs raised more money than business or labor PACs, they spent less on campaigns and gave less to candidates. None of the ten PACs that gave the most money to candidates in the 1986 election was ideological (see Table 5.5). This is because even a well-run ideological PAC must usually spend 50 cents on expensive direct-mail solicitation for

TABLE 5.5 Spending by Political-Action Committees (PACs), 1990

During the 1990 campaign more than three thousand PACs contributed about $150 million to congressional candidates, divided as follows:

	Contributions (in millions)						
	Election		Party		Incumbency		
PAC sponsor	Senate	House	Democratic	Republican	Incumbent	Challenger	Open
Corporations	$18.0	$35.4	$24.8	$28.6	$43.8	$4.9	$4.7
Labor unions	6.0	27.6	31.4	2.2	23.7	4.9	4.9
Trade and professional groups	10.0	32.5	23.5	19.1	34.7	3.2	4.5
"Nonconnected" (ie., ideological) groups	5.7	8.5	9.0	5.1	9.7	2.2	2.3

SOURCE: *Statistical Abstract of the United States, 1992,* Table 447.

every dollar it takes in. (Many spend even more.) By contrast, a typical business or labor PAC can inexpensively solicit money from the members of a single corporation or union.[40]

The popular image of rich PACs stuffing huge sums into political campaigns and thereby buying the attention, and possibly the favors, of the grateful candidates is a bit overdrawn. For one thing, the typical PAC contribution is rather small. The typical corporate PAC donation to a House candidate is about $500 (the average labor PAC donation is more than twice as much, but still small). Most PACs spread small sums over many candidates, and none can give more than $5,000 to any candidate.[41] And despite their great growth in numbers and expenditures, PACs still account for only about one-third of all the money spent by candidates for the House.[42]

Nor has systematic evidence been found that PAC contributions generally affect how members of Congress vote. On most issues, how legislators vote can be explained primarily by their general ideological outlook and the characteristics of their constituents; how much PAC money they have received turns out to be a trivial factor. There is, however, a slight correlation between PAC contributions and votes on issues in which most constituents have no interest and ideology provides little guidance. But even here, the correlation may be misleading, for the same groups that give money also wage intensive lobbying campaigns. These studies may therefore be measuring the effect of arguments, not money.[43]

Money probably affects legislative behavior in ways that will never appear in studies of roll-call votes in Congress. A representative or senator will be more willing to set aside time for a group that has given money than for a group that has not: the money has opened the door. Or contributions might influence how a member of Congress behaves on the committees to which he or she has been assigned. No one knows, because the research has not been done.

The "Revolving Door"

Interest groups could affect policy not by giving government officials things of value while they are in office but by holding out the prospect of lucrative jobs in private industry after they leave government.[44] For example, after Michael Deaver left the Reagan White House in 1985, he began representing, for a fat fee, various interests seeking to influence national politics. He had gone through the revolving door, but he went too far—he was convicted of perjury in a case arising out of charges that he had illegally used his political connections to line his own pocket.

It is hard to draw a clear line between making proper use of an ex-official's political expertise and improperly exploiting that expertise for unfair gain. The few studies done on the revolving door have focused on government agencies that regulate business. These studies have found some conspicuous abuses of power in return for business favors, but there seems to be no systematic pattern of abuse in the relationship of business employment to bureaucratic behavior.[45] On the other hand, in 1988 it was revealed that Pentagon insiders had been leaking valuable information to defense contractors in ways that helped them get new business.

Demonstrations

Public displays and disruptive tactics—protest marches, sit-ins, picketing, and violence—have always been a part of American politics, dating back to the struggle for independence in 1776.

Both ends of the political spectrum have used display, disruption, and violence. On the left, feminists, antislavery agitators, coal miners, auto workers, welfare mothers, blacks, antinuclear-power groups, public housing tenants, the American Indian Movement, Students for a Democratic Society, and the Weather Underground have created trouble ranging from peaceful sit-ins at segregated lunch counters to bombings and shootings. On the right, the Ku Klux Klan has used terror, intimidation, and murder; parents opposed to forced busing of schoolchildren have demonstrated; business firms once used strong-armed squads against workers; and an endless array of "anti-" groups have taken their disruptive turns on stage. Morally a sit-in demonstration is quite different from (for example) a lynching, but politically all these activities constitute a similar problem for a government official.

Protests, such as this one by antiabortion activists, have been a common tactic of interest groups since the 1960s.

To understand interest-group politics, it is important to remember that holding demonstrations and causing disruptions have become quite conventional political resources and are no longer the last resort of extremist groups. Making trouble is now an accepted political tactic of ordinary middle-class citizens as well as of the disadvantaged or the disreputable.

There is, of course, a long history of "proper" people using disruptive methods, dating back to early-twentieth-century British and American feminists who, campaigning for women's right to vote, would chain themselves to lampposts or engage in what we would now call sit-ins. Then, as now, the object was to disrupt the workings of some institution and force it to negotiate, or failing that, to gain the sympathy of third parties (including the media and other interest groups) who would call for negotiations—or, failing that, to goad the police into making martyrs.

The civil-rights and anti–Vietnam War movements of the 1960s gave experience in these methods to thousands of young people and persuaded others of the effectiveness of such methods under certain conditions. Though these earlier movements have abated or disappeared, their veterans and emulators have used such tactics in, for example, antiabortion and handicapped-rights demonstrations.

Government officials dread this kind of trouble. They usually find themselves in a no-win situation—accused of arrogance if they ignore it, encouraging more demonstrations if they give in, and risking bad publicity and lawsuits if they call in the police and violence ensues.

REGULATING INTEREST GROUPS

Interest-group activity is a form of political speech protected by the First Amendment to the Constitution; it cannot lawfully be abolished or even much curtailed. In 1946 Congress passed the Federal Regulation of Lobbying Act, which requires groups and individuals seeking to influence legislation to register with the secretary of the Senate and the clerk of the House and to file quarterly financial reports. The Supreme Court upheld the law but restricted its application to lobbying efforts involving direct contacts with members of Congress.[46] The act has had little practical effect. Not all lobbyists take the trouble to register, nor is there any guarantee that the financial statements filed are accurate or complete since no staff in the Senate or House is in charge of enforcing the law or of investigating violations of it.[47] And more general "grass-roots" interest-group activity may not be restricted at all by the government.

Several suggestions have been made for stricter or better-enforced laws. The issues involved are complex, and some important principles are at stake. One proposal, for example, would require that the names of contributors to an interest group be disclosed, much as contributors to an election fund must now be disclosed. This might well discourage people from giving money for fear of reprisals if their employer dislikes the cause they have supported or if disclosure entails personal embarrassment or worse (for example, if a covert homosexual contributes to a gay liberation group).

Even without disclosure rules, complex reporting requirements would place substantial burdens on smaller, less affluent interest groups that might well find the cost and bother of filling out endless forms so great as to make it difficult or impossible for them to function. Such rules might also give Congress access to essentially private correspondence.[48] Most lobbying groups, including the Naderites (but not Common Cause), oppose such a proposal. A comparable law in California has produced little beneficial effect.[49]

The significant legal constraints on interest groups come not from the current federal lobbying law (though that may change) but from the tax code and the campaign-finance laws. A nonprofit organization—which includes not only charitable groups but almost all voluntary associations that have an interest in politics—need not pay income taxes, and financial contributions to it can be deducted on the donor's income-tax return, provided the organization does not devote a "substantial part" of its activities to "attempting to influence legislation."[50] Many tax-exempt organizations do take public positions on political questions and testify before congressional committees. If the organization does any serious lobbying, however, it will lose its tax-exempt status (and thus find it harder to solicit donations and more expensive to operate). Exactly this happened to the Sierra Club in 1968 when the Internal Revenue Service revoked its tax-exempt status because of its extensive lobbying activities. Some voluntary associations try to deal with this problem by setting up separate organizations to collect tax-exempt money—for example, the NAACP, which lobbies, must pay taxes, but the NAACP Legal Defense and Educational Fund, which does not lobby, is tax exempt.[51]

Finally, the campaign-finance laws (described in detail in Chapter 6) limit to $5,000 the amount any PAC can spend on a given candidate in a given election. These laws have sharply curtailed the extent to which any single group can give money, though they may well have increased the total amount different groups in the same sector of society (labor, business, dairy farmers, lawyers) are providing.

Beyond making bribery or other manifestly corrupt forms of behavior illegal and restricting the sums that campaign contributors can donate, there is probably no system for controlling interest groups that would both make a useful difference and leave important constitutional rights unimpaired. Ultimately the only remedy for imbalances in interest-group representation is to devise a political system that gives all affected parties a reasonable chance to be heard on matters of public policy. Rightly or wrongly, that is exactly what the Founders thought they were doing.

SUMMARY

A political party exists in three arenas: among the voters who psychologically identify with it, as a grass-roots organization staffed and led by activists, and as a group of elected officials who follow its lead in lawmaking. In this chapter we have looked at the party primarily as an organization and seen the various forms it takes at the local level—the machine, the ideological party, the solidary group, the sponsored party, and the personal following.

Nationally the parties are weak, decentralized coalitions of these local forms. As organizations that influence the political systems, parties are getting weaker. Voters no longer strongly identify with one of the major parties as they once did. The spread of the direct primary has made it harder for parties to control who is nominated for elective office, thus making it harder for the parties to influence the behavior of these people once elected. Delegate-selection rules, especially in the Democratic party, have helped shift the center of power in the national nominating conventions. Because of the changes in rules, power has moved away from officeholders and party regulars and toward the more ideological wings of the parties.

The two-party system is maintained, and minor parties are discouraged, by an election system (winner-take-all, plurality elections) that makes voters reluctant to waste a vote on a minor party and by the ability of potential minor parties to wield influence within a major party by means of the primary system.

The decay of parties in recent decades has been paralleled by a vast proliferation of organized interest groups, or lobbies. Such groups in the United States are more numerous and fragmented than those in nations, such as Great

Britain, where the political system is more centralized and political parties are stronger.

The goals and tactics of interest groups reflect not only the interests of their members but also the size of the groups, the incentives with which they attract supporters, and the role of the professional staffs. Because of the difficulty of organizing large numbers of people, a group purporting to speak for mass constituencies will often have to provide material benefits to members or acquire an affluent sponsor (such as a foundation). The chief source of interest-group influence is information; public support, money, and the ability to create trouble are also important. The right to lobby is protected by the Constitution, but the tax and campaign-finance laws impose significant restrictions on how money donated to such groups may be used.

SUGGESTED READINGS

Bauer, Raymond A., Ithiel de Sola Pool, and Lewis A. Dexter. *American Business and Public Policy.* New York: Atherton, 1963. A study of how business organizations attempted to shape foreign trade policy, set in a broad analysis of how pressure groups and Congress operate.

Berry, Jeffrey M. *Lobbying for the People.* Princeton, N.J.: Princeton University Press, 1977. Discusses the general characteristics of more than eighty "public interest" lobbies, with a detailed discussion of two.

Chambers, William Nisbet, and Walter Dean Burnham, eds. *The American Party Systems: Stages of Political Development,* 2d ed. New York: Oxford University Press, 1975. Essays tracing the rise of the party system since the Founding.

Goldwin, Robert A., ed. *Political Parties in the Eighties.* Washington, D.C.: American Enterprise Institute, 1980. Essays evaluating parties and efforts to reform them.

Kayden, Xandra, and Eddie Mahe, Jr. *The Party Goes On.* New York: Basic Books, 1985. The new organizational strategies of the Democratic and Republican parties.

Key, V. O., Jr. *Southern Politics.* New York: Alfred A. Knopf, 1949. A classic account of how politics operated in the one-party South.

Kirkpatrick, Jeane. *The New Presidential Elite.* New York: Russell Sage Foundation, 1976. Detailed analysis of the delegates to the 1972 Democratic and Republican conventions.

Lowi, Theodore J. *The End of Liberalism.* New York: W. W. Norton, 1969. A critique of the role of interest groups in American government.

Malbin, Michael J. *Money and Politics in the United States.* Chatham, N.J.: Chatham House, 1984. Excellent studies of PACs and the influence of money on elections.

Olson, Mancur. *The Logic of Collective Action.* Cambridge, Mass.: Harvard University Press, 1965. A theory of interest-group formation from an economic perspective.

Ranney, Austin. *Curing the Mischiefs of Faction: Party Reform in America.* Berkeley: University of California Press, 1975. History and analysis of party "reforms" with special attention to the 1972 changes in the Democratic party rules.

Riordan, William L. *Plunkitt of Tammany Hall.* New York: Alfred A. Knopf, 1948 (first published in 1905). Amusing and insightful account of how an old-style party boss operated in New York City.

Schattschneider, E. E. *Party Government.* New York: Holt, Rinehart and Winston, 1942. An argument for a more disciplined and centralized two-party system.

Sundquist, James L. *Dynamics of the Party System,* rev. ed. Washington, D.C.: Brookings Institution, 1983. History of the party system, emphasizing the impact of issues on voting.

Truman, David B. *The Governmental Process,* 2d ed. New York: Alfred A. Knopf, 1971. An interpretation of American politics, first published in 1951, emphasizing the importance of groups and group conflict.

Wilson, James Q. *Political Organizations.* New York: Basic Books, 1973. A theory of interest groups and political parties that emphasizes the incentives they use to attract members.

———. *The Amateur Democrat.* Chicago: University of Chicago Press, 1962. An analysis of the issue-oriented political clubs that arose in the Democratic party in the 1950s and 1960s.

6

★ ★ ★

Campaigns and Elections

THERE ARE MORE ELECTIONS to fill more offices in the United States than in perhaps any other major democracy; public participation in American elections, however, is lower than in elections elsewhere. Moreover, political parties, as both organizations and labels, play a smaller role in American elections and campaigns than in other countries.

These three facts—the large number of offices filled by election, the low participation in those elections, and the weak condition of political parties—have important implications for a theory of democracy. As matters now stand, many offices (particularly the less important ones) are filled by people elected by less than a majority vote and with no political party accountable for their actions. If we were to get rid of many lesser elective offices in order to focus public attention—and participation—on a single elective office, we might get large turnouts and majority rule, but that majority would control only a small segment of the governmental structure.

Such is the case in Great Britain and other parliamentary democracies. Voters elect only one or two officials—their parliamentary representatives—who assemble in the parliament and form the government,

135

which in turn appoints all the rest of the country's officials. In most parliamentary democracies, voter participation is very high. Sometimes, as in Italy and Australia, compulsory voting yields turnouts well over 90 percent. But even where voting is voluntary, as in France and Great Britain, turnout regularly exceeds 70 or 80 percent of the eligible population. In the 1988 American presidential election, voter turnout was only about 50 percent.[1]

POLITICAL PARTICIPATION

People of different social and especially educational backgrounds not only have different political opinions but also participate in politics in different forms. Ordinarily we think of such participation in terms of voting, but there are many other—and probably more important—ways to participate: a citizen can join politically active organizations, contribute money to candidates, write to members of Congress, or simply talk politics with friends and neighbors.

Forms of Participation

Table 6.1 shows the results of asking Americans about their involvement in various kinds of political activities. As can be seen, voting is by far the most common form of political participation, while giving money to a candidate and being a member of a political organization are the least common. And even these figures are exaggerated: we know that since 1960 on average only 58 percent of the voting-age population have actually cast presidential ballots, far fewer than the number who claim they have voted.

An elaborate analysis by Sidney Verba and Norman Nie has identified six ways in which Americans participate in politics. About one-fifth (22 percent) of the population is **inactive:** they rarely vote, do not get involved in organizations, and probably do not even talk about politics very much. Compared with active citizens, they tend to have little education and low incomes and to be young and black. At the other extreme are the **complete activists,** constituting about one-ninth (11 percent) of the population, who are highly educated, have high incomes, and tend to be middle-aged rather than young or old. They participate in all forms of politics.

Between these extremes are four categories of limited forms of participation. The **voting specialists** are people who vote but do little else; they tend to have not much schooling or income and are substantially older than the average person. **Campaigners** not only vote but like to get involved in campaign activities as well. They are better educated than the average voter and are distinguished particularly for their interest in the conflicts and passions of politics, for their clear identification with a political party, and for their willingness to take strong positions. **Communalists** are much like campaigners in their social background but do not like the conflict and tension of partisan

TABLE 6.1 Political Involvement

Type of Political Participation	Percentage
1. Report regularly voting in presidential elections[a]	72%
2. Report always voting in local elections	47
3. Active in at least one organization involved in community problems	32
4. Have worked with others in trying to solve some community problems	30
5. Have attempted to persuade others to vote as they were	28
6. Have ever actively worked for a party or candidates during an election	26
7. Have ever contacted a local government official about some issue or problem	20
8. Have attended at least one political meeting or rally in last three years	19
9. Have ever contacted a state or national government official about some issue or problem	18
10. Have ever formed a group or organization to attempt to solve some local community problem	14
11. Have ever given money to a party or candidate during an election campaign	13
12. Presently a member of a political club or organization	8

[a]Composite variable created from reports of voting in 1960 and 1964 presidential elections. Percentage is equal to those who report they have voted in both elections.

SOURCE: Table 2.1, "Percentage Engaging in Twelve Different Acts of Political Participation," from *Participation in America,* by Sidney Verba and Norman H. Nie, p. 31. Copyright © 1972 by Sidney Verba and Norman H. Nie. Reprinted by permission of Harper & Row Publishers, Inc.

campaigns, tending instead to reserve their energies for community activities of a more nonpartisan nature. Finally, there are some **parochial participants** who do not vote and stay out of election campaigns and civic associations but will contact local officials about specific, often personal, problems.[2]

It is striking that more than 40 percent of Americans either do not participate in politics at all or limit that participation strictly to voting. There are a number of reasons why people do not get involved in politics, but one deserves special mention: for most people, politics offers few rewards. Even voting imposes a number of burdens (registering to vote, waiting in line, missing work, making sense of a long ballot), and hardly anybody ever casts a vote that affects the outcome of an election. The wonder is that the proportion of people who do vote is not smaller than it is.

Why People Participate

One reason for the high percentage of participants is that most Americans have a strong sense of civic duty. Their civic duty tells Americans that they ought to vote, and afterward they feel good about having voted. The sense of civic obligation is stronger in the United States than in many other democratic nations. But if more Americans than Britons (for example) say they *ought* to vote, are they hypocrites because fewer of them *actually* vote? Not really. As we shall see, Americans face greater difficulties in registering to vote than citizens of almost any other country. American political parties are less effective than their European counterparts in luring voters to the polls. And most important, Americans find being active in the community a more rewarding form of participation than merely voting.[3]

Who Participates?

Whatever the form of participation, those who are the most active tend to have more education (and, to a lesser degree, higher incomes) than those who are the least active. Indeed, educational differences explain more of the variations in political participation in the United States than they do in any other country in which comparable studies have been done. Older people are more active than younger ones, and men are more active than women.[4]

Overall, blacks participate in politics less frequently than whites, but among people of roughly the same income and level of education, blacks tend to participate *more* than whites.[5] This is particularly true for blacks who are financially better off or who are especially sensitive to racial issues. But the forms of participation among blacks are somewhat different from those of whites. Blacks, compared with whites, are less likely to contact public officials about their problems and are slightly less likely to vote, but are much more likely to join civic organizations or become active in political campaigns.[6]

There is much evidence that the rate at which people have been participating in politics in ways other than by voting has increased in recent years. One survey found that the proportion of citizens who had written a letter to a public official increased from about 17 percent in 1964 to more than 27 percent by 1976. Citizens also participate in politics (though they do not think of it in that way) whenever they make a demand on a government official, such as a welfare administrator or a highway planner. And since the 1960s, public demonstrations, protest marches, and sit-ins have become a much more common form of political participation.[7]

Government officials tend to be better informed about and more in agreement with the opinions of people most active in politics than with the views of the rank-and-file citizenry.[8] There is nothing particularly sinister about this: people who try to have influence on government are going to have more influence than people who do not try. Thus we should be especially interested in the political opinions of political activists. To recapitulate what we have said, activists tend to have more extreme views—whether liberal or conservative—than the citizens for whom they supposedly speak. Republican activists are often more consistently conservative than the average Republican; Democratic activists are more consistently liberal than the average Democrat.

HISTORICAL VOTING PATTERNS

It is ironic that relatively few citizens vote in American elections since it was in this country that the mass of people first became eligible to vote.

The Rise of the American Electorate

At the time the Constitution was ratified, the vote was limited to taxpayers or property owners (who, however, constituted a rather large proportion of the white male population), but by the administration of Andrew Jackson (1829–1837), it had broadened to include virtually all white males, except in a few southern states.

The most important changes in elections have been those that extended the suffrage to women, blacks, and eighteen-year-olds and made mandatory the direct popular election of United States senators. After the Civil War, the Fifteenth Amendment (1870) was ratified, stipulating that the "right of citizens of the United States to vote shall not be denied . . . on account of race, color, or previous condition of servitude." Nevertheless, throughout the South blacks were systematically barred from the polls by all manner of state stratagems after the end of Reconstruction. Between 1915 and 1944, the Supreme Court overturned some of these discriminatory rules, but still only a small proportion of the voting-age Southern blacks were able to register and vote. A dramatic change did not begin until 1965, with the passage of the Voting Rights Act. This law suspended the use of literacy tests (which had been used in a blatantly discriminatory fashion) and authorized the appointment of federal examiners who could order the registration of blacks in states and counties (mostly in the South) where fewer than 50 percent of the voting-age population were registered or had voted in the last presidential election. The law also provided criminal penalties for interfering with the right to vote.

Though implementation in some places was slow, the number of blacks who voted rose sharply throughout the South. In Mississippi, for example, the proportion of voting-age blacks who registered increased from 5 percent to more than 70 percent in just ten years.[9] In 1984 the campaign by a black, Jesse Jackson, for the Democratic presidential nomination helped increase black registration everywhere, but especially in the South, where nearly

When these blacks registered to vote in 1965 in Americus, Georgia, it was in the aftermath of days of racial violence. Beginning in that year, federal law empowered the national government to protect voting rights at the local level.

700,000 more blacks were registered in 1984 than in 1980. These changes had a profound effect on the behavior of many white southern politicians: for example, George Wallace stopped making prosegregation speeches and began courting the black vote.

Though women could vote in some state elections, it was not until the Nineteenth Amendment was ratified in 1920 that women were allowed to vote in all elections, including federal ones. At one stroke, the size of the eligible voting population almost doubled—but no dramatic change occurred in the conduct of elections, the identity of the winners, or the substance of public policy. Initially, at least, women voted more or less in the same manner as men, though not quite as frequently. From time to time, however, issues arose that created the gender gap described in Chapter 4.

The Twenty-Sixth Amendment, ratified in 1971, gave the vote to eighteen-year-olds, but the political impact of the youth vote was also less than expected. In the 1972 presidential election, the turnout of the voters between eighteen and twenty-one was lower than for the population as a whole. And those who did vote generally supported Richard Nixon rather than George McGovern. McGovern had counted on attracting a large youth vote but only received the support of college students.[10]

Voting Turnout

Given all the legal safeguards that now bring almost every aspect of voter eligibility under national standards, one might expect that participation in elections would have risen sharply. In fact, the proportion of the voting-age population that has gone to the polls in presidential elections for the last thirty years or so has remained about the same—between 53 percent and 60 percent of those eligible—and today appears to be much smaller than it was in the latter part of the nineteenth century (see Figure 6.1).

Scholars have vigorously debated the meaning of these figures. One view is that this decline in turnout, even allowing for the shaky data on which the estimates are based, has been real and the result of a decline in popular interest in elections and a weakening of the extent to which the two major parties are competitive. During the nineteenth century, according to this theory, the parties fought hard, got voters to the polls, made politics a participatory activity, kept registration procedures easy, and looked forward to close, exciting elections. But after 1896, when the South became a one-party Democratic region and the North heavily Republican, both parties became more conservative; national elections usually resulted in lopsided Republican victories; and citizens began losing interest.[11]

Another view, however, argues that the decline in voter turnout has been more apparent than real. Though nineteenth-century elections were certainly more of a popular sport than they are today, the parties were no more democratic in those days than now, and the voters then may have been more easily manipulated. Until the early twentieth century, vote frauds—including ballot-box stuffing—were common.[12] If votes had been legally cast and honestly counted, the statistics of nineteenth-century election turnouts might well have been much lower than the inflated figures we now have, so that the current decline in voter participation may not be as great as some have suggested.

Nevertheless, most scholars agree that, even accurately measured, voter turnout probably did decline somewhat after the 1890s, largely because of reforms promoted by Progressives to purify the electoral process. One such reform was the adoption of the **Australian ballot.** This ballot was printed by the government and secretly cast by the voter in a private booth, replacing the old party-printed ballot that was cast in public. The change helped reduce fraudulent voting. And voter-registration regulations became stricter, eliminating the participation of aliens and cutting back on that of blacks and transients.

Like most reforms in American politics, the Australian ballot and strict voter-registration procedures had some unintended consequences. Besides reducing fraudulent voting, these changes also reduced voting generally because they made it more difficult for certain groups of honest voters—those with little education, for example, or those who had recently moved—to register and vote. This was not the first time, and it will not be the last, that a reform designed to cure one problem created another.[13]

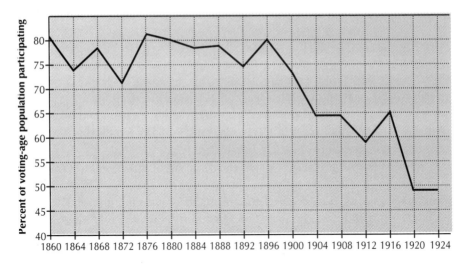

FIGURE   6.1 Voter Participation in Presidential Elections, 1860–1992

NOTE: Several southern states did not participate in the 1864 and 1868 elections.

SOURCE: For years 1860–1928. Bureau of the Census. *Historical Statistics of the United States, Colonial Times to 1970*, Pt. 2. p. 1071; and for years 1932–1984. *Statistical Abstract of the United States*, various years.

Even after all the legal changes are taken into account, citizen participation in elections has still declined. Between 1960 and 1980, the proportion of voting-age people casting ballots in presidential elections fell by about 10 percent, a drop that cannot be explained by how the ballots were printed or the registration rules written.

EXPLAINING—AND IMPROVING—
TURNOUT

Americans are often embarrassed by their low rates of voting in national elections. We often accuse each other of being "apathetic." But in fact apathy on election day is *not* the problem. Look at Table 6.2. If you compare democratic nations in terms of what percentage of their *voting-age population* went to the polls, the United States ranks near the bottom—fewer than 53 percent of us vote for president (column A). But if you compare these same nations in terms of what percentage of their *registered voters* went to the polls, the United States looks pretty good—almost 87 percent of our registered voters actually vote for president (column B).

The problem, obviously, is that a smaller fraction of our voting-age population registers to vote than is the case overseas. In 1984, only two-thirds of all

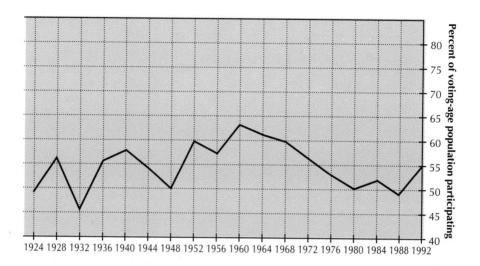

eligible voters were registered. Why is that? One big reason is that in this country the entire burden of registering falls on the citizens. They must learn how and when to register, take the trouble to get a registration form, fill it out, and deliver it (in a few states, mail it) to the local registrar. If they move to a new county or state, they must register all over again. In most European nations, registration is done for you by the government. Every adult citizen is automatically a registered voter.

Some American states have made things a lot easier by permitting people to register on the same day and at the same time as they vote.[14] One study estimated that if every state had such permissive registration requirements, voting turnout would be about 9 percent higher.[15] We could also raise turnout by making voting compulsory, as it is in Australia and some other countries.

But even allowing for legal differences, turnout is still lower here than abroad. One reason is that politics is not as important to Americans as it is to Swedes or Belgians. That is the case in part because government plays a smaller role in the lives of Americans than it does in the lives of Swedes or Belgians. A second reason is that political parties do not mobilize voters and get them to the polls with the same efficiency as do many European parties. Again, that is because parties do not play as large a role in our lives as they do in the lives of many Europeans.

This means that if you want voting turnout to be higher here, it is not enough to run advertising campaigns to "get out the vote." Those probably have almost no effect. What is required is simplified registration, compulsory voting, and a larger role for government in our daily lives. Given these alternatives, many Americans would probably decide that they prefer low voting turnouts.

TABLE **6.2** Two Ways of Calculating Voting Turnout, Here and Abroad

A Turnout as percentage of voting-age population		B Turnout as percentage of registered voters	
Austria	89.3%	Belgium	94.6%
Belgium	88.7	Australia	94.5
Sweden	86.8	Austria	91.6
Netherlands	84.7	Sweden	90.7
Australia	83.1	New Zealand	89.0
Denmark	82.1	West Germany	88.6
Norway	81.8	Netherlands	87.0
West Germany	81.1	UNITED STATES	86.8
New Zealand	78.5	France	85.9
France	78.0	Denmark	83.2
United Kingdom	76.0	Norway	82.0
Japan	74.4	United Kingdom	76.3
Canada	67.4	Japan	74.5
Finland	63.0	Canada	69.3
UNITED STATES	52.6	Finland	64.3
Switzerland	39.4	Switzerland	48.3

SOURCE: Adapted from tables in David Glass, Peverill Squire, and Raymond Wolfinger, "Voter Turnout: An International Comparison," *Public Opinion* (December-January 1984): 50, 52. Reprinted with permission of American Enterprise Institute for Public Policy Research.

POLITICAL CAMPAIGNS

Political campaigns, once mounted by party organizations, are today largely run by the personal followers of the candidate. The candidate creates a staff and an organization to work directly for him or her, but it is a temporary organization that goes out of existence the day after the election. Furthermore, campaigns for national offices are usually organized on behalf of an individual candidate, not a slate of candidates of the same party.

Several features of our political system have contributed to the rise of personal rather than party-run campaigns. Primary elections, as we have seen, have weakened or eliminated a major source of party power in many states—the ability of party leaders to select the party's nominee. Especially if a candidate wins the primary over the opposition of the party leadership, the party may feel little obligation to work hard for that person's victory in the general election.

Political funds and political jobs are increasingly under the control of candidates and officeholders, not party leaders. And as we shall see, the public financing of presidential campaigns means that most of the money used to help elect a candidate goes to the candidate, or his or her personal organization, and is not funneled through the party. The ability to reward followers with patronage jobs is, in many places, in the hands of an elected official rather than a party boss.

The increased reliance on the mass media for campaigning means that candidates purchase advertising and give interviews largely to bolster their own chances of victory. With the high cost of radio and television advertising, it hardly makes sense for one candidate to give any others a free ride by including them on a slate. Furthermore, electronic advertising is usually devoted to building a candidate's image—that is, to emphasizing his or her *personal* qualities—which cannot easily be done for a slate or a party ticket.

Finally, the decline in party identification has made any appeal to party loyalty a weaker basis for building a winning coalition than once was the case. Except in heavily Democratic or Republican areas, candidates today omit references to their party identification lest they alienate voters who might like them as individuals.

Assembling a Staff

The temporary, personal organizations of candidates tend to be composed of four distinct groups of workers. At the core is usually a small number of paid professionals, either hired for the occasion or drawn from an incumbent's office staff. A challenger must hire his or her own staff. As parties have declined, professional political consultants have grown in importance. These are individuals in the business of designing a campaign strategy, choosing the advertising, running the direct-mail campaign, and even telling the candidate what to wear and how much weight to lose. These professionals symbolize the evolution of American politics from torchlight parades and local ward bosses to centralized, computerized efforts at persuasion.

The second group of campaign workers are the unpaid senior advisers—usually old and trusted acquaintances of the candidate, most of whom have never held political office and have no personal political ambitions—to whom the candidate turns for counsel on major strategic questions.

The third group consists of citizen volunteers: young people looking for excitement, older people who are friends of the candidate, job seekers hoping for patronage appointments, and individuals attracted by the issues. They do routine, often boring, jobs. Some volunteers resent the power and privileges of the inner circle and especially of the paid staff; members of the inner circle,

KINDS OF ELECTIONS

★ ★ ★

There are two kinds of elections in the United States: general and primary. A **general** election is used to fill an elective office. A **primary** election is intended to select a party's candidates for an elective office, though in fact those who vote in a primary election may or may not consider themselves party members. Some primaries are **closed:** you must declare in advance, sometimes several weeks, that you are a registered member of the political party in whose primary you wish to vote. About forty states have closed primaries.

Other primaries are **open**—that is, you can decide when you enter the voting booth on election day in which party's primary you wish to participate. You are given every party's primary ballot; you may vote on one. Idaho, Michigan, Minnesota, Montana, North Dakota, Utah, Vermont, and Wisconsin have open primaries. A variant on the open primary is the **blanket** or "free love" primary—in the voting booth you mark a ballot that contains the candidates for nomination of all the parties, and thus you can help select the Democratic candidate for one office and the Republican candidate for another. Alaska and Washington have blanket primaries.

The differences among these kinds of primaries should not be exaggerated, for even the closed primary does not create any great barrier for a voter who wishes to vote in the Democratic primary in one election and the Republican in another. Some states also have a **runoff primary:** if no candidate gets a majority of the votes, there is a runoff between the two candidates with the most votes. Runoff primaries are common in the South.

on the other hand, frequently grumble about the inefficiency or meddle-someness of the volunteers.

A fourth group represents a new development in campaigns—the issue consultants. Candidates often believe they must have positions on the issues of the day, and many like to generate formal "position papers." Lawyers, professors, college students, and lobbyists are recruited to write these papers, most of which have little impact on the campaign or on the winner's subsequent term in office. As we shall see, campaigns are rarely organized around a detailed or extensive discussion of issues; ordinarily candidates take only general and equivocal positions on a few broad issues. Why, then, have issue consultants? Probably for three reasons: media and interest groups expect it, such tasks provide work for eager volunteers, and the candidate wishes to become better informed on matters with which he or she may have to deal.

A special kind of primary is used to pick delegates to the presidential nominating conventions of the major parties; these **presidential primaries** come in a bewildering variety. A simplified list of the kinds of presidential primaries looks like this:

1. **Delegate selection only**
   Only the names of prospective delegates to the convention appear on the ballot. They may or may not indicate their presidential preference.

2. **Delegate selection with advisory presidential preference**
   Voters pick delegates and indicate their preferences among presidential candidates. The delegates are not legally bound to observe these preferences.

3. **Binding presidential preference**
   Voters indicate their preferred presidential candidate. Delegates must observe these preferences, at least for a certain number of convention ballots. The delegates may be chosen in the primary or by a party convention.

In 1981 the Supreme Court decided that each political party, and not the state legislatures, has the right to decide how delegates to national conventions are selected. In particular, Wisconsin could not retain an "open" primary if the national Democratic party objected (*Democratic Party* v. *LaFollette,* 101 Sup. Ct. 1010, 1981). Henceforth, the parties can insist that only voters who declare themselves Democrats or Republicans can vote in presidential primaries. The Supreme Court's ruling may have relatively little practical effect, however, since the "declaration" might occur only an hour or a day before the election.

Strategy

A campaign, except one for a safe seat in Congress, is an exercise in uncertainty. No one knows in advance what will win or lose the election. Given the many divisions in public opinion, a winning majority is a coalition of many diverse parts; the campaigner must decide which parts can be taken for granted and which can be attracted. A strategy must be devised to attract wavering voters without irritating or alienating supporters.

The need to win the primary in order to win the nomination makes this problem all the harder. To win the primary, one must mobilize a relatively small number of enthusiasts. To win the general election, one must attract a much larger and perhaps much different group of supporters. If issues, rather than personality, dominate the primary campaign, there will be conflict. A candidate who has won a primary campaign by taking strong stands on controversial issues—for example, George McGovern in the 1972 presidential campaign—finds it difficult to move to the political center once he has the nomination. His opponent will not let the voters forget the positions he took while winning the primary, using his more extreme positions to hurt his standing with the voters. And if the candidate does start waffling on the controversial issues, his enthusiastic supporters may stop contributing time, effort, and money. McGovern found himself trapped by just this predicament, and Richard Nixon won reelection in a landslide.

In 1980, by contrast, Ronald Reagan won the primaries easily, largely on the basis of his personality. He did not have to mobilize his large following of militant conservatives and thus could avoid taking controversial stands. In the general election, the issue became Carter's record rather than Reagan's positions. Public financing of the campaign, which did not exist in 1972, also helped Reagan: unlike McGovern, he did not have to keep interrupting his campaign to make dramatic TV appeals to his militant supporters for money.

In 1988 Michael Dukakis avoided making strong issue appeals during the Democratic primaries by stressing the theme of "competence" (he was a successful Massachusetts governor at the time) and allowing Jesse Jackson to mobilize the issue-oriented, liberal voters. Voters unwilling to support Jackson (whether for reasons of philosophy or race) decided that Dukakis was the safe alternative. Meanwhile, George Bush was able to win the Republican nomination because he had been Ronald Reagan's vice president: Bush was strong in those states where Reagan had been strong. To hold this support, Bush found it necessary to stay close to Reagan positions. In the general-election campaign, Bush had to do a balancing act—convincing Reagan loyalists that he was faithful to the president's legacy and persuading swing voters that he was his own man with new ideas on controversial issues.

In 1992, Bill Clinton became the first Democrat in a quarter of a century to win his party's presidential nomination without mobilizing all of the issue-oriented activists in the party. Though he was clearly pro-choice, he did not take traditional liberal positions on crime, welfare, or the use of military force in international affairs. This meant that he had fewer political positions to explain away in the general election than had Dukakis, Mondale, or McGovern.

Events will often upset the best-laid plans, but at the beginning, at least, the candidate and his or her staff try to make some basic choices. Should they run a positive (build me up) or a negative (attack the opponent) campaign? What theme—a simple idea of broad appeal—should be developed? Should the campaign make a major effort early, or start slowly and build to a peak? What kinds of voters can be swayed by what appeals? Where shall most of the money be spent—on television, direct mail, or campaign trips?

Sometimes one has little choice in these matters. For example, an incumbent has to run on his or her record. For most voters an election is a retrospective judgment on the performance of whoever has been in office.

Incumbents enjoy great advantages in a campaign and are usually hard to unseat unless they have taken a controversial position, have been the subject of a scandal, or—like Jimmy Carter in 1980 and George Bush in 1992—have been besieged by economic problems.

If no incumbent is running, then the choice of strategies is wider, with one exception. A presidential candidate who is of the same party as the outgoing president will be saddled with the incumbent's record. Hubert Humphrey in 1968 had to defend the record of Lyndon Johnson, and George Bush in 1988 had to defend the policies of Ronald Reagan.

All these strategic considerations can go out the window if one candidate commits an apparent blunder. In a closely watched race, such as that for president, the media record every word and, in their need to have a daily headline, leap on every mistake. Two such blunders occurred in the 1976 campaign: Gerald Ford's slip of the tongue in a television debate implying that certain East European nations were independent of the Soviet Union, and Jimmy Carter's remark in an interview with *Playboy* magazine that he sometimes had lust in his heart. Every candidate lives in mortal fear of the fatal slip of the tongue or the skeleton in the closet. Bill Clinton was dogged by questions about his draft record during the Vietnam War.

At one time almost all campaigning was aimed at making personal contact with as many voters as possible through rallies, "whistle-stop" train or bus tours, and handshaking outside factory gates. This still goes on, but more and more candidates for statewide and national office devote their energies to getting on television. Television reaches more people than all other campaign methods put together, and voters say in polls that they get more of their political information from television than from any other single source, including newspapers. In 1992 Clinton revived the bus tour, with good effect.

Using Television

Though laws guarantee that candidates can buy time at favorable rates on television, not all candidates take advantage of this, for television is not always an efficient means of reaching voters. A television message is literally "broad cast"—spread out to a mass audience without regard to election districts. Presidential candidates, of course, always use television because their constituency is the nation as a whole. Candidates for senator or representative, however, may or may not use television depending on whether the boundaries of their state or district conform well to the boundaries of a television market.

There are two ways to use television—by running paid advertisements (**spots**) and by getting on the nightly news broadcasts (**visuals**). Much has been written—mostly by advertising executives, who are not known for underestimating their abilities—about packaging the candidate through the preparation of spots. No doubt spots can have an important effect in some cases, and occasionally a little-known candidate (like Jimmy Carter) can win a primary campaign through a clever use of spots.

But visuals—a brief filmed episode showing the candidate doing something—are at least as important. They cost the candidate nothing and, being "news," are likely to have greater credibility with the viewer.[16] To get on the air, visuals must seem newsworthy to TV editors. Thus the candidate must do something more interesting than giving a routine speech: he or she must make a charge or assert new facts, visit a nursing home or an unemployment line, or sniff the water of a polluted lake. This must be done before 3 P.M. in order to be on the 6 P.M. news, and obviously great pains are taken to schedule these visuals at times and in places where photographers will be present.

A special kind of television campaigning is the campaign debate. Incumbents or well-known candidates rarely have an incentive to debate their opponents. By so doing, they only give more publicity to lesser-known rivals, as Vice President Nixon did by debating John F. Kennedy in 1960 and as Ford did by debating Carter in 1976. Nixon and Ford lost. It is hard to know what effect TV debates have on election outcomes, but poll data suggest that voters who watched the debates in 1980 were reassured by Reagan's performance; after the second debate with Carter he took a lead in the polls that he never relinquished.[17] In 1984 most people believed Reagan lost the first debate but held his own in the second. Neither debate seems to have had much influence on the election outcome, nor did the 1988 debates change many minds.

THE EFFECTS OF CAMPAIGNS

No one knows whether campaigns make a difference, and, if so, which parts make what difference for which voters. This causes great uncertainty for candidates and great frustration for their managers. In a general election, perhaps two-thirds of the voters vote on the basis of their traditional party loyalties. In most congressional races, that is enough to ensure that the candidate of the locally dominant party will win. Presidential races, however, are usually much closer.

Nationally, more people identify with the Democratic than with the Republican party. Why then don't the Democrats always win? There are three reasons. First, people who consider themselves Democrats are less firmly wedded to their party than Republicans. Since 1952, at least 84 percent of Republican voters have supported the Republican candidate (omitting the unusual 1964 election when Goldwater ran). There has been a much higher rate of defection among Democratic voters.[18] Second, Republicans do much better than Democrats among the "independent" voters: except in 1964 and 1992, the Republicans have won most of the independents, who tend to be younger whites (see Table 6.3). Finally, a higher percentage of Republicans than of Democrats vote in elections.

TABLE **6.3** Percentage of Popular Vote by Groups in Presidential
Elections, 1956–1992

		National	Republicans	Democrats	Independents
1956	Stevenson	42%	4%	85%	30%
	Eisenhower	58	96	15	70
1960	Kennedy	50	5	84	43
	Nixon	50	95	16	57
1964	Johnson	61	20	87	56
	Goldwater	39	80	13	44
1968	Humphrey	43	9	74	31
	Nixon	43	86	12	44
	Wallace	14	5	14	25
1972	McGovern	38	5	67	31
	Nixon	62	95	33	69
1976	Carter	51	11	80	48
	Ford	49	89	20	52
1980[a]	Carter	41	11	66	30
	Reagan	51	84	26	54
	Anderson	7	4	6	12
1984	Mondale	41	7	73	35
	Reagan	59	92	26	63
1988	Dukakis	46	8	82	43
	Bush	54	91	17	55
1992	Clinton	43	10	77	38
	Bush	38	73	10	32
	Perot	19	17	13	30

[a]The 1980 figures fail to add up to 100 percent because of missing data.

SOURCE: Updated from Gallup poll data compiled by Robert D. Cantor, *Voting Behavior and Presidential Elections* (Itasca, Ill.: F. E. Peacock, 1975), p. 35, Gerald M. Pomper, *The Election of 1976* (New York: David McKay, 1977), p. 61, and Gerald M. Pomper, *The Election of 1980* (Chatham, N.J.: Chatham House, 1981), p. 71.

Most voters usually decide whom they will support for president soon after the nominating conventions are over. This was the case in 1972 and 1984. The campaign thus is aimed at the minority of voters who have not yet made up their minds. Just who these people are and what they want is the concern of the growing number of professional polling organizations hired by candidates. Scarcely any serious politician running for major office would dream of proceeding without a series of polls. These private polls are meant not to predict who will win but to find out how the voters perceive the candidates and what kinds of appeals will reach what kinds of undecided voters.

THE 1992 ELECTION

★ ★ ★

The presidential contest was over the day the Democrats nominated Governor Bill Clinton of Arkansas. Incumbent presidents, except those with extraordinary personal popularity, cannot survive an economic recession like the one that gripped this country in the early 1990s. And George Bush did not have that reservoir of personal popularity. Though Americans greatly admired the way he rallied American and allied forces to liberate Kuwait in Operation Desert Storm, the admiration was for his success and not for the man.

Whatever chance the Republicans might have had for winning depended on the Democrats choosing a candidate who appeared to be so far out of step with the public's core values that the people would have voted against him or her in spite of hard times. The Democrats had made that mistake before. George McGovern was too liberal for the 1972 electorate, Michael Dukakis too aloof and technocratic for the 1988 electorate. Clinton was neither.

WINNING THE NOMINATION

Clinton won the Democratic nomination for three main reasons. First, he was a Southerner who could carry the big block of Southern states that voted together on Super Tuesday. But for that to happen he had to hope that he would have no credible rival in the South. One such might have been Senator Al Gore of Tennessee, but back in 1991, when Bush looked invincible, Gore decided not to run. Another, far more potent, rival would have been Jesse Jackson. When Jackson decided not to run, he provided the second reason for Clinton's victory—the Southern primary vote would not be split between a white and a black candidate. The third factor was the decision of New York's Governor Mario Cuomo not to run. Cuomo was the only Northern liberal with a national reputation. With him out of the race, all Clinton had to do was defeat some relatively unknown regional candidates (Senators Tom Harkin of Iowa and Robert Kerrey of Nebraska and Paul Tsongas of Massachusetts) and the pesky but insubstantial Jerry Brown of California.

Clinton won the Democratic nomination without pushing all of the "hot buttons" that in the past had mobilized Democratic party activists. He positioned himself as a reformist governor of a Southern state with views on certain social issues that were not far from the mainstream of public opinion. Unlike Dukakis, he was not opposed to the death penalty; unlike Walter Mondale he was prepared to take a tough stance on welfare; unlike most congressional Democrats he did not clearly oppose U.S. participation in Desert Storm (but then he did not quite endorse it, either). Like any Democrat aspiring to the nomination, he supported the right to an abortion.

Bush also had to fight for the nomination, though not as hard. Like Gerald Ford in 1976, Bush was a centrist incumbent president who had to fight off a challenge from his party's right wing. Ford had to turn back Ronald Reagan, Bush had to overcome Pat Buchanan.

WINNING THE GENERAL ELECTION

With the economy in a prolonged recession, voters expressing deep dissatisfaction with President Bush, and Clinton perceived as a moderate, Bush's only chance to defeat Clinton was on the character issue. Charges during the primary campaign about Clinton's marital infidelity did not stick, but new charges of his having taken extraordinary steps to evade the draft during the Vietnam war and organized antiwar protest demonstrations lingered throughout the fall. Though Clinton never answered these attacks to everyone's satisfaction, most voters were not moved by what struck them as irrelevant or ancient history.

To insure that he would be seen in the right light, Clinton took pains to project a Middle American image, appearing with his running mate, Al Gore, in small cities in the Midwest and the South and avoiding an overly close identification with such traditional Democratic constituencies as the leaders of labor unions and big-city blacks. To help convey the impression of an affable, accessible person, Clinton appeared on television talk shows; on occasion, he played the saxophone for audiences. Everywhere they went, Clinton and Gore attacked President Bush for his failure to produce an economic recovery.

Though they waged a skillful and energetic campaign, the Democrats did not have to win votes so much as they had to avoid losing any. From September on, the polls showed Clinton ahead in enough states to give him the presidency, provided he made no mistakes. He made none.

THE PEROT FACTOR

In the summer, Ross Perot, a wealthy Texas businessman with a knack for vivid, homespun rhetoric, capitalized on public disgust with politicians by announcing that he would run if his backers got him onto the ballot as an independent candidate in all fifty states. To everyone's surprise, he quickly acquired a large following. For a while it appeared that his support might be large enough to carry enough states to deny either Bush or Clinton a clear Electoral College majority. If that had happened, the election would have been thrown into the House of Representatives, something that had not occurred since 1824. But unexpectedly, Perot withdrew from the race and then, just as unexpectedly, reentered it in October. Whatever the reasons for his apparent indecisiveness, he never regained his earlier momentum. Though he won 19 percent of the popular vote (the best showing by a third-party candidate since 1912), he carried no states and probably did not affect the outcome for Bush or Clinton

continued on page 154

continued from page 153

anywhere. Polls showed that if Perot had not been in the race, his supporters would have split their votes about evenly between the Democrat and the Republican. But perhaps because Perot was in the race and was an entertaining figure in the three-man presidential debates, turnout in this election rose to nearly 55 percent (from 50 percent in 1988).

THE PRESIDENTIAL RESULT

Clinton won 370 electoral votes (only 270 are needed for victory), carrying the Northeast, the Far West, and most of the states in the industrial Midwest. But there were some ominous clouds casting shadows on his victory. Clinton got less than half the popular vote (43 percent) and, despite being a Southerner, lost most of the Southern states, including Florida, North Carolina, and Texas, to Bush.

In 1992 the Democrats claimed a mandate, just as the Republicans had in 1980. But there was no clear policy mandate on either occasion. The voters simply wanted a change. In 1980 they were fed up with Carter, in 1992 with Bush.

Sometimes these polls can help the candidate: in 1952 Eisenhower learned from a poll that the public wanted some honorable end to the Korean War and went on television to announce that he would "go to Korea." The promise captured the public mood and helped elect Eisenhower. Usually,

THE CONGRESSIONAL ELECTION

The congressional races took on exceptional importance for several reasons. Reapportionment after the 1990 census added many new seats to the California, Florida, and Texas delegations and took away several from Illinois, Michigan, New York, Ohio, and Pennsylvania. The state struggle over redistricting cut heavily into some traditionally safe Democratic districts in these and other states, a problem made worse for the Democrats by the tendency to create seats for black and Latino candidates, thus putting Anglo incumbents at a disadvantage. In addition, popular resentment against Congress, intensified by the check-writing scandal in the House, caused many incumbents to feel deeply threatened.

For all of these reasons, a record number of incumbents decided not to stand for reelection or were defeated in the primaries. Sixty-six representatives and eight senators retired or decided to run for other offices; nineteen representatives and one senator lost in the primaries. Many people thought that the anti-incumbency mood would carry over into the general election. It did, but to a very modest extent. In fact, 88 percent of both the House and the Senate incumbents who ran were reelected. Nevertheless, because of all of the resignations, there were 110 new faces elected to the House, the biggest turnover since 1948.

Despite Bush's weaknesses and the faltering economy, the Republicans gained nine seats in the House. Clinton became the first Democratic president since Kennedy in 1960 to win the White House while his party was losing seats in the House. (Bush had won in 1988 while the Republicans were losing House seats.) There was no change in the Senate. The party composition of the 103d Congress that convened in January 1993 looked like this:

	House	Senate
Democrats	259	57
Republicans	175	43
Independent	1	0

however, the private polls will not suggest any masterstroke that can have a dramatic effect on the election. They will supply only general guidance about what campaign themes or tactics should be used—or avoided. Thus his private polls in 1980 told Reagan he should be reassuring, emphasizing such

themes as competence, experience, leadership, and moderation, advice he followed skillfully, drawing votes from middle-of-the-roaders and former Carter supporters.[19]

No one is sure what effect campaigns have on general elections, especially for president. Because the voter receives stimuli from so many sources, perhaps we shall never know which, if any, stimuli are of decisive importance. Probably a good rule of thumb is this: the fewer the other sources of voter information, the more the campaign will make a difference. Campaigns are more likely to be important (1) for low-visibility offices, (2) in primary campaigns where the voter is confronted with many candidates, all of whom have the same party label, and (3) in elections not extensively covered by the media. The less the voter can learn from other sources and the more confusing the choices he or she faces, the more helpful may be campaign literature, door-to-door canvassing, coffee parties, and speeches.

Single-Issue Groups

With the decline in the power of political parties has come, some observers believe, the rise in the influence of single-issue, ideological groups that urge their followers to vote for or against a candidate solely on the basis of some cause. In the 1980s one of the best known of such groups was Moral Majority, an organization of evangelical Christians headed by the Reverend Jerry Falwell; another was the National Conservative Political Action Committee (NCPAC, pronounced "nik-pak"). On the liberal side was the National Committee for an Effective Congress.

There is nothing new about such groups, however. In the nineteenth century, the Anti-Slavery Society and the National Woman Suffrage Association demanded that politicians take sides on emancipation for blacks and votes for women. During the early twentieth century, the Women's Christian Temperance Union made life miserable for candidates who tried to duck the question of prohibition. And during all this time, the parties were relatively strong, at least by today's standards.

Although they have become more powerful of late, it is not clear whether single-issue ideological groups have any large effect on elections. In the 1980 election, for example, NCPAC spent more than $7 million, mostly to defeat five liberal Democratic senators; four of them lost. But all four came from traditionally Republican states. Was NCPAC's effect on the campaign decisive? There is as yet little evidence that such ideological groups make a significant difference in a general election, at least for senator or president.[20]

However, they may make a difference in *primary* elections, which, as we have seen, can often be won by people who mobilize a small, dedicated following, especially if many candidates are running. The recent rise in the importance of primaries may give greater influence to single-issue or ideological groups. But there is no evidence with which to test this speculation.

Campaigns do have one indisputable effect: they provide for the passage of time between the nomination and the election. During that time—in a national election, roughly the beginning of September to the first week in November—several things happen. Traditional party loyalties start to reassert themselves. (Right after a presidential convention, the person just nominated tends to have a big lead in the polls. Usually, this lead quickly dwindles as time goes on.) The candidates have a chance to make mistakes. Generalized perceptions of the candidates' personalities begin to take hold in the voters' minds. Finally, events happen—strikes, riots, disasters, economic changes—and voters can watch how the candidates respond to these challenges.[21]

OPINION AND VOTING

One of the hottest issues among political scientists is this: Why do people vote for one candidate rather than another? To the voter, it all seems quite simple—he or she votes for either "the best person" or just as often the "least bad person."

Party Voting

But it is not so simple to scholars. People may say that they are voting for "the best person," but it may turn out that the best person is always a Democrat or always a Republican. Moreover, the voter, when interviewed, often turns out to be completely unfamiliar with any of the issues in the election or what positions his or her favored candidate has taken on these issues. So often is this the case that some scholars have argued that most voters chiefly choose a candidate on the basis of party identification.[22]

Of course, nobody ever claimed that party was the only factor that mattered. If that were the case, it would be impossible for a Republican candidate to win the presidency in a nation in which more people think of themselves as Democrats than Republicans. A popular Republican (Eisenhower in 1952 and Reagan in 1984) or an unpopular Democrat (George McGovern in 1972) can swing the election to the Republicans. But in general, some scholars say, issues play only a minor role in elections.

Issue Voting

A different and growing group of scholars has argued that voters do in fact respond to issues—and respond rationally. V. O. Key, Jr., looked at voters who switched from one party to another between elections and found that most of them switched in a direction consistent with their own interests. As he put it, the voters are not fools.[23]

The reason that voters often cannot answer questions about public issues may be because pollsters ask them questions of interest to scholars, not to voters. When the pollsters take the trouble to find out what is really worrying voters, it turns out that the voters are often aware of how the candidates differ on these vital matters and make their choices accordingly.[24]

The argument between those who explain voting on the basis of party and those who explain it on the basis of issues is far from settled, but if we bear in mind a few facts, it can be put into perspective. First, certain issues are easier for voters to have informed views about than others. Voters may be uninformed about our policy in Yugoslavia (so are many politicians!), and they may not know how the parties differ over how best to reduce the deficit (neither do many economists!), but they do know how they feel about such issues as crime, abortion, unemployment, and even the deficit.

Second, issues become more important in certain elections than in others. The studies that found party identification the key to voter choices were largely done in the 1950s, when there were few domestic issues and the parties did not seem to differ much. As we have seen, issues became much more important in the 1960s when the nation was convulsed by debates over crime, civil rights, campus protests, and the war in Vietnam. When issues become urgent, people are more likely to take them into account in casting their votes.[25]

Finally, people differ in how issues affect their vote. Most of us look back on the record of the party controlling the White House and ask whether, on the issues most important to us, things have gotten better or worse since that party took office. If we don't like how the current president has behaved, we vote for his opponent without closely examining the opponent's views. This is called making a **retrospective** voting decision. The biggest factor influencing retrospective judgments is usually the condition of the economy. The better off the nation is, the easier it is for the incumbent to win. Some of us, however, make a **prospective** voting decision, trying to figure out what the person seeking office has to offer by looking at his or her positions on the issues. In general, the average voter makes retrospective decisions; political activists and ideological voters are more likely to make prospective ones.[26]

A retrospective decision requires less information (you only have to know whether things have gotten worse or better) than does a prospective one (with it, you have to guess, on the basis of a candidate's statements and record, how he or she will behave in the future). But otherwise, both ways of deciding how to vote are examples of issue voting.

ELECTION OUTCOMES

To the candidates and perhaps to the voter, the only interesting outcome of an election is who wins. To a political scientist, the interesting outcomes are the broad trends in winning and losing and what they imply about the attitudes of voters, the operation of the electoral system, and the fate of political parties.

Figure 6.2 shows the trend in the popular vote for president since the rise of the party system. Before 1896 the two parties were hotly competitive. Beginning in 1896, the Republicans became the dominant party and, except for 1912 and 1916 when Democrat Woodrow Wilson won (owing to a split in the Republican party), the Republicans carried every presidential election until 1932. In that year of the Depression, Franklin D. Roosevelt put together what has since become known as the New Deal coalition, and the Democrats became the dominant party. They won every election until 1952, when Eisenhower, a Republican and a popular military hero, was elected for two terms.

Party Realignments

To help explain the alternations of dominance between the two parties, scholars have developed the notion of **critical,** or **realigning,** elections. During such periods a sharp, lasting shift occurs in the popular coalition supporting one or both parties. The issues that separate the two parties change, and so the kinds of voters supporting each party change. This shift may occur at the time of the election or just after, as the new administration draws to it new supporters.[27] There seem to have been five realignments so far, during or just after these elections: 1800 (when the Jeffersonian Republicans defeated the Federalists), 1828 (when the Jacksonian Democrats came to power), 1860 (when the Whig party collapsed and the Republicans under Lincoln came to power), 1896 (when the Republicans defeated William Jennings Bryan), and 1932 (when the Democrats under Roosevelt came into office). Some ob-

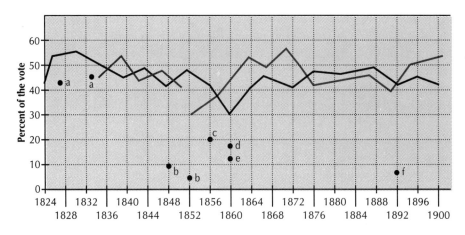

FIGURE 6.2 Partisan Division of the Presidential Vote in the Nation, 1824–1992

Other parties gaining at least 5 percent of the vote: [a]National Republican; [b]Free Soil; [c]American; [d]Southern Democratic; [e]Constitutional Union; [f]People's; [g]Bull Moose; [h]Progressive; [i]American Independent; [j]National Unity (Anderson); [k]United We Stand (Perot).

SOURCE: Updated from Historical Data Archive, Inter-university Consortium for Political Research, as reported in William H. Flanigan and Nancy H. Zingale, *Political Behavior of the American Electorate,* 3d ed., p. 32. Copyright © 1975 by William C. Brown Group. Reprinted with permission.

servers are struck by the fact that these realignments have occurred with marked regularity every twenty-eight to thirty-six years and have speculated on whether they are the result of inevitable cycles in American political life.

Such speculations need not concern us, for it is more important to understand why a realignment occurs at all. There are at least two kinds of realignments. In one, a major party is so badly defeated that it disappears and a new party takes its place. This happened to the Federalists in 1800 and to the Whigs between 1856 and 1860. In the other, the two existing parties continue, but voters shift their support from one to the other; this happened in 1896 and 1932. The three clearest cases of a critical election followed by a realignment seem to be 1860, 1896, and 1932.

In 1860, the central issue was slavery: the Democrats split between a southern group that defended slavery and a northern group that waffled on the issue. The remnants of the old Whig party tried to unite the nation by ignoring the issue; a new Republican party had formed four years earlier (in 1856) in clear-cut opposition to slavery. The Republicans won, eliminating the Whigs who had straddled the fence on slavery. The Civil War ensued, fixing new party loyalties deeply in the popular mind. Thus, the structure of party competition was set for nearly forty years.

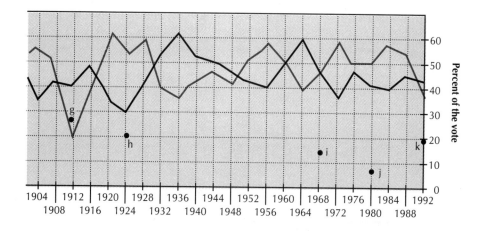

In 1896 economics and religion were at issue. A series of depressions hurt midwestern and southern farmers badly, and so they were prepared to turn against urban economic interests. At the same time, the cities were rapidly filling up with immigrant Catholics whose lifestyle offended many Protestant farmers. William Jennings Bryan captured the Democratic nomination and saw to it that the party adopted a platform responding to both the economic and cultural grievances of farmers. Anti-Bryan urban Democrats deserted the party in droves and helped elect the Republican William McKinley. The old split between North and South was partially replaced by an East versus West, urban versus rural cleavage. This alignment persisted until 1932.[28]

In 1932 the realignment was precipitated by a nationwide economic depression. The **New Deal coalition** that emerged brought together in the Democratic party urban workers, southern whites, northern blacks, and Jewish voters, making the Democrats the majority party. These disparate groups made for a strange coalition, but the federal government under Roosevelt supplied enough benefits to keep each of them loyal and to provide a new basis for party identification.

In short, an electoral realignment occurs when a new issue of utmost importance to voters cuts across existing party divisions and replaces old issues that were formerly the basis of party identification. Some observers have speculated that we are due for a new party realignment now, as tensions within the New Deal coalition become more evident and memories of Roosevelt and the Great Depression fade.

Did the Republican victories in 1980, 1984, and 1988 mark another realignment? Many of President Reagan's supporters thought so and talked of having received a mandate to make sweeping policy changes in line with the views of a "new majority." But a mandate is different from a realignment—the former refers to what a majority of the voters want the government to do

Republican Ticket

For all Republican candidates on this ballot (to vote a straight Republican ticket, make a voting mark (X or ✔) on or in this circle and do not make any other marks on this ballot).

FOR PRESIDENTIAL ELECTORS

For President
GEORGE BUSH

For Vice-President
DAN QUAYLE

REP.

Democratic Ticket

For all Democratic candidates on this ballot (to vote a straight Democratic ticket, make a voting mark (X or ✔) on or in this circle and do not make any other marks on this ballot).

FOR PRESIDENTIAL ELECTORS

For President
BILL CLINTON

For Vice-President
AL GORE

DEM.

Independent Ticket

For all Independent candidates on this ballot (to vote a straight Independent ticket, make a voting mark (X or ✔) on or in this circle and do not make any other marks on this ballot).

FOR PRESIDENTIAL ELECTORS

For President
ROSS PEROT

For Vice-President
JAMES STOCKDALE

IND.

ELECTORS OF PRESIDENT AND VICE PRESIDENT

To vote for Electors of President and Vice President, mark a cross **X** in the square at the right of the names.

Vote for ONE

BUSH and QUAYLE + + + + + + + + + + + Republican	
CLINTON and GORE + + + + + + + + + + + + Democrat	
MARROU and LORD + + + + + + + + + + + Libertarian	
PEROT and STOCKDALE + + + + + + + + + Independent	

SAMPLE BALLOTS
The party-column or "Indiana" ballot lists all candidates of one party under the party name or emblem, making it easier to vote a straight party ticket by putting an X in the emblem (or pulling the party lever on a voting machine). The office-bloc or "Massachusetts" ballot groups candidates of all parties by office, thereby making it harder to cast a straight party vote.

at the time of the election, the latter to the groups that have formed a lasting attachment to the majority party.

There is not much evidence that the Republicans received a clear mandate in their victories. Although most voters approved of some of Reagan's stands against big government and high taxes, poll data indicate that the voters continue to support federal spending on most domestic programs, such as health, education, the environment, and social security. Reagan won in 1980 because voters were dissatisfied with the performance of his predecessor, Jimmy Carter.[29] He won again in 1984 because they were satisfied with the condition of the economy. Bush won in 1988 because economic conditions continued to be good in most parts of the country and because his rival,

Dukakis, seemed too liberal on many social issues. When the economy turned sour in 1992, the voters rejected Bush.

But there is some evidence that a realignment of sorts has occurred, chiefly among white voters in the South. Well into the 1960s, these voters were overwhelmingly Democratic in their political preferences. Since the 1970s, they have moved steadily into the Republican camp—first at the presidential level, and now at the congressional level as well. This change has been so great that a region that once was solidly Democratic has now become (in presidential elections) almost as solidly Republican, at least so long as Democratic candidates are perceived as liberal and Republican ones as conservative. When the Democrats nominated Arkansas governor Bill Clinton, they revived their hopes of carrying at least part of the South, but carried only four of the eleven states.

Party Decline

The evidence that parties are decaying, not realigning, is of several sorts. We have already noted that the proportion of people identifying with one or the other party declined between 1960 and 1980. There has also been an increase in the proportion of people voting a split ticket. Whereas in the 1940s one party would carry a given district for both its presidential and congressional candidates, today more than a third of the districts split their votes. Public-opinion polls show the same thing. In 1948 about a third of the voters interviewed said they had split their tickets, by 1968 about half had, and in 1972 more than 60 percent divided their loyalty. This ticket splitting helped the Democrats keep control of Congress in the 1980s even when they lost the presidency.

Ticket splitting was almost unheard of in the nineteenth century, and for a very good reason: either the voter was given a ballot by the party of his choice, which he then dropped intact into the ballot box (thereby voting for everybody on the ticket), or he was given a government-printed ballot that listed all the candidates of each party in columns, at the top of which he could mark an X to vote for all the party's candidates. Around 1900, the Progressive party began to persuade states to adopt the **office-bloc** ballot, listing candidates by the office they were running for, not by party, and thus making straight-ticket voting more difficult. Not surprisingly, states using office-bloc ballots (or voting machines) show more ticket splitting than those that do not.[30]

A Winning Coalition

If the strength of each party's hold on the loyalty of its voters is declining, then we would expect the composition of each party's voting coalition to vary from election to election. This happens, though the persistence of party

TABLE 6.4 Who Likes the Democrats? Percentage of Various Groups Saying They Voted for the Democratic Presidential Candidate, 1956–1992

		1956	1960	1964	1968[a]	1972	1976	1980[c]	1984	1988	1992[f]
Sex	Men	45%	52%	60%	41%	37%	53%	37%	37%	41%	41%
	Women	39	49	62	45	38	48	45	42	49	46
Race	White	41	49	59	38	32	46	36	34	40	39
	Blacks	61	68	94	85	87	85	82	90	86	82
Education	College	31	39	52	37	37	42	35	40	43	44
	Grade school	50	55	66	52	49	58	43	49	56	55
Occupation	Professional and business	32	42	54	34	31	42	33	37	40	na
	Blue-collar	50	60	71	50	43	58	46	46	50	na
Age	Under 30	43	54	64	47	48	53	43	41	47	44
	60 and over	39[d]	46	59	41	36	52	41	39	49	50
Religion	Protestant	37	38	55	35	30	46	na	na	33[e]	38
	Catholic	51	78	76	59	48	57	40	44	47	42
	Jewish[b]	77	89	89	85	66	68	45	66	64	68
Southerners		49	51	52	31	29	54	47	36	41	42

[a]1968 election had three major candidates (Humphrey, Nixon, and Wallace).

[b]Jewish vote estimated from various sources; since the number of Jewish persons interviewed is often less than 100, the error in this figure, as well as that for nonwhites, may be large.

[c]1980 election had three major candidates (Carter, Reagan, and Anderson).

[d]For 1956–1976, refers to age 50 and over.

[e]For 1988, white Protestants only.

[f]1992 election had three major candidates (Clinton, Bush, Perot).

na = not available.

SOURCE: Gallup poll data as tabulated in Jeane J. Kirkpatrick, "Changing Patterns of Electoral Competition," in Anthony King, ed., *The New American Political System* (Washington, D.C.: American Enterprise Institute, 1978), pp. 264–265. Copyright © 1978 by the American Enterprise Institute. Reprinted by permission. 1980, 1984, 1988, and 1992 data from CBS News/*New York Times* survey and *Los Angeles Times* poll.

loyalty and policy preferences among various groups provides some continuity in the votes that each party receives.

There are two ways to examine a party's voting coalition. One is to ask what percentage of various identifiable groups in the population supported the Democratic or Republican candidate for president. The other is to ask what proportion of a party's total vote came from each of these groups. The answer to the first question tells us how *loyal* farmers, blacks, union members, and others are to the party or its candidate; the answer to the second tells us how *important* each group is to the party. These figures describe both the continuity and the changes within the coalitions supporting each party.

Blacks are the most loyal Democratic voters—85 to 90 percent vote Democratic (see Table 6.4). Jewish voters are the next most loyal—about two-thirds support the Democrats. Most Hispanics have been Democrats, though the label "Hispanic" conceals differences among Cuban-Americans (who often vote Republican) and Mexican-Americans and Puerto Ricans (who are strongly Democratic). The Democrats have lost their once-strong hold on Catholics, Southerners, and white blue-collar workers; these groups have become swing voters.

The Republican coalition is often described as the party of business and professional people. The loyalty of these groups to the Republican party is strong; only in 1964 did they desert the party to support Democrat Lyndon Johnson. Farmers have usually been Republican, but they are a volatile group, highly sensitive to the level of farm prices—and thus quick to change parties. They abandoned the Republicans in 1948 and 1964. Contrary to popular wisdom, the Republican party usually wins the votes of the poor (defined as those earning less than $5,000 a year). Only in 1964 did most poor people support the Democratic candidate. This can be explained by the fact that the poor include quite different elements—low-income blacks (who are Democrats) and many elderly, retired people (usually Republicans).

In sum, the loyalty of most identifiable groups to either party is not overwhelming. Only blacks, businesspeople, and Jews usually give two-thirds or more of their votes to one party or the other; other groups display tendencies, but none that cannot be changed.

The contribution each of these groups makes to the party coalitions is a different matter. Though blacks are overwhelmingly and persistently Democratic, they make up so small a portion of the total electorate that only in recent years have they accounted for as much as one-fifth of the total Democratic vote. The groups that make up the largest part of the Democratic vote—Catholics, union members, southerners—are also the least dependable parts of that coalition.[31]

When representatives of various segments of society make demands on party leaders and presidential candidates, they usually stress either their numbers or their loyalty, but rarely both. Black leaders, for example, sometimes describe the black vote as of decisive importance to Democrats and thus deserving of special attention from a Democratic president. But blacks are so loyal that a Democratic candidate can almost take their votes for granted and, in any event, they are not as numerous as other groups. Union leaders, by contrast, will emphasize how many union voters there are, but they cannot "deliver" the rank-and-file vote, much of which may well go Republican, whatever the union leaders say. Thus, for any president and for either party, a winning coalition must be put together anew in every election. Few voters can either be taken for granted or written off as a lost cause.

MODERN TECHNOLOGY AND POLITICAL CAMPAIGNS

In 1950 Estes Kefauver was a little-known senator from Tennessee. Then he chaired a special senate investigating committee that brought before it various figures in organized crime. When these dramatic hearings were televised to audiences numbering in the millions, Kefauver became a household name and subsequently emerged in 1952 as a leading contender for the Democratic nomination for president. He was a strong vote-getter in the primaries and actually led on the first ballot at the convention, only to lose to Adlai Stevenson. The lesson was not lost on other politicians. From that time on, developing a recognized name and a national constituency through the media became important to many candidates.

Today everyone believes the media have a profound effect, for better or for worse, on politics. Unfortunately very little scholarly evidence can prove or measure that effect, probably because scholars have chiefly tried to measure the effect of the media on election outcomes. But as we have seen, elections—especially general elections for important, highly visible offices—are occasions when the voter is bombarded with all manner of cues from friends, family, interest groups, candidates, radio, television, newspapers, memories, and loyalties. It would be very surprising if the effect of the media would be very strong, or at least very apparent, under these circumstances.

Television, Radio, and Newspapers

Efforts to see whether voters who watch a lot of television, or who see candidates on television frequently, vote differently from those who do not watch television at all, or who watch only nonpolitical messages, have generally proved unavailing.[32] This is quite consistent with studies of political propaganda generally. At least in the short run, television and radio suffer from processes called **selective attention** (the citizen sees and hears only what he or she wants) and **mental tune-out** (the citizen simply ignores or gets irritated by messages that do not accord with existing beliefs). Radio and television may tend to reinforce existing beliefs, but it is not clear they change them.[33] Besides, both sides will use commercially prepared TV spots; if they are well done, they are likely to cancel each other out.

Despite what most people think, commercial spots probably give viewers more information than visuals (and television newscasts generally). The best research we have suggests that news programs covering elections tend to convey very little information (they often show scenes of crowds cheering or candidates shouting slogans) and to make little or no impression on viewers. Spots, on the other hand, especially the shorter ones, often contain a good deal of information that is seen, remembered, and evaluated by a public quite capable of distinguishing between fact and humbug.[34]

Except in 1964, local newspapers have generally endorsed Republican presidential candidates throughout this century. Since the Democrats won eight of the thirteen presidential elections between 1932 and 1984, newspaper endorsements might seem worthless. They may have some value, however, under some circumstances. A careful study of the 1964 campaign found that, at least in the North, a newspaper endorsement may have added about five percentage points to what the Democrat, Lyndon Johnson, would otherwise have obtained.[35]

Computers and Direct Mail

Less visible than television, but perhaps just as important in campaigns, is the computer, which makes possible sophisticated direct-mail advertising and fund-raising. This in turn allows a candidate to address specific appeals to particular voters and to solicit people for campaign contributions.

Whereas television is heard by everybody—and thus leads candidates to avoid offending anyone—direct mail is aimed at particular groups to whom specific views can be expressed with much less risk of offending someone. So important are the lists of names of potential contributors to whom the computer sends appeals that a prize resource of any candidate, guarded as if it were a military secret, is "The List." Novices in politics must slowly develop their own lists or beg sympathetic incumbents for a peek at theirs.

Are Today's Voters "Manipulated"?

Citizens are not idiots: though they may try a deodorant because an ad catches their fancy, they know that the stakes are low and that they can change brands if they are dissatisfied. They can also tell a Democrat from a deodorant, know that government is more serious than smelling nice, and realize that they will be stuck with an elected official for years. Hence they evaluate political commercials more carefully. In short, it is not yet clear that a "gullible" public is being sold a bill of goods by slick Madison Avenue advertisers, whether the goods are automobiles or politicians.

The major effect of the media probably has less to do with how people vote in an election and much more to do with how politics is conducted, how candidates are selected, and how policies are formulated. To get elected, candidates must look attractive on television. Hitherto unknown persons can even become candidates by the skillful use of the media. And the media can put issues on the national agenda if they involve matters—such as foreign affairs—with which people are not familiar.[36] But people are much less likely to take their cues from the media on matters that affect them personally. Everyone who is unemployed, the victim of crime, or worried about high food prices will identify these matters as issues whether or not the media emphasize them.[37] In short, the media help set the political agenda on matters

citizens have little personal experience but have much less influ-
ᴸow people react to—and vote on—issues that touch their lives di-

ᴴe chief consequence of the new style of campaigning, with its exten-
ᴸreliance on sophisticated technology, is not, as some think, that it is more
ᴸmanipulative" than old-style campaigning (picnics with free beer and $5 bills
handed to voters can be just as manipulative as TV ads). Rather, the chief
consequence is that running the campaign has become divorced from the
process of governing. Formerly, party leaders who ran the campaign would
take an active part in the government once it was elected, and, since they
were *party* leaders, they had to worry about getting their candidate *re*elected.
Modern political consultants take no responsibility for governing, and by the
time the next election rolls around, they may be off working for somebody
else.

Elections and Money

"Money is the mother's milk of politics," a powerful California politician
once observed, and few candidates who have struggled to raise a campaign
chest would disagree. Indeed, raising money has become even more important to the candidate as party organizations have declined. If no machine can
supply battalions of precinct workers paid for with patronage jobs, then such
workers must either be dispensed with, hired on a temporary basis, or recruited from the sometimes undependable ranks of volunteers. Even more
important, increased reliance on television and radio advertising and on direct-mail campaigning has dramatically raised the cost of running for office.
A one-minute commercial on national television in prime time, for example, can cost $150,000 or more. And expenditures on the broadcast media can
account for about half of the campaign budget of a presidential candidate.
As Will Rogers said, "You have to be loaded just to get beat."

Impact of Money

In the twenty-nine presidential elections between 1860 and 1972, the winner
outspent the loser twenty-one times. This does not, however, mean that victory was the result of spending more money. People often donate money to
candidates who they think will win in order to get into their good graces.
Often, these candidates would in fact win even if they spent less. Since 1972
the major-party presidential candidates have spent the same amount of money
in general elections because the federal government has paid the bills.

The most careful effort to calculate the effect of spending on elections has
been done for congressional races. There are no legal limits on what congressional candidates can spend, but, since 1972, they have had to disclose their
campaign finances. Gary C. Jacobson used complex statistical techniques to

calculate whether, other things being equal (such as the candidates' parties and whether they are challengers or incumbents), spending more money produces more votes. In the elections of 1972, 1974, 1976, and 1978, how much an *incumbent* spent was apparently of little importance, but the *challengers* who spent more did better than those who spent less.[38] The money went to buy things like advertising that could be used to overcome the incumbents' natural advantages of name recognition and access to media.

If spending more money gives no edge to an incumbent but provides a significant edge for a challenger, then it is in the interest of incumbents to find some way—for example, by passing campaign-finance laws—to restrict the ability of candidates to raise money. As we shall see, this is exactly what they have done.

Where Does the Money Come From?

Many people think that well-heeled donors—fat cats—provide most of the money for political campaigns and do so in hopes of getting something for themselves out of government. For a long time that may have been the case. During a brief period in 1972, for example, President Nixon's reelection campaign raised nearly $20 million, mostly from wealthy contributors who preferred to remain anonymous. About 40 gave over $100,000 apiece, and a few contributed in excess of $1 million each. Some of these people just liked Nixon, but some wanted favors, ranging from special treatment in policymaking to an appointment as ambassador to some pleasant country. Nixon's rival, George McGovern, also got big individual contributions.[39] Some of Nixon's money was received in cash and was used to pay the men hired to break into the headquarters of the Democratic National Committee, located in the Watergate Hotel.

When the break-in was discovered, the Watergate scandal unfolded. One result was the passage of campaign finance reforms law that made it very hard for fat cats to operate in the old way. (For details, see the box on page 170.) Some key rules were these:

★ All contributions over $100 must be by check and publicly disclosed to the Federal Election Commission (FEC).

★ No individual can contribute more than $1,000 to any candidate in any given election.

★ No foreigners may contribute.

The new rules reduced the role of fat cats but did not reduce the amount of money spent on campaigns. On the contrary, the rules caused a vast increase in campaign contributions. The reason for this paradoxical result was that the law authorized the creation of political action committees. Once authorized, they mushroomed. A **political action committee,** or PAC, is an organization of at least fifty members that gives money to at least five different

MAJOR FEDERAL
CAMPAIGN-FINANCE RULES

★ ★ ★

GENERAL

★ All federal election contributions and expenditures are reported to a six-person Federal Election Commission with power to investigate and prosecute violators.

★ All contributions over $100 must be disclosed, with name, address, and occupation of contributor.

★ No *cash* contributions over $100; no foreign contributions.

★ No ceiling on amount a candidate or campaign may spend (unless a presidential candidate accepts federal funding).

INDIVIDUAL CONTRIBUTIONS

★ May not exceed $1,000 to any candidate in any election per year.

★ May not exceed $20,000 per year to a national party committee or $5,000 to a political action committee.

---

candidates in a federal election. A PAC can be sponsored by a corporation, a labor union, a trade association, or a professional society, or it can be just an organization of like-minded people. No PAC can give more than $5,000 to any candidate in any federal election (a primary and a general election each count as separate elections).

PACs were created in response to the failure of an older law that barred corporations and unions from giving money to candidates. That law had proved unworkable; many businesses and unions found it easy to evade it. Creating PACs was a way of bringing organizational contributions out into the open. Now, any corporation or union can form one (but only one) PAC; the money PACs spend must come from the voluntary contributions made by employees or members. The PACs must file complete financial reports with the FEC.

Authorizing PACs in effect authorized massive new fund-raising drives. There are now over four thousand PACs; in 1990 they gave about $160 million to congressional candidates. Some people think that PACs now control the politicians, but that is a considerable exaggeration. The typical corporate PAC will give small amounts (say, around $500) to each of several dozen candidates. This is enough money to insure that a phone call from the corporation gets returned by someone on the staff of the member of Congress, but not enough to guarantee (or much increase the chances) that the member will do exactly what the corporation (or union) wants.

★ No limit on individual expenditures for "independent advertising."

POLITICAL ACTION COMMITTEES (PACs)

★ A corporation, union, or other association may each establish one PAC.

★ A PAC must register six months in advance, have at least fifty contributors, and give to at least five candidates.

★ PAC contributions may not exceed $5,000 to a candidate per election, or $15,000 to a national party per year.

PRESIDENTIAL PRIMARIES

★ Federal matching funds, dollar for dollar, are available for all money raised by candidates from individual donors giving $250 or less.

★ To be eligible, a candidate must raise $5,000 in each of twenty states in contributions of $250 or less.

PRESIDENTIAL ELECTION

★ Federal government will pay all campaign costs (up to a certain ceiling) of major-party candidates and part of the cost of minor-party candidates (those winning between 5 and 25 percent of the vote).

There is, however, a way of increasing the effect of PAC (or individual) political contributions. It is called **bundling.** This involves taking checks from many individuals or PACs who think alike on some policy issue, bundling them together with a rubber band, and presenting them all at once to the politician. A big bundle might involve several hundred thousand dollars. That will definitely attract the attention of whoever receives it.

Not all the big PACs are connected with corporations or unions. One of the biggest nonconnected PACs is EMILY (which stands for Early Money Is Like Yeast), a feminist PAC that gives money to women running for Congress. In 1992 it raised more than $6 million to support 55 women, all Democrats, running for Congress.

Most nonconnected PACs, such as EMILY, are far more willing to support candidates running against incumbents than are connected PACs (those sponsored by corporations and unions). The latter are chiefly interested in maintaining influence with people already in office, and so give most of their money to incumbents. Since most incumbents are Democrats, business PACs often give more money to Democrats than to Republicans despite the ideological differences between corporate leaders and many Democrats.

Though PACs have grown in number and have become the target of political criticism, thay have never been the main source of political money. Most contributions still come from individuals. Since individuals can give no more than $1,000 to any candidate in any election, candidates must devise ways to reach large numbers of relatively small donors. The most effective way is the use of direct-mail advertising generated by computers into which lists of names are fed.[40]

There is one important exception to the $1,000 limit on individual contributions: congressional candidates. They can spend as much as they like out of their own bank accounts. (Congress tried to prevent this, but the Supreme Court overturned that restriction on the grounds that it abridged a candidate's right of free speech.)[41]

Presidential candidates operate under different rules than do people running for Congress. That is because the federal government pays most of the bills for presidential elections. It works this way: During the primary election, presidential candidates can receive **matching funds.** Any candidate who raises at least $5,000 (in individual contributions of $250 or less) in each of twenty states becomes eligible for matching funds. Once eligible, a candidate gets federal money to match, dollar for dollar, what he or she raises from individuals who contribute $250 or less. After the parties have chosen their nominees, the general-election campaign is entirely paid for by the government. (In 1992 Bush and Clinton each received $55 million.) If you are a minor party candidate (that is, candidate of a party that received less than 25 percent of the vote in the preceding election), you can get partial support from the government provided you win at least 5 percent of the vote in the election in which you are now running. If you take federal support, you cannot accept contributions from anybody else and you are limited to spending $50,000 of your own money. If you decide not to take the federal dollars, you can spend as much as you like. (In 1992, Ross Perot did not accept federal funding.)

There are at least two big loopholes in the federal campaign finance laws. The first is **soft money.** Individuals, unions, and corporations can give large sums of money to state political parties. Since this isn't going to the presidential candidate or to the national political parties, it is largely outside the federal rules. But obviously this state money can be spent in ways that help presidential candidates—for example, by conducting voter registration drives and get-out-the-vote campaigns on election day. Tens of millions of dollars of soft money were spent in the 1992 presidential campaign.

The second is **independent expenditures.** A PAC can spend unlimited amounts of money on advertising supporting or opposing a candidate, provided only that these expenditures are entirely independent of a candidate's campaign—that is, not at his or her direction and without his or her approval.

The Effects of Campaign-Finance Reform

The effects of these laws are not entirely clear, but some trends seem likely. First, candidates for federal office who are either personally wealthy or who can appeal successfully to many small donors by the use of television or direct-mail solicitation have an advantage. A candidate of modest means and little television appeal, however substantial his or her other qualifications and experience, is at a disadvantage.

Second, any congressional candidate who is not rich has to devote more time to fund-raising than before. Instead of raising a war chest by holding a few dinners with wealthy supporters, a candidate now must either become identified with powerful issues (as did Wallace, McGovern, or Reagan) or else spend much campaign time speaking to many small groups of potential donors. As yet there is no federal funding of congressional campaigns.

Third, incumbents continue to enjoy a substantial advantage in fund-raising. Now, as before, challengers probably must outspend incumbents to have any chance of winning. Yet in fact incumbents generally raise and spend more money than their challengers.[42] In raising money, incumbents have the advantage of being a known quantity, having a good chance of winning, and perhaps holding the power to act against the interests of those who support their opponent. (Remember, the names of contributors can no longer be secret.) These advantages explain why corporate PACs in 1990 gave more money to Democratic candidates for the House than to Republican ones: most incumbents were Democrats.

Fourth, late starters are likely to be discouraged. Candidates, who now must raise so much money from small groups, must begin early. It is no longer possible to enter a campaign late with the aid of well-heeled friends.

Fifth, the laws further weaken political parties by funneling most federal election grants to the candidates, not the parties, and by partially financing primary election campaigns. To compensate, however, the laws have been amended to help the parties: the Democratic and Republican congressional campaign committees can now spend more money on congressional candidates.[43]

Sixth, the role of celebrities in politics will increase. An efficient and perfectly legal fund-raising device is to have a movie star or rock group donate a benefit show that will attract thousands, with all proceeds (less expenses) going to the candidate. Such shows can generate huge sums.

These changes are the consequences of efforts to purify the electoral process. The object in every case has been to minimize the extent to which large contributors can unduly influence or even control the process of nomination and election. Elections since 1976 suggest that there have been no undue or improper solicitation of large givers. It has become extremely difficult to "sell" ambassadorships and harder for interest groups wanting special favors to conceal the money incentives they offer politicians under the guise of campaign contributions.

At the same time it should be recognized that the campaign-finance laws were not based on evidence that elected officials or policy decisions in the past had been for sale on a wholesale basis. Strong evidence indicates that milk price support levels may have been altered in recognition of large donations from the dairy industry and that a Securities and Exchange Commission investigation into a certain financial manipulator may have been terminated in reward for that person's large contributions. And some ambassadorships may have been given chiefly on the basis of money (though no person of ordinary means can afford the expenses of being an ambassador to a major foreign capital). Overall, however, there has been little evidence of systematic corruption of the political process.

The new laws governing campaign finance are based, at root, on the conviction that elections must not only be fair, they must also appear to be fair. Whether or not special-interest groups use campaign funds to buy and sell favors, the public is not likely to feel comfortable about a process in which—as *did* happen in the Nixon administration—millions of dollars are raised from a handful of people, funds are "laundered" in Mexico, or unaccounted-for cash is kept in safes and used to hire burglars.

THE EFFECTS OF ELECTIONS ON POLICY

Cynics complain that elections are meaningless. No matter who wins, crooks, incompetents, or self-serving politicians still hold office. People of a more charitable disposition may concede that elected officials are decent enough people but argue that public policy remains more or less the same no matter which official or which party is in office.

There is no brief and simple response to this view. One reason it is so hard to generalize about the policy effects of elections is that the offices to be filled are so numerous—and the ability of the political parties to unite behind a common policy is so weak—that any policy proposal must run a gauntlet of potential opponents. Though we have but two major parties, and though only one party can win the presidency, each party is a weak coalition of diverse elements that reflect the many divisions in public opinion. The proponents of a new law must put together a majority coalition almost from scratch, and a winning coalition on one issue tends to be somewhat different—quite often dramatically different—from a winning coalition on another issue.

Elections in parliamentary systems with strong parties, such as Great Britain, can often have a major effect on public policy because the winning party has the power to put its program into effect. American elections, unless accompanied by a national crisis such as a war or a depression, rarely produce changes of the magnitude of those that can occur in Britain. The constitutional system within which our elections take place was designed to moderate the pace of change—to make it neither easy nor impossible to adopt radical proposals.

But although the American system of government is intended to moderate the rate of change, it doesn't always work that way. Thus the election of 1860 brought to national power a party committed to opposing the extension of slavery and southern secession; it took a bloody war to vindicate that policy. The election of 1932 led to the New Deal, which produced the greatest single enlargement of federal authority since 1860. The election of 1964 gave the Democrats such a large majority in Congress (as well as control of the presidency) that an extraordinary number of new policies of sweeping significance emerged—Medicare and Medicaid, federal aid to education and to local law enforcement, two dozen environmental and consumer-protection laws, the Voting Rights Act of 1965, a revision of the immigration laws, and the new Department of Housing and Urban Development.

Of late, important economic changes have followed an election. In 1980 the voters brought into office the Reagan administration, determined to reverse the direction of policy over the preceding half-century; Reagan succeeded in obtaining large tax cuts, some reductions in the rate of spending increases on some major domestic programs, and changes in the policies of some regulatory agencies. The election of 1982 brought the Democrats some gains in the House and stiffened congressional resistance to change, a resistance that Reagan's reelection in 1984 did not greatly alter. Nonetheless, Reagan continued to press for major domestic spending cuts and a continued military buildup and joined some Democrats in calling for tax reform.

In view of all this, it is hard to argue that the pace of change in our government is always slow and that elections never make a difference. Studies confirm that elections are often significant, despite the difficulty of getting laws passed. One analysis of about 1,400 promises made between 1944 and 1964 in the platforms of the two major parties revealed that 72 percent were carried into effect.[44]

Why then do we so often think that elections make little difference? It is because public opinion and the political parties enter a phase of consolidation and continuity between periods of rapid change. During this phase the changes are, so to speak, digested, and party leaders adjust to the new popular consensus that may (or may not) evolve around the merits of these changes. Historically these periods of consolidation have followed the great realigning elections of 1860, 1896, and 1932.

Elections in these periods of consolidation are not "critical," are not fought out over a dominant issue, and provide the winners with no clear mandate. In most cases an election is little more than a retrospective judgment on the record of the incumbent president and the existing congressional majority. If times are good, incumbents win easily; if times are bad, incumbents may lose even though their opponents have no clear plans for change. But even a normal election can produce dramatic results if the winner is someone like Ronald Reagan, who helped give his party a distinctive political philosophy.

Elections have another, more complex effect on policy-making. The kinds of campaigns people must run in order to win affects the kinds of people who are willing to run. A century ago, presidential candidates did not even campaign. Television advertising did not become important until the 1960s. During the 1970s, political outsiders determined that they could run for president if they worked nonstop for three or four years. In the 1980s, campaign managers perfected the technique of learning how voters react to different messages and then feeding out those messages in ads and speeches.

People who can run successfully in campaigns organized this way may not have the ability to govern effectively once they are elected. Today's candidates, rather than being picked by knowledgeable peers in the party or in Congress, are self-selected. In any other democratic country in the world, people would be amazed to find candidates for the highest office running without having any experience in elective office (for example, Pat Buchanan, Jesse Jackson, and Ross Perot), or experience in state politics but not national politics (for example, Bruce Babbitt, Jimmy Carter, Bill Clinton, Michael Dukakis, and Ronald Reagan), or experience in Congress but not in any executive position (for example, Richard Gephardt, George McGovern, and Gary Hart). Some of these men might have made (or did make) good presidents, but there is no way to predict this from the experience they bring to the job.

Our election system rewards people who can mobilize small but strongly motivated constituencies, who can portray themselves as outsiders to the system they plan to run, who have the talent to utter newsworthy sound bites, and who are willing and able to spend three or four years campaigning.

SUMMARY

The United States has more elective offices and more elections than any other major nation. The decision on who is eligible to vote in those elections—originally made almost entirely by the states—is now largely under federal control. Though the franchise has gradually been extended to include all people eighteen years of age and over, we have seen an accompanying decline in voter participation in elections. This change may not be as significant as it appears because miscounting and vote frauds artificially inflated turnouts in the nineteenth century. But some decline has indisputably occurred, perhaps because politics is less interesting to citizens than it once was, perhaps also because the political parties have become weaker and less able to mobilize voters.

Political campaigns have increasingly become personalized, with little or no connection to formal party organizations, as a result of the decay of parties, the rise of the direct primary and the electronic media, and campaign-finance laws. Candidates face the problem of creating a temporary organization that can raise money from large numbers of small donors, mobilize enthusiastic supporters, and win a primary nomination in a way that will not harm their ability to appeal to a more diverse constituency in the general election. Campaigning has an uncertain effect on election outcomes, but election outcomes can have important effects on public policy, especially in those times—during *critical* or *realigning* elections—when new voters are coming into the electorate in large numbers, old party loyalties are weakening, or a major issue is splitting the majority party.

SUGGESTED READINGS

Burnham, Walter Dean. *Critical Elections and the Mainsprings of American Politics.* New York: Norton, 1970. An argument about the decline in voting participation and the significance of the realigning election of 1896.

Ehrenhalt, Alan. *The United States of Ambition.* New York: Random House, 1991. A brilliant analysis of the kinds of people willing and able to practice modern-day politics.

Fiorina, Morris P. *Retrospective Voting in American National Elections.* New Haven, Conn.: Yale University Press, 1981. A careful analysis of how voters judge politicians retrospectively—and rationally.

Jacobson, Gary C. *The Politics of Congressional Elections,* 2d ed. Boston: Little, Brown. How people are elected to Congress, with close attention to the role of money.

Kayden, Xandra. *Campaign Organization.* Lexington, Mass.: D. C. Heath, 1978. A close look at how political campaigns are organized, staffed, and led at the state level.

Key, V. O., Jr. *The Responsible Electorate.* Cambridge, Mass.: Harvard University Press, 1966. An argument, with evidence, that American voters are not fools.

Malbin, Michael J., ed. *Money and Politics in the United States: Financing Elections in the 1980s.* Chatham, N.J.: Chatham House, 1984. Articles on the sources and uses of campaign money with special attention to political parties and political action committees.

Page, Benjamin I. *Choices and Echoes in Presidential Elections.* Chicago: University of Chicago Press, 1978. Analyzes the interaction between the behavior of candidates and of voters in American elections.

Sundquist, James L. *Dynamics of the Party System: Alignment and Realignment of Political Parties in the United States,* rev. ed. Washington, D.C.: Brookings Institution, 1983. Historical analysis of realigning elections from 1860 to the nonrealignment of 1980.

Verba, Sidney, and Norman H. Nie. *Participation in America.* New York: Harper & Row, 1972. Analyzes the relationship between social class and political participation.

7

★ ★ ★

Congress

SENATOR DANIEL PATRICK MOYNIHAN OF NEW YORK once remarked that the United States is the only democratic government that has a legislative branch. Of course, lots of democracies have parliaments that pass laws. What he meant is that among the large democracies of the world, only the United States Congress has great powers that it can exercise independently of the executive branch. To see why this is the case, we must understand the difference between a congress and a parliament.

The United States (and most Latin American nations) have congresses; Great Britain and most Western European nations have parliaments. A **congress** is an assemblage of elected representatives empowered to make laws but not to select the chief executive of the nation; that individual is elected by the people. A **parliament** is an assemblage of elected representatives who both pass laws and select the nation's chief executive (usually called a prime minister).

Ordinarily a person becomes a member of a parliament (such as the British House of Commons) by being nominated by party leaders; voters generally choose between parties, not personalities; and thus par-

THE POWERS OF CONGRESS

★ ★ ★

The powers of Congress are found in Article I, section 8, of the Constitution:

* To lay and collect taxes, duties, imposts, and excises.
* To borrow money.
* To regulate commerce with foreign nations and among the states.
* To establish rules for naturalization (i.e., becoming a citizen) and bankruptcy.
* To coin money, set its value, and punish counterfeiting.
* To fix the standard of weights and measures.
* To establish a post office and post roads.
* To issue patents and copyrights to inventors and authors.
* To create courts inferior to (i.e., below) the Supreme Court.

liaments tend to be made up of people loyal to the national party leadership who meet to debate and vote on party issues. By contrast, a person becomes a member of the United States Congress by winning both a primary and a general election, elections in which personalities—not party identity—are usually most important to voters. Thus a congress tends to be made up of people who think of themselves as independent representatives of their districts or states and who, while willing to support their party on many matters, expect to vote as their (or their constituents') beliefs and interests require.

Members of a parliament usually can make only one important decision—whether or not to support the government (the government consisting of the prime minister and various cabinet officers selected from the party that has won the most seats in the last election). If members of a party in power in parliament vote against their leaders, a new government must be formed. Thus the party leaders insist that all party members vote together on most issues under pain of not being renominated.

In the United States, the voters, not the members of Congress, select the head of the executive branch of government, the president. This, however, makes members of Congress more, not less, powerful, for they can vote on proposed laws without worrying that their votes will cause the government to collapse and without fearing that a failure to support their party will lead to their removal from the ballot in the next election. Because Congress is con-

* To define and punish piracies, felonies on the high seas, and crimes against the law of nations.

* To declare war.

* To raise and support an army and navy and make rules for their governance.

* To provide for a militia (reserving to the states the right to appoint militia officers and to train the militia under congressional rules).

* To exercise exclusive legislative powers over the seat of government (i.e., the District of Columbia) and over places purchased to be federal facilities (forts, arsenals, dockyards, and "other needful buildings").

* To "make all laws which shall be necessary and proper for carrying into execution the foregoing powers, and all other powers vested by this Constitution in the government of the United States." (*Note:* This "necessary and proper" or "elastic" clause has been broadly interpreted by the Supreme Court, as will be explained in Chapter 10.)

stitutionally independent of the president and because its members are not tightly disciplined by party leaders, members are free to express their views, to vote as they wish, and to become involved in the minute details of creating laws, establishing budgets, and supervising agencies. They do this through an elaborate and growing set of committees and subcommittees.

Since members of a parliament have little independent power, they receive poor pay, few perquisites, little or no office space, and virtually no staff. But even the most junior member of the United States House of Representatives has power and is rewarded accordingly. A representative earns a substantial salary ($125,000 in 1991), receives generous retirement benefits, has at least a three-room suite of offices, is supplied with a staff of at least eighteen, can make thirty-three free trips to the home district each year, and can mail newsletters and certain other documents free under the "franking privilege." Representatives with more seniority and senators receive even more benefits.

THE EVOLUTION OF CONGRESS

The Framers chose to place legislative powers in the hands of a congress rather than a parliament for philosophical and practical reasons. They did not want to have all powers concentrated in a single government institution, even one that was popularly elected, because they feared that such a concentration could lead to rule by an oppressive or impassioned majority. At the same time, they knew that the states would never consent to a national constitution that did not protect their interests. Hence they created a **bicameral** (two-chamber) legislature, with a House of Representatives elected directly by the people and a Senate, consisting of two members from each state, chosen (originally) by the legislatures of each state. Though "all legislative powers" were to be vested in the Congress, those powers would be shared with a president (who could veto acts of Congress), limited to those explicitly conferred on the federal government, and, as it turned out, subject to the power of the Supreme Court to declare acts of Congress unconstitutional.

Although they designed these checks and balances to prevent legislative tyranny, the Framers nevertheless expected that Congress would be the dominant institution in the national government. And for at least a century and a half it was, except for a few brief periods when activist presidents (such as Andrew Jackson, Abraham Lincoln, and Theodore Roosevelt) were able to challenge congressional supremacy. During the twentieth century, the major struggles for national political power have not occurred between Congress and the president but rather *within* Congress—generally over issues of great national significance. At issue has been a disagreement over the distribution of power within Congress itself. Should Congress have a strong central leadership? Or should the power of individual members (and the constituencies they represent) be enhanced, a situation that could result in weak leadership, rules allowing for delay and extended discussion, and many opportunities for committee and subcommittee activity?

After nearly two centuries of growth and experimentation, the House has committed itself to the view that the autonomy and power of individual members are to be protected at the expense of opportunities for leadership. Though it flirted with strong party leadership in the late nineteenth century, the House has rejected the notion of playing the deliberative, party-controlled, general-policy role of a parliament. It has chosen instead to emphasize the importance of committees, subcommittees, and individual congressional offices. Thus legislative action must be achieved by an elaborate and necessarily slow process of building consent among individual members.

The Senate never even flirted with tight organization. Since they are so few in number, senators have always insisted on the right to unlimited debate and have always resisted the emergence of leaders with strong formal powers. A major change in the politics of the Senate occurred when the Constitution was amended in 1913 to require that senators be directly elected by the people instead of—as was originally the case—by state legislatures. The Seventeenth Amendment reflected in part popular revulsion against the appearance that the Senate had become a "millionaires' club," but its practical effect was small. Having a lot of money still helps (though it is not essential) if you wish to become a senator.

WHO IS IN CONGRESS?

Because Congress has such great power and because its internal structure, especially in recent years, has been so decentralized, the behavior of Congress is importantly affected by the kinds of people who are in it and how they get there. The barebones facts are these:

The Congress of the United States consists of two chambers, the House of Representatives and the Senate. The size of the House is fixed by law at 435 members, apportioned among the states roughly in accordance with their population. Each state must have at least one representative; how many more it has depends on its population. Every ten years, following the count of the nation's population by the Bureau of the Census, the House reapportions its seats among the states on the basis of a mathematical formula worked out many years ago. Because of population movements within the country, many of the northeastern states have been losing seats in the House in recent decades while many of the states in the South and Southwest have been gaining seats. A Supreme Court ruling requires that within each state, the districts from which representatives are elected be approximately equal in population.[1] Representatives serve for two-year terms.

The Senate consists of two senators from each state, each serving for six-year terms. Whereas federal law determines how many representatives each state has, the Constitution (Article I) requires that each state have two senators and prohibits the Constitution from being amended to change this allocation. The two senators from a given state serve staggered terms so that the two do not stand for reelection during the same year.

This constitutional and legal system has brought to both houses of Congress a total of 535 people who, *on the average,* are middle-age white males. The number of women in the House has increased—dramatically in the 1992 election—from 8 in 1947 to 48 in 1993; there are 6 women in the Senate. There are 39 blacks in the House and 1 in the Senate (see Table 7.1), and 19 Latinos in the House.

The importance of the personal characteristics (age, sex, or race) of members of Congress varies with the issues. On some matters, such as civil rights, they can be very important. Black members of the House will be far more solidly supportive of new civil-rights laws than will white members. But even civil-rights laws get a lot of support from white members. And in 1972 a male-dominated Congress proposed the Equal Rights Amendment to the Constitution. Support for aid to Israel wins consistent support from many non-Jewish members of Congress. Today, as in the past, some of the most affluent senators, such as Edward M. Kennedy, take the leadership in pressing for spending programs aimed at helping the poor.

Age, sex, and race are not nearly as important as seniority, partisanship, ideology, and constituency preferences in explaining how members of Congress vote.

TABLE 7.1 Blacks and Women in Congress 1949–1993

Congress	Senate		House	
	Blacks	Women	Blacks	Women
103d (1993–1995)	1	6	39	48
102d	0	2	25	28
101st	0	2	24	25
100th	0	2	23	23
99th	0	2	20	22
98th	0	2	21	22
97th	0	2	17	19
96th	0	1	16	16
95th	1	2	16	18
94th	1	0	15	19
93d	1	0	15	14
92d	1	2	12	13
91st	1	1	9	10
90th	1	1	5	11
89th	0	2	6	10
88th	0	2	5	11
87th	0	2	4	17
86th	0	1	4	16
85th	0	1	4	15
84th	0	1	3	16
83d	0	3	2	12
82d	0	1	2	10
81st (1949–1951)	0	1	2	9

SOURCE: Data from *Congressional Quarterly Almanac,* various years.

Years of Service

The most important change that has occurred in the composition of Congress has been so gradual that most people have not noticed it. In the nineteenth century, a majority of members often served only one term. Being in Congress was not regarded as a career, partly because the federal government's actions were not very important, partly because Washington was a distant, expensive, and unpleasant place to live, and partly because members of Congress were not well paid.

For the first time, one state (California) has two women senators: Dianne Feinstein (left) and Barbara Boxer.

Today serving in Congress has become a career, and there is relatively little turnover of members. From 1863 to 1969, the proportion of first-termers in the House fell from 58 percent to 8 percent, and then rose somewhat to about 16 percent in 1981. Today the typical representative has been in the House for about five terms.[2]

This change has an important implication for representative democracy: most members of the House face no serious electoral challenge. In the period 1946–1990, more than 90 percent of the incumbent representatives seeking reelection were returned to office. Furthermore, fewer incumbent members of Congress are now from "marginal" districts—those in which the winner gets less than 55 percent of the vote. In 1948 most races in which an incumbent representative was running were quite close: the winner got less than 55 percent of the vote. By 1970, however, the winner in three-fourths of these contests got 60 percent or more of the vote. Of late, the number of marginal districts has been getting even smaller. Senators, on the other hand, have faced riskier elections: in 1946–1984, only about three-fourths of the incumbents were reelected, and the proportion has decreased in recent years. And in fewer than half of their races does the incumbent receive at least 60 percent of the vote.[3] In 1992, with voter disgust at Congress at an all-time high, the percentage of incumbents reelected declined slightly.

Scholars do not entirely agree on why congressional seats should have become safer. Some feel that it is the result of television and other ways of reaching the voters through the media, but why don't challengers also bene-fit? Another possibility is that voters are more likely to vote for the person rather than the party, and thus to vote for the person they have heard of—the incumbent representative who can deluge the voters with free mailings, travel frequently (at public expense) to meet the voters, and get free publicity by sponsoring bills or conducting investigations. Challengers have much more difficulty gaining recognition. Finally, incumbents can use their powers to get programs passed (or to block unpopular ones) or to fund projects that benefit their districts—for example, by building highways, taking credit for federal grants, or making certain that a particular industry or union is protected by tariffs.[4]

Party

The tendency of voters to return incumbents to office means that, in ordi-nary times, no one should expect dramatic changes in the composition of Congress. Because the advantages of incumbency began to take effect after the Democrats were in control of Congress, these advantages help explain why the Democrats have so thoroughly dominated Congress for the last four decades. Other factors also explain this dominance: more voters consider themselves Democrats than Republicans, and many parts of the South still af-ford Republicans little chance of victory. Increasingly a majority of represen-tatives and senators come from one-party, or at least one-candidate, areas, though some of these districts are much more competitive in presidential elections than in congressional ones.

From time to time, major electoral convulsions alter the membership of Congress. The Democrats, for example, suffered severe losses in the elections of 1938, 1942, 1950, and 1966—but each time they still retained a majority of the House. In 1980 they lost control of the Senate for the first time since 1954 (they regained control in 1986). Because members of Congress do not always vote along strict party lines, the size of that majority is important. The kinds of bills that get passed will be affected by how many conservative Democrats are prepared to join with Republicans to form the so-called con-servative coalition. When the number of seats is rather evenly divided in Congress, one party may "control" Congress and still not be able to get all, or even most, of its legislative program approved.

GETTING ELECTED TO CONGRESS

To get elected to the House or Senate in most states, you need only win more votes than the other candidates running from your district or state in a given congressional election. You need not win a majority of the votes cast, only a plurality. In fact, most representatives and senators actually do receive a majority of the votes cast because most races involve no more than two candidates. Since voters almost always vote only for a Democrat or a Republican, you must have the word "Democrat" or "Republican" appear after your name on the general election ballot if you hope to win.

To acquire that party label, you must usually win a primary election (as described in Chapter 6). Ordinarily you enter a primary by collecting enough signatures on a petition to get your name listed on the primary ballot. In a hotly contested race, five or six names may be entered in the primary. In most states, plurality rule decides those primaries. This means that, in theory, you could win the primary with only 21 percent of the vote (if there are five candidates). Each candidate running in the general election could, in theory, be liked by only a small minority of the Democratic and Republican voters (which may explain why, in some races, the average voter isn't attracted to either candidate). To deal with this, some states, notably in the South, have a second or **runoff** primary in which the two top vote getters (if neither has won a majority of the votes) run against each other so that the final nominee will have a majority of the votes cast by his or her party's members.

Because of the primary system and because in most states party organizations cannot control who enters or wins the primary election, congressional campaigns have become highly personalized. This means that candidates try to develop among their constituents a good opinion of themselves as candidates and not of the party, of their party in Congress, or even of Congress itself. To the extent that they succeed in building trust in themselves, they can enjoy great freedom in how they vote on particular issues and have less need to explain away votes that displease their constituents. (Downplaying a record may be more difficult if a strong-minded, single-issue group concerned with gun control, abortion, or the like is active in their district.) Furthermore, many members of Congress cater to their constituents' heightened distrust of Congress and the federal government by promising to help "clean things up." Thus, paradoxically, opinion polls show that many Americans have a low opinion of Congress but a high opinion of their own member of Congress.[5]

THE ORGANIZATION OF CONGRESS: PARTIES AND INTERESTS

Congress is not a single organization; it is a vast and complex collection of organizations by which the business of Congress is carried on and through which members of Congress form alliances. Unlike the British Parliament, in which the political parties are the only important kind of organization, parties are only one of many important units in Congress. In fact, other organizations have grown in number as party influence has declined.

KEY FACTS ABOUT CONGRESS

★ ★ ★

QUALIFICATIONS

REPRESENTATIVE

* ★ Must be 25 years of age (when seated, not when elected).
* ★ Must have been a citizen of the United States for seven years.
* ★ Must be an inhabitant of the state from which elected. (*Note:* custom, but *not* the Constitution, requires that a representative live in the district he or she represents.)

SENATOR

* ★ Must be 30 years of age (when seated, not when elected).
* ★ Must have been a citizen of the United States for nine years.
* ★ Must be an inhabitant of the state from which elected.

JUDGING QUALIFICATIONS

Each house is the judge of the "elections, returns, and qualifications" of its members. Thus Congress alone decides disputed congressional elections. On occasion, it has excluded a person from taking a seat on the grounds that the election was improper.

Party Organization

The Democrats and Republicans in the House and the Senate are organized by party leaders, who in turn are elected by the full party membership within the House and Senate.

The Senate

The majority party (currently the Democratic party) chooses one of its members—usually the person with the greatest seniority—to be **president pro tempore** of the Senate. This is usually an honorific position, required by the Constitution so that the Senate will have a presiding officer when the vice president of the United States (according to the Constitution, the president of the Senate) is absent. In fact, both the president pro tem and the vice president usually assign the tedious chore of presiding to a junior senator.

The real leadership is in the hands of the majority and minority leaders. The **majority leader**'s principal task is to schedule the business of the

PRIVILEGES

Members of Congress have certain privileges, the most important of which, conferred by the Constitution, is that "for any speech or debate in either house they shall not be questioned in any other place." This doctrine of "privileged speech" has been interpreted by the Supreme Court to mean that members of Congress cannot be sued or prosecuted for anything they say or write in connection with their legislative duties.

When Senator Mike Gravel read the Pentagon Papers—some then-secret government documents about the Vietnam War—into the *Congressional Record* in defiance of a court order restraining their publication, the Court held this was "privileged speech" and beyond challenge [*Gravel* v. *United States*, 408 U.S. 606 (1972)]. But when Senator William Proxmire issued a press release critical of a scientist doing research on monkeys, the Court decided the scientist could sue him for libel because a press release was not part of the legislative process [*Hutchinson* v. *Proxmire*, 443 U.S. 111 (1979)].

THE SIZE OF CONGRESS

Congress decides the size of the House of Representatives. The House began with 65 members in 1790 and has had 435 members since 1912. Each state must have at least one representative. Regardless of its population, each state has two senators. Equal suffrage for states in the Senate is enshrined in Article I of the Constitution, the only provision that cannot be amended (see Article V).

Senate, usually in consultation with the **minority leader.** A majority leader with a strong personality who is skilled at political bargaining (such as Lyndon Johnson, the Democrats' leader in the 1950s) may also acquire much influence over the substance of Senate business. Johnson's successor in the 1960s, Mike Mansfield, was less assertive and had less influence.

A **whip,** chosen by each party, helps party leaders stay informed about what the party members are thinking, rounds up members when important votes are taken, and attempts to keep a nose count of how voting on a controversial issue is likely to go. He has several senators to assist him.

Each party also chooses a **Policy Committee** composed of a dozen or so senators who help the party leader schedule Senate business, choosing what bills are to be given major attention and in what order.

For individual senators, however, the key party organization is the group that assigns senators to the Senate's standing committees: for the Democrats, a twenty-two-member Steering Committee; for the Republicans, an eighteen-member Committee on Committees. For newly elected senators, their political careers, opportunities for favorable publicity, and chances for helping their states and constituents depend in great part on the committees to which they are assigned.

Achieving ideological and regional balance is a key—and delicate—aspect of selecting party leaders, making up important committees, and assigning freshmen senators to committees. Liberals and conservatives in each party will fight over the choice of majority and minority leaders.

The House of Representatives

The party structure is essentially the same in the House as in the Senate, though the titles of various posts are different. But leadership carries more power in the House than in the Senate because of the House rules. Being so large (435 members), the House must restrict debate and schedule its business with great care; thus leaders who do the scheduling and who determine how the rules shall be applied usually have substantial influence.

The **Speaker,** who presides over the House, is the most important person in that body. He is elected by whichever party has a majority. Unlike the president pro tem of the Senate, this position is anything but honorific, for the Speaker is also the principal leader of the majority party. Though Speakers as presiders are expected to be fair, Speakers as party leaders are expected to use their powers to help pass legislation favored by their party.

In helping his party, the Speaker has some important formal powers: he decides who shall be recognized to speak on the floor of the House; he rules whether a motion is relevant and germane to the business at hand; he decides (subject to certain rules) the committees to which new bills shall be assigned. He influences what bills are brought up for a vote and appoints the members of special and select committees. Since 1975 the Speaker has been able to select the majority-party members of the Rules Committee, which plays an important role in the consideration of bills.

The Speaker also has some informal powers: he controls some patronage jobs in the Capitol building and the assignment of extra office space. Even though the Speaker now is far less powerful than some of his predecessors, he is still an important person to have on one's side.

In the House, as in the Senate, the majority party elects a floor leader, called the **majority leader.** The other party chooses the **minority leader.** Traditionally, the majority leader becomes Speaker when the person in that position dies or retires—provided, of course, that his party is still in the majority. Each party also has a **whip,** with several assistant whips in charge of rounding up votes. For the Democrats, committee assignments are made and the scheduling of legislation is discussed in a Steering and Policy Committee, chaired by the Speaker. The Republicans have divided responsibility for committee assignments and policy discussion between two committees. Each party also has a congressional campaign committee to provide funds and other assistance to party members running for election or reelection to the House.

Party Voting

The effect of this elaborate party machinery can be crudely measured by the extent to which party members vote together in the House and the Senate. A **party vote** can be defined in various ways; naturally the more stringent the definition, the less party voting we will observe. Figure 7.1 shows two measures of party voting in the House of Representatives during this century. By the strictest measure, a party vote occurs when 90 percent or more of the Democrats vote together against 90 percent or more of the Republicans. A looser measure counts as a party vote when at least 50 percent of the Democrats vote together against 50 percent of the Republicans. As is plain by either measure, the extent of party voting is low and has declined since the turn of the century.

Given that political parties as organizations do not tightly control a legislator's ability to get elected, what is surprising is not that party votes are relatively rare, but that they occur at all. There are several reasons why congressional members of one party sometimes do vote together against a majority of the other party. First, members of Congress do not randomly decide to be Democrats or Republicans; at least for most members, these choices reflect some broad policy agreements. By tabulating the ratings that several interest groups give members of Congress for voting on important issues, it is possible to rank each member of Congress from most to least liberal in three policy areas—economic affairs, social questions, and foreign and military affairs. As can be seen in Table 7.2 on page 194, Democrats in the House and Senate were much more liberal than Republicans during 1991, just as they have been in most recent years. The ideological differences between the parties are so pronounced that even the average southern Democrat in the House is more liberal than the average northern Republican.

In addition to their personal views, members of Congress have other reasons for supporting their party's position at least some of the time: on many matters that come up for vote, members of Congress often have little information and no opinions. It is only natural that they look to fellow party members for advice. Furthermore, supporting the party position can work to the long-term advantage of a member interested in gaining status and influence in Congress. Though party leaders are weaker today than in the past, they are hardly powerless. Sam Rayburn reputedly told freshman members of Congress that "if you want to get along, go along." That is less true today, but still good advice.

In short, party *does* make a difference—not as much as it did eighty years ago and not nearly as much as it does in a parliamentary system—but party

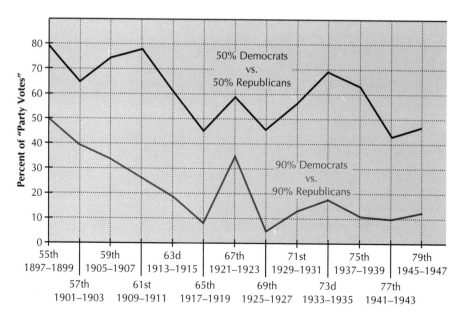

FIGURE 7.1 The Decline of Party Votes in the House of Representatives, 1897–1991

SOURCE: Updated from Joseph Cooper, David Brady, and Patricia Hurley, "The Electoral Basis of Party Voting: Patterns and Trends in the U.S. House of Representatives, 1887–1969," in *The Impact of the Electoral Process*, ed. Louis Maisel and Joseph Cooper (Beverly Hills, Calif.: Sage Publications, 1977), 139.

*No data on 90% versus 90% votes since 1969.

affiliation is still the single most important thing to know about a member of Congress. In fact, since 1980 the likelihood of a member voting with his or her party has increased sharply.

Caucuses

Congressional caucuses are a growing rival to the parties as a source of policy leadership. A **caucus** is an association of members of Congress created to advocate a political ideology or to advance a regional or economic interest. In 1959 only four such caucuses existed; by the early 1980s there were more than seventy. The more important ones include the Democratic Study Group (uniting more than two hundred liberal Democrats, though their names are not publicized to avoid embarrassing them with constituents), the Conservative Democratic Forum (or "Boll Weevils," a group of about forty southern representatives who generally supported Reagan's programs), the Wednesday Group (a moderately conservative Republican group), and the Gypsy Moths (twenty to thirty moderate or liberal Republicans who opposed some Reagan programs).

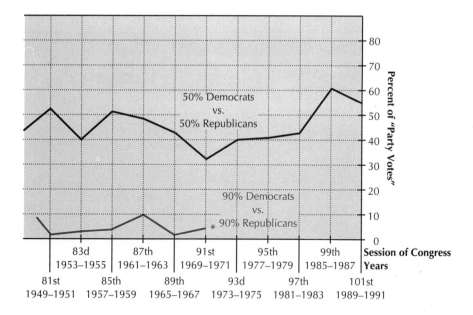

Other caucuses include the delegations from certain large states who meet on matters of common interest, as well as the countless groups dedicated to racial, ethnic, regional, and policy interests. The Congressional Black Caucus in the House is one of the best known of these and is probably typical of many in its operations. It meets regularly and employs a staff. As with most caucuses, some members are very active, others only marginally so. On some issues it simply registers an opinion; on others it attempts to negotiate with leaders of other blocs so that votes can be traded in a mutually advantageous way. It keeps its members informed, and on occasion presses to put a member on a regular congressional committee that has no blacks.

THE ORGANIZATION OF CONGRESS: COMMITTEES

The most important organizational feature of Congress is the set of legislative committees of the House and Senate. There the real work of Congress is done; in the chairmanship of these committees, and their subcommittees, most of the power of Congress is found. The number and jurisdiction of these committees are of the greatest interest to members of Congress since decisions on these subjects determine what groups of legislators with what political views will pass on legislative proposals, oversee the workings of agencies in the executive branch, and conduct investigations.

A typical Congress will have, in each house, about two dozen committees and well over one hundred subcommittees. Periodically efforts have been made to cut the number of committees to give each a broader jurisdiction

TABLE 7.2 Ideology and Party in the Congress in 1991

Senate	House
Of the 20 most conservative senators:	Of the 20 most conservative representatives:
All were Republicans	*All* were Republicans
Of the 20 most liberal senators:	Of the 20 most liberal representatives:
All were Democrats	*All* were Democrats

SOURCE: Calculated from data in Richard Cohen and William Schneider, "Partisan Polarization," *National Journal,* January 18, 1992, p. 134.

and to reduce conflict between committees over a single bill. But as the number of committees declined, the number of subcommittees rose, leaving matters about as they had been.

There are three kinds of committees: **standing committees** (more or less permanent bodies with specific legislative responsibilities), **select committees** (groups appointed for a limited purpose, which do not introduce legislation, and which exist for only a few years), and **joint committees** (on which both representatives and senators serve). An especially important kind of joint committee is the **conference committee,** made up of representatives and senators appointed to resolve differences in the Senate and House versions of a bill before final passage.

Though members of the majority party could, in theory, occupy all the seats on all the committees, in practice they take the majority of the seats, name the chairman, and allow the minority party to have the remainder of the seats. The number of seats varies from about six to more than fifty. Usually the ratio of Democrats to Republicans on a committee roughly corresponds to their ratio in the House or Senate.

Standing committees are the important ones because, with a few exceptions, they are the only committees that can propose legislation by reporting a bill out to the full House or Senate. Each member of the House usually serves on two standing committees (but members of the Appropriations, Rules, or Ways and Means committees are limited to one committee). Each senator may serve on two major committees and one minor committee (see boxes on pages 196–198), but this rule is not strictly enforced.

When party leaders in the past were stronger, committee chairmen were picked on the basis of loyalty to the leader. When this leadership weakened, seniority on the committee came to govern the selection of chairmen. Of late, however, even seniority has been under attack. In 1971 House Democrats decided in their caucus to elect committee chairmen by secret ballot; four years later they used that procedure to remove three committee chairmen who held their positions by seniority. And in 1985 they removed the chairman of the House Armed Services Committee.

Traditionally the committees of Congress were dominated by the chairmen. They did their most important work behind closed doors (though their hearings and reports were almost always published in full). In the early 1970s, Congress further decentralized and democratized its operations by a series of changes that some members regarded as a "bill of rights" for representatives and senators, especially those with little seniority. These changes, by and large, were made by the Democratic Caucus, but since the Democrats were in the majority, the changes, in effect, became the rules of Congress. In the House, the important changes included provisions for written committee rules and for guaranteeing minority-party members the right to call witnesses. In both Senate and House committees, the chairman now is elected by secret ballot, individuals are not permitted to chair more than one committee, and all meetings are open to the public unless members vote to close meetings for a special purpose, such as for considering defense secrets.

No matter what rules they operate under, many key committees have, because of their membership or leadership, a distinctive political coloration that must be recognized if one is to understand why Congress acts as it does. For example, bills pertaining to civil rights and courts often got a very different reception from the Senate Judiciary Committee when it was chaired by James Eastland of Mississippi, a staunch conservative, than they did from the House Judiciary Committee, chaired by the liberal Peter Rodino of New Jersey. Matters changed when Eastland retired in 1978 and the liberal Edward M. Kennedy became chairman of the Senate Judiciary Committee; they changed again when the Republicans took control of the Senate in 1981 and the conservative J. Strom Thurmond replaced Kennedy as chairman of the Judiciary Committee; they changed yet again when the Democrats returned to power and Joseph Biden became chairman.

Not only are the political colorations of congressional committees different, so also are their functions and operating styles. Some, such as the House Appropriations and Ways and Means committees and the Senate Foreign Relations and the Labor and Human Relations committees, have been attractive to members who want to influence public policy, who like to become experts on important issues, and who value having influence with their colleagues in Congress. Others, such as the House Interior and Insular Affairs Committee, the House Post Office and Civil Service committees (and their Senate counterparts), are attractive to members who value an opportunity to serve constituency groups and who worry more about solidifying their re-election prospects than about having influence with their congressional colleagues. Work on the first kind of committee—the Congress-oriented, policy-oriented type—does in fact give members more prestige and influence in Congress than work on the second kind, those that focus on external constituency concerns. The committee to which he or she is assigned thus significantly affects the kind of role a representative or senator will play.[6]

STANDING COMMITTEES OF THE SENATE

★ ★ ★

MAJOR COMMITTEES

(no senator is supposed to serve on more than two)

Agriculture, Nutrition, and Forestry

Appropriations

Armed Services

Banking, Housing, and Urban Affairs

Budget

Commerce, Science, and Transportation

Energy and Natural Resources

Environment and Public Works

Finance

Foreign Relations

THE ORGANIZATION OF CONGRESS: STAFFS AND SPECIALIZED OFFICES

In 1900 representatives had no personal staff, and senators averaged fewer than one staff member each. By 1979 the average representative had sixteen assistants and the average senator had thirty-six. To the more than ten thousand people on the personal staffs of members of Congress must be added another three thousand who work for congressional committees and yet another three thousand employed by various congressional research agencies. Congress has produced the most rapidly growing bureaucracy in Washington: the personal staffs of legislators have increased more than fivefold since 1947.[7] Though many staffers perform routine chores, many help draft legislation, handle constituents, and otherwise shape policy and politics.

Tasks of Staff Members

A major function of a legislator's staff is to help constituents solve problems and thereby help that member of Congress get reelected. Indeed, over the last two decades, a growing portion of congressional staffs have worked in the local (district or state) offices of the legislator, rather than in Washington. Almost all members of Congress have at least one (and most have two or more) such home offices. Some scholars believe that this growth in con-

Governmental Affairs

Judiciary

Labor and Human Resources

MINOR COMMITTEES

(no senator is supposed to serve on more than one)

Rules and Administration

Small Business

Veterans' Affairs

SELECT COMMITTEES

Aging

Ethics

Indian Affairs

Intelligence

NOTE: Despite the rules, some senators serve on more than two major committees.

stituency-serving staff helps explain why it is so difficult to defeat an incumbent.[8]

The legislative function of congressional staff members is also important. With each senator serving on an average of more than two committees and seven subcommittees, it is virtually impossible for members of Congress to become familiar in detail with all the proposals that come before them or to write all the bills that they feel ought to be introduced.[9] The role of staff members has expanded in proportion to the tremendous growth in Congress's workload.

The orientation of committee staff members differs. Some think of themselves as—and to a substantial degree they are—politically neutral professionals whose job it is to assist members of a committee, whether Democrats or Republicans, in holding hearings or revising bills. Others see themselves as partisan advocates, interested in promoting Democratic or Republican causes, depending on who hired them.

Those who work for individual members of Congress, as opposed to committees, see themselves entirely as advocates for their bosses. They often assume an entrepreneurial function, taking the initiative in finding and selling a policy to their boss—a representative or senator—who can take credit for it. Lobbyists and reporters understand this completely and therefore spend a lot of time cultivating congressional staffers.

STANDING COMMITTEES OF THE HOUSE

(CLASSIFIED IN ACCORDANCE WITH THE RULES OF THE HOUSE DEMOCRATIC CAUCUS)

★ ★ ★

EXCLUSIVE COMMITTEES

(member may not serve on any other standing committee, except Budget)

Appropriations

Rules

Ways and Means

MAJOR COMMITTEES

(member may serve on only one major standing committee)

Agriculture

Armed Services

Banking, Finance, and Urban Affairs

Education and Labor

Energy and Commerce

Foreign Affairs

Judiciary

Public Works and Transportation

The increased reliance on staff has changed Congress, mainly because the staff has altered the environment within which Congress does its work. In addition to their role as entrepreneurs promoting new policies, staffers act as negotiators: members of Congress today are more likely to deal with one another through staff intermediaries rather than through personal contact. Congress has thereby become less collegial, more individualistic, and less of a deliberative body.[10]

Staff Agencies

In addition to increasing the number of staff members, Congress has also created a set of staff agencies that work for Congress as a whole. These have come into being in large part to give Congress specialized knowledge equivalent to what the president has by virtue of his position as chief of the execu-

NONMAJOR COMMITTEES

(member may serve on one major and one nonmajor or two nonmajor standing committees)

Budget

District of Columbia

Government Operations

House Administration

Interior and Insular Affairs

Merchant Marine and Fisheries

Post Office and Civil Service

Science, Space, and Technology

Small Business

Standards of Official Conduct

Veterans' Affairs

SELECT COMMITTEES

Intelligence

(NOTE: In 1993, the House abolished four select committees: on aging, children, hunger, and narcotics.)

NOTE: The Republican party is not bound by these classifications or membership rules but generally tends to follow them, especially with respect to the exclusive committees.

tive branch. One of these, the *Congressional Research Service (CRS),* is part of the Library of Congress and employs almost nine hundred people; it is politically neutral, responding to requests by members of Congress for information and giving both sides of arguments. The *General Accounting Office (GAO),* once merely an auditing agency, now has about five thousand employees and investigates policies and makes recommendations on almost every aspect of government; its head, though appointed by the president for a fifteen-year term, is very much the servant of Congress rather than the president. The *Office of Technology Assessment (OTA)* studies and evaluates policies and programs that have a significant impact on technology. The *Congressional Budget Office (CBO),* created in 1974, advises Congress on the likely impact of different spending programs and attempts the difficult task of estimating future economic trends.

HOW A BILL BECOMES LAW

Some bills zip through Congress; others make their way painfully and slowly, sometimes emerging in a form very different from their original one. Congress is like a crowd, moving either sluggishly or, when excited, with great speed.

In the following account of how a bill becomes law (see Figure 7.2), keep in mind that the complexity of congressional procedures ordinarily gives powerful advantage to the opponents of any new policy. There are many points at which action can be blocked. This does not mean that nothing gets done, but that to get something done, a member of Congress must *either* slowly and painstakingly assemble a majority coalition *or* take advantage of enthusiasm for some new cause that sweeps away the normal obstacles to change.

Introducing a Bill

Any member of Congress may introduce a bill—in the House by handing it to a clerk or dropping it in a box; in the Senate by being recognized by the presiding officer and announcing the bill's introduction. Bills are then numbered and printed. If a bill is not passed within one session of Congress, it is dead and must be reintroduced during the next Congress.

We often hear that legislation is initiated by the president and enacted by Congress. The reality is more complicated. Congress often initiates legislation (for example, most consumer and environmental laws passed since 1966 originated in Congress), and even laws formally proposed by the president have often been incubated in Congress. Even when he is the principal author of a bill, a president usually submits it (if he is prudent) only after careful consultation with key congressional leaders. In any case, he cannot himself introduce legislation; he must get a member of Congress to do it for him.

In addition to bills, Congress can also pass resolutions. Either house can use **simple resolutions** for such matters as establishing operating rules. **Concurrent resolutions** settle housekeeping and procedural matters that affect both houses. Simple and concurrent resolutions are not signed by the president and do not have the force of law. A **joint resolution** requires approval by both houses and presidential signature; it is essentially the same as a law. A joint resolution is also used to propose a constitutional amendment; in this case it must be approved by a two-thirds vote in each house, but it does not require the signature of the president.

Study by Committees

A bill is referred to a committee for consideration by either the Speaker of the House or the Senate's presiding officer. If a chairperson or committee is known to be hostile to a bill, assignment can be a crucial matter. Rules gov-

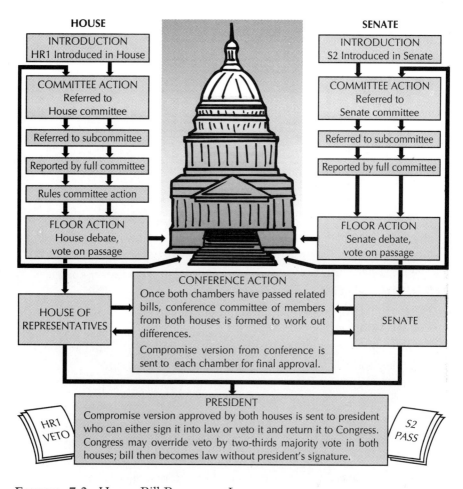

FIGURE 7.2 How a Bill Becomes a Law

ern which committee will get which bill, but sometimes a choice is possible. In the House, the Speaker's right to make such a choice (subject to appeal to the full House) is an important source of his power.

The Constitution requires that "all bills for raising revenue shall originate in the House of Representatives." The Senate can and does amend such bills, but only after the House has acted first. Bills that are not for raising revenue—that is, that do not alter tax laws—can originate in either chamber. In practice, the House also originates **appropriations bills** (bills that direct the spending of money). Because of the House's special position on revenue legislation, the committee that handles tax bills—the Ways and Means Committee—is particularly powerful.

Most bills die in committee. They are often introduced only to get publicity for various members of Congress or to enable them to say to a constituent or pressure group that they "did something" on some matter. Bills of

HOUSE-SENATE DIFFERENCES:

A SUMMARY

★ ★ ★

HOUSE	SENATE
435 members serving two-year terms	100 members serving six-year terms
House members have only one major committee assignment, thus tend to be policy specialists	Senators have two or more major committee assignments, tend to be policy generalists
Speaker referral of bills to committee is hard to challenge	Referral decisions easy to challenge
Committees almost always consider legislation first	Committee consideration easily bypassed
Scheduling and rules controlled by majority party	Scheduling and rules generally agreed to by majority and minority leaders
Rules Committee powerful; controls time of debate, admissibility of amendments	Rules Committee weak; few limits on debate or amendments
Debate usually limited to one hour	Unlimited debate unless shortened by unanimous consent or by invoking cloture
Nongermane amendments may not be introduced from floor	Nongermane amendments may be introduced

general interest—many of them drafted in the executive branch though introduced by members of Congress—are assigned to a subcommittee for a hearing where witnesses appear, evidence is taken, and questions are asked. These hearings are used to inform members of Congress, to permit interest groups to speak out (whether or not they have anything helpful to say), and to build public support for a measure favored by the majority on the committee.

Though committee hearings are necessary and valuable, they also fragment the process of considering bills dealing with complex matters. Both power and information are dispersed in Congress, and thus it is difficult to take a comprehensive view of matters cutting across committee boundaries. This has made it harder to pass complex legislation. For example, President Carter's energy proposals were cut up into small sections for the consideration of the various committees that had jurisdiction; after a year and a half, five laws emerged. But strong White House leadership and supportive public opinion can push controversial measures through both houses without great delay, as in the case of the Reagan budget cuts of 1981. It remains to be seen whether the slow energy package or the speedy budget cut is the wave of the future.

After the hearings, the committee or subcommittee will make revisions and additions (sometimes extensive) to the bill, but these changes do not become part of the bill unless they are approved by the entire house. If a majority of the committee votes to report a bill favorably to the House or Senate, it goes forward, accompanied by an explanation of why the committee favors it and why it wishes to see its amendments, if any, added; committee members who oppose the bill may include their dissenting opinions.

If the committee does not report the bill out to the house favorably, that ordinarily kills it, though there are complex procedures whereby the full House or Senate can get a bill that is stalled in committee out and onto the floor. But these procedures are rarely attempted and even more rarely succeed.

For a bill to come before either house, it must first be placed on a calendar. There are five of these in the House and two in the Senate. Though the bill goes onto a calendar, it is not necessarily considered in chronological order or even considered at all. In the House, the powerful Rules Committee—an arm of the party leadership, especially of the Speaker—reviews most bills and sets the **rule**—that is, the procedures—under which they will be considered by the House. A **restrictive** or **closed rule** sets strict limits on debate and confines amendments to those proposed by the committee; an **open rule** permits amendments from the floor. The Rules Committee is no longer as mighty as it once was, but it can still block any House consideration of a measure and can bargain with the legislative committee by offering a helpful rule in exchange for alterations in the substance of a bill. In the 1980s, closed rules became more common.

The House needs the Rules Committee to serve as a traffic cop; without some limitations on debate and amendment, nothing would ever get done. The House can bypass the Rules Committee in a number of ways, but it rarely does so unless the committee departs too far from the sentiments of the House.

No such barriers to floor consideration exist in the Senate where bills may be considered in any order at any time whenever a majority of the Senate chooses. In practice, bills are scheduled by the majority leader in consultation with the minority leader.

Floor Debate

Once on the floor, the bills are debated. In the House all revenue and most other bills are discussed by the **Committee of the Whole**—that is, whoever happens to be on the floor at the time, so long as at least one hundred mem-

The electronic voting system in the House of Representatives displays each member's name on the wall of the chamber. By inserting a plastic card in a box fastened to the chairs, a member can vote "Yea," "Nay," or "Present," and the result is shown opposite his or her name.

bers are present. The Committee of the Whole can debate, amend, and generally decide the final shape of a bill, but technically cannot pass it—that must be done by the House itself, for which the quorum is half the membership (218 representatives). The sponsoring committee guides the discussion, and normally its version of the bill is the version that the full House passes.

Procedures are a good deal more casual in the Senate. Measures that have already passed the House can be placed on the Senate calendar without a committee hearing. There is no Committee of the Whole and no rule (as in the House) limiting debate, so that **filibusters** (lengthy speeches given to prevent votes from being taken) and irrelevant amendments, called **riders,** are possible. Filibusters can be broken if three-fifths of all the senators agree to a **cloture** resolution. This is a difficult and rarely used procedure. (Both conservatives and liberals have found the filibuster useful, and therefore its abolition is unlikely.)

One rule is common to both houses: courtesy, often of the most exquisite nature, is required. Members always refer to each other as "distinguished" even if they are mortal political enemies. Personal or ad hominem criticism is frowned upon (though it has become more common), and only a few times have members taken a punch at each other, mostly in the nineteenth century.

Methods of Voting

There are several methods of voting in Congress. They can be applied to amendments to a bill as well as to the question of final passage. Some observers of Congress make the mistake of deciding who was for and who against a bill by the final vote. This can be misleading: often, a member of Congress will vote for final passage of a bill after having supported amendments which, if they had passed, would have made the bill totally different. To keep track of someone's voting record, therefore, it is often more important to know how that person voted on key amendments than how he or she voted on the bill itself.

Finding that out is not always easy, though it has become simpler in recent years. The House has four procedures for voting. A **voice vote** consists of the members shouting "aye" or "no"; a **division** (or standing) **vote** involves the members standing and being counted. In neither case are the names recorded of who voted which way. This is done only with a **recorded teller vote** (with the members depositing signed ballots in a box) or a **roll call.** Since 1973 an electronic voting system has been in use that greatly speeds up roll-call votes, and the number of recorded votes has thus increased sharply. Voting in the Senate is simpler: it votes by voice or by roll call; there are no teller votes or electronic counters.

If a bill passes the House and Senate in different forms, the differences must be reconciled if the bill is to become law. If they are minor, the last house to act may simply refer the bill back to the other house, which then accepts the alterations. Major differences must be ironed out in a **conference committee,** though only a minority of bills require a conference. Each house must vote to form such a committee. The members are picked by the chairmen of the standing committees that have been handling the legislation; the minority as well as the majority party is represented. No decision can be made unless approved by a majority of *each* delegation. Bargaining is long and hard; in the past it was also secret, but some sessions are now public. Often— as with Carter's energy bill—the legislation is substantially rewritten in conference. Theoretically nothing already agreed to by both the House and Senate is to be changed, but in the inevitable give-and-take, even those matters already approved may be changed.

Conference reports on spending bills usually split the difference between the House and Senate versions. Overall, the Senate tends to do slightly better than the House.[11] But whoever wins, conferees report their agreement back to their respective houses, which usually consider the report immediately. The report can be accepted or rejected; it cannot be amended. In the great majority of cases, it is accepted—the alternative is to have no bill at all, at least for that Congress. The bill, now in final form, goes to the president for **signature** or **veto.** A vetoed bill returns to the house of origin, where an effort can be made to override the veto. Two-thirds of those present (provided there is a quorum) must vote, by roll call, to override. If both houses override, the bill becomes law without the president's approval.

HOW MEMBERS OF CONGRESS VOTE

Voting on bills is not the only thing a member of Congress does, but it is among the more important and is probably the most visible. Since leaders in Congress are not nearly so powerful as those in a typical parliament, with political parties declining in influence, and since Congress has gone to great lengths to protect the independence and power of the individual member, it is by no means obvious what factors will lead a representative or senator to vote for or against a bill or amendment.

There are at least three kinds of explanations: representational, organizational, and attitudinal. A **representational** explanation is based on the reasonable assumption that members want to get reelected, and therefore they vote to please their constituents. The **organizational** explanation is based on the equally reasonable assumption that since most constituents do not know how their legislator has voted it is not essential to please them. However, it *is* important to please fellow members of Congress whose goodwill is valuable in getting things done and in acquiring status and power in Congress. The **attitudinal** explanation is based on the assumption that there are so many conflicting pressures on members of Congress that they cancel one another out, leaving them virtually free to vote on the basis of their own beliefs.

For decades political scientists have studied, tested, and argued about these (and other) explanations of voting in Congress, and never has a consensus emerged. Some facts have been established however.

Representational View

The representational view has some merit under certain circumstances, namely, when constituents have a clear view on some issue and a legislator's vote on that issue is likely to attract their attention. Such is often the case on civil-rights laws: representatives with significant numbers of black voters in their districts are not likely to oppose civil-rights bills.

One study of congressional roll-call votes and constituency opinion showed the correlation between the two was quite strong on civil-rights bills. There was also a positive (though not as strong) correlation between roll-call votes and constituency opinion on social-welfare measures. Scarcely any correlation, however, was found between congressional votes and hometown opinion on foreign-policy measures.[12] Foreign policy is generally remote from the daily interests of most Americans, and public opinion about such matters can change rapidly. It is not surprising therefore that congressional votes and constituent opinion should be different on such questions.

From time to time an issue arouses deep passions among the voters, and legislators cannot escape the need either to vote as their constituents want, whatever their personal views, or to anguish at length about which side of a divided constituency to support. Gun control has been one such question, the ratification of the Panama Canal treaties another, and the use of federal money to pay for abortions a third. Some fortunate members of Congress get unambiguous cues from their constituents on these matters, and no hard decision is necessary; others get conflicting views, and they know that whichever way they vote it may cost them dearly in the next election. Occasionally, members of Congress in this fix will try to be out of town when the matter comes up for a vote.

In general the problem with the representational explanation is that public opinion is not strong and clear on most measures on which Congress must vote. Many representatives and senators face constituencies that are divided on key issues. Some constituents go to special pains to make their views known. But as we indicated, the power of interest groups to affect congressional votes depends, among other things, on whether a legislator sees them as united and powerful in his or her district or as divided and unrepresentative.

This does not mean that constituents rarely have a direct influence on voting. The influence they have probably comes from the fact that legislators risk defeat should they steadfastly vote in ways that can be held against them by a rival in the next election. Even though most congressional votes are not known to most citizens, blunders (real or alleged) quickly become known when an electoral opponent exploits them.

Still, any member of Congress can choose the positions he or she takes on most roll-call votes (and on all voice or standing votes where names are not recorded). Furthermore, even a series of recorded votes that are against constituency opinion need not be fatal: a member of Congress can win votes in other ways—for example, by doing services for constituents or by appealing to the party loyalty of the voters.

Organizational View

When voting on matters where constituency interests or opinions are not vitally at stake, members of Congress respond primarily to cues provided by their colleagues. This is the organizational explanation of their votes. The principal cue is party; as already noted, what party a member of Congress belongs to explains more of his or her voting record than any other single factor. Additional organizational cues come from the opinions of colleagues with whom the member of Congress feels a close ideological affinity: for liberals in the House, it is the Democratic Study Group; for conservatives, it has often been the Republican Study Committee or the Wednesday Club. But party and other organizations do not have clear positions on all matters. For the scores of votes that do not involve the "big questions," a representative or senator is especially likely to be influenced by the members of his or her party on the sponsoring committee.

It is easy to understand why. Suppose you are a Democratic representative from Michigan who is summoned to the floor of the House to vote on a bill to authorize a new weapons system. You haven't the faintest idea what issues might be at stake. There is no obvious liberal or conservative position on this matter. How do you vote? Simple. You take your cue from several Democrats on the House Armed Services Committee that handled the bill. Some are liberal (such as Ron Dellums of California), others are conservative (such as Sonny Montgomery of Mississippi). If Dellums and Montgomery both support the bill, you vote for it unhesitatingly. If Dellums and Montgomery disagree, you vote with whichever Democrat is generally closest to your own political ideology. If the matter is one that affects your state, you can take your cue from members of your state's delegation to Congress.

Attitudinal View

Finally, there is evidence that a member of Congress's ideology affects how he or she votes. We have seen that Democratic and Republican legislators differ sharply on a liberal-versus-conservative scale. On both domestic and foreign-policy issues, many tend to be consistently liberal or conservative.

This consistency isn't surprising; as we saw in Chapter 4, political elites think more ideologically than the public generally.

On many issues the average member of the House has opinions close to those of the average voter, as seen in Table 7.3. Senators, by contrast, are often less in tune with public opinion. In the 1970s they were much more liberal than voters; in the early 1980s, more conservative. Two senators from the same state often mobilize quite different bases of support. The result is that many states, such as California, Delaware, and New York, have been represented by senators with almost diametrically opposed views.

The Democratic party is more deeply divided than the Republican. There are only a few liberal Republicans, but there are many conservative Democrats from the South and West. Southern Democrats often team up with Republicans to form a **conservative coalition.** In a typical year, a majority of Republicans and southern Democrats will vote together against a majority of northern Democrats about 20 to 25 percent of the time. When the conservative coalition does form, it usually wins: between 1970 and 1982, it won about two-thirds of the votes on which it held together. After the Reagan victory and the Republican gain of thirty-three seats in the House in 1981, the conservative coalition became even more effective, dominating key votes on the Reagan budget and tax plans. By the late 1980s, however, it had begun to lose influence.

TABLE 7.3 Comparison of Public and Congressional Opinion on Policy Issues, 1978

Issue	Public	House Members
Defense: Favor more money for national defense	23%	26%
Arms Control: Favor Strategic Arms Limitation Talks (SALT)	67	74
Health Insurance: Favor national health insurance fully paid for by the government	47	45
Tax-Cut: Oppose a "large" federal income-tax cut	53	51
Abortion: Favor government paying for abortion for the poor	41	35

SOURCE: CBS/*New York Times* poll, as reported in Robert S. Erikson, Norman R. Luttbeg, and Kent L. Tedin, *American Public Opinion,* 2d ed. New York: John Wiley & Sons, 1980, p. 240.

WHAT IT ALL MEANS

The combined effect of local representation; self-selected candidates; an elaborate system of committees, subcommittees, and caucuses; a big staff; a heavy work load; and weak party control over members is a legislature that

1. Has a localistic viewpoint
2. Is highly decentralized
3. Consists of individualists
4. Does not often engage in careful deliberation

When senators and representatives must get themselves nominated by running in primaries and then get themselves elected without much help from the parties, they are going to spend a lot of time providing services, speeches, and mail to their local constituents. This **localistic** viewpoint is inevitable. As former Speaker Tip O'Neill liked to put it, "in Congress all politics is local politics." Members who forget that may suddenly find that they are no longer members. What is surprising, given the role that they must play, is that members occasionally do vote contrary to their constituents' views. They did this when they deregulated the airlines in 1978 and when they reformed the tax code in 1986.

Because the real business of Congress is done in committees and subcommittees, the process of making policy is highly **decentralized.** More than 125 members of the House chair a committee or subcommittee; nearly half of all senators do the same. Each chairperson has a stake in shaping legislation, conducting hearings, and protecting his or her committee's jurisdiction (or turf) from that of rival committees. When a complex piece of legislation must be considered, it is often referred to several committees. If it passes the House and Senate, the conference committee convened to reconcile any differences may number more than a hundred people.

Men and women loyal to localities operating in a decentralized committee system are **individualists.** That is, rather than blindly following party leaders (as they do in England) in deciding how to vote, and they will try to get publicity for themselves. Though Democrats usually vote with other Democrats, and Republicans with other Republicans, this is not because anyone has cracked a whip; it is because of the ideological agreement within the parties. Being individualists, members will look for issues that they can make their own and bills that they can introduce that, if passed, they can take credit for.

These three factors have operated more or less continuously since the early decades of the nineteenth century. What has changed is the greatly increased size of the federal government, the vastly expanded scope of federal policies, and consequently the hugely increased work load of the members. There is **relatively little deliberation.** People often ridicule members for voting on bills they have not read (and sometimes have not even been printed in final form), but that is not a measure of the personal indifference or weaknesses of members; it is how we all would behave if we had to spend sixteen hours a day meeting visitors, going to hearings, speaking to the press, and traveling back and forth from our home districts to Washington.

ETHICS AND CONGRESS

The Framers hoped that members of Congress would be virtuous citizens, but they feared some would not be. They designed the system of checks and balances in part to minimize the chance that anybody, by gaining corrupt influence over one part of the government, would be able to impose his or her will on the other parts. But perhaps this very separation of powers made corruption more likely than it would be in a centralized nation. When bits and pieces of power are placed in many hands, there are many opportunities to exercise influence, and many officials have something to sell at a price many favor seekers can afford.

In all likelihood, the cruder forms of influence wielding are less common today than in the nineteenth and early twentieth centuries. Citizens are better educated and have higher standards of proper official conduct; party bosses have lost power; and the mass media have a strong incentive to find and expose improper influence and corruption.

But scandals continue to occur. From 1941 to 1981, nearly fifty members of Congress faced criminal charges; most were convicted.[13] A dramatic scandal—the Abscam affair—unfolded during the 96th Congress, when six representatives and one senator were indicted and eventually convicted for having accepted large bribes from undercover FBI agents posing as Arabs seeking po-

How Congress Responds to the Misconduct of Members

★ ★ ★

Under Article I, section 5, of the Constitution, Congress may "punish its members for disorderly behavior." There are two basic ways that Congress disciplines its members. Neither is used frequently.

CENSURE

★ May include condemnation, loss of seniority, and fines

★ Some memorable cases:

Senate motion to "condemn" Senator Joseph McCarthy of Wisconsin in 1954 for overzealous attacks on innocent citizens and officials accused of being communists or communist sympathizers

House vote to fine ($25,000) and exclude Representative Adam Clayton Powell, Jr., for the abuse of his official authority and congressional privileges

Censure of members who accepted bribes in the "Abscam" affair of the early 1980s

EXPULSION

★ Each chamber can expel a member by a two-thirds vote

★ Of 19 cases (4 in the House, 15 in the Senate), 17 occurred in the Civil War era

litical favors. All either resigned or were defeated for reelection. In 1991, the public was outraged to learn that House members had written checks against their House bank accounts without sufficient funds to cover them. (The Senate has no bank.)

When the criminal law is broken, the moral issues are clear. It is, after all, hard to maintain one's innocence when one is shown on videotape taking envelopes stuffed with money. Far harder to judge are cases in which members of Congress take advantage of their position in ways that are not clearly illegal but may be questionable. For example, what other sources of employment or income should members of Congress have? What kinds of campaign contributions should they accept? When does a legislator's attempt to influence a regulatory agency on behalf of a constituent become improper?

In 1977 the House and Senate each passed a new code of ethics, differing in some details but similar in broad outlines. (Other laws, described in Chapter 6, had already restricted campaign contributions.) The following are some key provisions of the 1977 ethics codes, as revised in the 1980s:

* Each member of Congress must annually file a financial-disclosure statement.
* No member of Congress may receive a fee (or "honorarium") for giving a speech.
* Former members may not lobby Congress for one year after leaving office.

The ethics code was based on the assumption that improper influence is associated with financial transactions, yet obviously that is not always the case. Many members of Congress who in the past earned substantial incomes from speaking and writing did not have their votes corrupted by such activities; other members who rarely take such fees may be heavily influenced, perhaps unduly so, by personal friendships and political alliances that have no direct monetary value at all. And no ethics code can address the bargaining among members of Congress, or between members of Congress and the president, involving the exchange of favors and votes. The ethics code was put to a major test in 1989 when former Speaker Jim Wright was charged by the House Committee on Standards of Official Conduct with having improperly accepted funds from constituents interested in legislation. Wright resigned.

As it stands, the ethics rules seem to favor people with inherited wealth or those who earned large sums before entering Congress and to penalize people of modest means who might want to take advantage of legitimate opportunities to give speeches for large fees while in Congress. Former Representative Otis G. Pike of New York decided not to seek reelection in part because of the new financial rules. Pike, an attorney, complained to a reporter: "If I get a hundred thousand dollars a year sitting on my ——— and collecting dividends, . . . I am ethical. If I work and earn [that amount], I am unethical. Our new no-work ethic makes no sense to me."

It might not have made sense to the Framers, either. Their objective was not to create a simon-pure Congress, but one that was powerful, that would be composed of representatives who (at least in the lower house) would be closely checked by the voters, and that would offer manifold opportunities for competing interests and opinions to check one another. Their goal was liberty more than morality, though they knew that in the long run the latter was essential to the former.

THE POWER OF CONGRESS

Almost all members of Congress and many scholars believe that since the 1930s, and especially during the 1960s, Congress lost power to the president. The president came to dominate the making of foreign policy, sent troops into combat without congressional approval, initiated most proposals for new domestic policies, refused to spend money Congress had appropriated, and sometimes denied to Congress, in the name of executive privilege, information and documents it sought.

This claim that Congress became weak as the president became strong is a bit overdrawn. As we shall see in the next chapter, the view from the White House is quite different. Recent presidents have complained bitterly of their inability to get Congress even to act on, much less to approve, many of their key proposals and have resented what they regard as congressional interference in the management of executive-branch agencies and the conduct of foreign affairs.

To any visitor from abroad, Congress seems extraordinarily powerful, probably the most powerful legislative body in the world (see box). But Congress has always been jealous of its constitutional independence and authority. Certain events—the increasingly unpopular war in Vietnam, which Congress supported with growing reluctance and despair, and the Watergate scandals, which revealed a White House meddling illegally in the electoral process—led Congress to reassert what it felt were its diminished powers.

In 1973 Congress passed, over a presidential veto, the **War Powers Act,** giving it greater voice in the use of American forces abroad. The following year it passed the **Congressional Budget and Impoundment Control Act,** which denied the president the right not to spend money appropriated by Congress and improved Congress's capacity to play a major role in the budget process. It passed laws containing a legislative veto over proposed presidential actions, especially with respect to the sale of arms abroad. Not all these steps withstood the tests of time or Supreme Court review, but together they symbolized the resurgence of congressional authority and helped set the stage for sharper conflicts between Congress and the presidency.

When different parties control the presidency and one or both houses of Congress, as during the Reagan and Bush administrations, those conflicts are likely to become especially sharp. They can even lead to a lengthy stalemate. For example:

★ Congress refused even to vote on the budget President Reagan submitted in the winter of 1985–1986. The standoff resulted from a profound disagreement over how best to reduce the budget deficit.

★ Congress steadily reduced the number of MX missiles the president planned to buy, from the hundred he originally wanted down to forty.

★ Repeatedly President Reagan asked for money to help the *contras* fighting against the Sandinista regime in Nicaragua; repeatedly Congress either turned him down or attached severe limitations to the amount and purpose of the aid.

★ The Senate refused to confirm John Tower, President Bush's choice for secretary of defense.

The Laws That Congress Can Ignore

★ ★ ★

One measure of the power and independence of Congress is its ability and willingness to pass laws that affect everybody *except* Congress. Here are some examples of laws that do not apply to Congress:

Civil Rights Act of 1964: Prohibits discrimination in employment

Equal Pay Act: Requires that men and women receive equal pay for equal work

Freedom of Information Act: Gives public the right to inspect most records of federal agencies

Privacy Act: Requires federal agencies to protect the confidentiality of files on individuals

National Labor Relations Act: Requires employers to recognize and bargain with employee unions

Occupational Safety and Health Act: Requires employers to meet certain safety and health standards

SOURCE: *Congressional Quarterly Weekly Report* (January 19, 1985), 104.

But conflict and stalemate are not inevitable. Even with the presidency and Congress in different partisan hands, a lot of legislation is adopted because both parties sense that the voters, or influential interest groups, want it. And sometimes Congress even surrenders a bit of its power. In 1976 Congress had passed a law that prevented President Ford from giving aid to a pro-Western faction fighting against a Marxist regime in Angola. A decade later, Congress allowed that law to lapse and President Reagan, freed of this restriction, moved quickly to supply aid (the civil war was still going on).

One of the reasons Congress is willing to follow the lead of even a president with whom it disagrees is that members of Congress are aware that no large legislative body can exercise leadership except in a few unusual cases. If a budget is to be prepared at all, the president must do it; if foreign affairs are to be conducted at all, the president must be the leader. Congress can come up with ideas and propose new legislation (Congress, not the president, wrote much of the environmental and consumer-protection legislation), but it cannot administer the executive branch or deal with foreign powers.

And perhaps most important, Congress is reluctant to challenge a popular president. It may delay, modify, or amend major presidential initiatives, but if the president is determined and persistent and effective, Congress cannot ignore those initiatives. How the president manages his resources—his execu-

In the United States, unlike in most nations with a parliamentary system of government, the legislature can investigate the executive branch. Here, John Poindexter testifies about his role in the Reagan administration's sending of arms to Iran in a vain attempt to obtain the release of American hostages.

tive powers and popular standing—to deal with a staunchly independent Congress is a major theme of the next chapter.

SUMMARY

Congress differs from a parliament in that it does not choose the nation's chief executive and is composed of members who attach greater importance to representing local constituencies than to supporting a national party leadership. Power in the American Congress is fragmented, specialized, and decentralized. Most of the important decisions are made in committees and subcommittees. Though there have been periods—such as the late nineteenth century—when party leaders in Congress were powerful, the general tendency, particularly in the last twenty years, has been to enhance the independence and influence of individual members of Congress.

The great majority of representatives are secure in their seats, a security that has been acquired chiefly by serving local constituency interests and by developing a personal following. The ability of political parties to determine who shall become a candidate for Congress has declined. As a result, votes in Congress are less likely to follow strict party lines than votes in most European parliaments. Nonetheless, party affiliation remains the most important influence on the behavior of members of Congress. In part this is because party loyalties in Congress correspond, to a degree, to the personal ideologies of members of Congress. Senators and representatives are more ideological than the public at large. Congressional Democrats are much more liberal than congressional Republicans. There are about forty conservative Democrats, mostly southerners, who often vote with Republicans.

The organization and procedures of the House are tightly structured to facilitate action and orderly debate. The committees therefore tend to dominate decisions made on the House floor. Senate procedures, on the other hand, permit lengthy debate and many floor amendments, with the result that individual senators have as much or more influence than Senate committees.

Congress does not simply respond to presidential needs for action; it initiates some proposals on its own and influences the kinds of proposals a president will offer. In shaping the policies of Congress, congressional staffs have become important. Though most of their time is spent on serving the constituency interests of members of Congress, the multiple committee assignments and heavy work load of senators and representatives mean that staffers often acquire substantial influence.

SUGGESTED READINGS

Arnold, R. Douglas. *The Logic of Action*. New Haven, Conn.: Yale University Press, 1990. Explains why Congress enacts the policies it does, especially those that serve general as opposed to special interests.

Dodd, Lawrence C., and Bruce I. Oppenheimer, eds. *Congress Reconsidered*, 3d ed. Washington, D.C.: Congressional Quarterly, 1985. Recent studies of congressional politics.

Fenno, Richard F., Jr. *Congressmen in Committees*. Boston: Little, Brown, 1973. Study of the styles of twelve standing committees.

Maass, Arthur. *Congress and the Common Good*. New York: Basic Books, 1984. Insightful account of congressional operations, especially those involving legislative-executive relations.

Malbin, Michael J. *Unelected Representatives*. New York: Basic Books, 1980. Study of the influence of congressional staff members.

Mayhew, David R. *Congress: The Electoral Connection*. New Haven, Conn.: Yale University Press, 1974. Argues that a member of Congress's desire to win reelection shapes his or her legislative behavior.

Rhode, David W. *Parties and Leaders in the Postreform House*. Chicago: University of Chicago Press, 1991. An account of the increase in partisanship in the House of Representatives since the 1970s.

Smith, Steven S., and Christopher J. Deering. *Committees in Congress*. Washington, D.C.: Congressional Quarterly, 1984. Analysis of how different kinds of congressional committees operate.

Sundquist, James L. *The Decline and Resurgence of Congress*. Washington, D.C.: Brookings Institution, 1981. A history of the fall and, after 1973, the rise of congressional power vis-à-vis the president.

8

★ ★ ★

The Presidency

PROFESSOR JONES SPEAKS to his political science class: "The president of the United States occupies one of the most powerful offices in the world. Presidents Kennedy and Johnson sent American troops to Vietnam, and President Reagan sent them to Grenada and Lebanon, all without war being declared by Congress. President Nixon imposed wage and price controls on the country. Presidents Carter and Reagan between them selected most of the federal judges now on the bench; thus the political philosophies of these two men were imposed on the courts. No wonder people talk about our having an 'imperial presidency.'"

A few doors down the hall, Professor Smith speaks to her class: "The president, compared to the prime ministers of other democratic nations, is one of the weakest chief executives anywhere. President Carter signed an arms limitation treaty with the Soviets, but the Senate wouldn't ratify it. President Reagan was not allowed even to test antisatellite weapons, and in 1986 Congress rejected his budget before the ink was dry. Subordinates who were supposedly loyal to Reagan regularly leaked his views to the press and undercut his programs before Congress. President Bush couldn't get his nominee for secretary of defense confirmed by the Senate. No wonder people talk about the president being a 'pitiful, helpless giant.'"

Can Professors Jones and Smith be talking about the same office? Who is right? In fact, they are both right. The American presidency is a unique office, with elements of both great strength and profound weakness built into it by its constitutional origins.

The popularly elected president is an American invention. Of the roughly five dozen countries in which there is some degree of party competition and thus, presumably, some measure of free choice for the voters, only sixteen have a directly elected president, and thirteen of these are nations of North and South America. The democratic alternative is for the chief executive to be a prime minister, chosen by and responsible to the parliament. This system prevails in most West European countries as well as in Israel and Japan. No purely presidential political system exists in Europe; France combines a directly elected president with a prime minister and parliament.[1]

One obvious result of the different ways presidents and prime ministers are chosen is that whereas the prime minister's party (or coalition of parties) always has a majority in the parliament (if it did not, somebody else would be prime minister), the president's party often does not have a majority in Congress. Of the ten presidents to hold office since Franklin D. Roosevelt, six had to deal with an opposition party that controlled one or both houses of Congress: Truman, Eisenhower, Nixon, Ford, Reagan, and Bush.

Other differences are less obvious but just as important. An American presidential candidate is nominated through primaries and conventions, whereas potential prime ministers are generally chosen by a caucus of veteran political leaders, with an eye to who can best hold the party together in parliament. Presidential candidates often have no experience in Congress, but potential prime ministers have always served in parliament. Once in office, a prime minister chooses cabinet officers primarily or exclusively from among members of his or her party in parliament and must appear regularly in parliament to defend the government's policies. The president of the United States, on the other hand, selects his cabinet officers and advisers not to control Congress but to reward personal followers, recognize important constituencies, and mobilize nongovernmental expertise; and he never has to answer hostile questions before Congress.

The results of these differences are clear. Prime ministers in two-party nations (such as Great Britain) have very great power because they can dominate the cabinet and the legislature. (In countries with multiparty systems, such as Italy or Israel, prime ministers are much weaker because the cabinet is usually an unstable coalition.) Although the president of the United States is elected by the people at large and occupies an office with powers derived from the Constitution, he may have great difficulty in exercising any legislative leadership at all owing to his inability to control Congress—even if, as in the case of John F. Kennedy, his own party has the majority in Congress.

THE POWERS OF THE PRESIDENT

The president's formal powers are few and vaguely defined; they are set forth in Article II of the Constitution:

Powers of the President Alone

- ★ Serve as commander in chief of the armed forces
- ★ Commission officers of the armed forces
- ★ Grant reprieves and pardons for federal offenses (except impeachment)
- ★ Convene Congress in special sessions
- ★ Receive ambassadors
- ★ Take care that the laws be faithfully executed
- ★ Wield the "executive power"
- ★ Appoint officials to lesser offices

Powers of the President Shared with the Senate

- ★ Make treaties
- ★ Appoint ambassadors, judges, and high officials

Powers of the President Shared with Congress as a Whole

- ★ Approve legislation

Interpreted narrowly, this list of powers is not very impressive. Obviously the president's authority as commander in chief is important, but most of the other constitutional grants amount to making the president a kind of chief clerk of the country. That is exactly how the office appeared a hundred years ago, even to as astute an observer as Woodrow Wilson in his 1885 book *Congressional Government*.[2] But Wilson was overlooking some examples of enormously powerful presidents, such as Lincoln, and was not sufficiently attentive to the potential for presidential power found in the more ambiguous clauses of the Constitution as well as in the political realities of American life. For example, the president's duty to "take care that the laws be faithfully executed," interpreted broadly, enabled Grover Cleveland to break a labor strike in the 1890s and Dwight Eisenhower to send troops to integrate a public school in Little Rock, Arkansas, in 1956. And the president's authority as commander in chief has grown—especially, but not only, in war time—to encompass not simply the direction of the military forces but the management of the economy and the direction of foreign policy as well. A quietly dramatic reminder of the awesome implications of the president's military power

Every successful modern president has worked hard at cultivating the press. Theodore Roosevelt was perhaps the first president to begin this courtship in earnest.

occurs at the precise instant a new president assumes office, when a military officer carrying a locked briefcase moves from the side of the outgoing president to the side of the new one. In the briefcase are the secret codes and orders that permit the president to authorize the launching of American nuclear weapons.

The greatest source of presidential power, however, is not found in the Constitution at all but in politics and public opinion. Increasingly since the 1930s, Congress has passed laws that confer on the executive branch grants of authority to achieve some general goals, leaving it up to the president and his deputies to define the regulations and programs that will actually be put into effect. Moreover, the American people look to the president—always in time of crisis, but increasingly as an everyday matter—for leadership and hold him responsible for a large and growing portion of our national affairs.

THE EVOLUTION OF THE PRESIDENCY

In 1787 few issues inspired as much debate or concern among the Framers of the Constitution as the problem of defining the powers of the chief executive. Fearing anarchy and monarchy in about equal measure, the delegates considered a number of proposals for an executive authority before finally deciding on a single president with significant powers. Most were reassured by the assumption that George Washington would be the first president, though some still feared that the presidency would become "the fetus of monarchy." The electoral college and the provision for the House settling inconclusive elections, for example, were designed to minimize the possibility of future presidents' attempts to hold office for life through bribery, intrigue, or force.

In retrospect, these concerns seem misplaced. The real sources of the expansion of the president's power—his role in foreign affairs, his ability to shape and lead public opinion, his position at the head of the executive branch—were hardly predictable in 1787. The pattern of relationships between the president and Congress that we see today is the result of a process of evolution extending over nearly two centuries.

Establishing the Legitimacy of the Presidency

The first problem for the Framers was to establish the legitimacy of the presidency itself; that is, to ensure, if possible, public acceptance of the office, its incumbent, and its powers, and to establish an orderly transfer of power from one incumbent to the next. Although we take this for granted, in much of the world today such peaceful transfers of power are still relatively unusual.

The first presidents were among the most prominent men in the new nation, and they tended to distrust the emerging political parties as "factions." (As it turned out, this hostility to party was unrealistic: parties are as natural to democracy as churches to religion.) The national government had relatively little to do, and the first presidents kept the office modest. Appointees to federal offices were men with standing in their communities. Presidents cast vetoes sparingly, and then only when they thought a proposed law was not only unwise but also unconstitutional. Washington established the precedent of a two-term presidency, and his immediate successors honored it. By treading cautiously, the first presidents did much to make their office legitimate to the citizenry.

The Jacksonians and the Reemergence of Congress

At a time roughly corresponding to the presidency of Andrew Jackson (1829–1837), broad changes began to occur in American politics. Mass political participation and modern political parties emerged. Together with the personality of Jackson himself, these changes altered the relations between president and Congress and the nature of presidential leadership. Seemingly old and frail, Jackson nevertheless used the powers of his office as no one before him had. He vetoed more bills than all his predecessors put together, on policy as well as on constitutional grounds, seeing himself as the only official elected by the entire voting citizenry, as the "Tribune of the People." Not shrinking from conflict with Congress, Jackson showed what a popular president could do. His view of a strong and independent presidency was ultimately to triumph, for better or worse.

THE ELECTORAL COLLEGE

★ ★ ★

The Constitution allots each state as many electoral votes as it has senators and representatives in Congress. Thus no state has fewer than three electoral votes. (The District of Columbia also gets three even though it has no members of Congress.) There are a total of 538 electoral votes; to win the presidency, a candidate must receive a majority, or 270.

In each state, each party runs a slate of electors pledged to that party's presidential and vice presidential candidates. The names of these electors usually do not appear on the ballots. The slate whose candidate wins more popular votes than any other is authorized to cast all the votes of that state in the electoral college.

This results in a "winner-take-all" effect. Since it is up to the state legislatures to decide how electors are chosen, they could devise systems that would produce a split in the states' electoral votes. Maine and Nebraska have done this by allowing some or all electors to be chosen by congressional district rather than at large.

If no candidate wins a majority, the House of Representatives chooses the president from among the three leading candidates, with each state casting one vote. By House rule, each state's vote is allotted to the candidate preferred by a majority of the state's House delegation. If there is a tie within a delegation, that state's vote is not counted.

The House has had to decide two presidential contests. In 1800 Thomas Jefferson and Aaron Burr tied in the electoral college because of a defect in the language of the Constitution—each state cast two electoral votes without indicating which was for president and which for vice president. (Burr was supposed to be vice president and, after much maneuvering, he was.) The Twelfth Amendment, ratified in 1804, corrected this problem. The only House decision under the modern system was in 1824 when it chose John Quincy Adams over Andrew Jackson and William H. Crawford, even though Jackson had more electoral votes (and probably more popular votes) than his rivals.

The chief political effects of the electoral college are these: The winner-take-all system probably discourages the emergence of serious third parties. The system encourages candidates to focus their campaigns on states, especially states whose vote may be in doubt. It especially encourages candidates to emphasize large, doubtful states. A candidate who carries the ten largest states wins 257 electoral votes, only thirteen short of a majority. These states are usually the most urbanized, industrialized, and politically competitive ones. A president seeking reelection has reason to be attentive to the needs of such states.

Proposals to alter or abolish the electoral college have been made, but none has come close to adoption. Among these are plans to elect the president by direct, national, popular vote; to divide each state's electoral votes in proportion to the popular vote received by each candidate in that state; to have electors

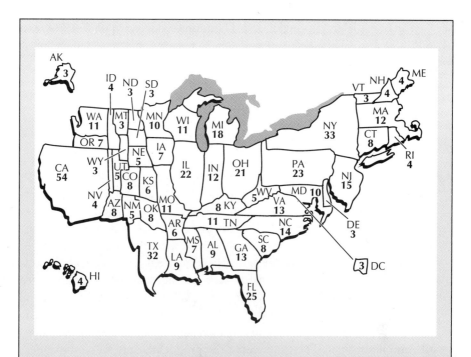

chosen by congressional district rather than at large; and to retain the electoral system but abolish the office of elector and thus the chance of a faithless elector.

The issues and arguments are complex. Those who want to preserve the electoral college generally believe that it is important for the states to have a role in choosing the president and for the president to have an electoral reason to attend to state interests. Those favoring direct popular election argue that the states are irrelevant in presidential elections and that each person's vote should count the same as every other person's regardless of where he or she lives.

With the end of Jackson's second term, however, Congress—and particularly the Senate—quickly reasserted itself, and for almost a century the presidency became the subordinate branch of the national government. This was an intensely partisan era, with public opinion sharply divided and most presidential elections very close. Only Lincoln broke new ground for presidential power. In response to the Civil War, he made unprecedented use of the vague gift of powers found in the Constitution, especially those he felt were implied or were inherent in the phrase "take care that the laws be faithfully executed," and in the express authorization for him to act as commander in chief.

After Lincoln, Congress reasserted its power; until the 1930s, Congress generally formulated legislative programs, and the president was at best a negative force—a source of opposition to, not leadership for, Congress. But Lincoln had made it abundantly clear that a national emergency could equip the president with great powers, and Theodore Roosevelt (1901–1909) and Woodrow Wilson (1913–1921) showed that a popular and strong-willed president could expand his powers even without an emergency. Wilson, for example, was the first president since John Adams to deliver personally the State of the Union address, and one of the first to develop and argue for a presidential legislative program.

THE MODERN PRESIDENCY

The popular conception of the president as the central figure of national government, devising a legislative program and commanding a large staff of advisers, is very much a product of the modern era and of the enlarged role of government. Only since the 1930s has the presidency been powerful no matter who occupied the office and whether or not there was a crisis.

Every modern president is the titular head of the huge federal administrative system (whether he is the real boss is another matter). Whereas once Grover Cleveland personally answered the White House telephone and Abraham Lincoln often answered his own mail, presidents today are surrounded by hundreds of assistants and by the trappings of power—helicopters, guards, and limousines. The resources at the president's disposal would appear awesome. In fact, he now confronts an army of assistants so large that it constitutes a bureaucracy he has difficulty controlling. Normally presidential assistants are influential in accordance with the Rule of Propinquity: power is wielded by persons who are in the room when a decision is made. Presidential appointments can thus be classified in terms of their proximity, physically and politically, to the president.

The White House Office

The White House Office consists of aides who are the president's personal staff; their appointments do not have to be confirmed by the Senate; he can hire and fire them at will. These are the men and women who have offices in the White House, usually in the West Wing of that building. Their titles often do not reveal the functions they actually perform: in general they oversee the political and policy interests of the president.

A president can organize his staff as a circle, a pyramid, or a cluster. In a **circle,** a few key assistants report to him. Jimmy Carter did this. In a **pyramid,** most report through one chief of staff. Eisenhower, Nixon, Reagan (after 1985), and Bush did this.[3] In a **cluster,** ad hoc task forces and key advisers have access to the president with no clear chain of command. Roosevelt did this; Clinton is now doing it.

Circles and clusters are favored by presidents who want to get personally involved in the details of policy; they provide a lot of information but at the price of confusion and conflict. Pyramids are favored by presidents who like order and clear lines of authority, even at the risk of reduced information.

THE PRESIDENT:
QUALIFICATIONS AND BENEFITS

★ ★ ★

QUALIFICATIONS

★ A natural-born citizen (can be born abroad of parents who are American citizens).

★ At least thirty-five years of age.

★ A resident of the United States for at least fourteen years (but not necessarily the fourteen years just preceding the election).

BENEFITS

★ A nice house.

★ A salary of $200,000 per year (taxable).

★ Expense account of $50,000 per year (taxable).

★ Travel expenses of $100,000 per year (tax-free).

★ Pension, on retirement, of $63,000 per year (taxable).

★ Staff support on leaving the presidency.

★ A White House staff of 400–500 persons.

★ A place in the country—Camp David.

★ A personal airplane—Air Force One.

★ A fine chef.

Typically, senior White House staff members are drawn from the ranks of the president's campaign staff—long-time associates in whom he has confidence. A few members, however, will be experts brought in after the campaign—for example, Nixon's assistant for national security affairs, Henry Kissinger. These men and women have to put up with small, cramped offices, but they willingly put up with any discomfort in return for the privilege (and the power) of being *in* the White House. The arrangement of offices (especially their proximity to the president's Oval Office) is a good measure of the relative influence of the people in them.

To an outsider, the amount of jockeying among the top staff for access to the president may seem comical or even perverse. But more than power plays and ego trips are involved. Who can see the president and who sees and "signs off" on memoranda going to him affect in important ways who influences policy and thus whose goals and beliefs become embedded in policy.

Executive Office of the President

The key agencies that make up the executive office of the president are the Office of Management and Budget (OMB), the Council of Economic Advisers, the Central Intelligence Agency (CIA), the Office of the U.S. Trade Representative, the Council on Environmental Quality, the Office of Science and Technology Policy, and the Office of Personnel Management. These agencies report directly to the president and perform staff services for him but are not located in the White House itself. Their individual members may or may not enjoy intimate contact with him; some of these agencies are rather large bureaucracies. The president appoints the heads of these organizations, but unlike White House staff positions, the Senate must confirm most of them.

In terms of the president's need for assistance in running the federal government, probably the most important of these agencies is the OMB. Besides assembling and analyzing the figures for the yearly national budget that the president submits to Congress, it also studies the operations of the executive branch, devises reorganization plans, improves the flow of information about government programs, and reviews the cabinet department's budgetary proposals. Its staff of more than six hundred is highly professional and traditionally nonpartisan, although in recent administrations the agency has played a major role in advocating rather than merely analyzing policies.

The Cabinet

At one time, the heads of the federal departments (such as State and Treasury) met regularly to discuss matters with the president, and some people (particularly those critical of strong presidents) would like to see this kind of cabinet decision making reestablished. But, in fact, the cabinet is largely a fiction. It is not even mentioned in the Constitution, and presidents from Washington on have found that it does not work as a presidential committee. Dwight Eisenhower is one of the only modern presidents who came close to making the cabinet a truly deliberative body; even under him, it neither had influence over presidential decisions nor helped him obtain more power over the government.

Cabinet officers are the heads of the fourteen administrative departments that, by custom or law, are considered part of the cabinet (see Table 8.1). Though the president, with the consent of the Senate, appoints the heads of these cabinet departments, his power over them is sharply limited. In only the large departments (such as the State Department) can the president appoint more than 1 percent of the employees, and many of these are ambassadors;

TABLE 8.1 The Cabinet Departments

Department	Created	Approximate Civilian Employment (1992)
State	1789	25,300
Treasury	1789	158,700
Defense[a]	1947	1,034,200
Justice	1789	83,900
Interior	1849	77,700
Agriculture[b]	1889	122,600
Commerce	1913	69,900
Labor	1913	17,700
Health and Human Services[c]	1953	124,000
Housing and Urban Development	1965	13,600
Transportation	1966	67,400
Energy	1977	17,700
Education	1979	4,800
Veterans' Affairs	1989	248,200

[a]Formerly the War Department, created in 1789. Figures are for civilians only.

[b]Agriculture Department created in 1862; made part of cabinet in 1889.

[c]Originally Health, Education, and Welfare; reorganized in 1979.

SOURCE: *Statistical Abstract of the United States,* 1992, p. 330.

the vast majority are civil-service personnel who cannot easily be fired. But the main reason for the cabinet's weakness is that its members are heads of vast organizations that they seek to defend, explain, and enlarge—often in sharp competition with one another. Thus cabinet officers can seldom give the president effective collective advice.

Independent Agencies, Commissions, and Judgeships

The president also appoints people to four dozen or so agencies and commissions that are not considered part of the cabinet and that by law often have a quasi-independent status. Many of these are regulatory commissions (such as the Federal Trade Commission and the Interstate Commerce Commission) whose members serve for fixed terms and can be removed only for cause. Other agencies, such as the Environmental Protection Agency, are headed by people who can be removed by the president at any time.

The president also appoints federal judges, subject to the consent of the Senate; they serve during "good behavior" (which usually means until they choose to retire). They can only be removed by impeachment and conviction. This tenure is required by the Constitution and is necessary to preserve the independence of the judiciary.

WHO GETS APPOINTED

Since so many of the departments employ permanent civil-service personnel, a president can make relatively few appointments: furthermore, he rarely knows more than a few of the people he does appoint. He is fortunate if most cabinet officers turn out to agree with him on major policy questions.

Usually cabinet officers and their immediate subordinates have had some prior federal experience, and many are "in and outers" who alternate between jobs in the federal government and ones in the private sector, especially in law firms and universities. At one time the cabinet included many people with strong political followings of their own, such as former senators and governors and powerful local party leaders. Of late, however, presidents have tended to place in their cabinet individuals known for their expertise or their administrative experience rather than for their political following. This has come about in part because political parties are now so weak that party leaders can no longer demand a place in the cabinet and in part because presidents want (or think they want) "experts."

A president's desire to appoint experts who do not have independent political power is modified—but not supplanted—by his need to recognize various politically important groups, regions, and organizations. It would be quite costly for a president *not* to appoint a woman and a black to every cabinet. The secretary of labor must be acceptable to the AFL-CIO, the secretary of agriculture to at least some organized farmers, and so on.

Because political considerations must be taken into account in making cabinet and agency appointments and because any head of a large organization will tend to adopt the perspective of that organization, an inevitable tension—even a rivalry—develops between the White House staff and the department heads. Staff members, many of them young and lacking in executive experience, see themselves as extensions of the president's personality and policies. Department heads see themselves as repositories of expert knowledge (often of knowledge of why the president's plans won't work). Department heads are often irritated when White House staffers tell them what to do and deny them access to the president.

Popularity and Influence

Every president strives for personal popularity because it is the key to congressional support (and improved chances for reelection). It is not obvious, of course, why Congress should care about a president's popularity. After all,

TABLE 8.2 Partisan Gains or Losses in Congress in Presidential Elections

Year	President	Party	Gains or Losses of President's Party in	
			House	Senate
1932	Roosevelt	Dem.	+90	+9
1936	Roosevelt	Dem.	+12	+7
1940	Roosevelt	Dem.	+7	−3
1944	Roosevelt	Dem.	+24	−2
1948	Truman	Dem.	+75	+9
1952	Eisenhower	Rep.	+22	+1
1956	Eisenhower	Rep.	−3	−1
1960	Kennedy	Dem.	−20	+1
1964	Johnson	Dem.	+37	+1
1968	Nixon	Rep.	+5	+7
1972	Nixon	Rep.	+12	−2
1976	Carter	Dem.	+1	+1
1980	Reagan	Rep.	+33	+12
1984	Reagan	Rep.	+16	−2
1988	Bush	Rep.	−3	−1
1992	Clinton	Dem.	−9	0

SOURCE: Updated from Congressional Quarterly, *Guide to U.S. Elections*, p. 928; and *Congress and the Nation*, Vol. IV (1973–1976), p. 28.

most members of Congress are now secure in their seats, and the president cannot ordinarily provide credible electoral rewards (or penalties) for them. Not even Franklin Roosevelt could purge members of Congress who opposed his program, and seldom does presidential support make a difference in a congressional race.

Careful studies of voter attitudes and of how presidential and congressional candidates fare in the same districts suggest that whatever the influence of presidential coattails once was, their effect has declined in recent years and is quite small today. The weakening of party loyalty and of party organizations, combined with the enhanced ability of members of Congress to build secure relations with their constituents, has tended to insulate congressional elections from presidential ones. When voters support members of Congress from the same party as an incoming president, they probably do so out of a desire for a general change and as an adverse judgment about the outgoing party's performance as a whole, and not because they want to support the new president with legislators favorable to him.[4] (See Table 8.2.) The unusu-

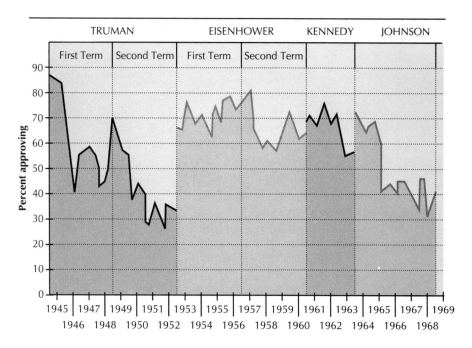

FIGURE 8.1 Presidential Popularity

NOTE: Popularity was measured by asking every few months, "Do you approve of the way ——— is handling his job as president?"

SOURCE: Thomas E. Cronin, *The State of the Presidency* (Boston: Little, Brown, 1975), pp. 110–111. Copyright © 1975 by Little, Brown and Company (Inc.). Reprinted by permission. Updated with Gallup poll data, 1976–1992.

ally big increase in Republican representatives and senators that accompanied the election of Ronald Reagan in 1980 was probably as much a result of the unpopularity of the outgoing president and the circumstances of various local races as it was of Reagan's coattails.

Nonetheless, a president's personal popularity may have a significant effect on how much of his program Congress passes. Though members of Congress may not fear a president who threatens to campaign against them, they do have a sense that it is risky to oppose too adamantly the policies of a popular president. It can be shown statistically that a president's popularity, as measured by the Gallup Poll (see Figure 8.1), is associated with the proportion of a president's legislative proposals that are approved by Congress (see Figure 8.2). Other things being equal, the more popular the president, the higher the proportion of his bills Congress will pass.[5]

The Decline in Popularity

Though presidential popularity is an asset, its value tends inexorably to decline. As can be seen from Figure 8.1, every president except Eisenhower and Reagan lost popular support between his inauguration and the time he left

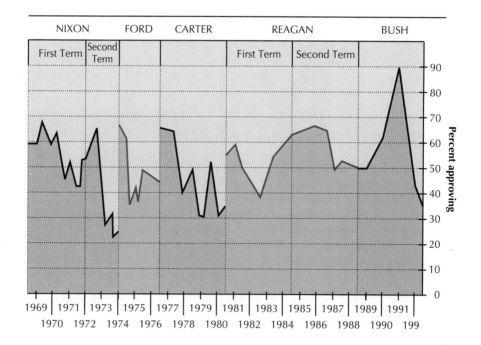

NIXON		FORD	CARTER	REAGAN		BUSH
First Term	Second Term			First Term	Second Term	

Percent approving

1969 1970 1971 1972 1973 1974 1975 1976 1977 1978 1979 1980 1981 1982 1983 1984 1985 1986 1987 1988 1989 1990 1991 199

office, except when his reelection gave him a brief burst of renewed popularity.

Because a president's popularity tends to be highest right after an election, political commentators like to speak of a "honeymoon," during which the president's love affair with the people and possibly with Congress can be consummated. Certainly Roosevelt, in his legendary "hundred days" after taking office in 1933, enjoyed a honeymoon during which he obtained from a willing Congress a vast array of new laws that created new agencies and authorized new policies. But those were extraordinary times of the Great Depression, with millions out of work, banks closed, farmers impoverished, and the stock market ruined. It would have been political suicide for Congress to have blocked, or even delayed, action on measures that appeared designed to help the nation out of the crisis. Other presidents, serving in more normal times, have not enjoyed such a honeymoon, though some have won a few victories. Reagan, in his first year in office, persuaded Congress to enact major cuts in taxes and spending on domestic programs.

The decay in the reputation of the president and his party in midterm is evident from the pattern of off-year elections. In every off-year election since 1934, the president's party has lost seats in one or both houses of Congress (see Table 8.3 on page 234).

PRESIDENTIAL CHARACTER

Every president brings to the White House a distinctive personality; the way the White House is organized and run reflects that personality. Moreover, the

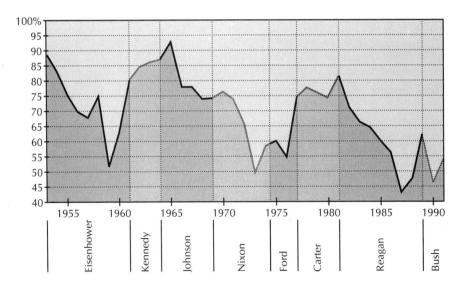

FIGURE 8.2 The percentage of roll-call votes in Congress in which the side publicly favored by the president won.

SOURCE: *Congressional Quarterly Weekly Report,* Dec. 28, 1991, p. 3754.

public judges the president not only in terms of what he has accomplished but also in terms of its perception of his character. Thus personality plays a more important role in explaining the presidency than it does in explaining Congress.

Dwight Eisenhower brought an orderly, military style to the White House. He was accustomed to delegating authority and to having careful and complete staff work done for him by trained specialists. Though critics often accused him of having a bumbling, incoherent manner of speaking, in fact much of that was a public disguise—a strategy for avoiding being pinned down in public on matters where he wished to retain freedom of action. His private papers reveal a very different Eisenhower—sharp, precise, deliberate.

John Kennedy brought a very different style to the presidency. He projected the image of a bold, articulate, and amusing leader who liked to surround himself with talented amateurs. Instead of clear, hierarchical lines of authority, there was a pattern of personal rule and an atmosphere of improvisation. Kennedy did not hesitate to call very junior subordinates directly and tell them what to do, bypassing the chain of command.

Lyndon Johnson was a master legislative strategist who had become majority leader of the Senate on the strength of his ability to persuade other politicians in face-to-face encounters. He was a consummate deal maker who, having been in Washington for thirty years before becoming president, knew everybody and everything. As a result he tried to make every decision himself. But the style that served him well in political negotiations did not

American presidents were always more powerful in wartime; the expansion in their peace-time powers began with Franklin D. Roosevelt, who came into office in the midst of the Great Depression.

serve him well in speaking to the country at large, especially when trying to retain public support for the war in Vietnam.

Richard Nixon was a highly intelligent man with a deep knowledge of and interest in foreign policy coupled with a deep suspicion of the media, his political rivals, and the federal bureaucracy. In contrast to Johnson, he disliked personal confrontations and tended to shield himself behind an elaborate staff system. Distrustful of the cabinet agencies, he tried first to centralize power in the White House and then to put into key cabinet posts former White House aides loyal to him. Like Johnson, his personality made it difficult for him to mobilize popular support. Eventually he was forced to resign under the threat of impeachment arising out of his role in the Watergate scandal.

Gerald Ford, before being appointed vice president, had spent his political life in Congress and was at home with the give-and-take, discussion-oriented procedures of that body. He was also a genial man who liked talking to people. Thus he preferred the circular to the pyramid system of White House organization. But this meant that many decisions were made in a disorganized fashion in which key people—and sometimes key problems—were not taken into account.

Jimmy Carter was an outsider in Washington and boasted of it. A former Georgia governor, he was determined not to be "captured" by Wash-

TABLE 8.3 Partisan Gains or Losses in Congress in Off-Year Elections

Year	President	Party	Gains or Losses of President's Party in	
			House	Senate
1934	Roosevelt	Dem.	+9	+9
1938	Roosevelt	Dem.	−70	−7
1942	Roosevelt	Dem.	−50	−8
1946	Truman	Dem.	−54	−11
1950	Truman	Dem.	−29	−5
1954	Eisenhower	Rep.	−18	−1
1958	Eisenhower	Rep.	−47	−13
1962	Kennedy	Dem.	−5	+2
1966	Johnson	Dem.	−48	−4
1970	Nixon	Rep.	−12	+1
1974	Ford	Rep.	−48	−5
1978	Carter	Dem.	−12	−3
1982	Reagan	Rep.	−26	0
1986	Reagan	Rep.	−5	−8
1990	Bush	Rep.	−8	−1

SOURCE: Updated from Congressional Quarterly, *Guide to U.S. Elections*, p. 928; and *Congress and the Nation*, Vol. IV (1973–1976), p. 28.

ington insiders. He also was a voracious reader with a wide range of interests and an appetite for detail. These dispositions led him to try to do many things and to do them personally. Like Ford, he began with a circular structure; unlike Ford, he based his decisions on reading countless memos and asking detailed questions. His advisers finally decided that he was trying to do too much in too great detail, and toward the end of his term he shifted to a pyramid structure.

Ronald Reagan was also an outsider, a former governor of California. But unlike Carter, he wanted to set the broad directions of his administration and leave the details to others. He gave wide latitude to subordinates and to cabinet officers, within the framework of an emphasis on lower taxes, less domestic spending, a military buildup, and a tough line with the Soviet Union. In the Iran-contra crisis, some of his subordinates let him down by doing a poor job of thinking through the secret exchange of arms for American hostages in the Middle East and by concealing from him the diversion of the profits from the arms sale to aid the civil war being waged by the contras in

Nicaragua. A report on the affair by a presidential commission concluded that Reagan's management style had been too lax and remote. At the same time, he was a superb leader of public opinion, earning the nickname, "The Great Communicator."

George Bush was, on paper, the best-prepared president since Richard Nixon. He had been a member of Congress, ambassador to China, director of the Central Intelligence Agency, and vice president of the United States. He was a close personal friend of many foreign leaders. These contacts and experiences were put to good use when he mobilized a coalition of nations to participate in Operation Desert Storm, the military operation that, with United Nations backing, ousted Iraqi troops from Kuwait. Despite his skill at one-on-one foreign diplomacy, he was unable to persuade Americans faced with an economic recession that he had a plan to get the nation moving again.

THE POWER TO SAY NO

Presidential character and skills are important, but a president also has a special bargaining chip: the power to say no. The Constitution gives the president the power to veto legislation. In addition, most presidents have asserted the right to **executive privilege**—the right to withhold information Congress may want to obtain from him or his subordinates—and some presidents have tried to impound funds appropriated by Congress. These efforts by the president to say no are not only a way of blocking action but also a way of forcing Congress to bargain with him over the substance of policies.

Veto

If a president disapproves of a bill passed by both houses of Congress, he may veto it in one of two ways. One way is by sending a **veto message** to Congress within ten days explaining his objections; the other way is by exercising a **pocket veto,** that is, by refusing to sign it within a ten-day period, during which time Congress adjourns. The Supreme Court ruled that a pocket veto can be used only just before Congress is about to adjourn at the end of its second session; it cannot be used if Congress merely recesses for a summer vacation or to permit its members to campaign during an off-year election.

A bill that is neither signed nor vetoed within ten days while Congress is still in session becomes a law automatically without the president's approval. A bill that has been returned to Congress with a veto message can be passed over the president's objections if at least two-thirds of each house vote to override the veto. A bill that has been pocket-vetoed obviously must be reintroduced in the next session if Congress wants to press the matter.

The president must accept or reject the entire bill; unlike most governors, he cannot exercise a **line-item veto,** rejecting some provisions and accepting others. Congress can take advantage of this fact by putting provisions a president wants into a bill he does not like, thereby forcing him to sign the entire bill, objectionable parts and all, to get what he wants.

Nevertheless, the veto power is a substantial one because Congress rarely has the votes to override. From George Washington through George Bush, less than 4 percent of presidential vetoes have been overridden. Often the vetoed legislation is revised by Congress and passed in a form suitable to the president. There is no tally of how often this happens, but it is frequent enough so that both branches of government recognize that the veto, or even the threat of it, is part of an elaborate process of political negotiation in which the president has substantial powers.

Executive Privilege

The Constitution says nothing about whether the president is obliged to divulge private communications between himself and his principal advisers, but presidents have acted as if they did have that privilege of confidentiality. The presidential claim is based (1) on the doctrine of the separation of powers, interpreted to mean that one branch of government does not have the right to inquire into the internal operations of another, and (2) on the principle that the president should be able to obtain confidential and candid information from subordinates, free of public scrutiny.

For almost two hundred years there was no challenge to the claim of presidential confidentiality, though Congress was never happy with it. But in 1973, during the Watergate scandal, the Supreme Court for the first time confronted the issue. The question was whether President Nixon could, by invoking executive privilege, deny a special prosecutor access to tape recordings of presidential conversations with his advisers. The Court ruled (8–0) that although there might be a sound basis for the claim, especially where sensitive military or diplomatic matters are involved, there is no "absolute unqualified Presidential privilege of immunity from judicial process under all circumstances."[6] To admit otherwise would be to block the constitutionally defined function of the federal courts to decide criminal cases. Thus Nixon had to surrender the disputed tapes. As a practical matter, however, it seems likely that presidential advisers will continue to be able to give the president private advice except in unusual cases such as Watergate, when allegations of criminal misconduct arise.

Impoundment of Funds

From time to time presidents have refused to spend money appropriated by Congress: the precedent for impounding funds goes back at least to Thomas Jefferson. But what has precedent is not thereby constitutional. The Constitution is silent on whether the president *must* spend the money Congress appropriates. The major test of the question came when President Nixon, hoping to reduce federal spending, impounded funds already appropriated by Congress. Congress responded by passing the Budget Reform Act of 1974 that, among other things, requires the president to spend all appropriated funds unless he first tells Congress what funds he wishes not to spend and Congress, within forty-five days, agrees to delete the items. It is not clear, however, that this will settle the matter, especially because the Supreme Court has subsequently declared the **legislative veto**—on which the Budget Reform Act depends—unconstitutional. Congress may have to rely instead on political pressure to get the money spent.

THE PRESIDENT'S PROGRAM

Imagine that you have just spent three or four years running for president, essentially giving the same speech over and over again. You have had no time to study the issues in any depth. To reach a large television audience, you have couched your ideas in rather simple—if not simple-minded—slogans. Your principal advisers are political aides, not legislative specialists.

You win. Now you must *be* president instead of just talking about it. Foreign governments and the stock market hang on your every word; soon you must make the State of the Union address and send an enormously complex budget to Congress. What will you do? What *will* you do?

The Constitution merely directs you to recommend "such measures" as you judge "necessary and expedient" and to "take care that the laws be faithfully executed." And at one time an incoming president was not expected to do very much. Today he must have something to say (and offer) to everybody.

Putting Together a Program

There are essentially two ways for a president to develop a program. Like President Carter, he can have a policy on almost everything, working endless hours trying to learn something about—and then state his position on—a large number of policies. Or like President Reagan, he can concentrate on a few major initiatives or themes, leaving everything else to subordinates.

But even when a president has a governing philosophy, as did Reagan, he cannot risk plunging ahead on his own. Before he fully commits himself, he must judge public and congressional reactions to the program, often by leaking part of it to the press. Reagan, for example, floated as a **trial balloon** his ideas on Social Security and tax reform to test the popular reaction; so did his opponents in the bureaucracy.

In addition to the risks of adverse reaction, the president faces three constraints on his ability to plan a program. First is the sheer limit on his time and attention span. Typically he must put in a ninety-hour week; even so he has great difficulty keeping up with all the proposed legislation he is supposed to know and make decisions about, including four hundred to six hundred bills that Congress passes each year. Second is the unexpected crisis: all modern presidents have had to respond to major domestic or foreign crises, usually when they least expect them. And third is the fact that the federal government and most federal programs, as well as the federal budget, can only be changed marginally, except in special circumstances. The vast bulk of federal expenditures are beyond his control in any given year: the money must be spent whether the president likes it or not. Many federal programs have sufficiently strong congressional or public support that they must be left intact or modified only slightly. And this means that most federal employees can count on being secure in their jobs, whatever a president's views on the size of the bureaucracy.

The result of these constraints is that the president, at least in ordinary times, must be selective about what he wants. If he wants to get the most return on his limited stock of influence and prestige, he must invest it carefully in enterprises that promise substantial gains—in public benefits and political support—at reasonable cost. Each newly elected president tends to speak in terms of changing everything at once. But beneath the rhetoric (of a "New Frontier," a "Great Society," or a "New Covenant"), he must identify a few specific proposals on which he wishes to bet his resources, remembering to keep a substantial stock in reserve to handle the inevitable crises. In recent decades events have required every president to devote a substantial part of his time and resources to two key issues: the state of the economy and foreign affairs. What he manages to do in addition to this depends on his personal views and his sense of what the nation, as well as his reelection, requires.

Measuring Success

There are two ways of measuring presidential success: by the proportion of measures the president submits to Congress that it approves, and by the proportion of the votes taken in Congress on which his position prevails. By the first method, the president usually wins less than half the time. By the second method (the line in Figure 8.2), he does better—he is on the winning side perhaps three-fourths of the time. This latter measure is misleadingly high, however, because it ignores bills the president favors that do not even come up for a vote and because it counts measures that he may only reluctantly support (with congressional amendments) after originally proposing them. (By contrast, in Great Britain, more than 90 percent of the prime minister's bills are passed by Parliament.) The most successful recent president was Lyndon Johnson, the least successful, Nixon.

PRESIDENTIAL TRANSITIONS

No president except Franklin Roosevelt has served more than two full terms and, since the ratification of the Twenty-second Amendment to the Constitution in 1951, no president may do so again. But more than tradition or the

Constitution escorts the president from office. Only a minority of all the presidents since George Washington have been elected to a second term. Four died in office during their first term. But the remainder either did not seek or more often could not obtain reelection. Of the eight presidents who died in office, four were assassinated (Lincoln, Garfield, McKinley, and Kennedy). At least six other presidents were the objects of unsuccessful assassination attempts.

The presidents who served two or more terms fall into certain periods such as the Founding (Washington, Jefferson, Madison, Monroe) or wartime (Lincoln, Wilson, Franklin Roosevelt, Lyndon Johnson), or happened to hold office in especially tranquil times (Monroe, McKinley, Eisenhower). When the country was deeply divided, as during the years before and after the Civil War, it was a rare president who was reelected. Reagan was the first president since Eisenhower to serve two full terms in the White House.

The Vice President

Eight times a vice president has become president because of the death of a predecessor. It happened first to John Tyler, who became president in 1841 when William Henry Harrison died peacefully after only one month in office. Tyler and the country faced a substantial question: was he simply the acting president and thus a kind of caretaker until a new president was elected, or was he *president* in every sense of the word? Despite criticism and what might perhaps have been the Framers' contrary intention, Tyler decided on the latter course and was confirmed in that decision by an act of Congress. Since then the vice president has automatically become president, in title and powers, on the death or resignation of the occupant of the White House.

But if vice presidents frequently acquire the presidency because of death, they rarely acquire it by election. Except for John Adams and Thomas Jefferson,* only three vice presidents have become president without their predecessor dying in office: Martin Van Buren (Jackson's vice president) in 1836, Richard Nixon (Eisenhower's vice president) in 1968, and George Bush (Reagan's vice president) in 1988. No one who wishes to become president should assume that the vice presidency is the best way to get there.

The office is just what so many of its occupants have said it is—a rather empty job. The vice president's only official task is to preside over the Senate and to vote in case of a tie; his leadership powers in the Senate are weak. From time to time presidents have found relatively minor tasks for their vice presidents, but essentially the vice president can do little more than endorse whatever the president does, and wait.

---

* Adams and Jefferson assumed the office under the original constitutional provision whereby the runner-up in the electoral college became vice president; this system proved unworkable with the appearance of political parties, and it was abandoned in 1804 when the Twelfth Amendment was adopted.

Problems of Succession

Since the time of John Tyler, it has been clear that if the president dies in office, the vice president is sworn in as president. But two questions remain: What if the president falls seriously ill, but does not die? And if the vice president steps up, who then becomes the new vice president?

The first question has arisen on a number of occasions. After President Garfield was shot in 1881, he lingered through the summer before dying. Woodrow Wilson collapsed from a stroke and was a virtual recluse for seven months in 1919 and an invalid for the rest of his term. Eisenhower had three serious illnesses while in office; Reagan was shot and seriously wounded.

The second question has arisen on eight occasions when the vice president became president owing to the death of the incumbent. In these cases no elected person was available to succeed the new president should he die in office.

The Twenty-fifth Amendment ratified in 1967 addressed both problems. First, it allows the vice president to serve as acting president in the case of presidential disability. **Disability** can be declared either by the president himself or by the vice president and a majority of the cabinet; the latter case is subject to a two-thirds vote of Congress. Second, it requires a vice president who has succeeded to the presidency to name a new vice president, subject to confirmation by a majority in Congress. Whenever there is no vice president, an earlier 1947 law still applies: next in line for the presidency are the Speaker of the House, the president pro tempore of the Senate, followed by the fourteen cabinet officers, beginning with the secretary of state.

The disability problem has not arisen as a major issue since the adoption of the amendment, but the succession problem has. In 1973 Vice President Spiro Agnew resigned, having pleaded no contest to criminal charges. President Nixon nominated Gerald Ford as vice president, who, after extensive hearings, was confirmed and sworn in. Then on August 9, 1974, Nixon resigned the presidency—the first man to do so—and Ford became president. Ford nominated as his vice president Nelson Rockefeller, who was confirmed by both houses of Congress—again, after extensive hearings—and was sworn in on December 19, 1974. For the first time in history, the nation had as its two principal executive officers men elected neither to the presidency nor to the vice presidency. It is a measure of the legitimacy of the Constitution that this arrangement caused no crisis in public opinion.

Impeachment

There is one other way—besides death, disability, or resignation—by which a president can leave office before his term expires, and that is by impeachment. Not only the president and vice president but also all "civil officers of the United States" can be removed from office by being impeached and convicted. As a practical matter, civil officers—cabinet officers, bureau chiefs, and the like—are never impeached because the president can remove them at any time and usually will if their behavior makes them a serious political liability. Federal judges, who serve during good behavior and are constitutionally independent of the president and Congress, have been subject to impeachment more frequently than anyone else.

An **impeachment** is like an indictment in a criminal trial: it is a set of charges against somebody voted by (in this case) a majority in the House of Representatives. To be removed from office, the impeached officer must be **convicted** by a two-thirds vote of the Senate, which sits as a court, hears the evidence, and makes its decision under whatever rules it wishes to adopt. Article II, Section 4, of the Constitution specifies "treason, bribery, or other high crimes and misdemeanors" as impeachable offenses. But no clear definition exists of what acts do (or do not) qualify as high crimes and misdemeanors, leaving Congress to decide as it wishes. Most scholars, however, agree that the charge must involve something illegal or unconstitutional, not just unpopular. Twelve persons have been impeached by the House, and four have been convicted by the Senate. The last conviction was in 1986 when a federal judge was removed from office for lack of integrity.

Only one president has been impeached—Andrew Johnson in 1868—but Richard Nixon almost surely would have been had he not first resigned. Johnson was not convicted on the impeachment, the effort to do so falling one vote short of the necessary two-thirds majority. Many historians feel that the effort to remove Johnson was entirely partisan and ideological in nature, for he was not charged with anything that they would regard as "high crimes and misdemeanors" within the meaning of the Constitution. The Congress detested Johnson's "soft" policy toward the defeated South after the Civil War and was determined to use any pretext to get him out of office. The charges against Nixon were far more grave, involving allegations of illegal acts arising out of his effort to cover up his subordinates' involvement in the burglary of the Democratic National Committee headquarters in the Watergate building.

Students may find the occasion of a president's misconduct or disability remote and the details of succession or impeachment tedious. But the problem is not remote—succession has occurred nine times and disability at least twice—and what may appear tedious goes, in fact, to the heart of the presidency. The first and fundamental problem is to make the office legitimate. That was the great task George Washington set himself, and that was the substantial accomplishment of his successors. Despite bitter and sometimes violent partisan and sectional strife, beginning almost immediately after Washington stepped down, presidential succession has always occurred peacefully, without a military coup or a political plot. For centuries, in the bygone times of kings as well as in the present times of dictators and juntas, peaceful succession has been a rare phenomenon among the nations of the world. Many of the critics of the Constitution believed in 1787 that peaceful succession would not happen in the United States either: somehow the president would connive to hold office for life or to handpick his successor. Their predictions were wrong, though their fears were understandable.

THE PRESIDENT AND PUBLIC POLICY

The President and Foreign Affairs

Most of the examples of the exercise of great presidential power given at the beginning of this chapter came from the area of foreign affairs. Because the president is commander in chief of the armed forces, because he appoints and receives ambassadors, and because Congress recognizes that it cannot negotiate with other nations, the president tends to be stronger in foreign than in domestic policy.

Until well into this century, and with only a few exceptions, foreign policy was often made and usually carried out by the secretary of state. As America became a permanent world power beginning with World War II, the president personally has become more deeply involved in managing our foreign relations. Franklin Roosevelt, John Kennedy, Lyndon Johnson, and Richard Nixon all played major roles in foreign policy and, accordingly, the power and stature of the secretary of state waned during their administrations. To ensure their control over foreign policy, Kennedy, Johnson, and Nixon brought into the White House a national security adviser who often was far more influential than the secretary of state. For example, when Nixon was getting ready to reopen diplomatic relations with the People's Republic of China (after decades during which we did not recognize that country), he gave the job to his national security adviser, Henry Kissinger, who did not even tell the secretary of state, William Rogers, what was going on until shortly before the public announcement. Later on, Kissinger replaced Rogers as secretary of state while still retaining his White House job as national security adviser, thereby making certain that no new White House staffer would challenge his power.

Some recent presidents, however, have relied more on their secretaries of state. Eisenhower deferred to John Foster Dulles, and Reagan usually supported his secretary of state, George Shultz, against his national security adviser. Reagan's security adviser rarely made highly publicized trips abroad; indeed he rarely sought out publicity at all. George Bush's secretary of state, James Baker, was a close personal friend, and so the secretary's influence was very great. But in general, the Department of State and the American ambassadors abroad have, since World War II, handled routine foreign-policy matters, with the big issues involving relations with the Soviet Union and China or crises in the Middle East being handled by either the national security adviser or a globe-trotting secretary of state who serves as the president's personal emissary.

Four major agencies support the president's conduct of foreign affairs. The Department of State is the oldest. Located in a part of the capital known as "Foggy Bottom," it is organized by geographic areas and staffed with career foreign-service officers. In Washington, it usually has the reputation for representing the interests of foreign nations *to* this country as much as it represents American interests abroad.

A major rival to the State Department is the Defense Department. Historically the military did not play much of a role in making foreign policy. But today, we have military alliances with and provide military aid to many nations, and hundreds of thousands of military personnel are stationed abroad. As a result, the Department of Defense (often referred to as DOD) has become a major influence in making foreign policy, especially if the secretary of defense is personally close to the president. The DOD, located in the Pentagon building across the Potomac River from downtown Washington, has its own miniature state department built into its organization. Headed by the assistant secretary of defense for international security affairs, this unit provides advice on foreign policy to the secretary of defense, who often becomes a major rival of the secretary of state for influence with the president.

The Central Intelligence Agency (CIA), based in Langley, Virginia, has intelligence officers serving abroad in scores of countries and intelligence analysts at work at headquarters. The director of the CIA (known as the Director of Central Intelligence or DCI) has the job of keeping the president informed on the actions, intentions, and capabilities of foreign powers. But giving information is not easily kept separate from giving advice, and so a strong DCI (such as William Casey, DCI for President Reagan) can be a major influence on foreign policy. Moreover, the CIA often carries out operations abroad that are usually referred to as "covert," though many of them—such as providing aid to the rebels fighting against the Sandinista government in Nicaragua and against the Soviet army in Afghanistan—have been hardly secret. Planning and implementing these operations deeply involve the CIA in the making of foreign policy.

Sometimes the desire to act covertly leads the government to conspire against itself. Frustrated by the restrictions on the CIA, DCI William Casey and other officials created a wholly unauthorized covert-action unit, in which the principal figure was Lieutenant Colonel Oliver North, a member of the White House staff. North led an effort to sell U.S. arms to Iran in exchange for the release of American hostages held in the Middle East and then diverted some of the profits of this sale to the contras fighting against the Marxist government of Nicaragua. The Iran-contra scandal, as it was known, became one of the major crises of the Reagan administration, leading to a prolonged congressional investigation and finally to criminal prosecution of many of its key figures, including North. (The convictions of North and his superior, John M. Poindexter, were later reversed on appeal.) President Bush

Lieutenant Colonel Oliver North was investigated by Congress and convicted in court of breaking the law when, as a member of President Reagan's National Security Council staff, he directed aid to the contras fighting against the Marxist government of Nicaragua.

pardoned many of the others who were prosecuted for withholding information from Congress about the matter.

The fourth organization, though the smallest, is perhaps the most influential. The National Security Council (NSC) is a committee, created by law and chaired by the president, on which sit (by law) the vice president and the secretaries of state and defense. The DCI and the chairman of the Joint Chiefs of Staff are regular advisers to the NSC. Assisting the council is a staff, headed by the national security adviser. Major foreign-policy issues are discussed by the NSC. The staff summarizes these discussions, carries out tasks assigned to it by the president, filters and manages the foreign-policy paperwork flowing to the president, and drafts decision memoranda for the president to sign. Though few in number, these staff people occupy a key position in the foreign-policy system because they are the ones who chiefly decide what the president will read and write on many foreign-policy issues.

Since the American people look to the president for leadership in foreign affairs and tend to support him in most foreign-policy crises, they may think he is more powerful than he actually is. Not only is he checked by disagreements among his principal advisers, but Congress plays an important role in setting the limits of presidential action. The Senate must confirm all ambassadorial appointments and ratify all treaties; Congress must approve all military spending; and only Congress can declare war. In the original draft of the

U.S. Marines training in Saudi Arabia for the battle that ousted Iraqi invaders from nearby Kuwait.

Constitution, Congress was given the power to "make war," but this was changed, presumably to allow the president to repel a sudden attack without waiting for Congress to assemble.

Since the early 1970s, Congress has tried to claim three additional powers over foreign policy. First, it passed laws that required the president to obtain congressional approval before he sold arms to other nations. (President Reagan, for example, had to lobby hard for congressional approval of the sale of certain military aircraft to Saudi Arabia.) The constitutionality of this requirement was brought into doubt by a 1983 Supreme Court ruling that declared the legislative veto to be unconstitutional (see full discussion in the next chapter, page 272).

Second, Congress in 1973 passed (over President Nixon's veto) the War Powers Act. This law, which every president from Nixon to Bush has claimed is unconstitutional, places the following restrictions on the president's ability to use military force:

1. He must report in writing to Congress within forty-eight hours after he introduces U.S. troops into areas where hostilities have occurred or are imminent.

2. Within sixty days after troops are sent into hostile situations, Congress must, by declaration of war or other specific statutory authorization, provide for the continuation of hostile action by U.S. troops.

3. If Congress fails to provide such authorization, the president must withdraw the troops (unless Congress has been prevented from meeting as a result of an armed attack).

4. If Congress passes a concurrent resolution (which the president may not veto) directing the removal of U.S. troops, the president must comply.

Sometimes the president has complied with the notification procedure, other times he has not. President Reagan sent marines into Lebanon and the army into Grenada but did not officially report this action as required by the War Powers Act; Congress itself authorized the marine deployment but took no action on the Grenada case. Many commentators believe the Act as written is politically unenforceable: if the president takes a popular action, the people will rally around him and Congress will have little say in the matter. In practice, almost every use of force by an American president has, in the short run, acquired popular support, even when (as with President Carter's efforts to rescue American hostages in Iran) the effort failed.

Third, Congress created two committees, one in the House and one in the Senate, to oversee the CIA. By law the president must keep each committee "fully and currently informed" on all intelligence activities, including covert operations. The committees do not have the power to disapprove of these activities, but they are still an important check on presidential authority since they pass on the CIA budget and can make public any activities they feel are questionable.

Ultimately, however, the decisive check on presidential authority is public opinion. In general, the public will support the president in most foreign-policy actions, even ones that backfire. The American people tend to "rally 'round the flag" when the president takes a bold foreign-policy step. When President Carter sent troops to rescue American hostages held captive in Iran, his standing in public opinion went up even though the mission was unsuccessful. When President Reagan sent troops into Grenada, his stock also rose, and some of the few congressional leaders who had criticized the move soon recanted so as not to appear to oppose a popular presidential move. When President Bush sent U.S. troops (along with many from our allies) to oust the Iraqi army from Kuwait, his popularity soared, especially when the land battle lasted only one hundred hours. But the public support will not last indefinitely. If a military involvement leads to a long-term stalemate (such as in Korea, Vietnam, and Lebanon), public support will begin to wither.

The President and Economic Policy

If the American people are supportive and forbearing with respect to the president's conduct of foreign policy, they are critical and quick-tempered regarding his conduct of economic policy. Voters, having no way to judge for themselves, will pretty much take the president's word when he describes U.S. interests abroad. But these same voters, having firsthand knowledge of unemployment, inflation, farm prices, and foreign competition for jobs, will hold the president strictly accountable for the condition of the economy. Elections are only occasionally won or lost over foreign-policy questions, but they are frequently won or lost over economic ones. George Bush knows this all too well: the stalled economy cost him his reelection in 1992.

This makes life difficult for the president, because he has far less control over economic policy than he does over foreign policy. For one thing, nobody really knows what makes the economy tick. Professional economists disagree over what policy we should follow and are not very good at predicting economic conditions even six months in advance.

For another, authority over economic policy is more widely dispersed in the government than is authority over foreign policy. The president gets economic advice from three key subordinates, but none of these has much direct influence over how the economy performs. The director of the Office of Management and Budget (OMB) tells the president how much the government is spending and taking in from taxes and helps him cut or increase the amounts some executive branch agencies are spending. But OMB and the president have little influence over most government spending, since nearly three-fourths of it is politically (and perhaps legally) uncontrollable: payments to retired and disabled people under Social Security, payments of benefits to veterans and others, payments to military contractors for equipment and supplies they have agreed to furnish—all these and more are virtually impossible to change from one year to the next. This means that a president such as Ronald Reagan, who wishes to cut spending, must find his cuts in the one-fourth of the budget that is controllable. And every item in this part of the budget is fiercely defended by agencies, interest groups, and congressional subcommittees.

The president also gets advice from the Council of Economic Advisers (CEA), and especially from its chairman. This group carries out important economic studies, mostly of high quality, but the limits of economic knowledge are such that a president can ignore such advice, or find economists who give him the advice he wants to hear, without too much difficulty. President Reagan's first CEA chairman, Harvard economist Martin Feldstein, regularly warned of what he felt were the dangers of a large federal deficit (that is, of the government spending more than it took in from taxes), but his warnings were largely ignored and in time he resigned.

The secretary of the treasury also gives advice that usually reflects the concerns of bankers here and abroad who worry about interest rates and the value of the dollar relative to that of other currencies (the British pound, the German mark, or the Japanese yen). Unlike the director of OMB or the chairman of the CEA, the secretary of the treasury has some important powers, such as the ability to buy and sell foreign currencies in an effort to influence the value of the dollar.

Perhaps the most important agency affecting economic policy is the Federal Reserve Board, but unlike the first three, it is not directly under presidential control. "The Fed," as it is often called, consists of seven persons who are appointed by the president and confirmed by the Senate and who serve for fourteen-year terms. One member is designated chairman for a term of four years. In theory, and to a large degree in practice, the Fed is independent of both the president and Congress. Its powers are very great, so great that many people regard the chairman of the Fed as the second most influential person in Washington.

The Federal Reserve Board influences both the supply of money and the price of money (that is, interest rates) in three ways. First, it buys and sells government securities (that is, notes and bonds issued by the Treasury Department in order to borrow money). When it buys securities, the Fed writes a check to the Treasury Department, which cashes the check and uses the money to pay government bills. But unlike the situation when you and I write checks, the Fed does not have any money in its bank account. When *it* writes a check, it is actually *creating* money. (Conversely, when the Fed sells treasury securities, it is taking money out of circulation.) Second, the Fed regulates the amount of money a bank that is a member of the Federal Reserve System must keep on hand as a reserve to back up the deposits its customers have made. The higher the reserve requirement, the less money the bank can lend out. Third, the Fed sets the interest rate it charges banks that wish to borrow money from it. The higher this rate, the more costly it is for banks to get additional funds and thus the higher the interest rates they charge their customers.

There are scores of other executive agencies that also influence economic policy—the State Department, the Commerce Department, and so on. Of late, presidents have created White House committees that try to coordinate how economic policy is made, but only occasionally have these efforts been very successful.

All of these agencies, together with Congress, come together in the annual fight over the federal budget. Under the current procedure, this is what is supposed to happen:

★ **First Monday in February:** The president submits his budget request to Congress. (For months before this, OMB has been compiling and adjusting budget requests from the separate departments and agencies.)

★ **February and March:** House and Senate budget committees discuss the president's proposed budget.

★ **April 15:** Congress is supposed to pass a **budget resolution** that states the total amount of allowable spending. Within the overall budget amount, there are supposed to be **caps** on total spending in four areas—

defense, foreign aid, entitlements (such as Medicare), and discretionary spending (most domestic programs). Any spending above these caps must be paid for by an equal reduction in spending in some other program in the same cap area.

★ **May and June:** Congress acts on thirteen **appropriations bills** that provide money to the departments and agencies. The total amount of money these bills provide is not supposed to exceed the amount in the budget resolution.

★ **Summer:** President signs or vetoes these appropriations bills.

★ **October 1:** The new fiscal year starts.

Having read the word *supposed* several times, you probably have guessed that things don't always work this way. And they don't. Congress may, and often does, miss these deadlines. The president and Congress may disagree over how much should be spent, as was often the case during the Reagan and Bush administrations. The result of such a disagreement is that the government has no budget on October 1. (When that occurs, Congress passes a set of **continuing resolutions** that allows the government to stay in business and pay its bills on the basis of how much it had to spend in the previous year.)

Haunting this entire process is the specter of the budget deficit. The **deficit** is the shortfall between what the government takes in from taxes and fees and what it spends. (The total **national debt** is the accumulation since 1789 of all of the annual deficits, less whatever may have been paid back as a result of running a surplus in some years. The government covers its debt by borrowing money. It does this by selling Treasury bonds that pay interest. In 1991 the government paid out $195 billion in interest on these bonds.) In the forty-two years from 1950 to 1992, there were only nine years when the federal government did not run a deficit. The deficits became especially large beginning in 1982.

Economists disagree on the economic effects of deficits. Contrary to many predictions, the big deficits of the 1980s did not prevent the nation from having a high level of prosperity. But the long-term effects may be very serious if government borrowing soaks up the nation's savings and thus reduces our ability to invest in new plant and equipment.

Politicians agree that the political effects of the red ink make it harder for them to pay for new programs or increase spending on old ones—harder, but not impossible. Spending on most domestic programs has continued to rise during the 1980s and 1990s. The president and Congress have never agreed on a way to cut the deficit dramatically. The reason is quite simple: To cut the deficit in the short run, you must either raise taxes or cut spending on the biggest and fastest-growing programs (such as Medicare) or both. Neither alternative is politically popular.

SUMMARY

A president, though chosen directly by the people, has less power than a British prime minister, even though the latter depends on the support of his or her party in Parliament. The separation of powers in the American system means that a president, however personally popular he may be, must deal with a political competitor—Congress—in setting policy and managing the executive branch.

The constitutional basis of presidential power is modest; the great growth in that power since the 1930s has resulted from the growth in the size and scope of the federal government, the increased importance of foreign affairs, and the president's enhanced ability to communicate directly with the people through radio and television.

Every president can depend on some support from his party's members in Congress but not enough to guarantee success, even when his party is in the majority in both houses (a rare event in the last thirty or so years). To increase his power, the president depends on personal popularity and on the bargaining power he has by virtue of his ability to veto bills.

In foreign affairs, the president has substantial power and, in a crisis, popular support. But Congress has reasserted some of its powers by bringing the CIA under congressional scrutiny and by passing the War Powers Act.

In economic policy, the president has less power but the public expects more of him. Elections often turn on economic issues, yet the president rarely has the knowledge, advice, or power to shape the economy to his liking. Congress is an especially important rival in this area because it controls the power of the purse. Since 1982, the president and Congress have made little progress in reducing the deficit.

SUGGESTED READINGS

General

Barber, James David. *The Presidential Character,* 3d ed. Englewood Cliffs, N.J.: Prentice-Hall, 1985. Analyzes how a president's personality evolves and shapes his conduct in office.

Corwin, Edward S. *The President: Office and Powers,* 5th ed. New York: New York University Press, 1984. Historical, constitutional, and legal development of the office.

Cunliffe, Marcus. *American Presidents and the Presidency.* New York: American Heritage Press/McGraw-Hill, 1972. Readable history of the presidency, with shrewd insights and ample anecdotes.

King, Gary, and Lyn Ragsdale. *The Elusive Executive.* Washington, D.C.: CQ Press, 1988. Compilation of and commentary about statistics on the presidency.

Neustadt, Richard E. *Presidential Power: The Politics of Leadership,* rev. ed. New York: Wiley, 1976. How presidents try to acquire and hold political power in the competitive world of official Washington, by a man who has been both a scholar and an insider.

On Particular Modern Presidents

FRANKLIN D. ROOSEVELT

—Burns, James MacGregor. *Roosevelt: The Lion and the Fox*. New York: Harcourt Brace, 1956.

—Leuchtenberg, William E. *Franklin D. Roosevelt and the New Deal, 1932–1940*. New York: Harper & Row, 1963.

HARRY S TRUMAN

—McCullough, David. *Truman*. New York: Simon & Schuster, 1992.Truman, Harry S *Memoirs*, 2 vols. Garden City, N.Y.: Doubleday, 1958.

DWIGHT D. EISENHOWER

—Greenstein, Fred I. *The Hidden-Hand Presidency: Eisenhower as Leader*. New York: Basic Books, 1982.

JOHN F. KENNEDY

—Paper, Lewis J. *The Promise and the Performance: The Leadership of John F. Kennedy*. New York: Crown, 1975.

—Sorenson, Theodore M. *Kennedy*. New York: Harper & Row, 1965.

LYNDON B. JOHNSON

—Evans, Rowland, and Robert Novak. *Lyndon B. Johnson: The Exercise of Power*. New York: New American Library, 1968.

—Kearns, Doris. *Lyndon Johnson and the American Dream*. New York: Harper & Row, 1976.

RICHARD M. NIXON

—Ambrose, Stephen E. *Nixon—The Education of a Politician, 1913–1962*. New York: Simon and Schuster, 1987.

9

★ ★ ★

The Bureaucracy

THERE IS PROBABLY not a man or woman in the United States who has not, at some time or other, complained about "the bureaucracy." Your letter was slow in getting to Aunt Minnie? The Internal Revenue Service took months to send you your tax refund? The Defense Department paid $435 for a hammer? The Occupational Safety and Health Administration told you that you installed the wrong kind of portable toilets for your farm workers? The "bureaucracy" is to blame.

For most people and politicians bureaucracy is a pejorative word implying waste, confusion, red tape, and rigidity. But for scholars—and for bureaucrats themselves—bureaucracy is a word with a neutral, technical meaning. A **bureaucracy** is a large, complex organization composed of appointed officials. By *complex* we mean that authority is divided among several managers; no one person is able to make all the decisions (see Figure 9.1). A large corporation is a bureaucracy; so are a big university and a government agency. With its sizable staff, even Congress has become, to some degree, a bureaucracy.

DISTINCTIVENESS OF THE AMERICAN BUREAUCRACY

Bureaucratic government has become an obvious feature of all modern societies, democratic and nondemocratic. In the United States, however, four aspects of our constitutional system and political traditions give to the bureaucracy and its operations a distinctive character. First, political authority over the bureaucracy is shared between the presidency and Congress—with its many committees and subcommittees—so that every senior appointed official has at least two masters. This divided authority encourages bureaucrats to play one branch of government against the other and to make heavy use of the media. All this is unknown in nations with parliamentary governments, like Great Britain, where the prime minister and cabinet control the bureaucracy.

Second, most federal agencies share their functions with related agencies in state and local government. Though some federal agencies deal directly with the people (for example, the Internal Revenue Service, the Federal Bureau of Investigation, and the Postal Service), many concerned with such matters as education, health, housing, and employment work with other organizations at state levels of government. In France, by contrast, such programs are centrally run with little or no control exercised by local governments.

Third, the institutions and traditions of American life, especially since the 1960s, have led to an expansion of personal rights. The defense of rights and claims, through lawsuits as well as political action, is now given central importance. A government agency in this country operates under closer public scrutiny and with a greater prospect of court challenges than in almost any other nation.

Fourth, the scope as well as the style of bureaucratic government differs. In most Western European nations, the government owns and operates large parts of the economy. Publicly operated enterprises account for about 12 percent of all employment in parts of Europe but for less than 3 percent in the United States.[1] The United States government, however, regulates privately owned enterprises to a degree not found in many other countries.

THE GROWTH OF THE BUREAUCRACY

The Constitution did not mention departments and bureaus, and it made scarcely any provision for an administrative system other than to give the president the power, subject to the Senate's advice and consent, to appoint officials.[2]

A crucial issue was decided in the First Congress of 1789. While considering a bill to create the Department of State, both houses debated long and heatedly over whether appointed officials could be removed by the president alone. At stake was the locus of power in what was to become the bureau-

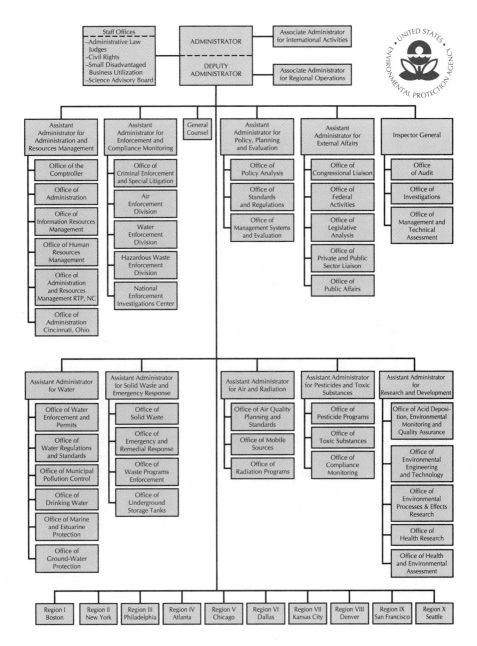

FIGURE 9.1 What a Bureaucracy Looks Like

SOURCE: U.S. Government Manual, 1986–1987.

cracy. Opponents wanted officials to be removable only with the Senate's consent. James Madison, who spoke for the Washington administration, argued that without the unfettered right of removal, the president would not be able to control his subordinates and thus would be unable to discharge his constitutional obligation to "take care that the laws be faithfully executed."[3]

By very narrow margins, Madison's view won (in the Senate, a tie vote had to be broken, in favor of the president, by Vice President Adams). The Department of State, and all cabinet departments subsequently created, would be run by people removable by the president.

That did not resolve the question of who would really control the bureaucracy, however. Congress retained the right to appropriate money, to investigate the administration, and to shape the laws that would be executed by the administration—more than ample power to challenge any president who claimed to have sole authority over his subordinates. And many members of Congress expected the cabinet departments, even though headed by people removable by the president, would report to Congress.

Bureaucracy Before the New Deal Era

The national government in Washington was at first minuscule. The State Department started with only nine employees; the War Department did not have eighty civilian employees until 1801. Only the Treasury Department, concerned with collecting taxes and finding ways to pay the public debt, had much power, and only the Post Office Department provided any significant service.

Small as the bureaucracy was, men struggled, often bitterly, over who would be appointed to it. From Washington's day to modern times, presidents have found making appointments one of their most important and difficult tasks. On it depended how the laws were interpreted, how effectively the public business would be discharged, and how strong the political party in power would be. And as John Adams remarked, every appointment creates one ingrate and ten enemies.

Congress was the dominant branch of government during most of this period, and so congressional preferences often controlled the appointment of officials. This meant that appointments were generally made with an eye to rewarding the local supporters of members of Congress or building up local party organizations—in a word, on the basis of political patronage. After the Civil War the patronage system became a major issue, galvanizing various reform movements that aimed to purify politics and raise the competence of the public service. Demands for reform culminated in 1883 with the passage of the Pendleton Act,* and there began a slow but steady transfer of federal jobs from the patronage to the merit system.

Many of the abuses that reformers complained about were real, but patronage served some useful purposes. The president could expect that his subordinates would be reasonably supportive of his policies, and he could

---

* The Pendleton Act (Civil Service Act of 1883) laid the foundation for the national government's personnel policies by establishing open, competitive tests and creating a Civil Service Commission.

use patronage as leverage on members of Congress. It also enabled party organizations to be built up to perform the necessary functions of nominating candidates and mobilizing voters.

Meanwhile there were more and more jobs to fight over. From 1816 to 1861 the number of federal employees increased eightfold, largely through the expansion of the Post Office.[4] The great watershed in bureaucratic development, however, was the Civil War when many new officials were hired. The war revealed the federal government's administrative weakness and spurred reformers' demands for a better civil service. Finally, the war was followed by rapid industrialization and the emergence of a national economy. The effects of these developments could no longer be managed by state governments acting alone.

More than 200,000 new federal employees were added from 1861 to 1901, many of them in new agencies created to deal with the new national economy, such as the Pension Office; the Departments of Agriculture, Labor, and Commerce; and the National Bureau of Standards. These agencies had one thing in common: their role was to serve—to do research, gather statistics, pass out benefits—but not to regulate. Not until the Interstate Commerce Commission (ICC) was created in 1887 did the federal government begin to regulate the economy (other than by managing the currency).

Late-nineteenth-century federal officials tended to avoid seeing themselves as regulators for several reasons. Belief in limited government and states' rights, and fear of concentrated discretionary power—the values that had shaped the Constitution—were still strong. And under the prevailing interpretation of the Constitution, only Congress had the power to regulate commerce among the states; any agency (such as the ICC) to which Congress might delegate its regulatory authority could function only if Congress first set down clear standards that would govern the agency's decisions. As late as 1935, the Supreme Court held that a regulatory agency could only apply the standards enacted by Congress. The Court's view was that the legislature may delegate its powers neither to the president nor to an administrative agency.[5]

These restrictions on what administrators could do were set aside during wartime: World War I, for example, saw an enormous expansion of government regulation of the economy.[6] Extraordinary grants of power generally ended with the war, but some changes in the bureaucracy did not. From the Civil War to the Vietnam War, each major conflict brought a sharp increase in the number of the government's civilian (as well as military) employees. And though there was some reduction in personnel afterwards, each war left a larger number of federal employees than before.[7]

A Change in Role

The bureaucracy as we know it is largely a product of two events: the Depression of the 1930s (and the concomitant New Deal programs of President Roosevelt) and World War II. Though many agencies have been added since, the basic features of the bureaucracy were set mainly as a result of changes in public attitudes and constitutional interpretation that occurred during these periods. The government was now expected to play an active role in dealing with economic and social problems. Reversing its earlier decisions, the Supreme Court began to uphold as constitutional laws that permitted Congress merely to authorize agencies to make whatever decisions seemed necessary to solve a problem or to serve "the public interest."[8]

World War II was the first occasion during which the government made heavy use of federal income taxes—on individuals and corporations—to finance its activities. Income taxes had been small between 1913 (when they were first authorized by the Sixteenth Amendment) and 1940 (when the average American paid only $7 in federal taxes). But between 1940 and 1945, total federal tax collections increased from about $5 billion to nearly $44 billion, and the end of the war brought no substantial tax reduction. World War II thus created the first great financial boom for the government, permitting the sustained expansion of a great variety of programs that in turn supported a large number of administrators.[9]

THE FEDERAL BUREAUCRACY TODAY

Presidents like to claim that the number of civilians working for the federal government has not increased significantly in recent years and is about the same today (3.2 million persons) as it was in 1970, and less than it was during World War II.[10] But this ignores the fact that as many as four persons earn their living *indirectly* from the federal government for every one person earning it directly. While federal employment has remained more or less stable, employment among federal contractors and consultants and in state and local governments has mushroomed.

The power of the bureaucracy cannot be measured by the number of employees, but rather by the extent to which appointed officials have **discretionary authority**—that is, their ability to choose courses of action and to make policies that are not spelled out in advance by law. In Figure 9.2 we see that the volume of regulations issued and the amount of money spent have risen much faster than the number of employees who write the regulations and spend the money.

By this test, the power of the federal bureaucracy has grown enormously. Congress has delegated substantial authority to administrative agencies in three areas: (1) paying subsidies to particular groups and organizations in society (farmers, veterans, retired people, scientists, schools, universities, hospitals); (2) transferring money from the federal government to state and local governments (the grant-in-aid program described in Chapter 3); and (3) devising and enforcing regulations (such as the pure food and drug laws). Congress closely monitors some of these administrative functions, such as grants-in-aid to the states; others, such as the regulatory programs, often

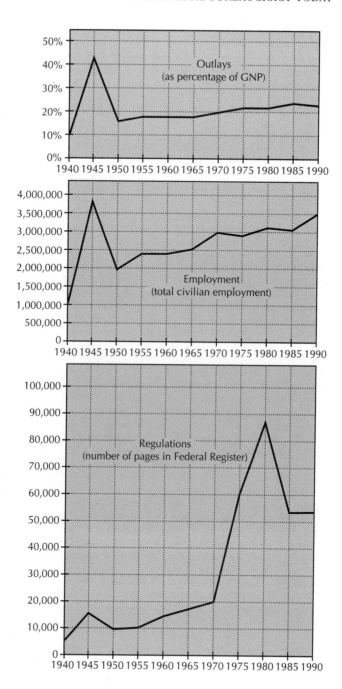

FIGURE 9.2 The Growth of the Federal Government in Money, People, and Rules, 1940–1990

SOURCES: Outlays: *Statistical Abstract of the United States, 1992,* Table 491 and *Historical Statistics of the United States,* Series F–32 and Y–340. Civilian employment and pages in the *Federal Register:* Harold W. Stanley and Richard G. Niemi, *Vital Statistics on American Politics,* 3d ed. (Washington, D.C.: CQ Press, 1992), Tables 8–8, 8–10.

operate with a large degree of independence. These delegations of authority, especially in the areas of paying subsidies and regulating the economy, did not become commonplace until the 1930s, and then only after the Supreme Court decided that such delegations were constitutional.

Delegated authority now permits appointed officials to decide, within rather broad limits, who shall own a television station, what safety features automobiles shall have, what kinds of scientific research shall be especially encouraged, what drugs shall appear on the market, which dissident groups shall be investigated, what fumes an industrial smokestack may emit, which corporate mergers shall be allowed, what use shall be made of national forests, and what price farmers shall receive for their products.

If appointed officials have this kind of power, then how they use it is crucial to understanding modern government. There are, broadly, four factors that explain the behavior of these officials:

1. The manner in which they are recruited and rewarded

2. Their personal attributes, such as their socioeconomic backgrounds and their political attitudes

3. The nature of their jobs: roles and mission

4. The way in which outside forces—political superiors, legislators, interest groups, journalists—influence how bureaucrats behave

Recruitment and Retention

About 62 percent of all appointed officials are part of the **competitive service.** This means that they are initially appointed only after they have passed a written examination administered by the Office of Personnel Management (OPM) or have met certain selection criteria devised by the hiring agency and approved by the OPM.

The other 38 percent of the civilian employees are part of the **excepted service**—that is, they are not appointed on the basis of qualifications designed or approved by the OPM. Most of these, however, are also appointed on a nonpartisan basis by various agencies that have merit-based appointment systems independent of the one run by the OPM. These include Postal Service employees, FBI agents, intelligence agents, foreign-service officers in the State Department, and doctors in the Public Health Service and the Department of Veterans' Affairs.

Some of the excepted employees—probably no more than 3 percent—are appointed on grounds other than or in addition to merit, narrowly defined. These legal exceptions exist to permit the president to select, for policy-making and politically sensitive posts, people who are in agreement with his policy views. Whereas in the nineteenth century practically every federal job was a patronage job, political appointments today constitute only a tiny fraction of all federal jobs. Such appointments are generally of three kinds:

1. **Presidential appointments** authorized by statute (cabinet and subcabinet officers, judges, U.S. marshals and U.S. attorneys, ambassadors, and members of various boards and commissions)
2. **Schedule C jobs** described as having a "confidential or policy-determining character" below the level of cabinet or subcabinet posts (including executive assistants, special aides, and confidential secretaries)
3. **Noncareer Executive Assignments** (NEA jobs) given to high-ranking members of the regular competitive civil service or to people brought into the civil service at these high levels as advocates of presidential programs or as participants in policy-making

The Buddy System

The actual recruitment of civil servants, especially in the middle- and upper-level jobs, is somewhat more complicated, and slightly more political, than the laws and rules might suggest. Though many people enter the federal bureaucracy by learning of a job opening, filling out an application, perhaps taking a test, and being hired, many also enter on a name-request basis. A **name-request job** is filled by a person whom an agency has already identified. In this respect, the federal government is not so different from private business: the head of a bureau decides in advance whom to hire. The agency must still send a form describing the job to the OPM, but it also names the person it wishes to get. Occasionally this name-request job is offered to a person at the insistence of a member of Congress who wants to repay a political supporter; more often it is made available because the bureaucracy itself has identified the individual it wishes to hire and wants to circumvent an elaborate search. This is sometimes called the "buddy system."

The buddy system does not necessarily produce poor employees. Indeed, it is often a way of hiring able people who are known quantities with specific skills. But it also opens up the possibility of hiring people whose policy views are congenial to those already in office. Bureaucrats in consumer-protection agencies, for example, recruit new staff from private groups with an interest in consumer protection, such as the various organizations associated with Ralph Nader, or from academics who have a proconsumer orientation.

Senior Executive Service

With the passage of the Civil Service Reform Act of 1978, Congress recognized that many high-level positions in the civil service have important policy-making responsibilities and that the president and his cabinet officers ought to have more flexibility in recruiting such people. Accordingly the law created a Senior Executive Service (SES) of about eight thousand top federal managers who could be hired, fired, and transferred more easily than ordinary civil servants. Moreover, members of the SES would be eligible for substantial cash bonuses if they were judged to have performed their duties well. (To protect the rights of SES members, anyone who is removed from the SES is guaranteed a job elsewhere in the government.)

Things did not work out quite as the sponsors of the SES had hoped. Only a modest proportion of higher-ranking positions in agencies were filled by transfers from other agencies; the cash bonuses did not prove to be an important incentive; and hardly any members of the SES were actually fired.

The great majority of bureaucrats who are part of the civil service and do not hold presidential appointments have jobs that are, for all practical purposes, beyond reach. Realistically no one is fired unless his or her superior is prepared to invest a great deal of time and effort in the attempt. In 1987 fewer than two-tenths of 1 percent of all civil-service employees were fired for misconduct or poor performance. Such a state of affairs would be inconceivable in any private organization. To cope, political executives devise various stratagems for bypassing or forcing out civil servants with whom they cannot work effectively.

Agency Point of View

When one realizes that most agencies are staffed with people recruited by that agency, sometimes on a name-request basis, and who are virtually immune to dismissal, it becomes clear that the recruitment and retention policies of the civil service ensure that most bureaucrats will share the agency's point of view. Even with the encouragement for transfers created by the SES, in 1980 only 10 percent of the people appointed to the three top civil-service grades in a given agency came from other agencies.[11]

The Senior Executive Service is not likely to change this pattern. Most government agencies are dominated by people who have grown up in that agency, have not served in any other agency, and have been in government service most of their lives. This situation has some advantages: most bureaucrats are expert in the procedures and policies of their agencies, and a substantial continuity in agency policy will be maintained, no matter which political party is in power. But it has costs as well. Political executives entering an agency and responsible for shaping its direction will discover that they must carefully win the support of their career subordinates. A subordinate has an infinite capacity for discreet sabotage and can make life miserable for a political superior by delaying action, withholding information, following the rule book with literal exactness, or appealing to those senators or representatives sympathetic to the bureaucrat's point of view.

Personal Attributes

Another factor that shapes the way bureaucrats behave is their personal attributes: social class, education, and personal political beliefs. The federal civil service looks very much like a cross section of American society in the education, sex, race, and social origins of its members (see Figure 9.3). But at the

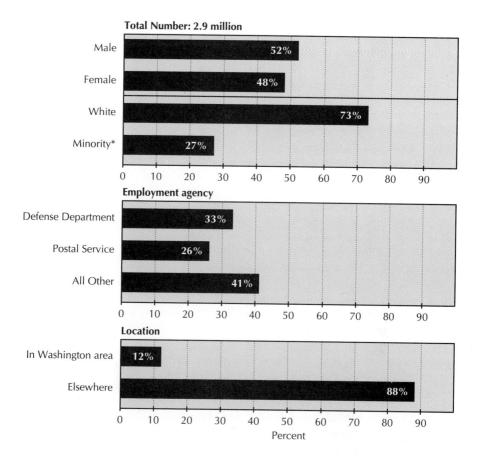

FIGURE 9.3 Characteristics of Federal Civilian Employees, 1990

ᵃBlack, Oriental, Native American, and Hispanic.

SOURCE: *Statistical Abstract of the United States, 1992,* Tables 514, 515, 517, 522.

higher-ranking levels where the most power is found, the typical civil servant is very different from the typical American. In the great majority of cases, the individual is a middle-aged white male with a college degree whose upbringing was somewhat more advantaged than the average (see Table 9.1).

Because the higher civil service is unrepresentative of the average American, some people speculate that people holding these top jobs think and act in ways very different from most Americans. Depending on their politics, these critics have concluded that the bureaucracy is either more conservative or more liberal than the country it helps govern.[12]

A recent survey of the attitudes of some two hundred top-level, nonpolitical federal bureaucrats suggests that they are, in fact, slightly more liberal than the average American voter, but considerably less liberal than key members of the media. About 56 percent of those interviewed in 1982 described themselves as liberals and said they had voted for the Democratic candidate for

TABLE 9.1 Women, Black, and Total Minority Employment in the Federal Bureaucracy, by Rank, 1990

Grade	% Female	% Black	% All minorities[a]
Lowest	75 (GS 1–6)	29 (GS 1–4)	42 (GS 1–4)
Moderate Low	51 (GS 7–10)	23 (GS 5–8)	33 (GS 5–8)
Moderate	30 (GS 11–12)	12 (GS 9–12)	21 (GS 9–12)
Moderate High	14 (GS 13–15)	6 (GS 13–15)	13 (GS 13–15)
Supergrades	7 (GS 16–18)	5 (GS 16–18)	8 (GS 16–18)
Totals, overall	48	17	27

[a]"All minorities" includes blacks, Native Americans, Orientals, and Hispanics.

SOURCE: *Statistical Abstract of the United States, 1992,* Tables 515, 522.

president in 1968, 1972, 1976, and 1980. (By contrast, a much smaller proportion of voters think of themselves as liberals, and most voted for Republican presidential candidates in 1968, 1972, and 1980.) But on most specific policy questions, bureaucrats do not have extreme positions. However, the kind of agency for which a bureaucrat works makes a difference. Those employed in "activist" agencies, such as the Federal Trade Commission, Environmental Protection Agency, and Food and Drug Administration, have much more liberal views than those who work for more traditional agencies, such as the departments of Agriculture, Commerce, and Defense.[13] (See Table 9.2.)

This association between attitudes and the kind of agency has been confirmed by other studies. Even when the bureaucrats come from roughly the same social backgrounds, their policy views seem to reflect the kind of government work they do. For example, those holding foreign-service jobs in the State Department are usually more liberal than those coming from similar family backgrounds who perform similar tasks in the Defense Department.[14] It is not clear whether the jobs produce these differences in attitudes or whether certain jobs attract people with certain beliefs. Probably both forces are at work.

We have only fragmentary evidence of the extent to which these differences in attitudes affect bureaucratic behavior. It may seem obvious that individuals will act in accordance with their beliefs, but that common-sense observation is only true when the nature of the job allows people to make decisions based on their beliefs. Sociologists call the different things people do in their lives **roles** and distinguish between roles that are loosely structured (such as being a voter) and those that are highly structured (such as being an air traffic controller). Personal attitudes greatly affect loosely structured roles and only slightly affect highly structured ones. Applied to the federal bureau-

TABLE 9.2 Political Attitudes of High-Level Federal Bureaucrats

Attitude	Percentage agreeing		
	All bureaucrats	"Traditional" agencies	"Activist" agencies
I am a liberal.	56%	48%	63%
I voted for:			
Humphrey (1968)	72	67	76
McGovern (1972)	57	47	65
Carter (1976)	71	65	76
Carter (1980)	45	34	55
Less regulation of business is good for the U.S.	61	66	57
U.S. military should be the strongest in the world, regardless of cost.	25	31	19
Women should get preference in hiring.	34	28	40
Blacks should get preference in hiring.	44	35	53
Homosexuality is wrong.	47	54	40
Nuclear plants are safe.	52	58	46

SOURCE: Stanley Rothman and S. Robert Lichter, "How Liberal Are Bureaucrats?" *Regulation* (Nov./Dec. 1983), pp. 17–18.

cracy, this suggests that civil servants performing tasks that are routinized (such as filling out forms), tasks that are closely defined by laws and rules (such as issuing welfare checks), or tasks that are closely monitored by others (such as supervisors, special-interest groups, or the media) will probably perform them in ways that are not much affected by their personal attitudes. But civil servants performing complex, loosely defined tasks that are not closely monitored may carry out their work in ways powerfully influenced by their attitudes.

One personal attribute has a clear effect on bureaucratic behavior—the **professional values** of a civil servant. An increasing number of bureaucrats are employed because they are lawyers, economists, engineers, and physicians. The values and ways of thinking that these professionals learned in training for their profession tend to weigh heavily when they make important policy decisions. For example, lawyers and economists in the Federal Trade Commission may differ over what kinds of antitrust cases to prosecute: the lawyers prefer to take on smaller cases they believe can be won, and the economists favor big cases that represent the greatest potential savings to consumers.

Roles and Mission

The tasks people are given often explain more of their behavior than the attitudes they have or the way in which they are hired or fired. We have already seen how a highly structured role often powerfully affects behavior, notwithstanding personal attitudes. But even a loosely structured role is also shaped by forces inside the bureaucracy that civil servants cannot easily ignore—especially those doctrines and attitudes that the agency instills in them and expects them to recall when they exercise discretionary authority.

When an organization has a clear view of its purpose and methods, a view that is widely shared by its members, we say it has a sense of **mission.** Some federal agencies have a sense of mission; some do not. The Forest Service, the Federal Bureau of Investigation, and the Public Health Service are examples of agencies that have, or have had, a powerful sense of mission.[15] This leads to easier management, higher morale, and tighter controls on behavior. But it also makes such organizations hard to change and sometimes resistant to political direction. This dilemma—whether to indoctrinate organization members with a sense of the mission of the agency or to keep them accountable to the public—is one of the central problems of bureaucratic government.

In addition to a consciously developed sense of mission, constraints are imposed on bureaucrats by government rules and laws. Civil-service regulations on hiring and firing staff, already discussed, are one example of these. There are many others:

★ The Freedom of Information Act gives citizens the right to inspect most of the files and records of agencies.

★ Various laws require careful accounting of all money spent.

★ Laws and orders oblige agencies to provide equal opportunities to minorities and women when hiring employees.

★ Environmental impact statements must be compiled before certain construction projects are undertaken.

★ The Administrative Procedure Act requires that interested people be notified of, and be given a chance to comment on, proposed new rules and be afforded an opportunity to introduce evidence at hearings that must be held before certain rules can be enforced.

Perhaps the most important constraint on bureaucratic power is that agencies are complicated organizations, the component parts of which do not always see things the same way. Before action can be taken, one part of an agency must consult with another part and get its agreement, and sometimes that agency must then consult with other agencies. This is called the process of **concurrences** and reflects the fragmentation of power in our government. Action requires persuading—rather than ordering—other people to go along. These constraints do not mean that the bureaucracy is feeble, but they do

For all their complaints about "bureaucrats," Americans like and find helpful most government employees with whom they have contact, such as this forest ranger.

mean that it is often easier to block an action than to implement one. Decisive action is likely only on those matters where just a few people need agree or where the action has little public visibility. In Washington, there are almost no such matters.

These limits on bureaucratic power are not obvious to people who object to how that power is used. But they are all too obvious to those who enter the government eager to take power and use it for what they regard as good ends.

External Forces

Bureaucrats do not operate in a vacuum. They exist in a constellation of political forces in and out of government that affect agency behavior. There are at least seven external forces with which a government bureau must cope: executive branch superiors (such as cabinet officers), the White House (especially the president's staff), congressional committees, interest groups, the media, the courts, and rival government agencies.

Not every agency is equally exposed to these external sources of influence. Much depends on the task the agency performs, the degree of public or political interest in the agency, and the extent to which those affected by its actions are organized, knowledgeable, and effective.

At the most general level, one can distinguish between those agencies that are more oriented toward presidential control and those that are more sensitive to congressional control. All of these agencies are nominally subordinate to the president; the difference in orientation is the result of political forces. **Presidential agencies** include those that carry out policies that do not distribute benefits among significant groups, regions, or localities within the United States. Thus they do not (usually) affect important congressional constituencies, or at least do not affect them differently in different places. They include the State, Treasury, and Justice departments, the Central Intelligence Agency, the Office of the Secretary of Defense, and the Arms Control and Disarmament Agency.

Congressional agencies are those whose actions have a more pronounced distributional effect within the country; among them are the departments of Agriculture, Interior, Housing and Urban Development, and Veterans Affairs; the Army Corps of Engineers; and the Small Business Administration. Many other agencies have neither a presidential nor a congressional orientation and can act somewhat independently of both.

Desire for Autonomy

Government bureaucrats, like people generally, prefer to be left alone so they can do their work as they wish. When they are left more or less alone, free of conflict with bureaucratic rivals and without close political supervision, we say an agency has **autonomy.** All agencies would like more autonomy than they have, and some have managed to get a great deal. The FBI, by skillful publicity and by some striking investigative successes, developed such strong public support during its first forty-five years that it was virtually immune to criticism, and thus to serious presidential or congressional supervision. It had acquired autonomy to an enviable degree. When the National Aeronautics and Space Administration (NASA) succeeded in landing a man on the moon, it was at the crest of a wave of popular support that conferred upon it substantial autonomy. But autonomy, like beauty, invariably fades. In the 1970s, when the FBI was publicly shown to have exceeded its powers, it lost much of its autonomy and came under the most searching congressional inspection and supervision. After the space shuttle Challenger exploded in 1986, NASA was subject to scathing criticism.

Agency Allies

Since many federal agencies were created explicitly to promote some sector of society—agriculture, business, labor, environmentalism, minorities—it is hardly surprising that organizations representing those sectors should have substantial influence over the agencies designed to serve them. Such relations exist between the American Legion (and other veterans' groups) and the Department of Veterans Affairs, the AFL–CIO and the Department of Labor, the NAACP and the Equal Employment Opportunity Commission, and the Environmental Defense Fund and the Environmental Protection Agency. These interest groups lobby to ensure that their favored agencies have ade-

The Treasury Department, because it does things (like print money) affecting the nation as a whole, is of less interest to Congress than the Transportation Department (headed by Federico Peña) because the latter's decisions affect particular localities—and thus particular congressional districts—differently.

quate funds and legal powers—and protest when the agency acts contrary to what the group prefers.

Given the conflict-ridden political environment that most government agencies face, these bureaucracies have a powerful incentive to develop strong allies in the private sector. They must often pay a price for that alliance, however, by deferring to the policy preferences of the ally.

Some scholars view these agency–interest group relations as so close that they speak of the agency as having been **captured** by the interest group and thus the interest group as having become the agency's client. This, indeed, happens. For example, it is inconceivable that the Department of Labor would ever recommend to Congress a decrease in the minimum wage even though many economists believe that a high minimum wage increases unemployment. The AFL-CIO would not tolerate such a position.

Iron triangle is another phrase often used to describe how external forces sometimes heavily influence agency decisions. Supposedly the three points on the triangle are:

1. An agency

2. An interest group

3. A congressional committee that ensures that the agency takes the views of the interest group seriously

An example of an iron triangle is the Department of Veterans' Affairs, organized veterans (such as the American Legion), and the House and Senate Veterans' Affairs committees.

Conflict Among Interest

"Iron triangle" is a vivid journalistic phrase that, while sometimes accurate, is often misleading. Most agencies are not part of a triangle, and what they are part of is not made of iron. The influences on agency behavior are too complex to be described by a simple piece of geometry. Many, probably most, agencies must deal with many conflicting interest groups and several, often conflicting, congressional committees and subcommittees. A secretary of agriculture will, of course, listen to farmers—but *which* farmers? Those in the National Farmers' Union (NFU), which favors high government subsidies, or those in the American Farm Bureau Federation (AFBF), which supports a phasing out of farm subsidies? Because a choice of interest-group allies is possible, we have had agriculture secretaries who have opposed high subsidies, those who have favored them, and those who have tried to take a middle-of-the-road position.[16]

In some agencies the conflict among interest groups is even sharper. The Occupational Safety and Health Administration must deal with corporations that oppose strict or expensive safety standards and labor unions that favor them; the Office for Civil Rights will hear from women's groups that want strong pressure placed on universities to hire more women professors and from universities that believe their hiring practices are already fair.

CONGRESSIONAL OVERSIGHT

Some interest groups are important to agencies mainly because they are important to Congress. Not every interest group in the country has substantial access to Congress, but those that do and that are taken seriously by the relevant committees or subcommittees must also be taken seriously by the agency. Furthermore, even apart from interest groups, members of Congress have constitutional powers over agencies and policy interests in how agencies function.

Congressional supervision of the bureaucracy takes several forms. First, no agency may exist (except for a few presidential offices and commissions) without congressional approval. Congress influences—and sometimes determines precisely—agency behavior by the statutes it enacts. In the past, Congress passed statutes that gave broad discretion to regulatory agencies, such as the Federal Communications Commission, but since the 1960s Congress has tended to sharply restrict agency discretion.

Second, no money may be spent unless it has first been authorized and appropriated by Congress. **Authorization** legislation originates in a legislative committee (such as Agriculture, Education and Labor, or Public Works) and states the maximum amount of money an agency may spend on a given program. This authorization may be permanent, it may be for a fixed number of years, or it may be annual (that is, it must be renewed each year or the program or agency goes out of business). Today most federal spending is done on the basis of permanent authorizations, especially the funds used to pay Social Security benefits and hire military personnel. Increasingly, however, there has been a trend toward annual authorizations to enable Congress to strengthen its control over certain executive agencies. Foreign aid, the State Department, NASA, and the procurement of military equipment by the Defense Department are now subject to annual authorizations.

Third, even funds that have been authorized by Congress cannot be spent unless (in most cases) they are also **appropriated.** Appropriations are usually made annually, and they originate not with the legislative committees but with the House Appropriations Committee and its various (and influential) subcommittees. An appropriation may be, and often is, for less than the amount authorized. The Appropriations Committee's action thus tends to have a budget-cutting effect. Some funds can be spent without an appropriation, but in virtually every part of the bureaucracy each agency is keenly sensitive to congressional concerns at the time that the annual appropriations process is going on.

The Appropriations Committee and Legislative Committees

Since an agency budget must be both authorized and appropriated, each agency serves not one congressional master but several, and these masters may be in conflict. The real power over an agency's budget is exercised by the Appropriations Committee; the legislative committees are especially important when a substantive law is first passed, when the agency is first created, or when an agency is subject to annual authorization.

The power of the Appropriations Committee in the past was rarely challenged: from 1947 through 1962, 90 percent of its recommendations on expenditures were approved by the full House without change.[17] Furthermore, the Appropriations Committee tends to recommend less money than an agency requests (except for some especially favored agencies, such as the FBI, the Soil Conservation Service, and the Forest Service). Finally, the process of **marking up** (revising, amending, and approving) an agency's budget requests gives the Appropriations Committee, or one of its subcommittees, substantial influence over the policies the agency follows.

The legislative and budget committees have begun to reclaim some of the power over agencies exercised by the Appropriations Committee by getting laws passed that entitle people to certain benefits (for example, Social Security or retirement payments) and creating **trust funds** to pay for them. These funds are not subject to annual appropriations. Legislative committees have also gained influence by making their annual authorizations more detailed and specific.[18]

There are informal ways by which Congress can control the bureaucracy. An individual member of Congress can call an agency head on behalf of a constituent—generally only to obtain information but sometimes to secure (or attempt to secure) special privileges. Congressional committees may also obtain the right to pass on certain agency decisions. This is called **committee clearance,** and though it is usually not legally binding on the agency, few agency heads will ignore the express wish of a committee chairperson that he or she be consulted before certain actions are taken.

The Legislative Veto

In the decades before 1983, Congress made increasing use of a technique for controlling both the president and the bureaucracy called the **legislative veto.** Here is an example of how it worked: Congress would pass a law giving the Federal Trade Commission (FTC) broad powers to regulate business practices. But included in the law would be a provision saying that before the FTC could issue a specific regulation (for instance, one affecting used-car dealers), it would have to send the proposed regulation to Congress. The regulation would not go into effect if, within a certain period of time (usually sixty or ninety days), either house of Congress passed a resolution that disapproved of—vetoed—the regulation. Sometimes the veto could be exercised by only one house; sometimes its exercise required the disapproval of both houses. Between 1932 and 1980, about two hundred laws were passed providing for a legislative veto. The idea behind them was to give to the executive branch broad authority (thus relieving Congress of the need to write detailed laws) but to reserve for Congress the power to block the exercise of that authority in particular cases.

Unlike a law, such veto resolutions did not have to be signed by the president. And that was their undoing. In 1983, in the *Chadha* case, the Supreme Court declared the legislative veto unconstitutional, ruling that Congress cannot take any action that has the force of law unless the president concurs in that action.[19] With a stroke of the pen, parts of some two hundred laws suddenly became invalid.

This decision may have a profound effect on congressional oversight of the bureaucracy if it means that Congress can no longer grant sweeping power to some agency, secure in the knowledge that it can later veto any specific action it does not like. But no one is yet quite certain whether that will happen. In fact, since the *Chadha* decision, Congress has passed a number of laws that contain legislative vetoes despite the Supreme Court's having ruled against them. (Somebody will have to go to court to test the constitutionality of these new provisions.) Opponents of the legislative veto hope that future Congresses will have to pass laws that state much more clearly than before what an agency may or may not do. But it is just as likely that Congress will continue to pass laws stated in general terms and require that agencies implementing those laws report their plans to Congress so that it will have a chance to enact and send to the president a regular bill disapproving of the proposed action. Or Congress may rely on informal (but scarcely weak) means of persuasion, including threats to reduce the appropriations of an agency that does not abide by congressional preferences.

Congressional Investigations

Perhaps the most visible and dramatic form of congressional supervision of an agency is the investigation. Since 1792 congressional investigations of the bureaucracy have been a regular feature—sometimes constructive, sometimes debasing—of legislative-executive relations. The investigative power is not mentioned in the Constitution but has been inferred from the power to legislate. The Supreme Court has consistently upheld this interpretation, though it has also said that such investigations should not be held solely to expose the purely personal affairs of private individuals and must not operate to deprive citizens of their basic rights.[20] Congress may compel a person to attend an investigation by issuing a subpoena. Anyone who ignores the subpoena may be punished for contempt: Congress can vote to send the person to jail or can refer the matter to a court for further action. As explained in Chapter 8, the president and his principal subordinates have refused to answer certain congressional inquiries on grounds of executive privilege.

Although many methods of congressional oversight—budgetary review, personnel controls, investigations—are designed to control the exercise of bureaucratic discretion, other provisions are intended to ensure the freedom of certain agencies from effective control, especially by the president. In dozens of cases Congress has authorized department heads and bureau chiefs to operate independently of presidential preferences. Congress has resisted, for example, presidential efforts to ensure that policies to regulate pollution do not impose excessive costs on the economy, and interest groups have brought suit to prevent presidential coordination of various regulatory agencies. If the bureaucracy sometimes works at cross-purposes, it is usually because Congress—or competing committees in Congress—wants it that way.

BUREAUCRATIC "PATHOLOGIES"

Everyone complains about bureaucracy in general (though rarely about bureaucratic agencies that one believes are desirable). This chapter should persuade you that it is difficult to say anything about bureaucracy "in general"; there are too many different kinds of agencies, kinds of bureaucrats, and kinds of programs to label the entire process with a single adjective. Nevertheless, many people who recognize the enormous variety among government agencies still believe that they all have some general features in common and suffer from certain shared problems or pathologies.

This is true enough, but the reasons for it—and the solutions, if any—are often not understood. There are five major problems with bureaucracies: red tape, conflict, duplication, imperialism, and waste. **Red tape** refers to the complex rules and procedures that must be followed to get something done. **Conflict** exists because some agencies seem to be working at cross-purposes with other agencies. **Duplication** occurs when two government agencies seem to be doing the same thing. **Imperialism** refers to the tendency of agencies to grow without regard to the benefits their programs confer or the costs they entail. **Waste** means spending more than what is necessary to buy some product or service.

These problems exist, but not necessarily because bureaucrats are incompetent or power-hungry. Most exist because of the very nature of government itself. Take red tape: it is also found in business and is in part the consequence of bigness. A great amount of governmental red tape also results from the need to satisfy legal and political requirements for fairness, accountability, and citizen access. Or take conflict and duplication: they do not occur because bureaucrats enjoy them. (Quite the contrary!) They exist because Congress, in setting up agencies and programs, often wants to achieve a number of different, partially inconsistent, goals.

Imperialism results largely from government agencies that seek goals so vague and so difficult to measure that it is hard to tell when they have been attained. When Congress is unclear as to exactly what an agency is supposed to do, the agency will often convert that vagueness into bureaucratic imperialism by taking the largest possible view of its powers—sometimes on its own, but more often because interest groups and judges rush to fill the vacuum left by Congress. Thus the Department of Transportation, under pressure from organized groups of handicapped people, converted a vague antidiscrimination provision in the 1973 Rehabilitation Act into a requirement that virtually every big-city bus have a device installed to lift wheelchairs on board—a prohibitively expensive solution to the problem. (The rule was later repealed.)

Waste is probably the biggest criticism that people have of the bureaucracy. Everybody has heard stories of the Pentagon's paying $91 for screws that cost 3 cents in the hardware store. President Reagan's "Private Sector Survey on Cost Control," generally known as the Grace Commission, after its chairman, J. Peter Grace, publicized these and other tales in a 1984 report.

No doubt there is waste in government. After all, unlike a business worried about maximizing profits, a government agency has only weak incentives to keep costs down. If a business employee cuts costs, he or she often receives a bonus or a raise, and the firm gets to add the savings to its profits. If a government official cuts costs, he or she receives no reward, and the agency cannot keep the savings—it goes back to the Treasury.

But many of the horror stories are either exaggerations or unusual occurrences. Most of the screws, hammers, and light bulbs purchased by the government are obtained at low cost by means of competitive bidding among several suppliers. When the government does pay outlandish amounts, the reason typically is that it is purchasing a new or one-of-a-kind item not available at your neighborhood hardware store—for example, a new bomber or missile.

Even when the government is not overcharged, it still may spend more money than a private firm in buying what it needs. The reason is red tape—rules and procedures designed to ensure that when the government buys something, it will do so in a way that serves the interests of many groups. For example, it must often buy from American rather than foreign suppliers even if the latter charge a lower price; it must make use of contractors that employ minorities; it must hire only union laborers and pay them the "prevailing" (that is, the highest) wage; it must allow public inspection of its records; it frequently is required to choose contractors favored by influential members of Congress; and so on. Private firms do not have to comply with all these rules and thus can buy for less.

From this explanation, it should be easy to see why these bureaucratic problems are so hard to correct. To end conflicts and duplication, Congress would have to make some policy choices and set some clear priorities, but with all the competing demands it faces, Congress finds it difficult to do that. You make more friends by helping people than by hurting them, and so Congress is more inclined to add new programs than to cut old ones, whether or not the new programs are in conflict with existing ones. To check imperialism, some way would have to be found to measure the benefits of government, but that is often impossible; government exists in part to achieve precisely those goals that are least measurable. Furthermore, what might be done to remedy some problems would make other problems worse: if you simplify rules and procedures to cut red tape, you are likely also to reduce the coordination among agencies and thus to increase the extent to which there is duplication or conflict. Waste could be reduced, but that might require turning over some government functions to competing private firms.

For all of these reasons, it is a mistake to think of the bureaucracy as some reckless, out-of-control monster. The main problem with executive agencies is not that they have too few controls but that they have too many; not that they are independent of political authority but that they are dependent on many rival authorities; not that they are wantonly wasteful or inefficient but that the system provides them with no incentives to save money and many incentives to spend everything they are given. In short, the problem of bureaucracy is inseparable from the problem of government in general.

SUMMARY

Bureaucracy is characteristic of almost all aspects of modern life, not simply the government. Government bureaucracies, however, pose special problems because they are subject to competing sources of political authority, must function in a constitutional system of divided powers and of federalism, and often have vague goals. The power of bureaucracy should be measured by its discretionary authority, not by the number of its employees or the size of its budget.

War and depression have been the principal sources of bureaucratic growth, aided by important changes in constitutional interpretation in the 1930s that permitted Congress to delegate broad grants of authority to administrative agencies. Congress has sought to check or recover those grants by controlling budgets, personnel, and policy decisions and by the exercise of legislative vetoes—with only partial success. The uses to which bureaucrats put their authority can be explained in part by their recruitment and job security (they have an agency orientation), their personal political views, and the nature of the tasks they are performing.

Many of the popular solutions for the problems of bureaucratic rule—red tape, duplication, conflict, and agency imperialism—fail to take into account that these problems are to a degree inherent in any government that serves competing goals and is supervised by rival elective officials.

SUGGESTED READINGS

Downs, Anthony. *Inside Bureaucracy.* Boston: Little, Brown, 1967. An economist's explanation of why bureaucrats and bureaus behave as they do.

Halperin, Morton H. *Bureaucratic Politics and Foreign Policy.* Washington, D.C.: Brookings Institution, 1974. Insightful account of the strategies by which diplomatic and military bureaucracies defend their interests.

Heclo, Hugh. *A Government of Strangers.* Washington, D.C.: Brookings Institution, 1977. Analyzes how political appointees attempt to gain control of the Washington bureaucracy and how bureaucrats resist those efforts.

Parkinson, C. Northcote. *Parkinson's Law.* Boston: Houghton Mifflin, 1957. Half-serious, half-joking explanation of why government agencies tend to grow.

Rourke, Francis E. *Bureaucracy, Politics, and Public Policy,* 3d ed. Boston: Little, Brown, 1984. Overview of bureaucratic influences on public policy.

Seidman, Harold, and Robert Gilmour. *Politics, Position, and Power,* 4th ed. New York: Oxford University Press, 1986. Perceptive account of relations between the White House and the bureaucracy.

Wilson, James Q. *Bureaucracy.* New York: Basic Books, 1989. How and why government agencies behave as they do.

NOTE: Two important magazines regularly cover the workings of the Washington bureaucracy: the *National Journal* (which appears weekly and has a frequently published index to its articles) and *The Washington Monthly,* which is more irreverent.

10

★ ★ ★

The Judiciary

ON JULY 1, 1987, President Ronald Reagan nominated Judge Robert Bork to be a justice of the United States Supreme Court. On October 23, 1987, after nearly four months of heated debate, the Senate voted, 42 to 58, to reject the nomination. Supporters of Bork argued that he would interpret the Constitution in a way that was faithful to the intent of its Framers. Opponents argued that Bork would interpret the Constitution in a way that would undermine civil rights. Both supporters and opponents produced long lists of prominent people and organizations that shared their views. The political struggle was intense, protracted, and televised. Millions of people watched the Judiciary Committee hearings. The final vote, with few exceptions, followed party lines. Four years later, a similar drama was played out over the nomination of Clarence Thomas. The issues were much the same. He was confirmed as a Justice, but by a very narrow margin.

Only in the United States would the selection of a judge produce so dramatic and bitter a conflict. The reason is simple: Only in the United States do judges play so large a role in making public policy.

One aspect of this power is **judicial review**—the right of the federal courts to declare laws of Congress and acts of the executive branch void and unenforceable if they are judged to be in conflict with the Constitution. Since 1789 the Supreme Court has declared more than one hundred federal laws unconstitutional. In Britain, by contrast, Parliament is supreme, and no court may strike down a law that it passes. As the second Earl of Pembroke is supposed to have said, "A parliament can do anything but make a man a woman and a woman a man." All that prevents Parliament from acting contrary to the (unwritten) constitution of Britain are the consciences of its members and the opinion of the citizens. About sixty nations do have something resembling judicial review, but in only a few cases does this power mean much in practice.[1]

Judicial review is the federal courts' chief weapon in the system of checks and balances on which the American government is based. Today few people would deny the courts the right to decide that a legislative or executive act is unconstitutional—though once that right was controversial. What remains controversial is the method by which such review should be conducted.

There are two competing views, each ardently pressed during the Bork fight. The first holds that judges should only judge—that is, they should confine themselves to applying those rules that are stated in or clearly implied by the language of the Constitution. This is often called the **strict constructionist** approach. The other view argues that judges should discover the general principles underlying the Constitution and its often vague language, amplify those principles on the basis of some moral or economic philosophy, and apply them to the case. This is sometimes called the **activist** approach.

The difference between strict constructionist and activist judges is not necessarily the same as the difference between liberals and conservatives. Fifty years ago judicial activists tended to be conservatives and strict constructionists tended to be liberals; today the opposite is usually the case.

THE DEVELOPMENT OF THE FEDERAL COURTS

Most Founders probably expected the Supreme Court to have the power of judicial review (though they did not say that in so many words in the Constitution), but they did not expect federal courts to play so large a role in making public policy. The traditional view of civil courts was that they judged disputes between people who had direct dealings with each other— they had entered into a contract, for example, or one had dropped a load of bricks on the other's toe—and decided which of the two parties was right. The court then supplied relief to the wronged party, usually by requiring the other person to pay him or her money (damages).

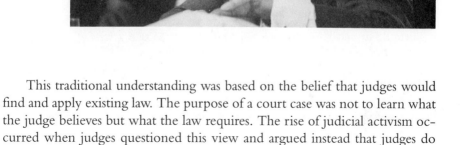

The Senate rejected Robert H. Bork (below) in 1987 and narrowly confirmed Clarence Thomas (left) in 1991 to be Supreme Court justices.

This traditional understanding was based on the belief that judges would find and apply existing law. The purpose of a court case was not to learn what the judge believes but what the law requires. The rise of judicial activism occurred when judges questioned this view and argued instead that judges do not merely find the law, they make the law.

The view that judges interpret the law and do not make policy made it easy for the Founders to justify the power of judicial review and led them to predict—as Hamilton did in *Federalist* No. 78—that the courts would play a relatively neutral, even passive, role in public affairs. Obviously things have changed since Hamilton's time. The evolution of the federal courts, especially the Supreme Court, toward the present level of activism and influence has been shaped by the political, economic, and ideological forces of three historical eras. From 1787 to 1865, the great issues were nation building, the legitimacy of the federal government, and slavery; from 1865 to 1937, the dominant issue was the relationship between government and the economy; from 1938 to the present, the major issues confronting the Court have involved personal liberty and social equality and the potential conflict between

MARBURY V. MADISON

★ ★ ★

The story of *Marbury* v. *Madison* is often told but deserves another telling because it illustrates so many features of the role of the Supreme Court—how apparently small cases can have large results, how the power of the Court depends not simply on its constitutional authority but on its acting in ways that avoid a clear confrontation with other branches of government, and how the climate of opinion affects how the Court goes about its task.

When President John Adams lost his bid for reelection to Thomas Jefferson in 1800, he—and all members of his party, the Federalists—feared that Jefferson and the Republicans would weaken the federal government and turn its powers to what the Federalists believed were wrong ends (states' rights, an alliance with the French, hostility to business). Feverishly, as his hours in office came to an end, Adams worked to pack the judiciary with fifty-nine loyal Federalists by giving them so-called midnight appointments before Jefferson took office.

John Marshall, as Adams's secretary of state, had the task of certifying and delivering these new judicial commissions. In the press of business he delivered all but seventeen; these he left on his desk for the incoming secretary of state, James Madison, to send out. Jefferson and Madison, however, were furious at Adams's behavior and refused to deliver the seventeen. William Marbury and three other Federalists who had been promised these commissions hired a lawyer and brought suit against Madison to force him to produce the documents. The suit requested the Supreme Court to issue a writ of mandamus (from the Latin, "we command") ordering Madison to do his duty. The right to issue such writs had been given to the Supreme Court by the Judiciary Act of 1789.

Marshall, the man who had failed to deliver the commissions to Marbury and his friends in the first place, had become the chief justice and was now in a position to decide the case. These days a justice who had been involved in an

---

the two. In the first period the Court asserted the supremacy of the federal government; in the second it placed important restrictions on the powers of that government; and in the third it enlarged the scope of personal freedom and narrowed that of economic freedom.

National Supremacy and Slavery

Under the leadership of Chief Justice John Marshall, the Supreme Court answered what has been called "that greatest of all the questions left unresolved by the Founders—the nation-state relationship."[2] The Court declared that the national law was in all instances the supreme law, with conflicting state law

issue before it came to the Court would probably disqualify himself or herself, but Marshall had no intention of letting others decide this question. He faced, however, not simply a partisan dispute over jobs but what was nearly a constitutional crisis. If he ordered the commissions delivered, Madison might still refuse, and the Court had no way—if Madison was determined to resist—to compel him. The Court had no police force, whereas Madison had the support of the president of the United States. And if the order were given, whether or not Madison complied, the Jeffersonian Republicans in Congress would probably try to impeach Marshall. On the other hand, if Marshall allowed Madison to do as he wished, the power of the Supreme Court would be seriously reduced.

Marshall's solution was ingenious. Speaking for a unanimous Court, he announced that Madison was wrong to withhold the commissions, that courts could issue writs to compel public officials to do their prescribed duty—*but* that the Supreme Court had no power to issue such writs in this case because the law (the Judiciary Act of 1789) giving it that power was unconstitutional. The law said that the Supreme Court could issue such writs as part of its "original jurisdiction"—that is, persons seeking such writs could go *directly* to the Supreme Court with their request (rather than to a lower federal court and then, if dissatisfied, appeal to the Supreme Court). Article III of the Constitution, Marshall pointed out, spelled out precisely the Supreme Court's original jurisdiction; it did not mention issuing writs of this sort and plainly indicated that on all matters not mentioned in the Constitution, the Court would have only appellate jurisdiction. Congress may not change what the Constitution says; hence the part of the Judiciary Act attempting to do this was null and void.

The result was that a showdown with the Jeffersonians was avoided—Madison was not ordered to deliver the commissions—but the power of the Supreme Court was unmistakably clarified and enlarged. As Marshall wrote, "It is emphatically the province and duty of the judicial department to say what the law is." Furthermore, "a law repugnant to the Constitution is void."

having to give way, and that the Supreme Court had the power to decide what the Constitution meant. In *Marbury* v. *Madison* in 1803 the Court, speaking through Marshall, held that the Supreme Court could declare an act of Congress unconstitutional. (See box.)

In *McCulloch* v. *Maryland,* decided in 1819, the Court, again speaking through Marshall, held that the power granted to the federal government flows from the people and should be generously construed so that any laws "necessary and proper" to the attainment of constitutional ends would be permissible, and that federal law is supreme over state law even to the point that the state may not tax an enterprise (such as a bank) created by the federal government.[3] In other decisions, the Marshall Court asserted broad powers to

John Marshall, chief justice of the United States, 1801– 1835, developed the principles of constitutional interpretation, established the right of the Court to declare acts of Congress unconstitutional, and expanded the powers of the federal government.

review any state court decision if that decision seemed to violate federal law or the federal Constitution, and it upheld the supremacy of federal law in regulating interstate commerce.[4]

All of this may sound rather obvious today, when the supremacy of the federal government is largely unquestioned. In the early nineteenth century, however, these were almost revolutionary decisions. The Jeffersonian Republicans were in power and had become increasingly devoted to states' rights. They were aghast at the Marshall decisions. President Andrew Jackson reportedly said of a later Court ruling he did not like, "John Marshall has made his decision—now let him enforce it!"[5]

In 1836 Roger B. Taney succeeded Marshall as chief justice, deliberately chosen by Andrew Jackson because he was an advocate of states' rights. Taney began to chip away at federal supremacy. But by this time another conflict had arisen that was even more divisive than any previous ones—slavery. In 1857 Taney wrote perhaps the most disastrous judicial opinion ever issued. In the *Dred Scott* case, Taney held that blacks were not citizens of the United States and could not become so, and that the federal law prohibiting slavery in northern territories—the Missouri Compromise—was unconstitutional.[6] The public outcry against this view was enormous, and the Court and Taney were discredited in at least northern opinion. A civil war was fought over what the Court mistakenly had assumed it could treat as a purely legal question.

Government and the Economy

The supremacy of the federal government may have been established by John Marshall and the Civil War, but the scope of the powers of that government, or even of the state governments, was still to be defined. During the period from the end of the Civil War to the early years of the New Deal, the dominant issue the Court faced was to decide under what circumstances the economy could be regulated by state or nation. The Court revealed a strong though not inflexible attachment to private property. In general it developed the view that the Fourteenth Amendment, adopted in 1868 primarily to protect black claims to citizenship from hostile state action, also protected private property and corporations from unreasonable state action. But the Court quickly found itself in a thicket: it began passing on the legality and constitutionality of so many efforts by government to regulate business or labor that its work load rose sharply, and its decisions were often inconsistent.

To characterize the Court during this period as "probusiness" or "antiregulation" is both simplistic and inexact. More accurately it was supportive of the rights of private property but unsure how to draw the lines that would distinguish reasonable from unreasonable regulation. The Court found itself trying to make detailed judgments it was not always competent to make and to invent legal rules where no clear legal rules were possible. In one area, however, the Court's judgments were clear—the Fourteenth and Fifteenth Amendments were construed so narrowly as to give blacks only the most limited benefits of their provisions. In a long series of decisions, the Court upheld segregation in schools and on railroad cars and permitted blacks to be excluded from voting in many states.

The Protection of Political Liberty and Economic Regulation

After 1936, the Supreme Court stopped imposing any serious restrictions on state or federal power to regulate the economy, leaving such matters in the hands of the legislatures. From 1937 to 1974, the Court did not overturn a single federal law designed to regulate business, but it did void thirty-six congressional enactments that violated personal political liberties.

This new direction began when one justice, Owen J. Roberts, changed his mind and began supporting Roosevelt's New Deal measures he had formerly opposed. This was the famous "switch in time that saved nine." Until then the justices had been striking down New Deal legislation by a five-to-four margin, prompting President Roosevelt to attempt to "pack" the Court. The attempt failed, but with Justice Robert's change of mind it was no longer necessary. He had yielded to public opinion in a way that Chief Justice Taney, a century before, had not, thus forestalling an assault on the Court by the other branches of government. Shortly thereafter several justices stepped down, and Roosevelt was able to make his own appointments. From then on, the Court turned its attention to new issues—political liberties and, in time, civil rights.

With the arrival in office of Chief Justice Earl Warren in 1953, the Court began its most activist period yet. The new activism involved the relationship between the citizen and the government and was especially concerned with protecting the rights and liberties of citizens from governmental trespass. In a large measure, the Court has always seen itself as protecting citizens from arbitrary government. Before 1937 that protection was of a sort that conservatives preferred; after 1937 it was of a kind that liberals preferred.

THE STRUCTURE OF THE FEDERAL COURTS

The only federal court that must exist is the Supreme Court, required by Article III of the Constitution. All other federal courts and their jurisdictions are creations of Congress. The Constitution, however, indicates neither how many justices shall be on the Supreme Court (there were originally six, now there are nine) nor what its jurisdiction as an appeals court should be.

Congress has created two kinds of lower federal courts to handle cases that need not be decided by the Supreme Court: constitutional and legislative courts. A **constitutional** court exercises the judicial powers found in Article III of the Constitution and, because of that, its judges are given constitutional protection: they may not be fired (they serve during good behavior) nor may their salaries be reduced while they are in office. The most important of the constitutional courts are the district courts (a total of ninety-four, with at least one in each state, the District of Columbia, and the Commonwealth of Puerto Rico) and the courts of appeals (one in each of eleven regions, or circuits, plus one in the District of Columbia). Certain specialized courts also have constitutional status, such as the Court of International Trade.

A **legislative** court is set up by Congress for some specialized purpose and staffed with persons who have fixed terms of office and can be removed or have their salaries reduced. Legislative courts include the Court of Military Appeals (Figure 10.1).

Since the judges on the constitutional courts serve for life and since they are the chief interpreters of the Constitution, how they are selected and what attitudes they bring to the bench are obviously important. All are nominated by the president and confirmed by the Senate; almost invariably the president nominates a member of his own party. Though presidents do sometimes manage to tilt the Supreme Court in a liberal or conservative direction by the appointments they make, it is not clear that party background makes a great

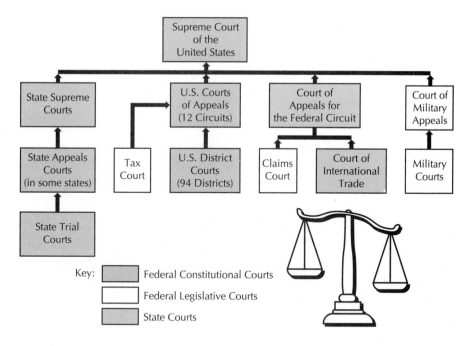

FIGURE 10.1 The Organization of the Federal Courts

deal of difference or even that a president can predict how a judge will be-have. Theodore Roosevelt, Franklin Roosevelt, and Richard Nixon all had reason to complain about the actions of some of their most important Supreme Court appointees—Oliver Wendell Holmes, Jr., Felix Frankfurter, and Warren Burger.[7] Ronald Reagan, an opponent of abortion, was probably disappointed when a justice he nominated, Sandra Day O'Connor, voted to uphold (with restrictions) the right to an abortion.

No president can exercise much control over the lower federal courts, though several have tried. For one thing, who becomes a district judge is heavily influenced by the preferences of the senators from the state in which the vacancy occurs. By the tradition of **senatorial courtesy,** the Senate will not confirm a judicial nominee if the senator from the candidate's state and of the president's party objects. Of late, many senators have created expert screening panels to advise them on candidates for appointment. But the process, of necessity, remains political: nominees who fail to get past their senators have little hope of appointment.

Of the 136 Supreme Court nominees presented to it, the Senate has re-jected 27, though only 5 in this century.[8] (In 1991 the Senate came within a few votes of rejecting Clarence Thomas.) The reasons for rejecting a Supreme Court nominee are complex—each senator may have a different reason—but have involved such matters as a record of hostility to civil rights, questionable personal financial dealing, a poor record as a lower court judge, and (in the

HOW PARTISANSHIP AFFECTS
JUDICIAL ATTITUDES

★ ★ ★

In 1984 more than one hundred federal judges were interviewed to learn about their background and attitudes. Although there were about equal numbers of Democrats and Republicans, they were quite similar in social background. The overwhelming majority were white males; their average age was sixty. Most had attended a prestigious college. Despite these similarities, they expressed quite different political views and applied quite different judicial philosophies.

	Judges appointed by	
Attitudes	**Democrats**	**Republicans**
Political ideology		
Liberal	75%	28%
Conservative	11	37
Policy positions		
Favor less government		
regulation of business	54	85

Bork case) Senate opposition to the nominee's legal philosophy. Nominations of district court judges are rarely defeated because, typically, no nomination is made unless the key senators approve in advance.

The judges who are confirmed in office are almost invariably of the same party as the president who nominated them. And they differ in more ways than their party label. In the box, we see the attitudes expressed by Democratic and Republican judges as of 1984. There were clear differences in ideology (Democrats were far more likely to be liberals than were the Republicans) and on a number of policy issues. These differences have some effect on certain issues the judges decide. But as we shall see, judging is a complex, technical process in which the facts of the case, the content of the law, and higher-court decisions all sharply restrict a judge's freedom to decide a matter in the way he or she may want. In most cases, ideological differences probably do not affect the outcomes.

When they do make a difference, much depends on the circuit in which the case is heard. By 1992, presidents Reagan and Bush had appointed a majority of the judges on most of the circuit courts of appeal, including the important D.C. circuit. But judges appointed by President Carter or earlier

Government should reduce income gap between rich and poor	78	44
Special preference should be given to blacks in hiring	62	41
Special preference should be given to women in hiring	47	22
A woman has the right to decide on abortion	81	80
Judicial philosophy Courts show too much concern for criminals	16	44
Judges should just apply the law, leave the rest to legislators	51	69
Judges need to supervise public bureaucracies	81	64

SOURCE: Althea K. Nagai, Stanley Rothman, and S. Robert Lichter, "The Verdict on Federal Judges," *Public Opinion* (November-December 1987): 52–56. Reprinted with the permission of the American Enterprise Institute for Public Policy Research, Washington, D.C.

presidents still occupied roughly half (in some cases more than half) of the seats on the fourth circuit (Maryland, the Carolinas, and Virginia) and the ninth circuit (California and other western states). Cases in these more liberal circuits are often decided differently than those in more conservative circuits.

Since the 1960s the number of women, blacks, and Latinos appointed to both the district and appeals courts has increased (see Figure 10.2). The biggest increase came under President Carter, but presidents Reagan and Bush continued to add appointees from these groups, especially women.

THE JURISDICTION OF THE FEDERAL COURTS

We have a dual court system—one state, one federal—and this complicates enormously the task of describing what kinds of cases federal courts may hear and how cases beginning in the state courts may end up in the Supreme Court. The Constitution lists the kinds of cases over which federal courts have jurisdiction (in Article III and the Eleventh Amendment); by implication, all other matters are left to state courts. Federal courts can hear all cases

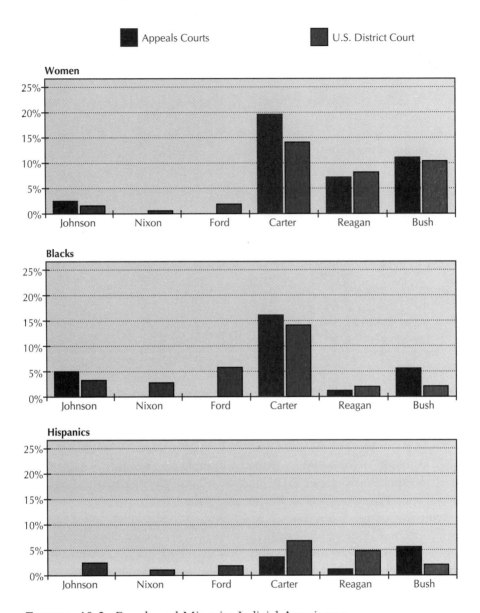

FIGURE 10.2 Female and Minority Judicial Appointees

SOURCE: Reprinted from *Congressional Quarterly Weekly Report,* January 19, 1991, p. 172.

"arising under the Constitution, the laws of the United States, and treaties" (these are **federal question cases**), and cases involving citizens of different states (**diversity cases**). In addition, certain cases can be heard in either federal or state courts. For instance, legal battles between citizens of different states where more than $50,000 is at stake may be heard in either federal or state courts. If a person robs a federally insured bank, he or she has broken both state and federal laws and hence can be prosecuted in either state or federal courts. Lawyers have become quite sophisticated in deciding whether, in a given civil case, their clients will get better treatment in state or federal court. Prosecutors often refer a person who has broken both federal and state law to whichever court system is likely to give the toughest penalty.

Furthermore, a matter that is exclusively in the province of a state court—for example, a criminal case in which the defendant is charged with violating only a state law—can be appealed to the Supreme Court of the United States under certain conditions, discussed below. Thus federal judges can supervise state court rulings even when they have no jurisdiction over the original matter. Under what circumstances this should occur is the subject of long-standing controversy between the state and federal systems.

Some matters, however, are exclusively under the jurisdiction of federal courts. When a federal criminal law is broken—but not a state one—the case is heard in federal district court. If you wish to appeal the decision of a federal regulatory agency, such as the Federal Communications Commission, you can only do so before a federal court of appeals. And if you wish to declare bankruptcy, you do so only in federal court. If there is a controversy between two state governments, the case can only be heard by the Supreme Court.

The vast majority of all cases heard by federal courts begin in the district courts. The volume of business there is huge. In 1990, the 500 or so district court judges received 218,000 civil cases and 48,000 criminal ones. Most of these cases involve rather straightforward applications of the law, and few lead to the making of new public policy. But those that do affect the interpretation of the law or the Constitution can begin with seemingly minor events. For example, a major broadening of the Bill of Rights—requiring for the first time that all accused persons in *state* as well as federal criminal trials be supplied with a lawyer, free if necessary—began when impoverished Clarence Earl Gideon, imprisoned in Florida, wrote an appeal in pencil on prison stationery and sent it to the Supreme Court.[9]

At one time a large number of matters could be appealed directly from district courts to the Supreme Court, but as the latter became overloaded with work, Congress passed laws giving the Court the power to control its work load by selecting, in most instances, the kinds of cases it wanted to hear.

The main route to the Supreme Court is by a writ of certiorari. **Certiorari** is a Latin term that means roughly "made more certain," and describes a procedure the Supreme Court can use whenever, in the opinion of at least four of its members, the decision of the highest state court involves a "substantial federal question" (the Supreme Court decides what that is). This procedure is also invoked when the decision of a federal court of appeals involves the interpretation of federal law or the Constitution. Either side in a case may ask the Supreme Court for certiorari, and the Court can decide whether or not to grant it without divulging its reasons.

THE JURISDICTION OF THE
FEDERAL COURTS

★ ★ ★

SUPREME COURT OF THE UNITED STATES

(1 court with 9 justices)

Original jurisdiction (cases begin in the Supreme Court) over controversies involving:

1. Two or more states

2. The United States and a state

3. Foreign ambassadors and other diplomats

4. A state and a citizen of a different state (if begun by the state)

Appellate jurisdiction (cases begin in another, lower court)
Hears appeals, at its discretion, from:

1. Lower federal courts

2. Highest state court

In exercising its discretion in granting certiorari, the Supreme Court is on the horns of dilemma. If it grants it frequently, it will be inundated with cases. As it is, the work load of the Court has risen from fewer than 900 cases in 1930 to more than 5,000 in recent years. If, on the other hand, the Court grants certiorari only rarely, then the federal courts of appeal have the last word on the interpretation of the Constitution and federal laws, and since there are twelve of these courts staffed by more than 160 judges, they may well be in disagreement. In fact, this diversity of constitutional interpretation has happened: because the Supreme Court reviews only about 1 percent of appeals court cases, applicable federal law may be different in different parts of the country.[10] One proposal to deal with this dilemma would be to devote the Supreme Court's time entirely to major questions of constitutional interpretation and to create a national court of appeals that would ensure that the twelve circuit courts of appeals are producing uniform decisions, but Congress has not found that idea attractive.[11]

UNITED STATES COURTS OF APPEALS

(1 in each of 11 "circuits" or regions plus 1 in the District of Columbia)

Hear only appeals; no original jurisdiction
Appeals from:

1. Federal district courts
2. U.S. regulatory commissions
3. Certain other federal courts

UNITED STATES DISTRICT COURTS

(1 in each of 94 districts)

Have only original jurisdiction; do not hear appeals
Original jurisdiction over cases involving:

1. Federal crimes
2. Civil suits under federal law
3. Civil suits between citizens of different states where the amount exceeds $50,000
4. Admiralty and maritime cases
5. Bankruptcy cases
6. Review of actions of certain federal administrative agencies
7. Other matters assigned to them by Congress

GETTING TO COURT

In theory the courts are the great equalizer in the federal government. To use the courts to settle a question, or even to alter fundamentally the accepted interpretation of the Constitution, one need not be powerful or rich. Once the contending parties are before the court, they are legally equal.

It is too easy to believe this theory uncritically or to reject it cynically. In fact, it is hard to get before the Supreme Court: it rejects about 95 percent of the applications for certiorari it receives. And the costs involved in getting to the Court can be high, though there are ways to lower them. If you are indigent—without funds—you can file and be heard as a pauper for nothing; about half the petitions arriving before the Supreme Court are **in forma pauperis,** such as that from Gideon described earlier. If your case began as a criminal trial in the district courts and you are poor, the government supplies a lawyer at no charge. If the matter is not a criminal case and you cannot afford to hire a lawyer, interest groups representing a wide spectrum of opinion sometimes are willing, if the issue in the case seems sufficiently important, to take up the cause.

Fee Shifting

Unlike most of Europe, each party to a lawsuit in this country must pay its own way. This is called the **American rule.** But various laws have made it increasingly easy to get someone else to pay. **Fee shifting,** as it is called, enables the plaintiff (the party that initiates the suit) to collect its costs from the defendant if the defendant loses. Even more important to individuals, Section 1983 of the *United States Code* allows a citizen to sue anybody acting in some legal capacity—say, a police officer or a school superintendent—who deprives the citizen of some constitutional right or withholds some benefit to which the citizen is entitled. If the citizen wins, he or she can collect money damages and lawyers' fees from the government. There has been a flood of such Section 1983 suits in the courts. The Supreme Court has restricted fee shifting to cases authorized by statute,[12] but it is clear that the drift of policy has made it cheaper for citizens to go to court—at least for some cases. In addition, foundations and private associations called public-interest law firms will sometimes pay the costs of important cases.

Standing

There is an important nonfinancial restriction on getting into federal court. To sue, one must have standing. **Standing** is a legal concept that defines who is entitled to bring a case. It is especially important in determining who can challenge the laws or actions of government itself. A complex and changing set of rules govern standing; some of the important ones are these:

1. There must be an actual controversy between real adversaries, not a "friendly" suit that you hope to lose in order to prove a friend right, nor a hypothetical or imaginary case in which you seek an advisory opinion.

2. You must show that you have been harmed by the law or practice about which you are complaining; it is not enough simply to dislike what the government or a corporation or a labor union does.

3. Merely being a taxpayer does not ordinarily entitle you to challenge the constitutionality of a federal government action. (You may not want your tax money spent in certain ways, but your remedy is to vote against the politicians doing the spending.)

Congress and the courts in recent years have made it easier to acquire standing. It has always been the rule that a citizen could ask the courts to order federal officials to carry out some act that they were under legal obligation to perform (such as issuing a welfare check) or to refrain from some action that was contrary to law. A citizen can also sue a government official personally in order to collect damages if the official acted contrary to law.

However, you cannot sue the government itself without its consent. This is the doctrine of **sovereign immunity.** By statute, Congress has increasingly given its consent for the government to be sued in many cases involving a dispute over a contract or damage done as a result of negligence. Over the years these statutes have made it easier and easier to take the government into court as a defendant.

Even some of the oldest rules defining standing have been liberalized. The rule that merely being a taxpayer does not entitle you to challenge in court a government decision has been relaxed in cases where the citizen claims that a right guaranteed under the First Amendment is being violated. The Supreme Court allowed a taxpayer to challenge a federal law that would have given financial aid to parochial (that is, church-related) schools on the grounds that this aid violated the constitutional separation between church and state. On the other hand, another taxpayer suit to force the CIA to make public its budget failed because the Court decided the taxpayer did not have standing in matters of this sort.[13]

Class-Action Suits

Under certain circumstances individual citizens can benefit directly from a court decision even though they have not gone into court themselves. This can happen by means of a **class-action suit:** a case brought into court by a person on behalf not only of himself or herself but of all other people in similar circumstances. One of the most significant of such cases was the school desegregation decision of the Supreme Court in 1954. In *Brown* v. *Board of Education* it found that Linda Brown, a black girl attending the fifth grade in the Topeka, Kansas, public schools, was denied the equal protection of the laws (guaranteed under the Fourteenth Amendment) because the schools in Topeka were segregated. The Court did not limit its decision to Linda Brown's right to attend an unsegregated school but extended it—as Brown's lawyers from the NAACP had asked—to cover all "others similarly situated."[14] It was not easy to design a court order that would eliminate segregation for black schoolchildren, but the principle was clearly established in this class action.

Many other groups have been quick to take advantage of the opportunity created by class-action suits. By this means, the courts could be used to give relief not simply to a particular person but to all those represented in the suit. Subsequent landmark class-action suits have involved malapportioned state legislatures,[15] civil-rights issues, the rights of prisoners, and antitrust actions against corporations. These suits became more common for three reasons: Congress was not addressing issues of concern to many people; it was often

When Linda Brown was refused admission to a white elementary school in Topeka, Kansas, the NAACP brought suit. The result was the 1954 landmark decision, Brown v. Board of Education, *making segregated schools unconstitutional. Today, in this classroom in Charlotte, North Carolina, black and white children study together.*

easier to make national policy through the courts than through the legislature; and lawyers often found it more profitable to bring a suit on behalf of thousands of people rather than on behalf of just one person.

The resulting flood of class-action suits greatly increased the Supreme Court's work load, and in 1974 it decided to tighten drastically the rules governing these suits. It held that it would not longer hear (except in certain cases defined by Congress, such as civil-rights matters) class-action suits seeking money damages unless each and every ascertainable member of the class was individually notified of the case. To do this is often prohibitively expensive, and so the number of such cases declined and the number of lawyers seeking them dropped.[16]

In sum, getting into court depends on having standing and having resources. The rules governing standing are complex and changing, but generally have been broadened to make it easier to enter the federal courts, especially for the purpose of challenging the actions of the government. Obtaining the resources is not easy but has become easier because laws in some instances now provide for fee shifting, because private interest groups are willing to finance cases, and because it is sometimes possible to bring inexpensively a class-action suit that lawyers find lucrative.

The Supreme Court in Action

If your case should find its way to the Supreme Court—and the odds are that it will not—you will be able to participate in one of the more impressive, sometimes dramatic ceremonies of American public life. The Court is in session in its white marble building for thirty-six weeks out of each year, from early October until the end of June. The nine justices read briefs in their individual offices, hear oral arguments in the large stately courtroom, and discuss their decisions with one another in a conference room where no outsiders are allowed.

Most cases, as we have seen, come to the Court on a writ of certiorari. The lawyers on each side may then submit their **briefs**—documents summarizing the lower-court decision, giving the arguments for their side, and discussing the other cases the Court has ruled on that bear on the issue. Then the lawyers are allowed to present their oral arguments in open court. These usually summarize the briefs or emphasize particular points in them, and are strictly limited in time—usually to no more than half an hour. The oral arguments give the justices a chance to question the lawyers, sometimes searchingly.

Since the federal government is a party—as either plaintiff or defendant—to about half the cases the Supreme Court hears, the government's top trial lawyer, the solicitor general of the United States, appears frequently before the Court. The solicitor general decides what cases the government will appeal from the lower courts and personally approves every case the government presents to the Supreme Court.

In addition to the arguments made by lawyers for both sides, written briefs and even oral arguments may also be offered by "friends of the court," or **amicus curiae.** An amicus brief is from an interested party not directly involved in the suit. For example, when Allan Bakke complained that he had been the victim of reverse discrimination when he was denied admission to a University of California medical school, fifty-eight amicus briefs were filed supporting or opposing his position. Before such briefs can be filed, both parties must agree or the Court must grant permission. These documents are a kind of polite lobbying of the Court which, though they sometimes offer new arguments, generally are a declaration of what interests are on which side. The ACLU, the NAACP, the AFL-CIO, and the United States government itself have been among the leading sources of such briefs.

These briefs are not the only source of influence on the justices' views. Leading legal periodicals, such as the *Yale Law Journal* and the *Harvard Law Review,* are frequently consulted and cited in decisions, so that the outside world of lawyers and law professors can help shape, or at least supply arguments for, the justices' conclusions.

The justices retire to their conference room every Friday where in complete secrecy they debate the cases they have heard. The chief justice speaks

This photo of the Supreme Court in session on February 8, 1932, may be the only one ever taken while the justices were actually hearing a case.

first, followed by the other justices in order of seniority. After the arguments they vote, traditionally in reverse order of seniority. In this process an able chief justice can exercise considerable influence—in guiding or limiting debate, in setting forth the issues, and in handling sometimes temperamental personalities. In deciding a case, a majority of the justices must be in agreement: if there is a tie, the lower-court decision is left standing. (There can be a tie among the nine justices if one is ill or disqualifies himself or herself because of prior involvement in the case.)

Though the vote is what counts, by tradition the Court usually issues a written decision. Sometimes this opinion is brief and unsigned (called a **per curiam** opinion); sometimes it is quite long and signed by the justices agreeing with it. If the chief justice is in the majority, he will either write the opinion or assign its writing to a justice who agrees with him. If he is in the minority, the senior justice on the winning side will decide who writes the Court's opinion. There are four kinds of signed opinions: **unanimous, majority** (the majority opinion of the Court when it is divided), **concurring** (an opinion by one or more justices who agree with the majority's conclusion but for different reasons that they wish to express), and **dissenting** (the opinion of one or more justices on the losing side).

The justices, like any group of people in public life, tend to take consistent positions on public issues and have certain political philosophies. When the Court must decide a case that raises philosophical issues (and that occurs only part of the time), it's not surprising to see rather clear voting blocs emerge. During the 1970s and 1980s, there were often three such blocs: a **liberal/activist bloc** (led by former Justice William Brennan and including former Justice Thurgood Marshall and sometimes Justice Blackmun and former Justice Lewis Powell), a **conservative/strict constructionist bloc** (of former Chief Justice Burger and Justices Rehnquist and O'Connor), and a **swing bloc** (composed of Justices White and Stevens).[17]

With the retirement of Powell, Brennan, Marshall, and Burger and the arrival of Justices Scalia, Kennedy, Souter, and Thomas, the liberal/activist bloc has more or less disappeared. There is now on many issues a conservative/strict-constructionist bloc of about six justices (seven on some issues): Rehnquist, O'Connor, Scalia, Kennedy, Souter, and Thomas, sometimes joined by White. Blackmun and Stevens often are dissenters, but they are not consistently liberal activists, except on the abortion issue.

But on many issues, voting blocs don't appear at all, and when they do appear individual justices may break ranks (as O'Connor did on some abortion cases). Supreme Court cases are complex, difficult issues that require the justices to think through legal precedents, participate in discussions with their colleagues, and react to the facts presented in briefs and the research of their law clerks.

THE POWER OF THE COURTS

The great majority of cases in federal courts have little to do with public policy: people accused of drug smuggling are tried, disputes over contracts are settled, and personal injury cases are heard. In most instances, the courts are simply applying a relatively settled body of law to a specific controversy.

The Power to Make Policy

But sometimes the courts make national policy. They do this whenever they interpret the law or the Constitution in a new way, extend the reach of existing laws to cover matters not previously thought to be covered, or design remedies for problems in ways that require the judges to act in administrative or legislative ways. By these tests, the courts have become exceptionally powerful.

One measure of that power is that more than 120 federal laws have been declared unconstitutional, though since 1937 relatively few of these had broad national significance. On matters where Congress feels strongly, it can often get its way by passing slightly revised versions of the voided law.

A second measure of judicial power is the frequency with which the Supreme Court changes its mind. An informal rule of judicial decision making has been **stare decisis,** meaning "let the decision stand." It is the principle of **precedent**—a court case today should be settled in accordance with prior decisions on similar cases. (What constitutes a similar case is not always clear.) There are two reasons why precedent is important. The practical reason should be obvious: if the meaning of the law continually changes, if the

The Supreme Court in 1993: Seated, left to right: John Paul Stevens, Byron R. White, William H. Rehnquist, Harry A. Blackmun, and Sandra Day O'Connor. Standing, left to right: David Souter, Antonin Scalia, Anthony Kennedy, and Clarence Thomas.

decisions of judges become wholly unpredictable, then human affairs affected by those laws and decisions become chaotic. The other reason is at least as important: if the principle of equal justice means anything, it means that similar cases should be decided in a similar manner. Of course times change and the Court can make mistakes; the Court will then change its mind. But however compelling the arguments for flexibility, the pace of change can become dizzying. By one count, the Court since 1810 has overruled its own previous decisions in more than 140 cases[18]—and in fact it may have done so more often (when it does not say it is abandoning a precedent but is merely distinguishing the present case from a previous one).

The third measure of judicial power is the degree to which courts are willing to handle matters once left to the legislature. The Supreme Court once regarded the determination of congressional district boundaries, for example, as a **political question** that it would leave to another branch of government—in this case, Congress—to decide for itself. Then in 1962 the Court decided that it was competent to deal with this question after all.[19]

A fourth indicator can be found in the kinds of remedies the courts will impose. A **remedy** is a judicial order setting forth what must be done to correct what a judge believes is wrong. In ordinary cases, the remedy is straightforward—for example, the loser pays the winner for some injury to the winner. Today, however, judges design remedies that go far beyond what is required to do justice to the parties who actually appear in court. The remedies now imposed often apply to large groups and affect the circumstances under which thousands or even millions work, study, or live; they affect, for example, inmates in a prison system that a judge orders revamped or people previously ineligible who are declared eligible for welfare.[20]

The basis for these sweeping court orders can sometimes be found in the Constitution. Others are based on court interpretations of federal laws, as when the Supreme Court interpreted the 1964 Civil Rights Act as meaning that the San Francisco school system must teach English to Chinese students unable to speak it.[21] Local courts and legislatures elsewhere decided that that same decision meant that classes must be taught in Spanish for Hispanic children. What Congress meant exactly by the Civil Rights Act's prohibition of discrimination on grounds of "race, color, or national origin" was not clear; what is important is that it was the Court, not Congress, that decided what Congress meant.

Views of Judicial Activism

Judicial activism has, of course, been controversial. Supporters argue that the federal courts must correct injustices when the other branches of the federal government, or the states, refuse to do so. The courts are the last resort for those without the influence to obtain new laws, and especially for the poor and powerless. State legislatures and Congress, after all, tolerated segregated public schools for decades. If the Supreme Court had not declared segregation unconstitutional in 1954, it might still be the law today.

Critics of the activist courts rejoin that judges usually have no special expertise in matters of school administration, prison management, or environmental protection. However desirable court-declared rights and principles may be, implementing those principles means balancing the conflicting needs of various interest groups, raising and spending tax monies, and assessing the costs and benefits of complicated alternatives, all things that judges are not good at. Finally, judges are appointed, not elected, and thus are immune to popular control. As a result, if they depart from their traditional role of making careful and cautious interpretations of what a law or the Constitution means and instead begin formulating wholly new policies, they become unelected legislators.

The Causes of Activism

Some people think that we have activist courts because we have so many lawyers. The more we take matters to courts for resolution, the more likely it is that the courts will become powerful. It is true that we have more lawyers in proportion to our population than most other nations. In 1982 there was one lawyer for every 400 Americans, but only one lawyer for every 1,600 Britons, every 3,400 French, and every 7,000 Japanese.[22] But this may well be a

SUPREME COURT JUSTICES IN ORDER OF SENIORITY, 1993

★ ★ ★

Name (Birthdate)	Home state	Prior experience	Appointed by (Year)
William H. Rehnquist, Chief Justice (1924)	Arizona	Justice; Assistant Attorney General	Reagan (1986) as chief; Nixon (1971) as justice
Byron R. White (1918)	Colorado	Deputy Attorney General	Kennedy (1962)
Harry A. Blackmun (1908)	Minnesota	Federal judge	Nixon (1970)
John Paul Stevens (1916)	Illinois	Federal judge	Ford (1975)
Sandra Day O'Connor (1930)	Arizona	State judge	Reagan (1981)
Antonin Scalia (1936)	New York	Federal judge	Reagan (1986)
Anthony Kennedy (1936)	California	Federal judge	Reagan (1988)
David Souter (1939)	New Hampshire	State judge	Bush (1990)
Clarence Thomas (1948)	Georgia	Federal judge	Bush (1991)

symptom, not a cause, of court activity. We have an adversary culture based on an emphasis on individual rights and an implicit antagonism between people and government. Generally speaking, lawyers do not create cases; contending interests do, thereby generating a demand for lawyers.

A more plausible reason has been the developments, discussed earlier in this chapter, that have made it easier for people to get into court, which in turn increases the number of cases being heard. Between 1961 and 1983 the increase in civil-rights, prisoner-rights, and Social Security cases was phenomenal: civil-rights cases rose by 6,567 percent, Social Security cases by 3,683 percent, and prisoner petitions by 2,490 percent.[23] Such matters are the fastest-growing portion of the courts' civil work load.

An increase in cases will not by itself lead to sweeping remedies. For change to occur, the law must be sufficiently vague to permit judges wide latitude in interpreting it, and the judges must want to exercise that opportunity to the fullest. The Constitution is filled with words of seemingly ambiguous meaning—"due process of law," the "equal protection of the laws," the "privileges and immunities of citizens." Such phrases may have been clear to the Framers, but the Court today finds them equivocal. How the Court has chosen to interpret such phrases has changed greatly over the last two hundred years—and particularly in the last thirty—in ways that can be explained in part by the justices' political beliefs.

Congress has passed laws that also contain vague language, thereby adding immeasurably to the courts' opportunities for designing remedies. Various civil-rights acts outlaw discrimination but do not say how one is to know whether discrimination has occurred or what should be done to correct it if it does occur. Implementation is left to the courts and the bureaucracy. Various regulatory laws empower administrative agencies to do what the "public interest" requires but say little about how the public interest is to be defined. Laws intending to alleviate poverty or rebuild neighborhoods speak of "citizen participation" but fail to identify the citizens who should participate, or how much power they should have.

Even clear laws can induce litigation. Almost every agency that regulates business makes decisions that cause the agency to be challenged in court—by business firms if the regulations go too far, by consumer or labor organizations if they do not go far enough. In 1974 the federal courts of appeal heard 506 cases in which they had to review the decisions of a regulatory agency. In two-thirds of those cases the agency's position was supported; in the other third the agency was overruled.[24] Perhaps one-fifth of those cases arose out of agencies or programs that did not even exist in 1960. The federal government is more likely to be on the defensive in court today than twenty or thirty years ago.

Finally, the attitudes of the judges powerfully affect what they will do, especially when the law gives them wide latitude. There have been very few studies of the attitudes of federal judges, but their decisions and opinions have been extensively analyzed—well enough at least to know that different judges often decide the same case in different ways.[25] Many judges and law professors believe the courts *ought* to make policy, and this belief probably affects what courts actually do.

CHECKS ON JUDICIAL POWER

No institution of government, including the courts, operates without restraint. The fact that judges are not elected does not make them immune to public opinion or to the views of the other branches of government. The importance of these restraints varies from case to case, but in the broad course of history they have been significant.

One restraint exists because of the very nature of courts. A judge has no police force or army; his or her decisions can sometimes be resisted or ignored *if* the resister is not highly visible *and* is willing to risk being caught and charged with contempt of court. For example, praying, Bible reading, and segregation continued in schools all over the country for years after the Supreme Court found them unconstitutional. But the courts' power is usually unchallenged when a failure to comply is easily detected and punished.

Congress and the Courts

Congress has a number of ways of checking the power of the judiciary. It can gradually alter the composition of the judiciary by the kinds of appointments the Senate is willing to confirm or it can impeach judges it does not like. In practice, however, impeachment proceedings can rarely be used to make much of an impact on the federal courts because simple policy disagreements are not generally regarded as adequate grounds for trying to impeach a judge, and most judicial appointments are not challenged.

But policy differences have become a major factor in confirmation hearings. The Senate rejected Robert Bork because it disagreed with his views and came close to rejecting Clarence Thomas because it disagreed with his. (In addition, Thomas had to face charges of sexual harassment brought by a former employee.) To cope with these difficulties, conservative presidents began to nominate candidates who either had not clearly taken a position on controversial issues such as abortion (as Reagan did when he nominated David Souter) or ones whom the Senate would find it difficult to reject on other grounds (as Bush did when he nominated Thomas, a black).

Congress can alter the number of judges, however, and by increasing the number sharply, it can give a president a chance to appoint judges to his liking. Franklin Roosevelt proposed to do this in his 1937 court-packing plan in order to change the political persuasion of the Supreme Court. In 1979, Congress created 152 new federal district and appellate judges to help ease the work load. This bill, combined with normal judicial retirements and deaths, allowed President Carter to appoint more than 40 percent of the federal bench. During and after the Civil War, Congress tried to influence Supreme Court decisions by changing the size of the Court three times in six years.

On rare occasions Congress and the states can also undo a Supreme Court decision interpreting the Constitution by amending that document. The Eleventh Amendment was ratified to prevent a citizen from suing a state in federal court; the Thirteenth, Fourteenth, and Fifteenth, to undo the *Dred Scott* decision regarding slavery; the Sixteenth, to make it constitutional for Congress to pass an income tax; and the Twenty-sixth, to give the vote to eighteen-year-olds in state elections. In 1983, a proposed amendment to authorize prayer in the public schools failed to get the necessary two-thirds vote of the Senate.

Sometimes Congress merely repasses a law that the Court has declared unconstitutional. That has occurred more than thirty times, as when a bill to aid farmers, voided in 1935, was accepted by the Court in a slightly revised form three years later.[26] (In the meantime, of course, the Court had changed its collective mind about the New Deal.)

One of the most powerful potential sources of control over the federal courts, however, is the authority of Congress to decide what the entire jurisdiction of the lower courts and the appellate jurisdiction of the Supreme Court shall be. In theory, Congress could prevent a matter on which it did not want federal courts to act from ever coming before the courts. In 1868, under the exceptional circumstances of Reconstruction in the South, it did just that—and the Court conceded Congress's right to do so.[27]

Congress has threatened to do this on other occasions, and the mere existence of the threat may have influenced the nature of Court decisions. In the 1950s, for example, congressional opinion was hostile to Court decisions on civil liberties and civil rights, and legislation was proposed that would have curtailed the Court's jurisdiction in these areas. It did not pass, but the Court may have allowed the threat to temper its decisions.[28] On the other hand, as congressional resistance to Roosevelt's court-packing plan shows, the Supreme Court enjoys a good deal of prestige in the nation, even among people who disagree with some of its decisions. Passing laws that would frontally attack it would not be easy, except perhaps in times of national crisis.

Furthermore, laws changing jurisdiction or restricting the kinds of remedies a court can impose are often blunt instruments that might not achieve their proponents' purposes. Consider, for example, the issue of school busing for racial balance. A law denying the Supreme Court appellate jurisdiction over school busing orders to achieve desegregation would leave lower federal and state courts free to go on ordering busing for this purpose. A law denying *all* federal courts the right to order busing as a remedy for racial imbalance would still leave them free to order busing for other reasons (such as to facilitate redistricting). And so on, to the ridiculous extreme of forbidding schoolchildren to enter a bus for any reason. Finally, the Supreme Court might well decide that if busing is essential to achieve a constitutional right, then any congressional law prohibiting such busing would itself be unconstitutional. Trying to think through how *that* dilemma would be resolved is like trying to visualize two kangaroos simultaneously jumping into each other's pouches.

Public Opinion and the Courts

Though not elected, judges read the same newspapers as members of Congress, and thus they too are aware of public opinion, especially elite opinion. While it may be going too far to say that the Supreme Court follows the election returns, it is nevertheless true that the Court is sensitive to certain bodies of opinion, especially of those elites—liberal or conservative—to which its members happen to be attuned. The justices will recall cases when, by defying opinion frontally, their predecessors very nearly destroyed the legitimacy of the Court itself. This was the case with the *Dred Scott* decision, which infuriated the North and was widely disobeyed. No such crisis exists today, but it is altogether possible that changing political moods will affect the kinds of remedies judges will think appropriate.

Opinion not only restrains the courts; it may also energize them. The most activist periods in Supreme Court history have coincided with times when the political system was undergoing profound and lasting changes. The assertion by the Supreme Court, under John Marshall's leadership, of the principles of national supremacy and judicial review occurred at the time when the Jeffersonian Republicans were coming to power and their opponents, the Federalists, were collapsing as an organized party. The proslavery decisions of the Taney Court came when the nation was so divided along sectional and ideological lines as to make almost any Court decision on this matter unpopular. Supreme Court review of economic regulation in the 1890s and 1900s occurred when the political parties were realigning and the Republicans acquiring dominance that was to last for several decades. The Court decisions of the 1930s corresponded to another period of partisan realignment.

Until the 1950s, the Court rarely struck out in new directions or used its powers very actively so long as there was a broad public consensus as to the correct course of action. Beginning with *Brown* v. *Board of Education* and accelerating with the Court decisions restricting police powers, requiring busing to integrate schools, and upholding affirmative-action plans, the Court was responsible for an extraordinary amount of policy making, often in the teeth of public opposition. This opposition has led Congress to consider bills that would weaken the Court's powers or change its jurisdiction, but none passed.

Public opinion may strongly object to certain Court *decisions* but it seems unprepared to attack the Court as an *institution*. Polls reveal that the percentage of people saying they have "a great deal of confidence" in the Court fell sharply from 1966 to 1971, went up again around 1974, seesawed back and forth for a few years, and then rose again after 1982. These trends seem to reflect the public's view not only of what the Court is doing but what the government generally is doing. From 1966 to 1971, the Court lost support, partly because of its controversial decisions but also because the government as a whole was losing support. In 1974 the Court gained strength because it was not tarnished by the Watergate scandal that afflicted the White House; after 1982 it gained support because the government as a whole was becoming (briefly) more popular.[29]

SUMMARY

An independent judiciary with the power of judicial review—the right to decide the constitutionality of acts of Congress, of the executive branch, and of state governments—can be a potent political force in American life. That influence has been realized from the earliest days of the nation when Marshall and Taney put the Supreme Court at the center of the most important issues of the time. From 1787 to 1865, the Supreme Court was preoccupied with the establishment of national supremacy. From 1865 to 1937, it struggled with defining the scope of political power over the economy. In the present era it has sought to expand personal liberties.

The scope of the courts' political influence has increasingly widened as various groups and interests have acquired access to the courts, as the judges serving on them have developed a more activist stance, and as Congress has passed more laws containing vague or equivocal language. Whereas in other political arenas (the electorate, Congress, the bureaucracy) the influence of contending groups is largely dependent on their size, intensity, prestige, and political resources, the influence of contending groups before the courts depends chiefly on their arguments and the attitudes of the judges.

Though the Supreme Court is the pinnacle of the federal judiciary, most decisions, including many important ones, are made by the twelve circuit courts of appeals and the ninety-four district courts. The Supreme Court can control its own work load by deciding when to grant certiorari. It has become easier for citizens and groups to gain access to the federal courts (through class-action suits, by amicus curiae briefs, by laws that require government agencies to pay fees, and because of the activities of private groups such as the NAACP and the ACLU).

At the same time, the courts have widened the reach of their decisions by issuing orders that cover whole classes of citizens or affect the management of major public and private institutions. However, the courts can overstep the bounds of their authority and bring upon themselves a counterattack from public opinion and from Congress. Congress has the right to control much of the courts' jurisdiction, but it rarely does so. As a result, the ability of judges to make laws is only infrequently challenged directly.

SUGGESTED READINGS

Abrahm, Henry J. *The Judicial Process,* 5th ed. New York: Oxford University Press, 1986. An excellent, comprehensive survey of how the federal courts are organized and function.

Bork, Robert H. *The Tempting of America.* New York: Free Press, 1990. A defense of judicial restraint and the doctrine of original intent.

Cardozo, Benjamin N. *The Nature of the Judicial Process.* New Haven, Conn.: Yale University Press, 1921. Important statement of how judges make decisions, by a former Supreme Court justice.

Carp, Robert A., and Robert Stidham. *The Federal Courts.* Washington, D.C.: Congressional Quarterly Press, 1985. Explains the workings of the lower federal courts.

Ely, John Hart. *Democracy and Distrust.* Cambridge, Mass.: Harvard University Press, 1980. Effort to create a theory of judicial review that is neither strict constructionist nor activist.

Hall, Kermit L., ed. *Oxford Companion to the Supreme Court.* New York: Oxford University Press, 1992. An encyclopedia with everything you ever wanted to know about the Supreme Court.

Lasser, William. *The Limits of Judicial Power.* Chapel Hill, N.C.: University of North Carolina Press, 1988. Explains why the Supreme Court has been able to make controversial decisions without suffering crippling political attacks.

McCloskey, Robert G. *The American Supreme Court.* Chicago: University of Chicago Press, 1960. Superb brief history of the Court and its role in American politics and thought.

Melnick, R. Shep. *Regulation and the Courts.* Washington, D.C.: Brookings, 1983. Careful study of how activist courts have shaped environmental regulations.

Pritchett, C. Herman. *Constitutional Civil Liberties.* Englewood Cliffs, N.J.: Prentice-Hall, 1984. Useful summary of the Court's interpretation of the Constitution on civil liberties and civil rights.

Rabkin, Jeremy. *Judicial Compulsions: How Public Law Distorts Public Policy.* New York: Basic Books, 1989. An argument against broad judicial review of administrative decisions.

11

★ ★ ★

Civil Liberties and Civil Rights

ONE OF THE DISTINCTIVE FEATURES of American politics is the extent to which it is concerned with, and shaped by, a concern for the rights and liberties of its citizens. We are all aware of individuals and groups that have had their rights ignored or their liberties violated, and we can recall periods, such as wartime, when certain rights have been sharply curtailed. But compared to the politics of almost any other democratic nation, American politics is defined by the people's and the government's preoccupation with rights.

Americans don't merely expect or ask for, or even demand, their social security benefits or welfare checks; they say they have the *right* to them. When we discuss abortion, we don't just talk about whether abortion on demand would have good or bad results; we argue about whether the fetus has a *right* to life or whether the mother has a *right* to control her own body. We frequently argue over whether industry and government are doing all they should to keep our air clean and our water pure; to a degree that would astonish Europeans, we carry on these arguments by claiming that we have a *right* to a certain quality of

RIGHTS AND LIBERTIES IN THE CONSTITUTION

★ ★ ★

FREEDOM OF EXPRESSION	AMENDMENT
Freedom of speech, press, assembly, and petition	First
Free exercise of religion	First
No "establishment of religion"	First

CITIZENSHIP RIGHTS	
Slavery prohibited	Thirteenth
All persons born or naturalized in U.S. are citizens	Fourteenth
Federal and state governments may not take "life, liberty, or property without due process of law"	Fifth and Fourteenth
States may not abridge "privileges and immunities" of citizens	Fourteenth
States may not deny "equal protection of the laws"	Fourteenth
The right to vote may not be denied on account of:	
★ race	Fifteenth
★ sex	Nineteenth
★ not paying poll tax	Twenty-fourth
★ age (if you are eighteen or over)	Twenty-sixth

air and water. Some people have said that every American has a *right* to a job and a decent standard of living.

None of these rights is mentioned in the Constitution. What is mentioned is a list of certain rights and liberties that can be grouped under three broad headings—freedom of expression, citizenship rights, and criminal and civil law—as shown in the box. Freedom of expression and freedom from arbitrary arrest and prosecution are usually called **civil liberties;** citizenship rights, including the right to vote and to be free from unjust discrimination, are usually called **civil rights.** The distinction is not very important, however, and many authors use "liberties" and "rights" interchangeably.

CRIMINAL AND CIVIL LAW

No bill of attainder[1]	Article I, sec. 9 and 10
No ex post facto law[2]	Article I, sec. 9 and 10
Right to habeas corpus[3]	Article I, sec. 9
Ban on "unreasonable" searches and seizures	Fourth
Right to due process of law	Fifth and Fourteenth
Ban on double jeopardy[4]	Fifth
Right to just compensation if property is taken for public use	Fifth
Ban on being forced to testify against oneself	Fifth
Right to a trial that is speedy, public, impartial, and fair (right to know the charges, confront one's accuser, call witnesses, have help of a lawyer)	Sixth
Trial by jury	Seventh
No excessive bail or fines and no "cruel and unusual punishment"	Eighth

[1] *Bill of attainder:* a law that declares a person, without a trial, guilty of a crime.
[2] *Ex post facto law:* a law that makes criminal an act that was legal when it was committed, or that increases the penalty for a crime after it was committed, or that changes the rules of evidence to make conviction easier; a retroactive criminal law.
[3] *Habeas corpus:* a court order directing police officers, sheriffs, or wardens to bring a person in their custody before a judge and show that they have legal grounds for detaining that person.
[4] *Double jeopardy:* being tried twice for the same crime unless the first trial led to no conclusion (a mistrial or a hung jury).

The Constitution guarantees these rights against infringement by the government (in general, there are no constitutional protections against actions by private individuals). When the Constitution was first presented to the states for ratification, it contained only a few guaranteed rights—those mentioned in Article I, sections 9 and 10. When people in various states complained that the Constitution, as drafted, would leave citizens inadequately protected against unreasonable government actions, the Framers promised to amend it after it was ratified by the states. The First Congress proposed twelve amendments. Ten were ratified by the necessary number of states, and these amendments became known as the **Bill of Rights.**

In 1971 Jesse Jackson was arrested at a sit-in held to demand that a grocery chain hire more blacks. In 1984 and again in 1988 he was a candidate for the Democratic presidential nomination.

The Bill of Rights protected the rights of citizens only from the actions of the *federal* government; except for Article I, section 10, state governments were limited only by their own constitutions.[1] This lack of protection from state governments began to change after the Civil War with the ratification of the Thirteenth, Fourteenth, and Fifteenth Amendments, all designed chiefly to protect the newly freed black slaves. Of these, the Fourteenth (ratified in 1868) was to become the most important. Section 1 contained two phrases that became, as interpreted by the Supreme Court, vehicles for applying much of the Bill of Rights to the states. These were the **due-process** clause (no state shall "deprive any person of life, liberty, or property, without due process of law") and the **equal-protection** clause (no state shall "deny to any person within its jurisdiction the equal protection of the laws").

In a series of cases beginning in 1925, the Supreme Court began interpreting "due process" and "equal protection" to mean what the Framers of the Bill of Rights had meant by such specific guarantees as freedom of speech, freedom of religion, and the right to a fair trial.[2] This became known as the doctrine of **incorporation:** the Bill of Rights became incorporated into the Fourteenth Amendment, so that most of its provisions would limit the powers of state governments, just as they had always limited those of the federal government.

The specific protections afforded by the Constitution are one reason why we are so preoccupied with rights, but there are other reasons as well. The Revolutionary War was fought out of a desire to assert the rights of colonists against the British government. When the new Constitution was written, the major argument over it concerned whether it had enough limitations against the new government to protect these hard-won rights. The Civil War was in part a struggle over the question of what rights, if any, slaves were to have. Later on, many immigrants came here from other lands because they suffered from religious or political persecution abroad, and so they arrived keenly sensitive to their rights. Finally, the existence of an independent judiciary has provided an arena wherein citizens can sue the government in order to protect their rights, even to the extent of getting judges to declare acts of Congress unconstitutional (see the discussion of "judicial review" in Chapter 10).

The results of these legal, cultural, and historical forces are evident to anyone: Americans go into court to sue one another more often than the citizens of virtually any other nation. We are always complaining about the myriad lawsuits that go on all about us. There is a cost to that, but there is a benefit as well: it is a measure of how committed (some would say overcommitted) we are to the assertion of rights.

That we always seem to be suing one another contains another important lesson—namely, rights are in conflict. Few, if any, rights are absolute. Someone may assert his right to publish what he wishes, but you will counter with your right to protect your children from his obscene books. Or if someone distributes classified documents, the government will counter with its right to protect vital secrets from the enemy. Or I may assert my right to a fair trial, but a journalist will assert his or her right to print stories about my trial—even if those stories arouse popular passions against me and so make it harder to have a fair trial. Or a high school student may think his or her locker is private, but the school principal will assert his or her right to search that locker if it seems necessary to preserve order or prevent the distribution of drugs. Even freedom of religion is not absolute: you may worship however you please, but you cannot use your religious beliefs to justify carrying out a ritual murder or preventing your child from receiving essential medical care.

Because rights are in conflict, the current definition of what our rights are represents an uneasy and changing balance between competing claims. We can illustrate this in four areas: freedom of expression, the relations between church and state, the role of the police, and equality under the law.

FREEDOM OF EXPRESSION

Over the last two centuries, the courts have more or less steadily broadened the area of free expression. In 1798 it was illegal to publish "any false, scandalous, and malicious writing" against the president or Congress. Today it is hard to imagine what anyone might write about any politician that could get its writer in trouble with the law. In 1918 it was illegal to utter or print any disloyal, profane, or scurrilous language intended to promote the cause of the nation's enemies. Today, condemning the United States in the most abusive manner or praising a foreign enemy in the most extravagant manner would not be grounds for a lawful arrest. As recently as the 1950s, local authorities regularly censored movies and banned books that contained four-letter words or any explicit discussion of sex. For example, in 1957 New York State banned a rather tame film, *Lady Chatterley's Lover,* on the grounds that its theme encouraged adultery. Today it is hard to find a large city that does not have many "adult" (that is, pornographic) bookstores and movie theaters. Indeed the Supreme Court has held that nude dancing and burning the American flag are forms of "speech" deserving of protection.[3]

Certain court-devised doctrines expanding the scope of permissible expression clearly place the burden on the government to prove that its restriction on speaking or publishing can be justified. These rules of thumb include the following:

1. **Preferred position:** The right of free expression, though not absolute, occupies a higher or more "preferred" position than any other constitutional rights, such as property rights.[4]

2. **No prior restraint:** With scarcely any exceptions, the courts will not allow the government to restrain or censor in advance any speaking or

writing, even when they will allow punishment after the fact for publishing libels or obscenity.[5]

3. **Imminent danger:** You may utter inflammatory statements or urge people to consider committing dangerous actions, but unless there is an "imminent danger" that the utterances will actually lead to an illegal act, they are constitutionally protected.[6]

4. **Neutrality:** If the government requires a license for a parade, it must be neutral—that is, not favor one group more than another.[7]

5. **Clarity:** If the law forbids some form of expression, such as obscenity, it must contain a clear definition of it.[8]

6. **Least means:** If it is necessary to restrict the rights of one person to speak or publish in order to protect the rights of another, the restriction should involve the least intrusive means to achieve its end. For instance, restricting press coverage of a trial in order to ensure a fair trial should involve the least intrusive means (for example, transferring the case to another town rather than issuing a "gag order" against the press).[9]

Despite the stringency of these rules, not all forms of expression are protected by the Constitution. There are these exceptions:

First, **libel** is not protected speech. If you harm another person by writing or publishing statements that defame his or her character, you can be sued by the injured party and cannot claim in defense that your freedom to speak and write is constitutionally guaranteed. However, the Court has made it very difficult for public officials (and even "public figures" or celebrities) to protect themselves against false and defamatory statements provided they were not uttered with "actual malice"—that is, uttered with reckless disregard of their accuracy or while knowing them to be false.[10]

Second, you cannot ordinarily claim that illegal *action* should go unpunished because that action is meant to convey a political or social message. For example, if you burn your draft card to protest the foreign policy of the United States, you can be punished for the illegal act (burning the draft card) even if your intent was to communicate your political beliefs. The Court felt that if "symbolic speech" were given the same constitutional protection as actual speech or writing, then virtually any action—murder, arson, rioting—could be excused on the grounds that its perpetrator meant to send a message.[11] But when Texas authorities arrested a man for burning an American flag in order to send a message, the Court held that the statute that made flag burning illegal was an unconstitutional infringement of free speech. What, then, is the difference between burning a draft card and burning a flag? The Court argued that since the government has the right to run a military draft, it can protect the draft cards that are a necessary part of this process. But the only motive that government has in banning flag burning is to restrict a form of speech, and that is impermissible under the Constitution. Similarly, when a Des Moines high school punished some students for wearing black arm bands to class, the Court ruled that the arm bands were a protected form of speech.[12]

Third, you cannot freely use words that **incite** others to commit illegal acts or that directly and immediately provoke another person to violent behavior. As we have already seen, the Court has steadily expanded the protection afforded those who advocate illegal actions so long as that incitement to action is not immediate and direct. But the Court has sustained state laws that make it illegal to insult a person to his or her face in a way that provokes a fight; it has insisted, however, that laws prohibiting "fighting words" be carefully drawn and narrowly applied.[13] The provocation would probably have to be severe and person-to-person before the Court would allow it to be punished. When a group of American Nazis in 1977 wanted to parade through Skokie, Illinois, a community with a large Jewish population, lower courts (acting after Supreme Court prodding) held that, as noxious and provocative as their anti-Semitic slogans might be, the Nazis had a constitutional right to speak and parade peacefully.[14]

Fourth, **obscenity** is not protected by the First Amendment. The Court has always held that obscene materials, because they have no redeeming social value or are calculated chiefly to appeal to one's sexual rather than political or literary interests, can be regulated by the state. The problem, of course, arises with the meaning of "obscene." In one eleven-year period, 1957 to 1968, the Court decided thirteen major cases involving the definition of obscenity, which resulted in fifty-five separate opinions.[15] Some justices, such as Hugo Black, believed that the First Amendment protected all publications, even wholly obscene ones. Others believed that obscenity deserved no protection and struggled heroically to define the term. Still others shared the view of former Justice Potter Stewart who objected to "hard-core pornography" but admitted that the best definition he could offer was "I know it when I see it."[16]

It is unnecessary to review in detail the many attempts by the Court at defining obscenity. The justices have made it clear that nudity and sex are not, by definition, obscene and that they will provide First Amendment protection to anything that has any arguable political, literary, or artistic merit, allowing the government to punish only the distribution of "hard-core pornography." Their most recent (1973) definition of this is as follows: To be obscene, the work, taken as a whole, must be judged by "the average person applying contemporary community standards" to appeal to the "prurient interest" or to depict "in a patently offensive way, sexual conduct specifically defined by applicable state law" and to lack "serious literary, artistic, political, or scientific value."[17]

Though the Court has taken a hard look at efforts to prohibit the distribution of pornography, it has been willing to allow cities to determine where in a city that distribution can occur. When one city adopted a zoning ordinance prohibiting an "adult" movie theater from being located within one thousand feet of any church, school, park, or residential area, the Court upheld it. The purpose of the law, it said, was to regulate not speech or press but the use of land. Since the "adult" theater still had 5 percent of the city's land area in which to find a location, it was not being barred from operating.[18]

The American people clearly have fairly broad rights of expression. But who are "the people?" Do they include associations? Corporations? High-school students? Or just adult individuals? The Court has not said that corporations have all the rights of individuals, but they do enjoy a large number of them. A state cannot prevent a bank from spending money to influence votes in a local election, nor can an electric utility be required to enclose in its monthly bills statements written by groups attacking the utility.[19] Lobbying organizations enjoy First Amendment rights, as do their members.[20]

But high-school students do not have exactly the same rights as adults. In 1988 the Supreme Court held that the principal of a high school could censor the school's student newspaper by ordering it not to print stories about student pregnancies and parental divorces. It was important to the decision in this case that the paper was published using school money and edited as part of a school journalism class. The Court held that while students cannot be punished for expressing their personal views on campus, what they do in class or as participants in school-sponsored activities can be controlled.[21]

Though the Constitution provides the legal basis for freedom of expression, that freedom would be—and in the past, has been—weak if public opinion did not provide reasonable support for it. The overwhelming majority of Americans have always supported freedom of expression in the abstract, but when we get down to concrete cases they have not always been so tolerant. Liberals tend to be intolerant of the rights of the ultraconservatives, and conservatives tend to be intolerant of the rights of ultraliberals. For example, most liberals don't believe that a member of the John Birch Society should be allowed to speak or teach in schools, while most conservatives don't believe that a member of the Communist party should be permitted to speak or teach. In general, however, the average American is willing to allow even rather unpopular groups, such as communists and atheists, to speak out, and the proportion willing to tolerate such acts has increased.

CHURCH AND STATE

Everybody knows, correctly, that the plain language of the First Amendment protects freedom of speech and the press, though most people are not aware of how complex the law applying these terms has become. But many people also believe, wrongly, that the language of the First Amendment clearly requires the "separation of church and state." It does not.

What that amendment actually says is quite different and maddeningly unclear. It has two parts: The first, often referred to as the **free-exercise clause,** states that Congress shall make no law prohibiting the "free exercise" of religion. The second, called the **establishment clause,** states that Congress shall make no law "respecting an establishment of religion."

The Free-Exercise Clause

The "free-exercise" clause is the clearer of the two, though by no means free of ambiguities. It obviously means that Congress cannot, for example, pass a law prohibiting Catholics from celebrating Mass. Since the First Amendment has been applied to the states via the due-process clause of the Fourteenth Amendment, it means that state governments cannot pass such a law either. In general the courts have treated religion like speech: you can pretty much do what you want so long as it does not cause some serious harm to others.

Even some laws that do not initially appear to apply to churches may be unconstitutional if their enforcement imposes particular burdens on churches or greater burdens on some churches than others. For example, a state cannot require a door-to-door solicitor to pay a license fee when the solicitor is a Jehovah's Witness selling religious tracts.[22]

Having the right to exercise your religion freely does not, however, exempt you from laws binding other citizens, even when the law goes against your religious beliefs. A man cannot have more than one wife, even if (as once was the case with Mormons) polygamy is thought desirable on religious grounds.[23] For religious reasons, you may oppose being vaccinated or having blood transfusions, but if the state passes a compulsory vaccination law or orders that a blood transfusion be given a sick child, the courts will not on grounds of religious liberty prevent such things from being carried out.[24] And in an issue that remains bitterly controversial to this day, the courts have allowed local authorities to close down schools operated by fundamentalist religious groups if the schools were not accredited by the state.[25]

Conflicts between religious belief and public policy are always difficult to settle. What if you believe on religious grounds that war is immoral? The draft laws have always exempted a conscientious objector from military duty, and the Court has upheld such exemptions. But the Court has gone further: it has said that people cannot be drafted even if they do not believe in a Supreme Being or belong to any religious tradition so long as their "consciences, spurred by deeply held moral, ethical, or religious beliefs, would give them no rest or peace if they allowed themselves to become part of an instrument of war."[26] Do exemptions on such grounds create an opportunity for some people to evade the draft because of their political preferences? Or the opportunity to create a "religion" for the sole purpose of staying out of the army? In trying to answer such questions, the courts have had to try to define a religion—no easy task.

The Supreme Court has banned prayer in public schools, but this has not prevented children from being asked to observe a moment of silence.

And even when there is no question about your membership in a bona fide religion, the circumstances under which you may claim exemption from laws that apply to everybody else are not really clear. What if you, a member of the Seventh-Day Adventists, are fired by your employer for refusing on religious grounds to work on Saturday, and then it turns out you can't collect unemployment insurance because you refuse to take an available job—one that also requires you to work on Saturday? Or what if you are a member of the Amish sect, which refuses, contrary to state law, to send its children to public schools past the eighth grade? The Court has ruled that the state must pay you unemployment compensation and cannot require you to send your children to public schools beyond the eighth grade.[27]

The Establishment Clause

What in the world did the members of the First Congress mean when they wrote into the First Amendment language prohibiting Congress from making a law "respecting" an "establishment" of religion? The Supreme Court has more or less consistently interpreted this vague phrase to mean that the Constitution erects a "wall of separation" between church and state.

That phrase, so often quoted, is neither in the Bill of Rights nor in the debates in the First Congress that drafted the Bill of Rights; it comes from the pen of Thomas Jefferson, who was opposed to having the Church of England as the established church of his native Virginia. (At the time of the Revolutionary War, there were established—that is, official, state-supported—churches in at least eight of the thirteen former colonies.) But it is not clear that Jefferson's view was the majority view.

During much of the debate in Congress, the wording of this part of the First Amendment was quite different and much plainer than what finally emerged. Up to the last minute, the clause was intended to read "no religion shall be established by law" or "no national religion shall be established." The meaning of those words seems quite clear: whatever the states may do, the federal government cannot create an official, national religion or give support to one religion in preference to another.[28]

Congress instead adopted an ambiguous phrase, leaving the Supreme Court to decide what it meant. The Court subsequently declared that these words do not simply mean "no national religion" but mean as well no governmental involvement with religion at all, even on a nonpreferential basis. They mean, in short, erecting a "wall of separation" between church and state.[29] Though the proper interpretation of the establishment clause remains a topic of great controversy among judges and scholars, the Court has more or less consistently adopted the "wall of separation" interpretation.

Its first statement of this interpretation was in 1947 in a case involving a New Jersey town that reimbursed parents for the costs of transporting their children to school, including parochial (in this case, Catholic) schools. The Court decided that this reimbursement was constitutional, but it clearly stated that the establishment clause of the First Amendment applied (via the Fourteenth Amendment) to the states and that it meant, among other things, that the government cannot require a person to profess a belief or disbelief in any religion; it cannot aid one religion, some religions, or all religions; and it cannot spend any tax money, however small, in support of any religious activities or institutions.[30] The reader may wonder, in view of the Court's reasoning, why it allowed the town to pay for busing children to Catholic schools. Its answer was that busing is a religiously neutral activity, akin to providing fire and police protection to Catholic schools. Busing, available to public- and private-school children alike, does not breach the wall of separation.

Since 1947 the Court has applied the "wall of separation" theory to strike down as unconstitutional every effort to have any form of prayer in public schools, even if it is nonsectarian,[31] voluntary,[32] or limited to reading a passage from the Bible.[33] Moreover, the Court has held that laws prohibiting teaching the theory of evolution or requiring giving equal time to "creationism" are religiously inspired and thus unconstitutional.[34] A public school may not allow its pupils to take time out from their regular classes for religious instruction if this occurs within the schools, though "released-time" instruction is all right if it is done outside the public-school buildings.[35] The school prayer decisions in particular have provoked a storm of controversy, but efforts to get Congress to propose to the states a constitutional amendment authorizing such prayers have failed.

Court-imposed restrictions on public aid to parochial schools have been almost as controversial, though here the wall of separation principle has not been used to forbid any and all forms of aid. For example, it is permissible for the federal government to provide aid for constructing buildings on denominational (as well as nondenominational) college campuses[36] and for state governments to loan free textbooks to parochial school pupils,[37] grant tax-exempt status to parochial schools,[38] and allow parents of parochial school children to deduct their tuition payments on their income tax returns.[39] But the government cannot pay a salary supplement to teachers who teach secular subjects in parochial schools,[40] reimburse parents for the cost of parochial school tuition,[41] supply parochial schools with services such as counseling,[42] or give money to parochial schools to purchase instructional materials.[43]

If you find it confusing to follow the twists and turns of Court policy in this area, you are not alone. The "wall of separation" principle has not been easy to apply, and with its membership undergoing change, the Supreme Court has begun to alter its position on church-state matters. The Court has tried to sort out the confusion by developing a three-part test to decide under what circumstances government involvement in religious activities is improper.[44] That involvement is constitutional if it meets these tests:

1. It has a secular purpose.

2. Its primary effect neither advances nor inhibits religion.

3. It does not foster an excessive government entanglement with religion.

But no sooner had the test been developed than the Court decided that it was all right for the government of Pawtucket, Rhode Island, to erect a Nativity scene as part of the Christmas display in a local park. But not every Christmas display will win the Court's approval. In 1989 Pittsburgh put up both a crèche (a Christian Nativity scene) and a menorah (the nine-branched candelabra used to celebrate the Jewish holiday of Chanukah) in front of the county courthouse. The Court said that the crèche had to go (because it was too close to the courthouse and thus implied a government endorsement), but the menorah could stay (because it was next to a Christmas tree and would not lead people to think that Pittsburgh was endorsing Judaism).[45] If there is a principle that rationalizes these bewildering distinctions, it is not obvious.

Tradition seems to count for as much as doctrine in reaching these decisions. Though the Court has struck down prayers in schools, it has upheld prayers in Congress. Since the First Congress in 1789, the House and the Senate have hired chaplains to open each session with a prayer. Therefore, when somebody complained that it was unconstitutional for the Nebraska legislature to do this, the Court disagreed.[46]

Despite its efforts to set forth clear rules governing church-state relations, the Court's actual decisions are hard to summarize. It is deeply divided— some would say deeply confused—on these matters, and so the efforts to define the "wall of separation" will continue to be as difficult as the Court's earlier effort to decide what was interstate and what was local commerce (see Chapter 3).

CRIME AND DUE PROCESS

Whereas the central problem in interpreting the religion clauses of the First Amendment has been to decide what they mean, the central problems in interpreting those parts of the Bill of Rights that affect people accused of a crime have been to decide not only what they mean but how to put them into effect. It is not obvious what constitutes an "unreasonable search," but even if we settle that question, we still must decide how best to protect people against such searches in ways that do not unduly hinder criminal investigations.

There are at least two ways to provide that protection. One is to let the police introduce in court evidence relevant to the guilt or innocence of a person, no matter how it was obtained, and then, after the case is settled, punish the police officers (or their superiors) if the evidence was gathered improperly (for example, by an unreasonable search). The other way is to exclude improperly gathered evidence from the trial in the first place, even if it is relevant to determining the guilt or innocence of the accused.

Most democratic nations, including England, use the first method; the United States uses the second. Because of this, many of the landmark cases decided by the Supreme Court have been bitterly controversial. Opponents of these decisions have argued that a guilty person should not go free just because the police officer blundered, especially if the mistake was minor.[47] Supporters rejoin that there is no way to punish errant police officers effectively other than by excluding tainted evidence; moreover, nobody should be convicted of a crime except by evidence that is above reproach.[48]*

---

* We shall consider here only two constitutional limits—those bearing on searches and confessions. Thus we will omit many other important constitutional provisions affecting criminal cases, such as rules governing wiretapping, prisoner rights, the right to bail and to a jury trial, the bar on ex post facto laws, the right to be represented by a lawyer in court, the ban on "cruel and unusual" punishment, and the rule against double jeopardy.

The Exclusionary Rule

The American method relies on what is called the **exclusionary rule.** That rule holds that evidence gathered in violation of the Constitution cannot be used in a trial. The rule has been used to implement two provisions of the Bill of Rights—the right to be free from unreasonable searches or seizures (Fourth Amendment) and the right not to be compelled to give evidence against oneself (Fifth Amendment).

Not until 1949 did the Supreme Court consider whether to apply the exclusionary rule to the states. In a case decided that year, the Court made it clear that the Fourth Amendment prohibited the police from carrying out unreasonable searches and obtaining improper confessions but held that it was not necessary to use the exclusionary rule to enforce those prohibitions. It noted that other nations did not exclude improperly gathered evidence from a criminal trial. The Court said that the local police should not gather and use evidence improperly, but if they did, the remedy was to sue the police department or punish the officer.[49]

But in 1961 the Supreme Court changed its mind about the use of the exclusionary rule. It all began when the Cleveland police broke into the home of Dollree Mapp in search of drugs and, finding none, arrested her for possessing some obscene pictures they found there. The Court held that this was an unreasonable search and seizure because the police had not obtained a search warrant, though they had ample time to do so. Furthermore, such illegally gathered evidence could not be used in the trial of Mapp.[50] Beginning with this case—*Mapp* v. *Ohio*—the Supreme Court used the exclusionary rule as a way of enforcing a variety of constitutional guarantees.

There were two reasons for adopting the exclusionary rule. The first was deterrence: If the police could not use illegally obtained evidence in court, they would be deterred from using illegal means to gather evidence. The second was justice: Nobody should be convicted of a crime by the use of tainted evidence. Since the rule was first adopted, scholars have argued about both reasons, but mostly over the first. Some claim that the rule has only made crimes harder to solve without improving police conduct; others claim that the rule has not impeded investigations and has made the police more law-abiding.

Search and Seizure

After the Court decided to exclude improperly gathered evidence, the next problem was to decide what evidence was improper. What happened to Dollree Mapp was an easy case: hardly anybody argued that it was reasonable for the police without a warrant to break into someone's home, ransack one's belongings, and take whatever they could find that might be incriminating. But that left a lot of hard choices still to be made.

Just when is a police search reasonable? Under two circumstances—when they have a search warrant and when they have lawfully arrested you. A **search warrant** is an order from a judge authorizing the search of a place; the order must describe what is to be searched and seized, and the judge can issue it only if persuaded by the police that they have good reason **(probable cause)** to believe that a crime has been committed and the evidence bearing on that crime will be found at a certain location. (The police can also search a building if the occupant gives permission.)

You can also be searched when you are being lawfully arrested. When can you be arrested? If a judge has issued an arrest warrant for you, if you commit a crime in the presence of a police officer, or if the officer has probable cause to believe that you have committed a serious crime (usually a felony). If you are arrested and no search warrant has been issued, the police, and not a judge, decide what they can search. What rules should they follow?

In trying to answer that question, the courts have elaborated a set of rules that are complex, subject to frequent change, and quite controversial. In general the police, after arresting you, can search:

1. you

2. things in plain view

3. things or places under your immediate control

As a practical matter, "things in plain view" or "under your immediate control" mean the room in which you are arrested but not other rooms in the house.[51] If the police want to search the rest of your house or a car parked in your driveway, they first have to go to a judge to obtain a search warrant. But if the police arrest a college student on campus for drinking under age and then accompany him back to his dormitory room so he can get proof that he was old enough to drink, the police can seize drugs that are in plain view in that room.[52] And if marijuana is growing in plain view in an open field, the police can enter and search that field even though it is fenced off with a locked gate and a "No Trespassing" sign.[53]

But what if you are arrested while driving your car—how much of it can the police search? The answer has changed almost yearly. In 1979 the Court ruled that the police could not search a suitcase taken from a car of an arrested person and in 1981 extended this protection to any "closed, opaque container" found in the car.[54] But the following year the Court decided that all parts of a car, closed or open, could be searched, if the officers had probable cause to believe it contained contraband (that is, goods illegally possessed).[55]

The law may be confusing but the purpose is clear—to find ways of protecting those places in which a person has a "reasonable expectation of privacy." Your body is one such place, and so the Court has held that the police cannot force you to undergo surgery to remove a bullet that might provide evidence of your guilt.[56] But the police can require you to take a Breathalyzer

The constitutional ban against unreasonable searches has been interpreted to permit the police to use a Breathalyzer on persons suspected of driving while intoxicated.

test to find out whether you have been drinking while driving (driving is a privilege, not a right).[57] Your house is another place where you have an expectation of privacy, but the barn next to your house is not, nor is your backyard viewed from an airplane, nor is your house if it is a motor home that can be easily driven away. The police therefore need no warrant to look in those places.[58]

If you work for the government, you may have an expectation that your desk and files are private; nonetheless, your supervisor may search them without a warrant provided that he or she is looking for something related to your work.[59] If your brother is a high-school student, you may think his high-school locker is private, but school officials can search it without a warrant if they have a "reasonable suspicion" that he is hiding marijuana or other contraband in it.[60]

But since the Bill of Rights protects people against *government* action, a private employer has much more freedom to search your desk, files, or locker. Because of this, the Constitution does not restrict the power of corporations to require employees to undergo drug tests (state or federal law may, however, impose some restrictions).

Government testing for drugs and for AIDS (acquired immune deficiency syndrome) has opened up a new dimension for civil-liberties issues. In 1987

President Reagan called for AIDS tests for immigrants, federal prisoners, and certain other categories of persons, and in 1986 he signed an executive order requiring drug testing for many federal employees. Are such tests, in the absence of any reasonable suspicion that an immigrant, a prisoner, or an employee has contracted AIDS or is using drugs, an unreasonable search that the Constitution prohibits? Not all of the answers are in, but in 1989 the Supreme Court upheld federal rules requiring drug tests of train crews involved in accidents and of customs officers who carry firearms or are involved in enforcing drug laws.[61] The Court also clearly stated that a private employer who requires his or her workers to take drug tests is not violating the federal Constitution. (It may, however, violate some *state* constitutions.)

Confessions and Self-Incrimination

The constitutional ban on being forced to give evidence against oneself was originally intended to prevent the use of torture or "third-degree" police tactics to extract confessions. But it has since been extended to cover many kinds of statements uttered not out of fear of torture but from lack of awareness of one's rights, especially the right to remain silent whether in the courtroom or the police station.

For many decades the Supreme Court had held that involuntary confessions could not be used in federal criminal trials but had not ruled that they were barred from state trials. In the early 1960s it changed its mind in two landmark cases—*Escobedo* and *Miranda*.[62] The story of the latter and the controversy it provoked is worth telling.

Ernesto A. Miranda was convicted in Arizona of the rape-kidnapping of a young woman. The conviction was based on a written confession that Miranda signed after two hours of police questioning. (The victim also identified him.) Two years earlier the Court had decided that the rule against self-incrimination applied to state courts.[63] Now the question arose, what constitutes an "involuntary" confession? The Court decided that a confession would be presumed involuntary unless the person in custody had been fully and clearly informed of his or her right to be silent, to have an attorney present during any questioning, and to have an attorney provided free of charge if he or she could not afford one. The accused may waive these rights and offer to talk, but the waiver must be truly voluntary. Since Miranda did not have a lawyer present when he was questioned and had not knowingly waived his right to a lawyer, the confession was excluded from evidence in the trial and his conviction was overturned.[64]

Miranda was tried and convicted again, this time on the basis of evidence supplied by his girlfriend who testified that he had admitted to her that he was guilty. Nine years later he was released from prison; four years after that he was killed in a barroom fight. When the Phoenix police arrested the prime suspect, they read him his rights from a "Miranda card."

The Miranda Rules

★ ★ ★

The Supreme Court has interpreted the due-process clause to require that local police departments issue warnings of the sort shown below to people they are arresting.

PHILADELPHIA POLICE DEPARTMENT

STANDARD POLICE INTERROGATION CARD

WARNINGS TO BE GIVEN ACCUSED

We are questioning you concerning the crime of (state specific crime).

We have a duty to explain to you and to warn you that you have the following legal rights:

A. You have a right to remain silent and do not have to say anything at all.

B. Anything you say can and will be used against you in Court.

C. You have a right to talk to a lawyer of your own choice before we ask you any questions, and also to have a lawyer here with you while we ask questions.

D. If you cannot afford to hire a lawyer, and you want one, we will see that you have one provided to you free of charge before we ask you any questions.

E. If you are willing to give us a statement, you have a right to stop any time you wish.

75-Misc.-3   (Over)

(6-24-70)

Everyone who watches cops-and-robbers shows on television probably knows the "Miranda warning" by heart since the police now read it routinely to people they arrest, both on and off television. It is not clear whether it has much impact on who does or does not confess or what effect, if any, it may have on the crime rate.

In time the Miranda rule was extended to mean that you have a right to a lawyer when you appear in a postindictment police lineup[65] and when you are questioned by a psychiatrist to determine if you are competent to stand trial.[66] The Court threw out the conviction of a man who had killed a child because the accused, without being given the right to have a lawyer present, had led the police to the victim's body.[67]

Relaxing the Exclusionary Rule

Cases such as *Miranda* were highly controversial and led to an effort in Congress during the 1960s to modify or overrule the decisions by statute—without much success. But as the rules governing police conduct became increasingly complex, pressure mounted to find an alternative. Some thought any evidence should be admissible, with the question of police conduct left to lawsuits or other ways of punishing official misbehavior. Others felt that the exclusionary rule served a useful purpose but had simply become too technical to be an effective deterrent to police misconduct (the police cannot obey rules they cannot understand). And still others felt the exclusionary rule was a vital safeguard to essential liberties and should be kept intact. Bills to enact the first and second positions were introduced in Congress during the 1980s.

The courts themselves began to adopt the second position, deciding a number of cases in ways that retained the exclusionary rule but modified it by limiting its coverage (police were given greater freedom to question juveniles[68]) and by incorporating what was called a **good-faith exception.** For example, if the police obtain a search warrant that they believe is valid, the evidence they gather will not be excluded if it later turns out that the warrant was defective for some reason (such as the judge having used the wrong form).[69] And the Court decided that "overriding considerations of public safety" may justify questioning a person without first reading him his rights.[70] Moreover, the Court changed its mind about the killer who led the police to the place where he had disposed of his victim's body. After the man was convicted a second time and again appealed, the Court in 1984 held that the body would have been discovered anyway; evidence will not be excluded if it can be shown that it would "inevitably" have been found.[71]

EQUAL PROTECTION OF THE LAWS

If the government passes a law that treats different groups of citizens differently, that law is not necessarily unconstitutional. Most laws classify people into groups. For example, the income-tax laws classify people according to how much money they earn and then apply different tax rates to each group. For a law to violate the equal-protection clause of the Fourteenth Amendment, it must make an *unreasonable* classification or impose an *unreasonable* burden. The Supreme Court's opinion as to what classifications are reasonable has changed, as we can see by looking at how it has reacted to classifications based on race and sex.

Race and "Strict Scrutiny"

Until 1954, classifying people on the basis of race for the purpose of assigning them to schools was accepted by the Supreme Court. It held that as long as the schools that blacks and whites attended were substantially equal in quality,

The protest march from Selma to Montgomery (Alabama) in 1965 was a milestone in the campaign to strengthen federal civil rights laws.

then having racially segregated schools was not unconstitutional. In 1954, in the famous case of *Brown* v. *Board of Education,* the Court held that "separate educational facilities are inherently unequal," thus denying to blacks the equal protection of the law.[72] The authors of the Fourteenth Amendment probably had not intended the equal-protection clause to bar segregated schools (the schools of Washington, D.C., were segregated at the time Congress was debating the amendment, and no one seemed to think that the amendment was going to change that). But by 1954 the Court believed public education had become so important and segregated schools had become so harmful to blacks that the continued existence of such schools was incompatible with the concept of equality under the law.

Beginning with the *Brown* case, virtually every form of racial segregation imposed by law has been struck down. Race has become a **suspect classification** such that any law making racial distinctions is now subject to **strict scrutiny.** No law may require that blacks be segregated in any public facility (such as a voting booth, public school, or municipal swimming pool). But the equal-protection clause only limits the action of state *governments;* it is not a limitation on purely private behavior. To ban discrimination in *private* transactions, it was necessary for Congress to pass a series of civil-rights laws that, beginning in 1964, made it illegal to discriminate on the grounds of race,

KEY PROVISIONS OF
MAJOR CIVIL-RIGHTS LAWS

★ ★ ★

1957   Made it a federal crime to try to prevent a person from **voting** in a federal election. Created the Civil Rights Commission.

1960   Authorized the attorney general to appoint federal referees to gather evidence and make findings about allegations that blacks were being deprived of their right to **vote.** Made it a federal crime to use interstate commerce to threaten or carry out a **bombing.**

1964   **Voting:** Made it more difficult to use administrative devices or literacy tests to bar blacks from voting.

Public accommodations: Barred discrimination on grounds of race, color, religion, or national origin in restaurants, hotels, lunch counters, gasoline stations, movie theaters, stadiums, arenas, and lodging houses with more than five rooms.

Schools: Authorized the attorney general to bring suit to force the desegregation of public schools on behalf of citizens. Did not authorize issuing orders to achieve racial balance in schools by busing.

Employment: Outlawed discrimination in hiring, firing, or paying employees on grounds of race, color, religion, national origin, or sex. Eventually covered all firms employing twenty-five workers or more.

Federal funds: Barred discrimination in any activity receiving federal assistance. Authorized cutting off federal funds to activities where discrimination was practiced.

color, religion, or national origin in public accommodations, such as restaurants, theaters, sports stadiums, or hotels, or in employing workers (provided that the firm employs more than twenty-five workers or has a federal contract). Subsequent laws banned discrimination in the sale or rental of most housing (see box).

That race is a suspect category does not mean that the government cannot treat the races differently. The federal government can require that contractors doing business with the government hire a certain proportion of black workers. Public schools can be required to bus black pupils to white schools. State universities can take race into account in admitting students to colleges, law schools, and medical schools provided that no strict numerical quota is used and provided that the special consideration given to race is designed to help rather than hurt blacks.[73]

1965 **Voting registration:** Authorized appointment by the Civil Service Commission of voting examiners who would require registration of all eligible voters in federal, state, and local elections, general or primary, in areas where discrimination was found to be practiced or where less than 50 percent of voting-age residents were registered to vote in the 1964 election.

Literacy tests: Suspended use of literacy tests or other devices to prevent blacks from voting. Directed the attorney general to bring suit challenging the constitutionality of poll taxes.

1968 **Housing:** Banned, by stages, discrimination in sale or rental of most housing (excluding private owners who sell or rent their homes without the services of a real estate broker).

Riots: Made it a federal crime to use interstate commerce to organize or incite a riot.

1972 **Education:** Prohibited sex discrimination in education programs that receive federal aid.

1988 **Discrimination:** If any part of an organization receives federal aid, no part may discriminate on the basis of race, sex, age, or physical handicap.

1991 **Civil Rights:** Reversed Supreme Court decisions that had narrowed the interpretation of federal civil-rights laws as they affected disputes between employees and employers over racial or gender discrimination.

Race norming: Made it illegal for the government to adjust, or "norm," test scores by race.

In short, the Supreme Court has not held that the Constitution is "color-blind." The law may make racial distinctions if their purpose is benign or intended to remedy the consequences of past discrimination. This interpretation of the Constitution is controversial. Many people believe that policies designed to make it easier for blacks to get into state universities or to get government contracts are merely "reverse discrimination" and that busing to achieve racial balance in the schools is undesirable. These individuals argue that what is necessary is **equality of opportunity,** and to this end the Constitution should be color-blind. But other people believe that the harmful effects of centuries of slavery and segregation can only be overcome if the government is allowed to take race into account in making policy. This is especially the case, they hold, if informal social forces lead blacks and whites to live in separate neighborhoods, thereby minimizing the amount of contact they have with one another and reducing black access to certain kinds of jobs and schools. These people argue that what is necessary is **equality of result,** and that to this end the Constitution should permit compensatory or **affir-mative-action** programs.

The Supreme Court has wrestled with this issue many times, and the results are not easily summarized. In general it has allowed race to be taken into account in giving people access to jobs and schooling *if* there has been a past practice of discrimination and *if* race is used for benign purposes. But there remains a lot of confusion in the law. Here are some important Court decisions on this matter:

1. *Schools can be required to admit black students even after they have repealed laws and rules that once kept blacks out. Giving blacks "freedom of choice" is not enough.* Formerly all-white schools can actually be required to have black students in attendance and to use busing to bring in black children.[74]

2. *The courts will order busing only within a city, unless it can be shown that the suburban areas have in fact practiced segregation.* Busing limited to the central city has been approved in Charlotte, Boston, Detroit, Atlanta, Denver, Indianapolis, and Richmond, among other places; busing across city lines has been approved in Louisville and Wilmington.[75]

3. *A university medical school can "take race into account" in admitting students but cannot use explicit racial quotas.* Allen Bakke, a white, was wrongly excluded from the medical school of the University of California at Davis because it had used a numerical quota to give preference to blacks.[76]

4. *If an industry or occupation has a past history of racial discrimination, quotas may be used by voluntary agreement or government requirement to remedy the effects of that discrimination.* Where there was a history of discrimination, contractors can be required to set aside 10 percent of their contract funds to purchase services from minority-owned businesses, unions can be required to recruit black members, and state police departments and municipal fire departments can be required to hire blacks on the basis of a quota system. But if there is no clear showing of past discrimination, setting aside a percentage of city contracts for minority-owned businesses is unconstitutional. A factory and a union can voluntarily adopt a quota system for selecting black workers for a training program.[77]

5. *If there is no past history of discrimination, no mandatory hiring or promotional plan favoring blacks is permissible.* Black teachers cannot be given preferential promotions over whites when it has not been proven that the school system has discriminated.[78] But even without a history of past discrimination, a voluntary affirmative-action plan can be used to hire women in preference to men.[79]

The passage of expanded civil-rights laws and the court decisions on key civil-rights cases have not occurred in a vacuum. Since the 1960s, the propor-

Federal courts held that opening formerly all-white schools to blacks was not enough: where past discrimination had existed, black students would have to attend those schools even if it meant bringing them by bus.

tion of whites who have expressed (and probably acted on) more tolerant views regarding race relations has increased steadily (see Figure 11.1). At the same time, the number of blacks holding elective office at all levels of government has grown sharply (see Table 11.1). The shift in opinion and the growth in black political power help explain why the Civil Rights Restoration Act of 1988 passed Congress by lopsided majorities, compared to the narrower victories won by the civil-rights laws of the 1960s.

Sex and "Reasonable Classifications"

While race is a "suspect" classification, sex is not. One reason may be that laws putting women in a special category had a different history and a different justification than laws putting blacks in a special category. Segregationist laws were designed to separate blacks from whites and thereby subjugate them to white rule. Laws limiting the opportunities of women did not aim at segregating them from men and were supposedly intended to protect women. For example, in 1908 the Supreme Court upheld an Oregon law that limited female laundry workers to a ten-hour work day (men were allowed to work as long as they wished). The Court held that men and women differed in strength, functions, and self-reliance, and so women required special protection.[80]

Percentage of white respondents not objecting

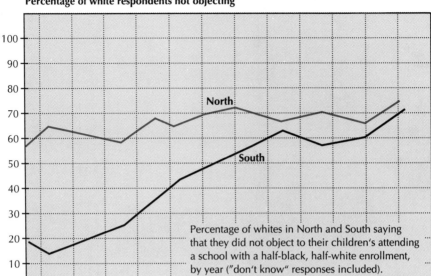

FIGURE 11.1 Changing White Attitudes Toward School Integration

SOURCE: Howard Schuman, Charlotte Steeh, and Lawrence Bobo, *Racial Attitudes in America* (Cambridge, Mass.: Harvard University Press, 1985), 69.

The feminist movement has, of course, challenged the claim that men and women differ in ways that require different legal treatment. In response, Congress and state legislatures have passed laws that eliminate many of the old gender-based distinctions. Today discrimination based on sex in employment and education is (in general) illegal: men and women must receive equal pay for equal work, and male and female students must receive equal opportunities in colleges and universities receiving federal funds.

At the same time, the Supreme Court began altering the standards it applied to laws and practices that treated men and women differently. The traditional standard, as we saw in the 1908 case, reflected a kind of protective paternalism; under it, no state law was ever held unconstitutional because of sex discrimination. In 1971, however, the Court overturned an Idaho statute that gave men preference over women in the appointment of administrators of the estates of deceased children. A unanimous Court set down a new standard: to be constitutionally permissible, any law that classifies people on the basis of sex "must be reasonable, not arbitrary, and must rest on some ground of difference having a fair and substantial relation to the object of the legislation so that all persons similarly circumstanced shall be treated alike."[81]

TABLE 11.1 Increase in Number of Black Elected Officials

Office	1970	1990
Congress and state legislatures	182	440
City and county offices	715	4,481
Judges and sheriffs	213	769
Boards of education	362	1,645
Total	1,472	7,335[a]

SOURCE: *Statistical Abstract of the United States, 1992,* Table 432.

[a]Of this total, 5,037 are in the South.

This was a milder test than the one the Court had developed to judge racial classifications, which were always "suspect" and thus had to survive the strict scrutiny of the Court. In a later decision, some justices wanted to abandon the standard of reasonableness applied to sex and replace it with the same standard governing laws involving race—that they are "inherently suspect." But there was no majority for this view.[82]

Under the **reasonableness standard,** the courts have overturned some distinctions based on sex and have permitted others. Here are some examples.

Decisions Barring Differences Based on Sex:

★ A state cannot set different ages at which men and women become legal adults.[83]

★ A state cannot set different ages at which men and women are allowed to buy beer.[84]

★ Women cannot be barred from jobs by arbitrary height and weight requirements.[85]

★ Employers cannot require women to take mandatory pregnancy leaves.[86]

★ Girls cannot be barred from Little League baseball teams.[87]

★ The Junior Chamber of Commerce and the Rotary Club, though private associations, cannot exclude women from membership.[88]

★ Though women as a group live longer than men, an employer must pay women monthly retirement benefits equal to those received by men.[89]

★ High schools must pay coaches of girls' sports the same as they pay coaches of boys' sports.[90]

The civil-rights law of 1964 bans discrimination in employment on the grounds of sex as well as race.

Decisions Allowing Differences Based on Sex:

★ A law that punishes males but not females for statutory rape is permissible; men and women are not "similarly situated" with respect to sexual relations.[91]

★ All-boy and all-girl public schools are permitted if enrollment is voluntary and quality is equal.[92]

★ States can give widows a property-tax exemption not given to widowers.[93]

★ The navy may allow women to remain officers longer than men without being promoted.[94]

Perhaps the most far-reaching cases defining the rights of women have involved the draft and abortion. In 1981 the Court held in *Rostker* v. *Goldberg* that Congress may draft men but not women without violating the due-process clause of the Fifth Amendment.[95] In the area of national defense, the Court will give greater deference to congressional policy (Congress has already decided to bar women from combat roles). The controversy over whether women should be treated the same as men in the military was one of the major issues in the debate over the Equal Rights Amendment. If the ERA had been ratified, it would have overturned *Rostker* v. *Goldberg.*

Abortion

State laws forbidding abortions were ruled unconstitutional in 1973 in the case *Roe* v. *Wade*[96], a decision reaffirmed in other cases. This bitterly controversial decision gave rise to two competing social movements—the opponents of abortion want to amend the Constitution to permit such state laws, and the defenders of abortion hope to get federal laws changed to allow the use of government funds to pay for abortions for poor women.

Neither movement has succeeded. Congress has refused to adopt the constitutional amendment and has passed, with the Court's blessing, a series of laws (the best known is the "Hyde Amendment") barring the use of federal funds for abortions in all but a few special circumstances. The Supreme Court has upheld the constitutionality of such laws, as well as that of even more restrictive state ones.[97]

For sixteen years the Court defended *Roe* v. *Wade* by, for example, striking down a state law that required an underage girl to have her parents' consent before getting an abortion. But in 1989, under the influence of justices appointed by President Reagan, the court began to uphold some state restrictions on abortions.[98]

When that happened, many people predicted that in time *Roe* v. *Wade* would be overturned, especially if President Bush appointed more justices. Although he appointed two (Souter and Thomas), *Roe* survived. Justices O'Connor, Souter, and Kennedy cast the key votes. In 1992, in its *Casey* decision, the Court by a vote of 5–4 explicitly refused to overturn *Roe*. It upheld a variety of restrictions imposed by the state of Pennsylvania on women seeking abortions. These included a mandatory twenty-four-hour waiting period between the request for and the performance of an abortion, the obligation of teenagers to obtain the consent of one parent (or, in special circumstances, of a judge), and a state requirement that a woman contemplating an abortion be given pamphlets about alternatives. Similar restrictions had been enacted in many other states, all of which looked to the Pennsylvania case for guidance as to whether they could be enforced. The Court, however, struck down a state law that would have required a married woman to obtain the consent of her husband. In allowing these restrictions, the Court overruled some of its earlier decisions. The key provisions of the *Casey* decision are summarized in the box on page 336.[99]

The ERA

The extension to women, by law and court order, of a wide range of rights was sufficiently steady to make it seem for a while that the passage of an Equal Rights Amendment (ERA) to the Constitution was a foregone conclusion.

THE CONSTITUTIONAL POSITION OF ABORTION LAWS AS OF 1992

★ ★ ★

THIS IS WHAT THE MAJORITY OF THE
COURT HELD IN THE CASEY DECISION:

1. "It is a constitutional liberty of the woman to have some freedom to terminate her pregnancy. . . . No state may prohibit a woman from terminating her pregnancy" before the fetus becomes "viable."

2. After the fetus has become viable, a state may "regulate, and even proscribe, abortion except where it is necessary . . . for the preservation of the life and the health of the mother."

   Note: The point at which a fetus becomes "viable"—that is, capable of living outside the mother's womb—may change with changes in medical science. The old distinction in *Roe* between the first, second, and third trimesters was discarded in the *Casey* decision.

3. States may put restrictions on the right to an abortion, but these restrictions must not place an "undue burden" on the exercise of a woman's rights.

An "undue burden" is defined as a legal restriction that has the "purpose or effect" of placing a "substantial obstacle in the path of a woman seeking an abortion before the fetus attains viability." Parental notification and waiting periods were not judged to be undue burdens.

THIS IS THE CORE ARGUMENT OF THE
JUSTICES WHO DISSENTED FROM THE
CASEY DECISION:

Roe was wrongly decided and should be overturned because nothing in the Constitution provides for a right to abortion. It should be left to the political process in the states to decide this issue.

That amendment, which had been before Congress since 1923, read in its operative clause: "Equality of rights under the law shall not be denied or abridged by the United States or any State on account of sex."

When Congress in 1972 passed this amendment and sent it to the states for consideration, the prospects for its prompt ratification seemed excellent. It had sailed through Congress by votes of 84–8 in the Senate and 354–24 in the House; every president from Harry Truman to Jimmy Carter and both political parties had endorsed it; opinion polls showed the public to be in favor of it; and women—the group that would benefit from it—accounted for half the voting population.

The optimism of its backers appeared for the moment to be justified. Within the first year, the legislatures of twenty-two states ratified the ERA, most by overwhelming votes. By 1974–1975, however, the amendment was clearly in trouble: it barely squeaked through the Montana senate and the North Dakota house, and two states (Nebraska and Tennessee) voted to rescind their earlier ratifications. By 1978 the ratification effort was stalled. Thirty-five states had ratified, three short of the necessary three-fourths; three states had rescinded their earlier ratifications; and repeated efforts to get the ERA ratified in such key states as Illinois and Florida had failed. Moreover, the time originally allowed for the ratification process—until March 22, 1979—was about to expire.

Congress was persuaded to extend the period allowed for ratification to June 30, 1982, but not one of the fifteen states refusing to ratify changed its position. Thus the ERA is no longer before the states. How can the reversal of this measure be explained?

What began as an apparently noncontroversial matter ended by being deeply controversial. That fact alone worked against it: since three-fourths of the states must ratify, the opponents needed only 13 of the 99 state legislative houses to vote no.* And legislators do not like to take positions on controversial matters, especially after it becomes evident that many of the supposed beneficiaries—in this case, women—were themselves opposed. One particularly important issue was the draft: many legislators and voters otherwise favoring the ERA worried that its passage would require that women be drafted for combat duty. Proponents of the ERA, such as the National Organization for Women (NOW), had difficulty countering that argument. Another issue was whether the ERA would eliminate laws that protected women in the workplace (such as maximum-hour or minimum-wage laws). This was a concern of the Mormon Church and of the National Council of Catholic Women.

In the end the ERA became an issue that symbolized the conflict over a broad range of cultural values in the United States. In 1980 the Republican party withdrew its endorsement of the ERA, and the people elected a president known to oppose it. Then in 1982, a federal judge in Idaho held that Congress had acted unconstitutionally when it extended the deadline for ratification and when it refused to allow states to rescind their earlier ratifications. As of 1993, Congress has not produced the two-thirds majority necessary to resubmit the ERA to the states.

New laws and court interpretations of existing laws and of the equal-protection clause of the Fourteenth Amendment could in time achieve most of what the ERA supporters had contemplated. However, one effort to expand

---

*Forty-nine states have two-house (bicameral) legislatures; one state, Nebraska, has a one-house (unicameral) legislature.

women's rights by law and court ruling has become deeply controversial. This effort seeks to guarantee that women be paid not only equal pay for equal work but also equal pay for *comparable* work. The **comparable-worth** movement would require, for example, that librarians (most of whom are women) be paid the same as, say, truck drivers (most of whom are men). Several local governments have adopted comparable-worth pay policies over the objections of those who say only the market—and not the government—can determine whether one job is worth as much as another.

SUMMARY

Civil liberties and civil rights are limitations placed by the Constitution—and by court interpretations of it—on what powers the government can exercise over people. The most important of these rights are listed in the first ten amendments, called the Bill of Rights. But few, if any, rights and liberties are absolute: most of the time rights are in conflict.

Over the years, the right of free expression has been greatly enlarged so that few important governmental limits exist on what we can say or write or on how we can worship. Government support of church-related activities remains controversial. At the same time, the rights of people accused of crimes have been broadened mostly by means of the **exclusionary rule**—the court-devised doctrine that makes it illegal to introduce into a trial evidence that was improperly gathered.

The equal-protection and due-process clauses of the Fourteenth Amendment restrict the power of the states to treat different groups of people differently. Different treatment is unconstitutional if it is unreasonable. In deciding what treatment is unreasonable, the courts have subjected classifications based on race, but not those based on sex, to strict scrutiny. A racial classification is always suspect; a gender classification is not inherently suspect but it must be reasonable.

SUGGESTED READINGS

Berns, Walter. *The First Amendment and the Future of American Democracy.* New York: Basic Books, 1976. A fresh look at what the Founders intended by the First Amendment that takes issue with contemporary Supreme Court interpretations of it.

Clor, Harry M. *Obscenity and Public Morality.* Chicago: University of Chicago Press, 1969. Argues for the legitimacy of legal restrictions on obscenity.

Emerson, Thomas I. *Toward a General Theory of the First Amendment.* New York: Random House, 1966. Argues, contrary to Walter Berns (cited above), that the First Amendment confers an absolute protection of speech.

Flexner, Eleanor. *Century of Struggle: The Women's Rights Movement in the United States,* rev. ed. Cambridge, Mass.: Harvard University Press, 1975. A historical account of the feminist movement and its political strategies.

Franklin, John Hope. *From Slavery to Freedom,* 4th ed. New York: Knopf, 1974. A survey of black history in the United States.

Kluger, Richard. *Simple Justice.* New York: Random House/Vintage, 1977. Detailed and absorbing account of the school desegregation issue, from the Fourteenth Amendment to the *Brown* case.

Levy, Leonard W. *Legacy of Suppression: Freedom of Speech and Press in Early American History.* Cambridge, Mass.: Harvard University Press, 1960. Careful study of what the Founders and the early leaders meant by freedom of speech and press.

Mansbridge, Jane J. *Why We Lost the ERA.* Chicago: University of Chicago Press, 1986. Analyzes the politics of the Equal Rights Amendment.

Orfield, Gary. *Congressional Power: Congress and Social Change.* New York: Harcourt Brace Jovanovich, 1975. Analysis of the legislative politics of the major civil rights laws.

Pritchett, C. Herman. *Constitutional Civil Liberties.* Englewood Cliffs, N.J.: Prentice-Hall, 1984. Chapters 10 and 12 provide an excellent summary of the constitutional basis of civil rights.

Sindler, Allan P. *Bakke, DeFunis, and Minority Admissions.* New York: Longman, 1978. History and analysis of the landmark Supreme Court case on affirmative action and quotas in college admissions.

12

★ ★ ★

Politics and Public Policy

TALK TO ALMOST ANY CITIZEN about American government and you will get a long list of complaints that generally fall into two groups. The first are gripes about politics: "Politicians are self-serving captives of special-interest groups, interested only in their own reelection. Judges are too liberal (or too conservative). The media are too interested in trivial scandals (or not interested enough in important scandals). The president and Congress are in gridlock, unable or unwilling to take decisive action." The second group are grievances about policies: "It's outrageous that we have this budget deficit; why can't we manage to live within our means? Why can't the government do something about (take your pick) crime, drug abuse, racism, poor schools, air pollution, welfare dependency, or Japanese competition?"

A lot of people think that there is a connection between our political problems and our policy failures. In their opinion, we don't solve the problems of the deficit, or crime, or racism, or Japanese competition *because* our politicians are self-serving, the press doesn't do its job right, the courts are filled with wrong-headed judges, and special-interest groups are too powerful. Many people who think that way decided to support Ross Perot when the Texas businessman announced that he would run for president as an independent in 1992. They apparently were saying that we could solve our problems if only we had strong, dedicated leaders.

This view of how to fix the system, or even whether the system needs fixing at all, has some truth to it, but for the most part it is too simple. Having read this book so far, you should understand that the way our system works is not mainly the result of the people in charge of it, but mainly (though not entirely) the result of the Constitution that shapes it. The Constitution was written not to make governing easy but to make it hard; not to facilitate choices, but to impede them; not to empower leaders, but to frustrate them. The written and unwritten constitutions of European democracies are very different: they were designed to allow the government to govern, subject only to the periodic checks of a popular election. Here, popular participation is encouraged; there, it is discouraged. Here, the courts can overturn presidential and congressional actions; there, they cannot. Here, many officials have the power to say "no" and none has the power to say "yes" and make it stick; there, a prime minister can say "yes" and make it stick.

How the American System Affects Policy-Making

This system for making policy creates quite predictable results, and among them are the very aspects of politics that so many Americans find distasteful. Consider the effects of four constitutional provisions on how we make policy:

1. *The separation of powers:* This has at least two important results. First, the president and Congress will be rivals, even when they are from the same political party. The White House and Congress will compete for power over the policies and personnel of the government. Stalemates will be the rule, not the exception, and they will only be overcome by a national crisis, a powerful tide of public opinion, or tough political bargaining. For example, if the president wants to cut the deficit by reducing spending and Congress wants to cut it by increasing taxes, a political standoff will occur, as during much of the Reagan and Bush administrations. Second, members of Congress will first and foremost represent their districts and states. Virtually no bill will become a law unless it is first adjusted to reflect the differing demands of local constituencies. A president may complain that members of Congress work to get "unnecessary" benefits—roads, bridges, parks, and airports—for their districts, but he forgets that this is exactly what the voters want from their members. Calling it "pork-barrel politics" doesn't change that fundamental political reality.

2. *Federalism:* The states have an independent political position. As a result, it will be very hard to have a truly "national" policy on anything. And

When the economy goes sour, a president has to make that his number one priority—even if he can't do much about it. After Bill Clinton defeated George Bush on this issue, he convened a summit meeting of economists, labor leaders, and business executives to discuss what he should do.

even when we do have a national policy, the states will play a big role in implementing it. For example, the states have a large say in setting and administering welfare benefits, enforcing pollution-control programs, and building major highways, even though most of the money comes from Washington. And they play the dominant role in schooling, law enforcement, and land-use controls and pay most of those bills.

3. *Judicial review:* The federal courts can declare an act of the president or Congress unconstitutional and can decide suits brought by people arguing either that a federal agency has exceeded its legal authority or that it has not done all that the law requires. The courts have obviously played a decisive role in racial integration and civil-liberties cases, but they also play an important, though less visible, role in implementing laws affecting the environment, occupational safety and health, and highway construction.

4. *Freedom of speech and assembly:* The First Amendment guarantees the right of individuals to speak their minds and lobby their senators and representatives. This right cannot be preserved for individuals and denied to groups; after all, groups are just collections of like-minded individuals. As

a result, placing any meaningful restrictions on the activities of lobbyists is next to impossible (except, of course, to ensure that they do not engage in corruption, such as bribery).

When you add together the effects of these four features of our Constitution, you get a uniquely American system of government policy-making. Though it has many distinctive features, the best word to describe our system of government is **adversarial**—that is, a system that encourages participation by people who have an incentive to fight rather than cooperate. Freedom of speech protects a person's right to participate; the separation of powers and federalism means that any participant can usually find a political ally; the decentralized organization of Congress (which is one effect of federalism and the separation of powers) gives each member an incentive to call attention to himself or herself by making speeches, taking positions, and (above all) attacking adversaries; and the courts provide a convenient (though expensive) arena in which to wage endless struggles.

One can see our adversarial system at work in many policy arenas. Business and government fight over what environmental protection rules to enforce. (You may be surprised to learn that in much of Europe, they cooperate rather than fight in deciding the rules.) Pro-environment groups attack business, portraying it in the worst possible light; antiabortion groups attack proabortion groups (and vice versa). Anyone offering a plan to reduce the deficit quickly discovers that every interest that might be adversely affected (either by paying higher taxes or receiving smaller benefits) is highly organized and ready to do battle. When a government agency issues an unpopular order, we don't usually respond by obeying but by claiming that our rights have been violated and threatening to sue or hold a protest march.

Not all of these situations occur as the inevitable result of our Constitution; the next chapter discusses the historical forces that have intensified these problems in recent decades. But however much events have aggravated these tendencies, the tendencies themselves arise directly from the kind of government that we have chosen.

Adversarial politics puts a premium on the ability to dramatize issues, gain publicity, mount demonstrations, and attack opponents. It downplays the ability to conduct quiet negotiations, make commitments, or accept personal responsibility.

In making policy in a participatory, adversarial system, politicians have no incentive to say that the government shouldn't tackle a problem or doesn't know how to solve it and every incentive to claim that government must "do something" and they know just what to do. The more such things are done, the more interest groups will have an incentive to organize lobbying efforts and open offices in Washington. The more such offices are opened, the greater the pressure to draft more bills and the smaller the chances that any given bill will make much sense.

Adversarial politics also colors our judgment as to the actual level of corruption and misconduct in our government. The checks and balances of our constitutional system and the individualistic style of political campaigning give everybody an incentive to dig up dirt and blow the whistle on a rival. By contrast, in parliamentary regimes such as those in Europe, these checks and balances and individualistic rivalries are much less common, and therefore the incentive to expose a rival also diminishes. As a result, lying and corruption seem more prevalent here than abroad when in fact we may have less; it is just that here more gets exposed—or invented.

Given these features of our system, what is surprising is that anything gets done at all. But it does. Preoccupied as we are with all the government's failings, we sometimes forget its accomplishments. Since the end of World War II, our government has built an interstate highway system, passed a set of civil-rights laws, created the Medicare program for the elderly, adopted a series of increasingly tough environmental laws, explored outer space, deregulated the airlines, waged and won a forty-five-year Cold War against the former Soviet Union, and sustained a level of economic growth and freedom sufficient to make millions of people from all parts of the world want to immigrate to this country. It paid a price, of course, for all of this: higher taxes, more regulations, and new groups to assimilate.

How Things Get Done

Since our complex political system makes it easy for all kinds of people and groups to wield at least some power, we should not expect policies to get made in only one way. If we had a less participatory, less adversarial system, it would be much easier to explain policy-making. In Japan, for example, appointed officials—bureaucrats—have much more power than their American counterparts, and so much Japanese policy-making is the result of government agencies making proposals that are only modestly changed, if changed at all, by the legislature. In Great Britain, the prime minister enjoys a great deal of power for as long as his or her party has a majority in the House of Commons, and so discussing British policy-making involves explaining why the prime minister favors one policy over another.

In the United States, everybody gets into the act. Some policies are proposed by the president and enacted (after many changes) by Congress; others are proposed by members of Congress and enacted despite presidential objections. (The Congress may override the president's veto or sufficiently modify the proposal to get him to withhold his veto.) When a congressional majority forms around a proposal, it is not always the result of one party (say, the Democrats) outvoting the other (the Republicans); rather, the majority often consists of a coalition of Democrats and Republicans winning out over a smaller coalition of other Democrats and Republicans.

FOUR KINDS OF POLITICAL COALITIONS

The key to understanding policy-making in the United States is understanding how these coalitions form. There are various theories of coalition formation. Many will be familiar to you even though you may not have thought of them as "theories" or given them these labels.

Client Politics

In this view, a small group that would benefit from the policy rounds up the necessary votes. The group may be dairy farmers who want federal subsidies for the milk they produce, labor unions that want to ensure that only union members can get jobs working on federal projects, sugar-beet growers who want to restrict imports of cheaper sugar produced abroad, or a town that wants a new airport. These groups are called "clients" because they will be beneficiaries of the policy if it is adopted. Many people have this in mind when they talk about "special-interest" or "pork-barrel" politics.

The reason such groups can win is that nobody else stands to lose enough to make it worthwhile to organize and fight against the policy. Subsidies to dairy farmers or restrictions on importing foreign-made sugar will raise the price of milk and sugar for the consumer, but usually not by enough for consumers to worry about it. And even if the price increase is large, most consumers will not be aware of it. (Dairy subsidies may cost people about twenty cents per gallon of milk, but hardly anyone knows that and those who know don't care that much.) And even if consumers know and care, it would be very hard for them to organize any opposition to these policies. Imagine trying to persuade your friends to protest against the dairy lobby just to get the price of milk reduced—maybe!—by twenty cents a gallon. Most people would say it wasn't worth the time and trouble. The same is true of policies that require that workers be paid the "prevailing" wage (which is usually the union wage) for building a new federal courthouse. Hardly anybody cares enough about the amount by which this policy increases the cost of the building to do anything about it. And most people don't care whether Jonesville gets a new airport or Smithtown gets a new bridge; all they care about is getting these things for their towns, too. It is easy to see why Congress votes for these proposals. Somebody who stands to gain a lot supports each proposal, often with campaign contributions, personal lobbying, and threats of voter reprisals if the group gets turned down. Hardly anyone opposes it, and those who do rarely represent any well-organized or highly motivated group. Voting for these things is, in political jargon, a no-brainer. Any idiot would do it.

Because there is a clear beneficiary and no real opponent, client politics usually does not involve the political parties. Both Democrats and Republicans favor these proposals, albeit not unanimously (there are always a few in each party who want to defend the unorganized interests that may be adversely affected).

Some people think that all politics is client politics. They talk about how the "fat cats" and the "big interests" always get their way in Congress. But all politics is not client politics. For example, just about every organized interest in Washington opposed the 1986 tax reform act, because they feared they would lose some cherished tax loopholes. But they lost anyway. The auto industry opposed the auto safety act of 1966, but they lost. Most of the airlines opposed the airline deregulation bill of 1978, but they lost. To see why, we have to look at other ways by which political coalitions form and congressional votes are rounded up.

Entrepreneurial Politics

This theory explains why client groups sometimes lose. In this case, a very unusual kind of coalition is formed consisting of people who claim, rightly or wrongly, to speak on behalf of the large number of people who would benefit from a policy that imposes heavy costs on some small group. As we saw above, client groups often win because the average citizen has too small a stake in the outcome to take the trouble to fight. But sometimes a leader or a few activists will have the ability or good luck to be regarded as the spokespersons for the unorganized majority. To the extent they are successful in being perceived this way, they can often defeat client groups, either by repealing some policy the client group already enjoys or by imposing some new tax, regulation, or restriction on it.

The people who can do this are called **policy entrepreneurs.** Ralph Nader is a familiar example. For decades, he has successfully portrayed himself as the champion of the consumer. He has taken on automobile companies (by arguing for safety regulations) and even Congress itself (by fighting its efforts to vote itself a pay increase). But there are many other examples, not all of them from the liberal side of the political spectrum. The late Howard Jarvis mobilized voters in California to vote for a ballot measure (called Proposition 13) that sharply restricted the ability of local governments to levy property taxes or increase tax assessments.

Becoming a successful policy entrepreneur is not easy. Washington is filled with people who want to lead various causes; they spend countless hours wandering from one congressional office to the next looking for allies, usually finding none. Though some of their causes are nutty, some are worthwhile, but winning allies takes more than just having a good cause.

The key requirement is the ability to dramatize the issue. This usually means making it front-page news. Ralph Nader is a master at this, beginning with his revelation that General Motors had attempted to spy on him when he was leading a campaign for an auto-safety law. Instantly the issue was transformed from auto safety (in which few Americans were interested) into "ruthless big business" (in which many were interested). Events can create policy entrepreneurs. The oil spill on the beaches of Santa Barbara, California, in 1968, made it easier for the organizers of the first Earth Day to dramatize environmental problems. Since then, the environmental movement has highlighted (not always accurately) other events to further its gains, such as the story about toxic waste supposedly harming the residents of Love Canal or apples treated with the chemical Alar allegedly harming people who ate them.

Dramatizing an issue is easier when you can portray the opponent of your policy as not just wrong but evil, when your opponent has made a newsworthy blunder, if friendly reporters and editors willingly print or broadcast the story, if the story can be cast in terms with which the public readily sympathizes, and when like-minded congressional staffers are willing to persuade a member of Congress to hold a well-publicized hearing to investigate the issue. Understanding entrepreneurial politics, therefore, involves understanding the kinds of symbols and appeals to which attentive members of the public, journalists, and congressional staffers respond. These will change from generation to generation. Once "Americanism" and "anticommunism" were powerful symbols; today, "cancer" and "the spaceship earth" are powerful. The proponents of handgun control labored for years to find a compelling symbol that would produce votes for their proposal and almost found it when James Brady, President Reagan's former press secretary, was shot in the head during a failed attempt to assassinate the president. Bills restricting access to handguns soon became known as "Brady bills," and Brady himself testified in support of them. But for many Americans, the "right to bear arms" is an even more powerful symbol than the sight of a seriously wounded public official, and so only modest restrictions have been enacted.

Interest-Group Politics

This theory says that policies are made as a result of the pulling and hauling of rival, organized interests. Some political scientists call it the **pluralist** theory of politics. In this view, the winning coalition consists of whichever side has amassed the most votes. There is generally no way to predict which side that will be; everything depends on the relative size, strength, and energy of rival interest groups. But in any particular case, you may be able to predict the winner by measuring size, strength, and energy. You might ask, for example, which side has the most members, makes the biggest campaign contributions through political action committees (PACs), or has the best access to the mass media. For example, when the occupational safety and health bill was first proposed in the late 1960s, labor unions favored it and most businesses opposed it. There was a furious struggle that the unions won, in part because they had more members whom they could mobilize.

Interest-group politics occurs whenever some specific group, town, occupation, or industry stands to gain significantly from the proposal and some other specific group, town, occupation, or industry stands to lose a lot. Each side will have enough at stake to make it worthwhile to organize, spend money, buy advertisements, mail letters, and buttonhole legislators. That occurs, for example, when labor unions want a law restricting a business from closing a plant and businesses oppose such a law; or when American automakers and unionized autoworkers want a law reducing the importation of Japanese-built cars and people who sell Japanese cars want no such reductions. For interest-group politics to occur, the stakes do not have to involve money. People may feel so strongly about some issue that they will fight tooth and nail even though they stand to gain nothing of monetary value. This is obviously the case with the struggle between proabortion and antiabortion groups. Many of the participants in these battles will not personally be affected by the outcome, but they have strong convictions nonetheless.

Members of Congress don't like an intense, evenly matched interest-group battle because it forces them to take sides. This is especially true of members who have in their districts large numbers of people on both sides of the issue. As citizens, we are often irritated by the tendency of politicians to be mealy-mouthed, talking about important issues in ways that avoid taking a clear position. We should realize that this tendency does not reveal a flaw in their character, however. If we were in their shoes, we would probably do exactly the same thing unless, of course, we didn't care about getting reelected. And if winning office wasn't important, you wouldn't be in politics in the first place.

Political parties usually don't play a very big role in settling interest-group conflicts for the same reason individual members wish that they didn't have to take sides. Most such conflicts split the parties right down the middle. Because both the Democrats and the Republicans would like to win the support of autoworkers, union members, or business leaders, party leaders are careful to not go too far in backing one side or another. Some interest-group issues, however, happen to coincide with party labels. Abortion is one of these: though most Americans tend to take a middle position (tolerating abortion, but only under certain limited circumstances), those who strongly favor free choice are usually concentrated in the Democratic party while those who strongly oppose it are overwhelmingly Republican.

Interest-group politics doesn't end when Congress decides the issue. Each side will lobby hard to influence the kinds of people who get appointed to carry out the law. In many cases, the losing side will take its case to the courts, trying to block or modify enforcement of the law, and in all cases the struggle will continue before whatever administrative agency is charged with implementing it. Since there are so many places in American government where interest groups can plead their case—the president, the White House staff, the bureaucratic agency, the media, various congressional committees—the struggle is never over.

Some writers like to describe American politics as involving nothing but interest-group competition, or pluralism. But as we have seen with client politics, this isn't always the case. And it also isn't the case with the fourth kind of politics.

Majoritarian Politics

In this kind of political coalition the great majority of the people stand to benefit in some significant way and the great majority must pay the cost. This is what many people have in mind when they say, "the people ought to rule." Here they do. The only question is whether the benefits people expect to get will or will not exceed the costs they expect to pay. If the perceived benefits exceed the perceived costs, the proposal will have a lot of support.

That was the case when the Social Security Act was passed in 1935 and when Medicare was enacted thirty years later. These were popular measures because they held out to people the prospect of getting a lot—a retirement check, free medical care when they were old—in exchange for paying what started out as a rather small payroll tax. When people thought the United States was being pushed around by foreign countries—at one time, the Soviet Union; later, Iraq—they supported higher defense spending. When they thought these threats had lessened, they called for cuts in defense spending.

Obviously public opinion is the key factor in determining the outcome of majoritarian politics. Interest groups may reinforce what the public believes, but the group effort is usually not the decisive factor. For example, the American Association of Retired Persons (AARP) opposes cuts in Social Security benefits, but this popular program is unlikely to experience any cuts even if the AARP did not exist. Political parties don't play much of a role, either, because popular programs get support from both sides of the aisle. The only exception to this occurs when a new policy is first debated and no one is certain how popular it will be. Then, one party may favor it and the other oppose it. This happened when the Democrats backed Social Security and the Republicans were initially critical of it; it also occurred more recently when the Republicans backed military action against Iraq (Operation Desert Storm) and most congressional Democrats opposed it. But both parties quickly jump onto the same bandwagon when public opinion about the policy is clear (as the Republicans did with Social Security in the 1950s and the Democrats did with the Persian Gulf War in the 1990s).

Majorities in Congress can be produced by any one of these four types of politics. As a result, no single explanation of policy-making is correct, and the careful student should avoid using slogans that imply that there *is* a single explanation. Some people complain that the rich rule (but that statement isn't consistent with their tax rate, which is higher than that of the nonrich), some say that big business dominates (but that doesn't smuare with the passage of so many environmental policies opposed by business), some argue that organized labor calls the shots (but that theory can't explain why free-trade policies opposed by labor generally win out), and still others claim that party bosses or congressional leaders have all the clout (but this argument doesn't account for the small role that the party leaders play in client or majoritarian politics and the difficulty they have keeping their party members in Congress toeing the line). *On any given issue,* one or another group may be very powerful, but no group is powerful across all or even most issues.

SOME CAUTIONARY REMARKS

Having described these four types of politics, I want to caution the reader against certain common mistakes in applying this schema. First, not every issue fits neatly into one or another of these categories. Many don't fit at all and some fit into two simultaneously; this is especially true for foreign policy. Second, how people perceive the effects of a policy will change, in turn changing the political coalitions around that policy. For example, making less-polluting cars seemed like a good idea to everybody until some of the newer cars turned out to be less powerful and more expensive than the previous models. At that point, some autoworkers began worrying that they would lose their jobs because foreign manufacturers were doing a better job of complying with the new rules than were American carmakers. Similarly, Social Security looked like a great idea until the taxes to pay for it got very high, making it harder to increase benefits. At one time, federal subsidies for tobacco farmers seemed like a harmless case of client politics; people who bought cigarettes didn't care that they cost a few pennies more because of the subsidies. But when the adverse health consequences of smoking became better known, many members of Congress began to question the wisdom of such subsidies.

The words *client, entrepreneurial,* or *majoritarian* are intended only to explain the policy process, not to label the policies as good or bad. Client politics can be good (as when some very deserving group, such as crippled children, is the object of tax-supported research) or dubious (as when somebody receives subsidies to produce something that they ought to be able to produce without the subsidy). Entrepreneurial politics can lead to good outcomes (as when big cities reduce their smog levels) or questionable outcomes (as when useful drugs are kept off the market for years because of the fear that a few cases will yield adverse side effects). Majoritarian politics is certainly consistent with popular rule, but the public doesn't always see its own interests clearly. People may love the idea of having their medical bills paid in part by Medicare without understanding the inefficiencies that it can produce. They may like the idea of cleaner air but not see that one good way to achieve this is to tax gasoline so that people drive less.

Finally, bear in mind that the confusion and deadlocks of American politics, since they are caused largely by our constitutional system, cannot easily be corrected without changing that system fundamentally. Very few quick fixes or clever new leaders can make much of a difference. Moreover, the system that produces these problems also provides some very great advantages. The Constitution may encourage an adversarial system, but such a system is less likely to trample on our personal liberties than one that is less adversarial, less participatory, and more orderly. We all want our leaders to have the guts to make the tough decisions, but sometimes what we have in mind by way of a "tough decision" is something that gores the other fellow's ox. Strong leaders can gore your ox, too.

SUMMARY

American politics is a confusing, sometimes dispiriting spectacle because so many people have a chance to get into the act and the system encourages adopting an adversarial tone. Many people think they have little influence in government; that is sometimes true, but it is true because so many people try to have influence. This participatory, adversarial system arises directly out of our constitutional arrangements, especially the separation of powers, federalism, political freedom, and judicial review. That system also makes it very difficult for any one group to dominate the policy-making process. There are four different ways in which winning coalitions are pulled together to enact a policy: client politics, entrepreneurial politics, interest-group politics, and majoritarian politics.

SUGGESTED READINGS

Derthick, Martha, and Paul J. Quirk. *The Politics of Deregulation.* Washington, D.C.: Brookings Institution, 1985. A brilliant analysis of how three industries—airlines, trucking, and telecommunications—were deregulated despite industry opposition.

Kingdon, John W. *Agendas, Alternatives, and Public Policies.* Boston: Little, Brown, 1984. Insightful account of how issues, especially those involving health and transportation, get on (or drop off) the federal political agenda.

Polsby, Nelson W. *Political Innovation in America.* New Haven, Conn.: Yale University Press, 1984. Explains how the federal government adopted eight policy innovations.

Wilson, James Q., ed. *The Politics of Regulation.* New York: Basic Books, 1980. Analyzes regulatory politics in nine agencies using the four types of politics described in this chapter.

13

★ ★ ★

American Government: Continuity and Change

IN WRITING A CONSTITUTION intended to reconcile the competing demands of public order and personal liberty, the Framers devised a
political system in which it would be difficult to adopt new policies. For
any new policy to take effect, the House and the Senate have to agree
on a bill, the president has to sign it, and the courts have to accept it as
constitutional. Since the president and the members of Congress are
elected separately, neither branch of government can readily use a political party to control the other branch, and so no party system can (except under unusual circumstances) centralize by informal means what
the Constitution had decentralized by formal ones.

Moreover, the states enjoy special constitutional protection (for a
while, the state legislatures even chose the United States senators); this
means that the sphere in which the federal government can act—assuming it decides to take any action at all—is quite limited. To obtain a new
policy, its proponents have to navigate a difficult obstacle course, persuading hundreds of independent legislators that the new policy is in
their interests, does not violate states' rights, and will serve the common

The federal government has found it easy to devise programs to help the elderly but not so easy to stop drug abuse.

good. To defeat a new policy, its opponents need only persuade the majority of one key committee.

If the American political system is biased against action, how has it become so large, powerful, and expensive? If it is so hard for Congress and the president to agree, how is it that the federal government now spends a sum equal to one-fourth of the gross national product, has piled up a federal debt of nearly three *trillion* dollars, and employs more than three million civilians and nearly two million military personnel? If the federal government is so hedged in with constitutional restrictions, what enables that government to manage a vast welfare and retirement system, set rules determining how factories and businesses shall operate, strike down laws banning abortions, require that private colleges allow women to participate in intercollegiate sports, search our luggage before we board an airplane, compel all eighteen-year-old males to register for the draft, and insist (until recently) that the states impose a fifty-five mile per hour speed limit on all their highways?

The most striking change in American government since its founding has been the vast increase in the scope of its activities and the reach of its powers. For the first century and a half, the government in Washington behaved pretty much as the Framers had anticipated. It regulated foreign commerce, distributed the mail, and occasionally went to war. It carried on passionate debates about slavery and the right of women to vote, but dealt with the former only when an irrepressible conflict broke out and with the latter only after decades of agitation. Generally it spent no more money than it took in

from taxes, and these taxes were mostly on imported goods, not on personal incomes. During wartime, the government would get larger and run up a debt, but after the war it would shrink in size and return to pay-as-you-go financing. The standing army was minuscule. During an economic recession, a major argument would arise over whether something other than gold should be the basis for American currency (if dollar bills could be redeemed for silver, for example, more dollar bills could be printed and so money would be easier to get), but for the most part the advocates of maintaining a hard, gold-backed currency prevailed. A few efforts were made to regulate large corporations, especially the railroads, but in general government regulation of business was left to the states. And sometimes the Supreme Court prevented even the states from regulating businesses.

Until the mid-twentieth century, who ruled in Washington—and to what ends—made little difference in the lives of most citizens except in time of war or economic crisis. Governors and mayors were more in the public eye than presidents or members of Congress. Most senators and representatives served only one or two terms in office; there didn't seem to be much point in becoming a career legislator since Congress didn't do much, didn't pay much, and wasn't in session very often. If the Republicans were in power, the government tended to seek high tariffs; if the Democrats were in power, lower tariffs. Today, who rules and to what ends affect almost every aspect of our lives. Members of the House serve, on the average, five terms in office. What can explain the growth of the federal government?

In a sense, the question ought to be turned around. In a government whose leaders are chosen by a competitive struggle for the people's votes, candidates for office have a strong incentive to offer new programs to voters in order to win their support. It is hard to excite people by promising to do less for them; it is only natural therefore that politicians usually promise to do more. In acting this way, politicians are not behaving badly; they are behaving democratically. If politicians foster new programs, the interesting questions become these: What kept the federal government from growing rapidly in size from its very first years of existence? Why did it not become large and powerful until nearly the middle of this century?

RESTRAINTS ON GROWTH

There were three restraints on the growth of government in the nineteenth and early twentieth centuries. First, the Constitution was interpreted in a way that sharply limited what policies the federal government could adopt. For a century or more, the Supreme Court held that the federal government had only very limited powers to regulate business and commerce and that Congress could not delegate such powers as it had to administrative agencies. Similarly the Supreme Court for a long time maintained that the Bill of Rights only limited what the federal government could do, and so there was little or no basis for challenging in federal court what state governments were doing. For example, not until 1963 was there a federal constitutional right to have a lawyer appointed to represent a poor person in a state criminal trial. The ratification of the Fourteenth Amendment in 1868 in theory brought more state action under federal court scrutiny (it held that no state could "deprive any person of life, liberty, or property without due process of law"), but the Court interpreted this provision narrowly so that, for example, the amendment provided no basis for attacking school segregation as unconstitutional. The Court even held that a federal income tax was unconstitutional.

The Supreme Court could not have maintained its interpretation for as long as it did if that position had not been pretty much in accord with public opinion. This opinion was the second restraint on the growth of government. There was little or no popular demand for a federal welfare or retirement system, federal aid to local public education, a federal program to deal with crime, or federal action against segregation. Not even organized labor demanded a major federal role in industrial affairs. The American Federation of Labor, led by Samuel Gompers, resisted federal involvement in labor-management disputes and was not especially outspoken in calling for a national social security program. Even as late as the 1930s, during the depths of the Great Depression, public-opinion polls suggested that as many as half the voters were opposed to a federal unemployment compensation program. There were frequent popular demands by farmers for federal control over the railroads and by progressives for reforming the federal civil service, but these were matters well within the accepted limits of federal constitutional authority.

Even if people had wanted the federal government to do more, many of them lacked the political resources to back up their demands. This is the third reason that Washington had so small an agenda for so long. Although labor unions existed in the nineteenth century, it was not until after their right to organize was guaranteed in 1935 that they grew rapidly in numbers and influence. Whatever policies women might have wanted to see adopted did not stand much chance until women had won the vote, and that did not occur until 1920. Those elites who wanted to organize people concerned about the environment, consumer safety, and public health did not have the computerized mailing lists, foundation grants, and sympathetic journalists necessary to convert a cause into a campaign. Public-interest law firms, willing and able to pursue policy goals through the courts, scarcely existed.

RELAXING THE RESTRAINTS

In recent decades, each of these constraints on federal action has weakened or disappeared altogether. First, the courts have altered their interpretation of the Constitution in ways that have not only permitted but sometimes even required government action. The Bill of Rights has been extended so that almost all of its important provisions are now regarded as applying to the states (by having been incorporated into the due-process clause of the Fourteenth Amendment). This means that a citizen can use the federal courts to alter state policy to a greater degree than ever before. (Overturning state laws that ban abortions or require racially separate schools are two important examples of this change.) The special protection that the courts once granted property rights has been substantially reduced so that business can be regulated to a greater degree than previously. The Court has permitted Congress to give broad discretionary powers to administrative agencies, allowing bureaucrats to make decisions that once only Congress could make.

Second, public opinion has changed in ways that support an expanded role for the federal government. The public demanded action to deal with the Great Depression (the programs that resulted, such as Social Security, survived in part because the Supreme Court changed its mind about the permissible scope of federal action). Political elites changed their minds faster than the average citizen. Well-educated, politically active people began demanding federal policies regarding civil rights, public welfare, environmental protection, consumer safety, and foreign aid well before the average citizen became concerned with such things.

Once in place, most of these programs proved popular and so their continuance was supported by mass as well as elite opinion. The cumulative effect of this process was to blur, if not erase altogether, the line that once defined what the government had the authority to do. At one time, a new proposal was debated in terms of whether it was *legitimate* for the federal government to do it at all. Federal aid to education, for example, was usually opposed

Two turning points in American history: Women campaign to get the vote before the Nineteenth Amendment was ratified in 1920 and large industrial unions organize mass-production workers (here, Ford auto-workers in 1941).

because many people feared it would lead to federal control of local schools. But after so many programs (including federal aid to education) had been passed, people stopped arguing about whether a certain policy was *legitimate* and argued instead about whether it was *effective*.

Third, political resources have become more widely distributed. The number and variety of interest groups have increased enormously. The funds available from foundations for organizations pursuing specific causes have grown. It is now easier to get access to the federal courts than formerly was the case, and once in the courts the plaintiffs are more likely to encounter judges who believe that the law and the Constitution should be interpreted broadly to permit particular goals (for example, prison reform) to be attained by legal rather than legislative means. Hundreds of magazines and newsletters have arisen to provide policy information to specialized segments of opinion. The techniques of mass protest, linked to the desire of television to show pictorially interesting accounts of social conflict, have been perfected in ways that convey the beliefs of a few into the living rooms of millions.

Campaign-finance laws and court rulings have given legal status and constitutional protection to thousands of political-action committees (PACs) that raise and spend tens of millions of dollars from millions of small contributors.

College education, once the privilege of a tiny minority, has become the common experience of millions of people, so that the effects of college—in encouraging political participation and in shaping political beliefs—are now widely shared. The ability of candidates to win nomination for office no longer depends on their ability to curry favor with a few powerful bosses; it now reflects their skill at raising money, mobilizing friends and activists, cultivating a media image, and winning a primary election.

So great have been the changes in the politics of policy-making in this country starting in the 1930s that we can refer, with only slight exaggeration, to one policy-making system having been replaced by another (see box on pages 360 and 361).

The Old System

The Old System had a small agenda. Though people voted at a high rate and often took part in torchlight parades and other mass political events, political leadership was professionalized in the sense that the leadership circle was small, access to it was difficult, and the activists in social movements were generally kept out. Only a few major issues were under discussion at any time. A member of Congress had a small staff (if any at all), dealt with his or her colleagues on a personal basis, deferred to the prestige of House and Senate leaders, and tended to become part of some stable coalition (the farm bloc, the labor bloc, the southern bloc) that persisted across many issues.

When someone proposed adding a new issue to the public agenda, a major debate often arose over whether it was legitimate for the federal government to take action at all on the matter. A dominant theme in this debate was the importance of "states' rights." Except in wartime, or during a very brief period when the nation expressed an interest in acquiring colonies, the focus of policy debate was on domestic affairs. Members of Congress saw these domestic issues largely in terms of their effect on local constituencies. The presidency was small and somewhat personal; there was only a rudimentary White House staff. The president would cultivate the press, but there was a clear understanding that what he said in a press conference was never to be quoted directly.

For the government to take bold action under this system, the nation usually had to be facing a crisis. War presented such a crisis, and so the federal government during the Civil War and World Wars I and II acquired extraordinary powers to conscript soldiers, control industrial production, regulate the flow of information to citizens, and restrict the scope of personal liberty. Each succeeding crisis left the government bureaucracy somewhat larger than it had been before, but when the crisis ended, the exercise of extraordinary powers ended. Once again, the agenda of political issues became small, and legislators argued about whether it was legitimate for the government to enter some new policy area, such as civil rights or industrial regulation.

HOW AMERICAN POLITICS HAS CHANGED

★ ★ ★

OLD SYSTEM	NEW SYSTEM
CONGRESS:	CONGRESS:
Chairmen relatively strong	Chairmen relatively weak
Small staffs	Large staffs
Few subcommittees	Many subcommittees
INTEREST GROUPS:	INTEREST GROUPS:
A few large blocs (farmers, business, labor)	Many diverse interests that form ad hoc coalitions
Rely on "insider" lobbying	Mobilize grass roots
PRESIDENCY:	PRESIDENCY:
Small staff	Large staff
Reaches public via press conferences	Reaches public via radio and television

The New System

The New System began in the 1930s but did not take its present form until the 1970s. It is characterized by a large policy agenda, the end of the debate over the legitimacy of government action (except in the area of First Amendment freedoms), the diffusion and decentralization of power in Congress, and the multiplication of interest groups. The government has grown so large that it has a policy on almost every conceivable subject, and so the debate in Washington is less often about whether it is right and prudent to take some bold new step and more often about how the government can best cope with the strains and problems that arise from implementing existing policies. As someone once said, the federal government is now more concerned with managing than with ruling.

For example: In 1935 Congress debated whether the nation should have a Social Security retirement system at all; in the 1980s it debated whether the system could best be kept solvent by raising taxes or by cutting benefits. In the 1960s Congress argued over whether there should be any federal civil-rights laws at all; by the 1980s it was arguing over whether those laws should be administered in a way that simply eliminated legal barriers to equal opportunity for racial minorities or in a way that by affirmative action made up for the disadvantages that burdened such minorities in the past. As late as the 1950s, the president and Congress argued over whether it was right to adopt

OLD SYSTEM	NEW SYSTEM
COURTS:	COURTS:
Allow government to exercise few economic powers	Allow government to exercise broad economic power
Take narrow view of individual freedoms	Take broad view of individual freedoms
POLITICAL PARTIES:	POLITICAL PARTIES:
Are dominated by state and local party leaders meeting in conventions	Are dominated by activists chosen in primaries and caucuses
BRIEF POLICY AGENDA	LONG POLICY AGENDA
KEY QUESTION:	KEY QUESTION:
Should the federal government enter a new policy area?	How can we fix or pay for an existing policy?
KEY ISSUE:	KEY ISSUE:
Would a new federal program abridge states' rights?	Would a new federal program prove popular?

a new program if it meant that the government had to borrow money to pay for it. Today the existence of a huge federal deficit is taken for granted, and the debate in Washington now focuses on the best way to slow its rate of growth or cut it back slightly. As late as the 1960s, many members of Congress believed the federal government had no business paying for the health care of its citizens; today hardly anyone argues against having Medicare but many worry about how best to control its rising cost.

The differences between the Old and New Systems should not be exaggerated. The Constitution still makes it easier for Congress to block the proposals of the president, or for some committee of Congress to defeat the preferences of the majority of Congress, than is true in almost any other democratic government. The system of checks and balances operates as before. The essential differences between the Old and the New Systems are these:

1. Under the Old System, the checks and balances made it difficult for the federal government to *start* a new program, and so the government remained relatively small. Under the New System, these checks and balances made it hard to *change* what the government is already doing, and so the government remains large.

2. Under the Old System, power was *somewhat centralized* in the hands of party and congressional leaders. There was still plenty of conflict, but the number of people who had to agree before something could be done was

not large. Under the New System, power is much more *decentralized,* and so it is harder to resolve conflict because so many more people—party activists, interest-group leaders, individual members of Congress, heads of government agencies—must agree.

The transition from the Old to the New System occurred chiefly during two periods in American politics. The first was in the early 1930s when a catastrophic depression led the government to explore new ways of helping the needy, regulating business, and preventing a recurrence of the disaster. Franklin Roosevelt's New Deal was the result. The huge majorities enjoyed by the Democrats in Congress coupled with popular demands to solve the problem led to a vast outpouring of new legislation and the creation of dozens of new government agencies. Though initially the Supreme Court struck down some of these measures as unconstitutional, a key member of the Court changed his mind and others retired from the bench; by the late 1930s, the Court had virtually ceased opposing any economic legislation.

The second period was in the mid-1960s, a time of prosperity. There was no crisis akin to the Great Depression of World War II, but two events helped change the face of American politics. One was an intellectual and popular ferment that we now refer to as the spirit of "the sixties"—a militant civil-rights movement, student activism on college campuses aimed at resisting the Vietnam War, growing concern about threats to the environment, the popular appeal of Ralph Nader and his consumer-protection movement, and an optimism among many political and intellectual leaders that the government could solve whatever problems it was willing to address. The other was the 1964 election that returned Lyndon Johnson to the presidency with a larger share of the popular vote than any other president in modern times. Johnson swept into office with him huge Democratic majorities in both the House and Senate.

The combination of organized demands for new policies, elite optimism about the likely success of those policies, and extraordinary majorities in Congress meant that President Johnson was able, for a few years, to get almost any program he wanted enacted into law. So large were his majorities in Congress that the conservative coalition of Republicans and southern Democrats was no longer large enough to block action; northern Democratic liberals were sufficiently numerous in the House and Senate to take control of both bodies. And so much of Johnson's "Great Society" legislation became law. This included (1) the passage of Medicare (to help pay the medical bills of retired people) and Medicaid (to help pay the medical bills of people on welfare), (2) greatly expanded federal aid to the states to assist them in fighting crime, rebuilding slums, and running transit systems, (3) the enactment of major civil-rights laws and of a program to provide federal aid to local schools, (4) the creation of a "War on Poverty" that included various job-training and community-action agencies, and (5) the enactment of a variety of laws regulating business for the purpose of reducing auto fatalities, improving the safety and health of industrial workers, cutting back on pollutants entering the atmosphere, and safeguarding consumers from harmful products.

These two periods—the early 1930s and the mid-1960s—changed the political landscape in America. Of the two, the latter was perhaps the more important, for not only did it witness the passage of so much unprecedented legislation, but also it saw major changes in the pattern of political leadership. It was during this time that the great majority of the members of the House of Representatives came to enjoy relatively secure seats, the primary elections came to supplant party conventions as the decisive means of selecting presidential candidates, interest groups increased greatly in number, and television began to play an important role in shaping the political agenda and perhaps influencing the kinds of candidates that are nominated. (At least one major change in the political process occurred after the 1960s—the passage of the campaign-finance laws.)

Some people believed that the election of Ronald Reagan in 1981 meant that we had begun a new era of bold changes. No doubt the Reagan administration was more conservative than any other in a half a century; no doubt it made a major effort to alter how certain laws (such as in the area of civil rights) are administered. But rather little in the way of a legislative breakthrough occurred comparable to the breakthroughs of Franklin Roosevelt and Lyndon Johnson. Domestic spending was cut in certain areas; though the effect of a few of these cuts has been keen, there was no reduction in total outlays. (Federal spending, domestic as well as military, *increased* during the Reagan years.) There was a significant personal income-tax cut in 1981, but it was partially offset by increases in Social Security and business taxes in subsequent years. There was a buildup in our military, but even before Reagan left office the buildup had ended.

The politics of the deficit illustrate the features of the New System. The huge (approximately $300 billion) gap between what the government took in from taxes and what it spent on programs in 1992 would not exist in a government that had not acquired a large policy agenda—an expensive medical-care program, high levels of peacetime military spending, and many subsidies to various domestic interest groups. But the great difficulty the government experienced in trying to cut the deficit revealed, among other things, the effects of decentralized and fragmented political power: no group of officials could impose its preferences on the others.

SHOULD THE SYSTEM BE CHANGED?

Almost from the day it was ratified, the Constitution has been the object of debate over ways in which it might be improved. These debates have rarely involved the average citizen, who tends to revere the document even if he or she cannot recall all of its details. Because of this deep and broad popular support, scholars and politicians have been wary of attacking it or suggesting many wholesale changes. But such attacks have occurred, and during 1987, when we celebrated the bicentennial of its adoption, we heard a variety of suggestions for improving the Constitution, ranging from particular amendments to wholesale revisions. In general, there are today, as in the eighteenth century, two kinds of critics—those who think the federal government is too weak and those who think it too strong.

Reducing the Barriers to Action

To the first kind of critic, the chief difficulty with the Constitution is the separation of powers. By making every decision the uncertain outcome of the pulling and hauling between the president and Congress, the Constitution precludes the emergence, except perhaps in times of crisis, of the kind of effective national leadership the country needs. In this view our nation today faces a number of challenges that require prompt, decisive, and comprehensive action. Our position of international leadership and the need to find ways of stimulating economic growth (while reducing our dependence on foreign oil and conserving our environment) all require that the president be able to formulate and carry out policies free of some of the pressures and delays from interest groups and local-minded members of Congress.

This increase in presidential authority not only would make for better policies, these critics argue, but also it would help the voters hold the president and his party accountable for their actions. As matters now stand, nobody in government can be held responsible for policies: everybody takes the credit for successes and nobody takes the blame for failures. This is because the president, who tends to be the major source of new programs, cannot get his policies adopted by Congress without long delays and much bargaining, the result of which may be some watered-down compromise that neither the president nor Congress really likes but which each must settle for if anything is to be done at all.

Finally, critics of the separation of powers complain that the government agencies responsible for implementing a program are exposed to undue interference from members of Congress and the special interests that can capture a member's ear. In this view, the president is supposed to be in charge of the bureaucracy, but in fact he has to share that authority with countless legislators and legislative committees.

Not all critics of the separation of powers agree with all these points, nor do they all agree on what should be done about the problems. But they all have in common a fear that the separation of powers makes the president too weak and insufficiently accountable.

Their proposals for reducing the separation of powers include the following:

★ Allow the president to appoint members of Congress to serve in the cabinet (the Constitution forbids members from holding any federal appointive office while in Congress).

★ Allow the president to dissolve Congress and call for a special election (elections now can be held only on the schedule determined by the calendar).

★ Allow the Congress to require a president who has lost its confidence to face the country in a special election before his term would normally end.

★ Require the presidential and congressional candidates to run as a team in each congressional district so that each voter would have to vote for the team as a whole. Thus a presidential candidate who carries a given district could be sure that the congressional candidate of his party would also win in the district.

★ Have the president serve a single six-year term instead of being eligible for up to two four-year terms; this would presumably free him to lead without having to worry about reelection.

★ Lengthen the terms of members of the House of Representatives from two to four years so that the entire House would stand for reelection at the same time as the president.

Some of these proposals are offered out of a desire to make the American system of government work a bit more like the British parliamentary system in which the prime minister is the undisputed leader of his or her majority in the British parliament. The parliamentary system is the major democratic alternative in the world today to the American separation-of-powers system. Another way of describing the aims of these reforms is that they would combine the somewhat greater centralization of power characteristic of the Old System of making policy with the larger agenda and bigger government characteristic of the New System.

Both the diagnosis and the remedies proposed by these critics of the separation of powers have been challenged. Many defenders of the present Constitution believe that other nations with a more unified political system, such as Great Britain, have done no better than the United States in dealing with the problems of economic growth, national security, and environmental protection. Moreover, they argue, close congressional scrutiny of presidential proposals has improved those policies more often than it has weakened them. Finally, congressional "interference" in the work of government agencies is a good way of ensuring that the average citizen can fight back against the bureaucracy. Without that so-called interference, citizens and interest groups might be helpless before big, powerful agencies.

Each of the specific proposals, defenders of the present system argue, would either make matters worse or have at best uncertain effects. Adding a few members of Congress to the president's cabinet would not help him much in getting his programs through Congress: of the 535 senators and representatives, only about half a dozen would probably be in the cabinet. Giving either the president or Congress the power to call a special election between the regular elections (every two or four years) would cause needless confusion and great expense; the country would live under the threat of being in a perpetual political campaign with even weaker political parties. Linking the fate of the president and representatives by having them run as a team in each district would reduce the stabilizing and moderating effect of having them separately elected: if a Republican presidential candidate won, he would have a Republican majority in the House; if a Democratic candidate won, he would have a Democratic majority. With a linked ticket we might expect dramatic changes in policy as the political pendulum swung back and forth. Giving the president a single six-year term would indeed free him from the need to worry about reelection, but it is precisely that worry that keeps the president reasonably concerned about what the American people want.

Finally, defenders of the present system simply do not agree that the separation of powers makes government inert. They marvel at the sweeping domestic- and foreign-policy initiatives taken during this century. How, they ask, can a governmental system capable of launching a New Deal, a Great Society, and a rocket to the moon, of mobilizing for World War I, World War II, and Vietnam, and of readying to impeach a president for violating his oath of office be characterized as antiquated or prone to inaction?

Defenders believe that problems in the system may result less from the separation of powers and more from the inability (or unwillingness) of key political leaders to work within it. They point, for example, to Jimmy Carter's first years in office. Carter did relatively little to persuade Congress to support his early domestic initiatives. His party had a majority in both houses of Congress but that did not seem to matter. Several of his efforts to court the press and the public were bungled. If the separation of powers, and not a lack of political skills, explains the policy stalemate suffered by President Carter, then how, defenders ask, did his immediate successor in the Oval Office, Ronald Reagan, succeed in getting Congress to act quickly on his major domestic proposals?

Increasing the Barriers to Action

The second kind of critic of the Constitution thinks the government does too much, not too little. Though the separation of powers at one time may have slowed the growth of government and moderated the policies it adopted, in the last few decades government has grown helter-skelter. The problem, these critics argue, is not that democracy is a bad idea, but that democracy can produce bad, or at least unintended, results if the government caters to the special-interest claims of the citizens rather than to their long-term values.

To see how these unintended results might occur, imagine a situation in which every citizen thinks the government is too big, taxes too heavily, and spends too much. Each citizen wants the government made smaller by reducing the benefits other people get—but not by reducing the benefits he or she gets. In fact this citizen may even be willing to see his or her own benefits cut, provided everybody else's are cut as well, and by a like amount.

But the political system attends to individual wants, which may or may not be in the public interest. It gives aid to farmers, contracts to industry, grants to professors, pensions to the elderly, and loans to students. As someone once said, the government is like an adding machine: during elections, candidates campaign by promising to do more for whatever group is dissatisfied with what the present officeholders are doing for it. As a result, most elections bring to office men and women who are committed to doing more for somebody. The grand total of all these additions is more for everybody. No politician has an incentive to do less for anybody.

Moreover, a big government is hard to manage. When the government tries to do too much, it does nothing well. To these critics, our government is big without being strong, fat but not effective.

To remedy this state of affairs, these critics suggest various mechanisms, but principally a constitutional amendment that would either set a limit on the amount of money the government could collect in taxes each year, or require that each year the government have a balanced budget (that is, not spend more than it collects in taxes), or both. In some versions of these plans, an extraordinary majority (say, 60 percent) of Congress could override these limits, and the limits would not apply in wartime.

The effect of such amendments, the proponents claim, would be to force Congress and the president to look at the big picture—the grand total of what they are spending—rather than just to operate the adding machine by repeatedly pushing the "add" button. If they could only spend so much during a given year, they would have to allocate what they spend among all the rival claimants, comparing the worth of each claimant to that of every other one. For example, if more money were spent on the poor, less would be spent on the military, or vice versa. In this way, we could no longer add to the national debt by continuing to run up big deficits.

Some critics of an overly powerful federal government think these amendments will not be passed or may prove unworkable. Instead they favor enhancing the president's power to block spending by giving him a **line-item veto.** The president must now sign or veto a bill as a whole, take it or leave it. Most state governors, with a line-item veto, can disapprove a particular part of a bill and approve the rest. The theory is that such a veto would better equip the president to stop unwarranted spending without vetoing the other provisions of a bill that he approves of.

Finally, some of these critics of a powerful government feel that the real problem arises not only from an excess of "adding-machine" democracy but also from the growth in the power of the federal courts. These critics would like to devise a set of laws or constitutional amendments that would narrow the authority of federal courts.

The opponents of these constitutional amendments argue that to restrict the level of taxes and to require a balanced budget are unworkable suggestions, even assuming—which they do not—that a smaller government is desirable. There is no precise, agreed-upon way to measure how much the government spends or to predict in advance how much it will receive in taxes during the year; thus defining and enforcing a "balanced budget" is no easy matter. The government has shown great ingenuity in spending money in ways that never appear as part of the regular budget (for example, Social Security).

The line-item veto may or may not be a good idea, these people argue, but we can never know without trying it since the states, where some governors now have the veto power, differ markedly from the federal government in power and responsibilities. And if we tried it, we might discover that the president would use it not to spend less but to spend more—by threatening to veto something of modest cost that Congress wants in order to get Congress to vote for something expensive that the president wants.

Finally, proposals to curtail judicial power are thinly veiled attacks, the opponents argue, on the ability of the courts to protect essential citizen rights. If Congress and the people do not like the way the Supreme Court has interpreted the Constitution, they can always amend the Constitution to change that specific ruling. There is no need to adopt some general, across-the-board limitation on court powers.

Term Limits

A change that might make our system either more or less democratic is to limit the number of terms that people can serve in Congress. Already, the president is limited to two terms. The most common proposal is to limit members of the House to six terms (a total of twelve years) and members of the Senate to two (also a total of twelve years). In 1992, the people in fourteen states adopted proposals that, if upheld in the courts, will impose term limits on their delegations to Congress.

But it is far from clear that the courts will uphold these measures. The Constitution makes Congress the sole judge of the qualifications of its members and limits the states to determining the time, place, and manner of holding congressional elections. We will probably see a court challenge when these term limits begin to take effect.

It is also not clear what effect such limits might have. Proponents argue that it will once again make members of Congress "citizen legislators," not career politicians. Knowing that they can serve only twelve years, they will be free, at least toward the end of their last term in office, to do what is right rather than what is demanded by interest groups or required by their own desire for reelection.

But opponents argue that short-term legislators will never master the intricacies of federal politics and policies, and so they will become dependent on unelected staff members and Washington lobbyists. And they point to the many long-term legislators who are widely admired. Finally, they argue that the voters are the best judges of who should stay in office and so should have the right to keep reelecting their own representatives and senators if they wish.

There is no way to settle this issue by arguments or theories. We will learn what difference term limits make only if we try them. But there is a risk: if we try them and don't like them, it will be very hard to get rid of them. In any event, term limits may be hard to try because Congress doesn't like them and Congress must approve a constitutional amendment to impose them (unless, of course, two-thirds of the state legislatures demand the calling of a constitutional convention to consider them).

Who Is Right?

Some of the arguments of these various critics of the Constitution may strike you as plausible or even entirely convincing. But one should not make or remake a Constitution based entirely on abstract reasoning or unproven factual arguments. Even when the Constitution was first written in 1787, it was not an exercise in abstract philosophy but rather an effort by the Framers to solve pressing, practical problems in the light of a theory of human nature, the lessons of past experience, and a close consideration of how governments in other countries had worked.

Just because the Constitution is now two hundred years old does not mean that it is out of date. The crucial questions are these: How well has it worked over the long sweep of American history? And how well has it worked compared to the constitutions of other democratic nations?

The only way to answer these questions is to study American government closely, with special attention to its historical evolution, the way it makes particular policies, and the practices of other nations. This book has provided only the briefest introduction to the workings of American government and has said very little about how it works in comparison to other governments or how it handles particular policy issues. Therefore, you should not try to make up your mind about what, if anything, needs to change in our Constitution from what you have learned here. Learn more.

Nonetheless, by reviewing these competing proposals for revising the Constitution, you will at least be able to understand the central features of our system of government and the controversies that system has engendered, as well as how that system has changed over the last half century.

Appendix

The Declaration of Independence

IN CONGRESS, JULY 4, 1776
THE UNANIMOUS DECLARATION OF THE
THIRTEEN UNITED STATES OF AMERICA

When, in the course of human events, it becomes necessary for one people to dissolve the political bands which have connected them with another, and to assume, among the powers of the earth, the separate and equal station to which the laws of nature and of nature's God entitle them, a decent respect to the opinions of mankind requires that they should declare the causes which impel them to the separation.

We hold these truths to be self-evident: That all men are created equal; that they are endowed by their Creator with certain unalienable rights; that among these are life, liberty, and the pursuit of happiness; that, to secure these rights, governments are instituted among men, deriving their just powers from the consent of the governed; that whenever any form of government becomes destructive of these ends, it is the right of the people to alter or to abolish it, and to institute new government, laying its foundation on such principles, and organizing its powers in such form, as to them shall seem most likely to effect their safety and happiness. Prudence, indeed, will dictate that governments long established should not be changed for light and transient causes; and accordingly all experience hath shown that mankind are more disposed to suffer, while evils are sufferable, than to right themselves by abolishing the forms to which they are accustomed. But when a long train of abuses and usurpations, pursuing invariably the same object, evinces a design to reduce them under absolute despotism, it is their right, it is their duty, to throw off such government, and to provide new guards for their future security. Such has been the patient sufferance of these colonies; and such is now the necessity which constrains them to alter their former systems of government. The history of the present King of Great Britain is a history of repeated injuries and usurpations, all having in direct object the establishment of an absolute tyranny over these states. To prove this, let facts be submitted to a candid world.

He has refused to assent to laws, the most wholesome and necessary for the public good.

He has forbidden his governors to pass laws of immediate and pressing importance, unless suspended in their operation till his assent should be obtained; and, when so suspended, he has utterly neglected to attend to them.

He has refused to pass other laws for the accommodation of large districts of people, unless those people would relinquish the right of representation in the legislature, a right inestimable to them, and formidable to tyrants only.

He has called together legislative bodies at places unusual, uncomfortable, and distant from the depository of their public records, for the sole purpose of fatiguing them into compliance with his measures.

He has dissolved representative houses repeatedly, for opposing, with manly firmness, his invasions on the rights of the people.

He has refused for a long time, after such dissolutions, to cause others to be elected; whereby the legislative powers, incapable of annihilation, have returned to the people at large for their exercise; the state remaining, in the mean time, exposed to all the dangers of invasions from without and convulsions within.

He has endeavored to prevent the population of these states; for that purpose obstructing the laws for naturalization of foreigners; refusing to pass others to encourage their migration hither, and raising the conditions of new appropriations of lands.

He has obstructed the administration of justice, by refusing his assent to laws for establishing judiciary powers.

He has made judges dependent on his will alone, for the tenure of their offices, and the amount and payment of their salaries.

He has erected a multitude of new offices, and sent hither swarms of officers to harass our people and eat out their substance.

He has kept among us, in times of peace, standing armies, without the consent of our legislatures.

He has affected to render the military independent of, and superior to, the civil power.

He has combined with others to subject us to a jurisdiction foreign to our constitution, and unacknowledged by our laws, giving his assent to their acts of pretended legislation:

For quartering large bodies of armed troops among us;

For protecting them, by a mock trial, from punishment for any murders which they should commit on the inhabitants of these states;

For cutting off our trade with all parts of the world;

For imposing taxes on us without our consent;

For depriving us, in many cases, of the benefits of trial by jury;

For transporting us beyond seas, to be tried for pretended offenses;

For abolishing the free system of English laws in a neighboring province, establishing therein an arbitrary government, and enlarging its boundaries, so as to render it at once an example and fit instrument for introducing the same absolute rule into these colonies;

For taking away our charters, abolishing our most valuable laws, and altering fundamentally the forms of our governments;

For suspending our own legislatures, and declaring themselves invested with power to legislate for us in all cases whatsoever.

He has abdicated government here, by declaring us out of his protection and waging war against us.

He has plundered our seas, ravaged our coasts, burned our towns, and destroyed the lives of our people.

He is at this time transporting large armies of foreign mercenaries to complete the works of death, desolation, and tyranny already begun with circumstances of cruelty and perfidy scarcely paralleled in the most barbarous ages, and totally unworthy the head of a civilized nation.

He has constrained our fellow-citizens, taken captive on the high seas, to bear arms against their country, to become the executioners of their friends and brethren, or to fall themselves by their hands.

He has excited domestic insurrections among us, and has endeavored to bring on the inhabitants of our frontiers the merciless Indian savages, whose known rule of warfare is an undistinguished destruction of all ages, sexes, and conditions.

In every stage of these oppressions we have petitioned for redress in the most humble terms; our repeated petitions have been answered only by repeated injury. A prince, whose character is thus marked by every act which may define a tyrant, is unfit to be the ruler of a free people.

Nor have we been wanting in our attentions to our British brethren. We have warned them, from time to time, of attempts by their legislature to extend an unwarrantable jurisdiction over us. We have reminded them of the circumstances of our emigration and settlement here. We have appealed to their native justice and magnanimity; and we have conjured them, by the ties of our common kindred, to disavow these usurpations, which would inevitably interrupt our connections and correspondence. They, too, have been deaf to the voice of justice and of consanguinity. We must, therefore, acquiesce in the necessity which denounces our separation, and hold them, as we hold the rest of mankind, enemies in war, in peace friends.

We, therefore, the representatives of the United States of America, in General Congress assembled, appealing to the Supreme Judge of the world for the rectitude of our intentions, do, in the name and by the authority of the good people of these colonies, solemnly publish and declare, that these United Colonies are, and of right ought to be, FREE AND INDEPENDENT STATES; that they are absolved from all allegiance to the British crown, and that all political connection between them and the state of Great Britain is, and ought to be, totally dissolved; and that, as free and independent states, they have full power to levy war, conclude peace, contract alliances, establish commerce, and do all other acts and things which independent states may of right do. And for the support of this declaration, with a firm reliance on the protection of Divine Providence, we mutually pledge to each other our lives, our fortunes, and our sacred honor.

JOHN HANCOCK [*President*]
[*and fifty-five others*]

The Constitution of the United States

We the People of the United States, in Order to form a more perfect Union, establish Justice, insure domestic Tranquility, provide for the common defence, promote the general Welfare, and secure the Blessings of Liberty to ourselves and our Posterity, do ordain and establish the Constitution for the United States of America.

ARTICLE I

Section 1. All legislative Powers herein granted shall be vested in a Congress of the United States, which shall consist of a Senate and House of Representatives.

Section 2. The House of Representatives shall be composed of Members chosen every second Year by the People of the several States, and the Electors in each State shall have the Qualifications requisite for Electors of the most numerous Branch of the State Legislature.

No Person shall be a Representative who shall not have attained to the age of twenty five Years, and been seven Years a Citizen of the United States, and who shall not, when elected, be an Inhabitant of that State in which he shall be chosen.

Representatives and direct Taxes shall be apportioned among the several States which may be included within this Union, according to their respective Numbers, which shall be determined by adding to the whole Number of free Persons, including those bound to Service for a Term of Years, and excluding Indians not taxed, three fifths of all other Persons.[1] The actual Enumeration shall be made within three Years after the first Meeting of the Congress of the United States, and within every subsequent Term of ten Years, in such Manner as they shall by Law direct. The Number of Representatives shall not exceed one for every thirty Thousand, but each State shall have at Least one Representative; and until

---

[1] Changed by the Fourteenth Amendment, Section 2.

Note: Excluding the Preamble and Closing, those portions set in italic type have been superseded or changed by later amendments.

such enumeration shall be made, the State of New Hampshire shall be entitled to chuse three, Massachusetts eight, Rhode-Island and Providence Plantations one, Connecticut five, New-York six, New Jersey four, Pennsylvania eight, Delaware one, Maryland six, Virginia ten, North Carolina five, South Carolina five, and Georgia three.

When vacancies happen in the Representation from any State, the Executive Authority thereof shall issue Writs of Election to fill such Vacancies.

The House of Representatives shall chuse their Speaker and other Officers; and shall have the sole Power of Impeachment.

Section 3. The Senate of the United States shall be composed of two Senators from each State, *chosen by the Legislature thereof,*[2] for six Years; and each Senator shall have one Vote.

Immediately after they shall be assembled in Consequence of the first Election, they shall be divided as equally as may be into three Classes. The Seats of the Senators of the first Class shall be vacated at the Expiration of the second Year, of the second Class at the Expiration of the fourth Year, and of the third Class at the Expiration of the sixth Year, so that one third may be chosen every second Year; *and if Vacancies happen by Resignation, or otherwise, during the Recess of the Legislature of any State, the Executive thereof may make temporary Appointment until the next Meeting of the Legislature, which shall then fill such Vacancies.*[3]

No Person shall be a Senator who shall not have attained to the Age of thirty Years, and been nine Years a Citizen of the United States, and who shall not, when elected, be an Inhabitant of that State for which he shall be chosen.

The Vice President of the United States shall be President of the Senate, but shall have no Vote, unless they be equally divided.

The Senate shall chuse their other Officers, and also a President pro tempore, in the Absence of the Vice President, or when he shall exercise the Office of President of the United States.

The Senate shall have the sole Power to try all Impeachments. When sitting for that Purpose, they shall be on Oath or Affirmation. When the President of the United States is tried the Chief Justice shall preside: And no Person shall be convicted without the Concurrence of two thirds of the Members present.

Judgment in Cases of Impeachment shall not extend further than to removal from Office, and disqualification to hold and enjoy any Office of honor, Trust or Profit under the United States: but the Party convicted shall

---

[2] Changed by the Seventeenth Amendment.

[3] Changed by the Seventeenth Amendment.

nevertheless be liable and subject to Indictment, Trial, Judgment and Punishment, according to Law.

Section 4. The Times, Places and Manner of holding Elections for Senators and Representatives, shall be prescribed in each State by the Legislature thereof; but the Congress may at any time by Law make or alter such Regulations, except as to the Places of chusing Senators.

The Congress shall assemble at least once in every Year, and such Meeting shall be on the *first Monday in December, unless they shall by Law appoint a different Day.*[4]

Section 5. Each House shall be the Judge of the Elections, Returns and Qualifications of its own Members, and a Majority of each shall constitute a Quorum to do Business; but a smaller Number may adjourn from day to day, and may be authorized to compel the Attendance of absent Members, in such Manner, and under such Penalties as each House may provide.

Each House may determine the Rules of its Proceedings, punish its Members for disorderly Behaviour, and, with the Concurrence of two thirds, expel a Member.

Each House shall keep a Journal of its Proceedings, and from time to time publish the same, excepting such Parts as may in their Judgment require Secrecy; and the Yeas and Nays of the Members of either House on any question shall, at the Desire of one fifth of those Present, be entered on the Journal.

Neither House, during the Session of Congress, shall, without the Consent of the other, adjourn for more than three days, nor to any other Place than that in which the two Houses shall be sitting.

Section 6. The Senators and Representatives shall receive a Compensation for their Services, to be ascertained by Law, and paid out of the Treasury of the United States. They shall in all Cases, except Treason, Felony and Breach of the Peace, be privileged from Arrest during their Attendance at the Session of their respective Houses, and in going to and returning from the same; and for any Speech or Debate in either House, they shall not be questioned in any other Place.

No Senator or Representative shall, during the time for which he was elected, be appointed to any civil Office under the Authority of the United States, which shall have been created, or the Emoluments whereof shall have been encreased during such time; and no Person holding any Office under the United States, shall be a Member of either House during his Continuance in Office.

---

[4] Changed by the Twentieth Amendment, Section 2.

Section 7.   All Bills for raising Revenue shall originate in the House of Representatives; but the Senate may propose or concur with Amendments as on other Bills.

Every Bill which shall have passed the House of Representatives and the Senate, shall, before it become a Law, be presented to the President of the United States; If he approve he shall assign it, but if not he shall return it, with his Objections to that House in which it shall have originated, who shall enter the Objections at large on their Journal, and proceed to reconsider it. If after such Reconsideration two thirds of that House shall agree to pass the Bill, it shall be sent, together with the Objections, to the other House, by which it shall likewise be reconsidered, and if approved by two thirds of that House, it shall become a Law. But in all such Cases the Votes of both Houses shall be determined by yeas and Nays, and the Names of the Persons voting for and against the Bill shall be entered on the Journal of each House respectively. If any Bill shall not be returned by the President within ten Days (Sundays excepted) after it shall have been presented to him, the Same shall be a Law, in like Manner as if he had signed it, unless the Congress by their Adjournment prevent its Return, in which Case it shall not be a Law.

Every Order, Resolution, or Vote in which the Concurrence of the Senate and House of Representatives may be necessary (except on a question of Adjournment) shall be presented to the President of the United States; and before the Same shall take Effect, shall be approved by him, or being disapproved by him, shall be repassed by two thirds of the Senate and House of Representatives, according to the Rules and Limitations prescribed in the Case of a Bill.

Section 8.   The Congress shall have Power To lay and collect Taxes, Duties, Imposts and Excises, to pay the Debts and provide for the common Defence and general Welfare of the United States; but all Duties, Imposts and Excises shall be uniform throughout the United States;

To borrow Money on the credit of the United States;

To regulate Commerce with foreign Nations, and among the several States, and with the Indian Tribes;

To establish an uniform Rule of Naturalization, and uniform Laws on the subject of Bankruptcies throughout the United States;

To coin Money, regulate the Value thereof, and of foreign Coin, and fix the Standard of Weights and Measures;

To provide for the Punishment of counterfeiting the Securities and current Coin of the United States;

To establish Post Offices and post Roads;

To promote the Progress of Science and useful Arts, by securing for limited Times to Authors and Inventors the exclusive Right to their respective Writings and Discoveries;

To constitute Tribunals inferior to the Supreme Court;

To define and punish Piracies and Felonies committed on the high Seas, and Offences against the Law of Nations;

To declare War, grant Letters of Marque and Reprisal, and make Rules concerning Captures on Land and Water;

To raise and support Armies, but no Appropriation of Money to that Use shall be for longer Term than two Years;

To provide and maintain a Navy;

To make Rules for the Government and Regulation of the land and naval Forces;

To provide for calling forth the Militia to execute the Laws of the Union, suppress Insurrections and repel Invasions;

To provide for organizing, arming, and disciplining, the Militia, and for governing such Part of them as may be employed in the Service of the United States, reserving to the States respectively, the Appointment of the Officers, and the Authority of training the Militia according to the discipline prescribed by Congress;

To exercise exclusive Legislation in all Cases whatsoever, over such District (not exceeding ten Miles square) as may, by Cession of Particular States, and the Acceptance of Congress, become the Seat of the Government of the United States, and to exercise like Authority over all Places purchased by the Consent of the Legislature of the State in which the Same shall be, for the Erection of Forts, Magazines, Arsenals, dock-Yards, and other needful Buildings; — And

To make all Laws which shall be necessary and proper for carrying into Execution the foregoing Powers, and all other Powers vested by this Constitution in the Government of the United States, or in any Department or Officer thereof.

Section 9. The Migration or Importation of such Persons as any of the States now existing shall think proper to admit, shall not be prohibited by the Congress prior to the Year one thousand eight hundred and eight, but a Tax or duty may be imposed on such Importation, not exceeding ten dollars for each Person.

The Privilege of the Writ of Habeas Corpus shall not be suspended, unless when in Cases of Rebellion or Invasion the public Safety may require it.

No bill of Attainder or ex post facto Law shall be passed.

No Capitation, or other direct, Tax shall be laid, *unless in Proportion to the Census or Enumeration herein before directed to be taken.*[5]

No Tax or Duty shall be laid on Articles exported from any State.

No Preference shall be given by any Regulation of Commerce or Revenue to the Ports of one State over those of another; nor shall Vessels bound

---

[5] Changed by the Sixteenth Amendment.

to, or from, one State, be obliged to enter, clear or pay Duties in another.

No Money shall be drawn from the Treasury, but in Consequence of Appropriations made by Law; and a regular Statement and Account of the Receipts and Expenditures of all public Money shall be published from time to time.

No Title of Nobility shall be granted by the United States: And no Person holding any Office of Profit or Trust under them, shall, without the Consent of the Congress, accept of any present, Emolument, Office, or Title, of any kind whatever, from any King, Prince, or foreign State.

Section 10. No State shall enter into any Treaty, Alliance, or Confederation; grant Letters of Marque and Reprisal; coin Money; emit Bills of Credit; make any Thing but gold and silver Coin a Tender in Payment of Debts; pass any Bill of Attainder, ex post facto Law, or Law impairing the Obligation of Contracts, or grant any Title of Nobility.

No State shall, without the Consent of the Congress, lay any Imposts or Duties on Imports or Exports, except what may be absolutely necessary for executing its inspection Laws: and the net Produce of all Duties and Imposts, laid by any State on Imports or Exports, shall be for the Use of the Treasury of the United States; and all such Laws shall be subject to the Revision and Controul of the Congress.

No State shall, without the Consent of Congress, lay any Duty of Tonnage, keep Troops, or Ships of War in time of Peace, enter into any Agreement or Compact with another State, or with a foreign Power, or engage in War, unless actually invaded, or in such imminent Danger as will not admit of delay.

ARTICLE II

Section 1. The executive Power shall be vested in a President of the United States of America. He shall hold his Office during the term of four Years, and, together with the Vice President, chosen for the same Term, be elected, as follows

Each State shall appoint, in such Manner as the Legislature thereof may direct, a Number of Electors, equal to the whole Number of Senators and Representatives to which the State may be entitled in the Congress: but no Senator or Representative, or Person holding an Office of Trust or Profit under the United States, shall be appointed an Elector.

The Electors shall meet in their respective States, and vote by Ballot for two Persons, of whom one at least shall not be an Inhabitant of the same State with themselves. And they shall make a List of all the Persons voted for, and of the Number of Votes for each; which List they shall sign and certify, and transmit sealed to the Seat of the Government of the United States, directed to the President of the Senate. The President of the Senate shall, in the Presence of the Senate and House of Representa-

tives, open all the Certificates, and the Votes shall then be counted. *The Person hav-ing the greatest Number of Votes shall be the President, if such Number be a Majority of the whole Number of Electors appointed; and if there be more than one who have such Majority, and have an equal Number of Votes, then the House of Representa-tives shall immediately chuse by Ballot one of them for President; and if no Person have a Majority, then from the five highest on the List the said House shall in like Manner chuse the President. But in chusing the President, the Votes shall be taken by States, the Representation from each State having one Vote; a quorum for this Purpose shall consist of a Member or Members from two thirds of the States, and a Majority of all the States shall be necessary to a Choice. In every Case, after the Choice of the President, the Person having the greatest Number of Votes of the Electors shall be the Vice President. But if there should remain two or more who have equal Votes, the Senate shall chuse from them by Ballot the Vice President.*[6]

The Congress may determine the Time of chusing the Electors, and the Day on which they shall give their Votes; which Day shall be the same throughout the United States.

No Person except a natural born Citizen, or a Citizen of the United States, at the time of the Adoption of this Constitution, shall be eligible to the Office of President; neither shall any person be eligible to that Office who shall not have attained to the Age of thirty five Years, and been fourteen Years a Resident within the United States.

In Case of the Removal of the President from Office, or of his Death, Resig-nation, or Inability to discharge the Powers and Duties of the said Office, the Same shall devolve on the Vice President, and the Congress may by Law provide for the Case of Removal, Death, Resignation or Inability, both of the President and Vice Presi-dent, declaring what Officer shall then act as President, and such Officer shall act accord-ingly, until the Disability be removed, or a President shall be elected.[7]

The President shall, at stated Times, receive for his Services, a Com-pensation, which shall neither be encreased nor diminished during the Period for which he shall have been elected, and he shall not receive within that Period any other Emolument from the United States, or any of them.

Before he enter on the Execution of his Office, he shall take the follow-ing Oath or Affirmation: —"I do solemnly swear (or affirm) that I will faith-fully execute the Office of President of the United States, and will to the best of my Ability, preserve, protect and defend the Constitution of the United States."

Section 2.   The President shall be Commander in Chief of the Army and Navy of the United States, and of the Militia of the several States, when called into the actual Service of the United States; he may require the

---

[6] Superseded by the Twelfth Amendment.

[7] Modified by the Twenty-Fifth Amendment.

Opinion, in writing, of the principal Officer in each of the executive Departments, upon any Subject relating to the Duties of their respective Offices, and he shall have Power to grant Reprieves and Pardons for Offences against the United States, except in Cases of Impeachment.

He shall have Power, by and with the Advice and Consent of the Senate, to make Treaties, provided two thirds of the Senators present concur; and he shall nominate, and by and with the Advice and Consent of the Senate, shall appoint Ambassadors, other public Ministers and Consuls, Judges of the supreme Court, and all other Officers of the United States, whose Appointments are not herein otherwise provided for, and which shall be established by Law: but the Congress may by Law vest the Appointment of such inferior Officers, as they think proper, in the President alone, in the Courts of Law, or in the Heads of Departments.

The President shall have Power to fill up all Vacancies that may happen during the Recess of the Senate, by granting Commissions which shall expire at the End of their next Session.

Section 3. He shall from time to time give to the Congress Information of the State of the Union, and recommend to their Consideration such Measures as he shall judge necessary and expedient; he may, on extraordinary Occasions, convene both Houses, or either of them, and in Case of Disagreement between them, with Respect to the Time of Adjournment, he may adjourn them to such Time as he shall think proper; he shall receive Ambassadors and other public Ministers; he shall take Care that the Laws be faithfully executed, and shall Commission all the Officers of the United States.

Section 4. The President, Vice President and all civil Officers of the United States, shall be removed from Office on Impeachment for, and Conviction of, Treason, Bribery, or other high Crimes and Misdemeanors.

ARTICLE III

Section 1. The judicial Power of the United States, shall be vested in one supreme Court, and in such inferior Courts as the Congress may from time to time ordain and establish. The Judges, both of the supreme and inferior Courts, shall hold their Offices during good Behaviour, and shall, at stated Times, receive for their Services, a Compensation, which shall not be diminished during their Continuance in Office.

Section 2. The judicial Power shall extend to all Cases, in Law and Equity, arising under this Constitution, the Laws of the United States, and Treaties made, or which shall be made, under their Authority; — to all Cases affecting

Ambassadors, other public Ministers and Consuls; — to all Cases of admiralty and maritime Jurisdiction; — to Controversies to which the United States shall be a party; — to Controversies between two or more States; — *between a State and Citizens of another State;* [8]— between Citizens of different States; — between Citizens of the same State claiming Lands under Grants of different States, and between a State, or the Citizens thereof, and foreign States, Citizens or Subjects.

In all Cases affecting Ambassadors, other public Ministers and Consuls, and those in which a State shall be Party, the supreme Court shall have original Jurisdiction. In all the other Cases before mentioned, the supreme Court shall have appellate Jurisdiction, both as to Law and Fact, with such Exceptions, and under such Regulations as the Congress shall make.

The Trial of all Crimes, except in Cases of Impeachment, shall be by Jury; and such Trial shall be held in the State where the said Crimes shall have been committed; but when not committed within any State, the Trial shall be at such Place or Places as the Congress may by Law have directed.

Section 3. Treason against the United States, shall consist only in levying War against them, or in adhering to their Enemies, giving them Aid and Comfort. No Person shall be convicted of Treason unless on the Testimony of two Witnesses to the same overt Act, or on Confession in open Court.

The Congress shall have Power to declare the Punishment of Treason, but no Attainder of Treason shall work Corruption of Blood, or Forfeiture except during the Life of the Person attainted.

ARTICLE IV

Section 1. Full Faith and Credit shall be given in each State to the public Acts, Records, and judicial Proceedings of every other State. And the Congress may by general Laws prescribe the Manner in which such Acts, Records and Proceedings shall be proved, and the Effect thereof.

Section 2. The Citizens of each State shall be entitled to all Privileges and Immunities of Citizens in the several States.

A person charged in any State with Treason, Felony, or other Crime, who shall flee from Justice, and be found in another State, shall on Demand of the executive Authority of the State from which he fled, be delivered up, to be removed to the State having Jurisdiction of the Crime.

No Person held to Service or Labour in one State, under the Laws thereof, escaping into another, shall, in Consequence of any Law or Regulation therein, be

---

[8] Modified by the Eleventh Amendment.

discharged from such Service or Labour, but shall be delivered up on Claim of the Party to whom such Service or Labour may be due.[9]

Section 3. New States may be admitted by the Congress into this Union; but no new State shall be formed or erected within the Jurisdiction of any other State; nor any State be formed by the Junction of two or more States, or Parts of States, without the Consent of the Legislatures of the States concerned as well as of the Congress.

The Congress shall have Power to dispose of and make all needful Rules and Regulations respecting the Territory or other Property belonging to the United States; and nothing in this Constitution shall be so construed as to Prejudice any Claims of the United States, or of any particular State.

Section 4. The United States shall guarantee to every State in this Union a Republican Form of Government, and shall protect each of them against Invasion; and on Application of the Legislature, or of the Executive (when the Legislature cannot be convened) against domestic Violence.

Article V

The Congress, whenever two thirds of both Houses shall deem it necessary, shall propose Amendments to this Constitution, or, on the Application of the Legislatures of two thirds of the several States, shall call a Convention for proposing Amendments, which, in either Case, shall be valid to all Intents and Purposes, as Part of this Constitution, when ratified by the Legislatures of three fourths of the several States, or by Conventions in three fourths thereof, as the one or the other Mode of Ratification may be proposed by the Congress; Provided that no Amendment which may be made prior to the Year One thousand eight hundred and eight shall in any Manner affect the first and fourth Clauses in the Ninth Section of the first Article; and that no State, without its Consent, shall be deprived of its equal Suffrage in the Senate.

Article VI

All Debts contracted and Engagements entered into, before the Adoption of this Constitution, shall be as valid against the United States under this Constitution, as under the Confederation.

This Constitution, and the Laws of the United States which shall be made in Pursuance thereof; and all Treaties made, or which shall be made,

---

[9] Changed by the Thirteenth Amendment.

under the Authority of the United States, shall be the supreme Law of the Land; and the Judges in every State shall be bound thereby, any Thing in the Constitution or Laws of any State to the Contrary notwithstanding.

The Senators and Representatives before mentioned, and the Members of the several State Legislatures, and all executive and judicial Officers, both of the United States and of the several States, shall be bound by Oath or Affirmation, to support this Constitution; but no religious Test shall ever be required as a Qualification to any Office or public Trust under the United States.

ARTICLE VII

The Ratification of the Conventions of nine States, shall be sufficient for the Establishment of this Constitution between the States so ratifying the Same.

Done in Convention by the Unanimous Consent of the States present the Seventeenth Day of September in the Year of our Lord one thousand seven hundred and Eighty seven and of the Independence of the United States of America the Twelfth In witness whereof We have hereunto subscribed our Names,

Go. Washington–*Presidt.*
and deputy from Virginia

New Hampshire	{ JOHN LANGDON { NICHOLAS GILMAN		
		Delaware	{ GEO. READ { GUNNING BEDFORD JUN { JOHN DICKINSON { RICHARD BASSETT { JACO. BROOM
Massachusetts	{ NATHANIEL GORHAM { RUFUS KING		
Connecticut	{ WM. SAML. JOHNSON { ROGER SHERMAN	**Maryland**	{ JAMES MCHENRY { DAN OF ST. THOS. JENIFER { DANL. CARROLL
New York	ALEXANDER HAMILTON	**Virginia**	{ JOHN BLAIR– { JAMES MADISON JR.
New Jersey	{ WIL. LIVINGSTON { DAVID BREARLEY { WM. PATERSON { JONA. DAYTON	**North Carolina**	{ WM. BLOUNT { RICHD. DOBBS SPAIGHT { HU WILLIAMSON
Pennsylvania	{ B FRANKLIN { THOMAS MIFFLIN { ROBT. MORRIS { GEO. CLYMER { THOS. FITZSIMONS { JARED INGERSOLL { JAMES WILSON { GOUV MORRIS	**South Carolina**	{ J. RUTLEDGE { CHARLES COTESWORTH { PINCKNEY { CHARLES PINCKNEY { PIERCE BUTLER
		Georgia	{ WILLIAM FEW { ABR BALDWIN

[The first ten amendments, known as the "Bill of Rights," were ratified in 1791.]

Amendment I

Congress shall make no law respecting an establishment of religion, or prohibiting the free exercise thereof; or abridging the freedom of speech, or of the press; or the right of the people peaceably to assemble, and to petition the Government for a redress of grievances.

Amendment II

A well regulated Militia, being necessary to the security of a free State, the right of the people to keep and bear Arms, shall not be infringed.

Amendment III

No Soldier shall, in time of peace be quartered in any house, without the consent of the Owner, nor in time of war, but in a manner prescribed by law.

Amendment IV

The right of the people to be secure in their persons, houses, papers, and effects, against unreasonable searches and seizures, shall not be violated, and no Warrants shall issue, but upon probable cause, supported by Oath of affirmation, and particularly describing the place to be searched, and the persons or things to be seized.

Amendment V

No person shall be held to answer for a capital, or otherwise infamous crime, unless on a presentment or indictment of a Grand Jury, except in cases arising in the land or naval forces, or in the Militia, when in actual service in time of War or public danger; nor shall any person be subject for the same offence to be twice put in jeopardy of life or limb; nor shall be compelled in any criminal case to be a witness against himself, nor be deprived of life, liberty, or property, without due process of law; nor shall private property be taken for public use, without just compensation.

Amendment VI

In all criminal prosecutions, the accused shall enjoy the right to a speedy and public trial, by an impartial jury of the State and district wherein the crime shall have been committed, which district shall have been previously ascertained by law, and to be informed of the nature and cause of the accusation; to be confronted with the witnesses against him; to have compulsory process for obtaining witnesses in his favor, and to have Assistance of Counsel for his defence.

AMENDMENT VII

In Suits at common law, where the value in controversy shall exceed twenty dollars, the right of trial by jury shall be preserved, and no fact tried by a jury, shall be otherwise reexamined in any Court of the United States, than according to the rules of the common law.

AMENDMENT VIII

Excessive bail shall not be required, nor excessive fines imposed, nor cruel and unusual punishments inflicted.

AMENDMENT IX

The enumeration in the Constitution, of certain rights, shall not be construed to deny or disparage others retained by the people.

AMENDMENT X

The powers not delegated to the United States by the Constitution, nor prohibited by it to the States, are reserved to the States respectively, or to the people.

AMENDMENT XI [*RATIFIED IN 1795.*]

The Judicial power of the United States shall not be construed to extend to any suit in law or equity, commenced or prosecuted against one of the United States by Citizens of another State, or by Citizens or Subjects of any Foreign State.

AMENDMENT XII [*RATIFIED IN 1804.*]

The Electors shall meet in their respective states and vote by ballot for President and Vice President, one of whom, at least, shall not be an inhabitant of the same state with themselves; they shall name in their ballots the person voted for as President, and in distinct ballots the person voted for as Vice President, and they shall make distinct lists of all persons voted for as President, and of all persons voted for as Vice President, and of the number of votes for each, which lists they shall sign and certify, and transmit sealed to the seat of the government of the United States, directed to the President of the Senate; — The President of the Senate shall, in the presence of the Senate and House of Representatives, open all the certificates and the votes shall then be counted; — The person having the greatest number of votes for President, shall be the President, if such number be a majority of the whole number of Electors appointed; and if no person have such majority, then from the persons having the highest numbers not exceeding three on the list of those voted for as President, and the House of Representatives shall choose immediately, by ballot, the President. But in choosing the President, the votes shall be taken by states, the representation from each state having one vote; a quorum for this purpose shall consist of a member or members from two-thirds of the states, and a majority of all the states shall be necessary to a choice. *And if the House of Representatives shall not choose a President whenever the right of choice shall devolve upon them, before the fourth day of March next following, then the Vice President shall act as President, as in the case of the death or other constitutional disability of the President.*—[10] The person having the greatest number of votes as Vice President, shall be the Vice President, if such number be a majority of the whole number of Electors appointed, and if no person have a majority, then from the two highest numbers on the list, the Senate shall choose the Vice President; a quorum for the purpose shall consist of two-thirds of the whole number of Senators, and a majority of the whole number shall be necessary to a choice. But no person constitutionally ineligible to the office of President shall be eligible to that of Vice President of the United States.

AMENDMENT **XIII** [*RATIFIED IN 1865.*]

Section 1.   Neither slavery nor involuntary servitude, except as a punishment for crime whereof the party shall have been duly convicted, shall exist within the United States, or any place subject to their jurisdiction.

Section 2.   Congress shall have power to enforce this article by appropriate legislation.

AMENDMENT **XIV** [*RATIFIED IN 1868.*]

Section 1.   All persons born or naturalized in the United States and subject to the jurisdiction thereof, are citizens of the United States and of the State wherein they reside. No State shall make or enforce any law which shall abridge the privileges or immunities of citizens of the United States; nor shall any State deprive any person of life, liberty, or property, without due process of law; nor deny to any person within its jurisdiction the equal protection of the laws.

---

[10] Changed by the Twentieth Amendment, Section 3.

Section 2. Representatives shall be apportioned among the several States according to their respective numbers, counting the whole number of persons in each State, excluding Indians not taxed. But when the right to vote at any election for the choice of electors for President and Vice President of the United States, Representatives in Congress, the Executive and Judicial officers of a State, or the members of the Legislature thereof, is denied to any of the male inhabitants of such State, being *twenty-one*[11] years of age, and citizens of the United States, or in any way abridged, except for participation in rebellion, or other crime, the basis of representation therein shall be reduced in the proportion which the number of such male citizens shall bear to the whole number of male citizens twenty-one years of age in such State.

Section 3. No person shall be a Senator or Representative in Congress, or elector of President and Vice President, or hold any office, civil or military, under the United States, or under any State, who, having previously taken an oath, as a member of Congress, or as an officer of the United States, or as a member of any State legislature, or as an executive or judicial officer of any State, to support the Constitution of the United States, shall have engaged in insurrection or rebellion against the same, or given aid or comfort to the enemies thereof. But Congress may by a vote of two-thirds of each House, remove such disability.

Section 4. The validity of the public debt of the United States, authorized by law, including debts incurred for payment of pensions and bounties for services in suppressing insurrection or rebellion, shall not be questioned. But neither the United States nor any State shall assume or pay any debt or obligation incurred in aid of insurrection or rebellion against the United States, or any claim for the loss or emancipation of any slave; but all such debts, obligations and claims shall be held illegal and void.

Section 5. The Congress shall have power to enforce, by appropriate legislation, the provisions of this article.

AMENDMENT **XV** [*RATIFIED IN 1870.*]

Section 1. The right of citizens of the United States to vote shall not be denied or abridged by the United States or by any State on account of race, color, or previous condition of servitude.

---

[11] Changed by the Twenty-Sixth Amendment.

Section 2. The Congress shall have power to enforce this article by appropriate legislation.

AMENDMENT **XVI** [*RATIFIED IN 1913.*]

The Congress shall have power to lay and collect taxes on incomes, from whatever source derived, without apportionment among the several States, and without regard to any census or enumeration.

AMENDMENT **XVII** [*RATIFIED IN 1913.*]

The Senate of the United States shall be composed of two Senators from each State, elected by the people thereof, for six years; and each Senator shall have one vote. The electors in each State shall have the qualifications requisite for electors of the most numerous branch of the state legislatures.

When vacancies happen in the representation of any State in the Senate, the executive authority of such State shall issue writs of election to fill such vacancies: *Provided,* That the legislature of any State may empower the executive thereof to make temporary appointments until the people fill the vacancies by election as the legislature may direct.

This amendment shall not be so construed as to affect the election or term of any Senator chosen before it becomes valid as part of the Constitution.

AMENDMENT **XVIII** [*RATIFIED IN 1919.*]

Section 1. *After one year from the ratification of this article the manufacture, sale, or transportation of intoxicating liquors within, the importation thereof into, or the exportation thereof from the United States and all territory subject to the jurisdiction thereof for beverage purposes is hereby prohibited.*

Section 2. *The Congress and the several States shall have concurrent power to enforce this article by appropriate legislation.*

Section 3. *This article shall be inoperative unless it shall have been ratified as an amendment to the Constitution by the legislatures of the several States, as provided in the Constitution, within seven years from the date of the submission hereof to the States by the Congress.*[12]

---

[12] Repealed by the Twenty-First Amendment.

AMENDMENT XIX [*RATIFIED IN 1920.*]

The right of citizens of the United States to vote shall not be denied or abridged by the United States or by any State on account of sex.

Congress shall have power to enforce this article by appropriate legislation.

AMENDMENT XX [*RATIFIED IN 1933.*]

Section 1. The terms of the President and Vice President shall end at noon on the 20th day of January, and the terms of Senators and Representatives at noon on the 3d day of January, of the years in which such terms would have ended if this article had not been ratified; and the terms of their successors shall then begin.

Section 2. The Congress shall assemble at least once in every year, and such meeting shall begin at noon on the 3d day of January, unless they shall by law appoint a different day.

Section 3. If, at the time fixed for the beginning of the term of the President, the President elect shall have died, the Vice President elect shall become President. If a President shall not have been chosen before the time fixed for the beginning of his term, or if the President elect shall have failed to qualify, then the Vice President elect shall act as President until a President shall have qualified; and the Congress may by law provide for the case wherein neither a President elect nor a Vice President elect shall have qualified, declaring who shall then act as President, or the manner in which one who is to act shall be selected, and such person shall act accordingly until a President or Vice President shall have qualified.

Section 4. The Congress may by law provide for the case of the death of any of the persons from whom the House of Representatives may choose a President whenever the right of choice shall have devolved upon them, and for the case of the death of any of the persons from whom the Senate may choose a Vice President whenever the right of choice shall have devolved upon them.

Section 5. Sections 1 and 2 shall take effect on the 15th day of October following the ratification of this article.

Section 6. This article shall be inoperative unless it shall have been ratified as an amendment to the Constitution by the legislatures of three-fourths of the several States within seven years from the date of its submission.

AMENDMENT XXI [RATIFIED IN *1933*.]

Section 1. The eighteenth article of amendment to the Constitution of the United States is hereby repealed.

Section 2. The transportation or importation into any State, Territory, or possession of the United States for delivery or use therein of intoxicating liquors, in violation of the laws thereof, is hereby prohibited.

Section 3. This article shall be inoperative unless it shall have been ratified as an amendment to the Constitution by conventions in the several States, as provided in the Constitution, within seven years from the date of the submission hereof to the States by the Congress.

AMENDMENT XXII [RATIFIED IN *1951*.]

Section 1. No person shall be elected to the office of the President more than twice, and no person who has held the office of President, or acted as President, for more than two years of a term to which some other person was elected President shall be elected to the office of the President more than once. But this Article shall not apply to any person holding the office of President when this Article was proposed by the Congress, and shall not prevent any person who may be holding the office of President, or acting as President, during the term within which this Article becomes operative from holding the office of President or acting as President during the remainder of such term.

Section 2. This Article shall be inoperative unless it shall have been ratified as an amendment to the Constitution by the legislatures of three-fourths of the several States within seven years from the date of its submission to the States by the Congress.

AMENDMENT XXIII [RATIFIED IN *1961*.]

Section 1. The District constituting the seat of Government of the United States shall appoint in such manner as the Congress may direct:

A number of electors of President and Vice President equal to the whole number of Senators and Representatives in Congress to which the District would be entitled if it were a State, but in no event more than the least populous State; they shall be in addition to those appointed by the States, but they shall be considered, for the purposes of the election of President and Vice President, to be electors appointed by a State; and they shall meet in the District and perform such duties as provided by the twelfth article of amendment.

Section 2. The Congress shall have power to enforce this article by appropriate legislation.

AMENDMENT XXIV [RATIFIED IN 1964.]

Section 1. The right of citizens of the United States to vote in any primary or other election for President or Vice President, for electors for President or Vice President, or for Senator or Representative in Congress, shall not be denied or abridged by the United States or any State by reason of failure to pay any poll tax or other tax.

Section 2. The Congress shall have power to enforce this article by appropriate legislation.

AMENDMENT XXV [RATIFIED IN 1967.]

Section 1. In case of removal of the President from office or of his death or resignation, the Vice President shall become President.

Section 2. Whenever there is a vacancy in the office of the Vice President, the President shall nominate a Vice President who shall take office upon confirmation by a majority vote of both Houses of Congress.

Section 3. Whenever the President transmits to the President pro tempore of the Senate and the Speaker of the House of Representatives his written declaration that he is unable to discharge the powers and duties of his office, and until he transmits to them a written declaration to the contrary, such powers and duties shall be discharged by the Vice President as Acting President.

Section 4. Whenever the Vice President and a majority of either the principal officers of the executive departments or of such other body as Congress may by law provide, transmit to the President pro tempore of the Senate and the Speaker of the House of Representatives their written declaration that the President is unable to discharge the powers and duties of his office, the Vice President shall immediately assume the powers and duties of the office as Acting President.

Thereafter, when the President transmits to the President pro tempore of the Senate and the Speaker of the House of Representatives his written declaration that no inability exists, he shall resume the powers and duties of his office unless the Vice President and a majority of either the principal officers of the executive department or of such other body as Congress may by law provide, transmit within four days to the President pro tempore of the Senate and the Speaker of the House of Representatives their written declaration that the President is unable to discharge the powers and duties of his office. Thereupon Congress shall decide the issue, assembling within forty-eight hours for that purpose if not in session. If the Congress, within twenty-one days after receipt of the latter written declaration, or, if Congress is not in session, within twenty-one days after Congress is required to assemble, determines by two-thirds vote of both Houses that the President is unable to discharge the powers and duties of his office, the Vice President shall continue to discharge the same as Acting President; otherwise, the President shall resume the powers and duties of his office.

AMENDMENT XXVI [*RATIFIED IN 1971.*]

Section 1. The right of citizens of the United States, who are eighteen years of age or older, to vote shall not be denied or abridged by the United States or by any State on account of age.

Section 2. The Congress shall have power to enforce this article by appropriate legislation.

AMENDMENT XXVII [*RATIFIED IN 1992.*]

No law varying the compensation for the service of Senators and Representatives shall take effect until an election of Representatives shall have intervened.

The Federalist No. 10
James Madison
November 22, 1787

Among the numerous advantages promised by a well constructed Union, none deserves to be more accurately developed than its tendency to break and control the violence of faction. The friend of popular governments, never finds himself so much alarmed for their character and fate, as when he contemplates their propensity to this dangerous vice. He will not fail therefore to set a due value on any plan which, without violating the principles to which he is attached, provides a proper cure for it. The instability, injustice and confusion introduced into the public councils, have in truth been the mortal diseases under which popular governments have every where perished; as they continue to be the favorite and fruitful topics from which the adversaries to liberty derive their most specious declamations. The valuable improvements made by the American Constitutions on the popular models, both ancient and modern, cannot certainly be too much admired; but it would be an unwarrantable partiality, to contend that they have as effectually obviated the danger on this side as was wished and expected. Complaints are every where heard from our most considerate and virtuous citizens, equally the friends of public and private faith, and of public and personal liberty; that our governments are too unstable; that the public good is disregarded in the conflicts of rival parties; and that measures are too often decided, not according to the rules of justice, and the rights of the minor party; but by the superior force of an interested and over-bearing majority. However anxiously we may wish that these complaints had no foundation, the evidence of known facts will not permit us to deny that they are in some degree true. It will be found indeed, on a candid review of our situation, that some of the distresses under which we labor, have been erroneously charged on the operation of our governments; but it will be found, at the same time, that other causes will not alone account for many of our heaviest misfortunes; and particularly, for that prevailing and increasing distrust of public engagements, and alarm for private rights, which are echoed from one end of the continent to the other. These must be chiefly, if not wholly, effects of the unsteadiness and injustice, with which a factious spirit has tainted our public administrations.

By a faction I understand a number of citizens, whether amounting to a majority or minority of the whole, who are united and actuated by some common impulse of passion, or of interest, adverse to the rights of other citizens, or to the permanent and aggregate interests of the community.

There are two methods of curing the mischiefs of faction: the one, by removing its causes; the other, by controlling its effects.

There are again two methods of removing the causes of faction: the one by destroying the liberty which is essential to its existence; the other, by giving to every citizen the same opinions, the same passions, and the same interests.

It could never be more truly said than of the first remedy, that it is worse than the disease. Liberty is to faction, what air is to fire, an aliment without which it instantly expires. But it could not be a less folly to abolish liberty, which is essential to political life, because it nourishes faction, than it would be wish the annihilation of air, which is essential to animal life, because it imparts to fire its destructive agency.

The second expedient is as impracticable, as the first would be unwise. As long as the reason of man continues fallible, and he is at liberty to exercise it, different opinions will be formed. As long as the connection subsists between his reason and his self-love, his opinions and his passions will have a reciprocal influence on each other; and the former will be objects to which the latter will attach themselves. The diversity in the faculties of men from which the rights of property originate, is not less an insuperable obstacle to a uniformity of interests. The protection of these faculties is the first object of Government. From the protection of different and unequal faculties of acquiring property, the possession of different degrees and kinds of property immediately results: and from the influence of these on the sentiments and views of the respective proprietors, ensues a division of the society into different interests and parties.

The latent causes of faction are thus sown in the nature of man; and we see them every where brought into different degrees of activity, according to the different circumstances of civil society. A zeal for different opinions concerning religion, concerning Government and many other points, as well of speculation as of practice; an attachment to different leaders ambitiously contending for pre-eminence and power; or to persons of other descriptions whose fortunes have been interesting to the human passions, have in turn divided mankind into parties, inflamed them with mutual animosity, and rendered them much more disposed to vex and oppress each other, than to co-operate for their common good. So strong is this propensity of mankind to fall into mutual animosities, that where no substantial occasion presents itself, the most frivolous and fanciful distinctions have been sufficient to kindle their unfriendly passions, and excite their most violent conflicts. But the most common and durable source of factions, has been the various and unequal distribution of property. Those who hold, and those who are without property, have ever formed distinct interests in society. Those who are creditors, and those who are debtors, fall under a like discrimination. A landed interest, a manufacturing interest, a mercantile interest, a monied interest, with many lesser interests, grow up of necessity in civilized nations, and divide them into different classes, actuated by different sentiments and views. The regulation of these various and interfacing interests forms the principal task of modern Legislation, and involves the spirit of party and faction in the necessary and ordinary operations of Government.

No man is allowed to be a judge in his own cause; because his interest would certainly bias his judgment, and, not improbably, corrupt his integrity. With equal, nay with greater reason, a body of men, are unfit to be both judges and parties, at the same time; yet, what are many of the most important acts of legislation, but so many judicial determinations, not indeed concerning the rights of single persons, but concerning the rights of large bodies of citizens; and what are the different classes of legislators, but advocates and parties to the causes which they determine? Is a law proposed concerning private debts? It is a question to which the creditors are parties on one side, and the debtors on the other. Justice ought to hold the balance between them. Yet the parties are and must be themselves the judges; and the most numerous party, or, in other words, the most powerful faction must be expected to prevail. Shall domestic manufactures be encouraged, and in what degree, by restrictions on foreign manufactures? are questions which would be differently decided by the landed and the manufacturing classes; and probably by neither, with a sole regard to justice and the public good. The apportionment of taxes on the various descriptions of property, is an act which seems to require the most exact impartiality; yet, there is perhaps no legislative act in which greater opportunity and temptation are given to a predominant party, to trample on the rules of justice. Every shilling with which they over-burden the inferior number, is a shilling saved to their own pockets.

It is in vain to say, that enlightened statesmen will be able to adjust these clashing interests, and render them all subservient to the public good. Enlightened statesmen will not always be at the helm: Nor, in many cases, can such an adjustment be made at all, without taking into view indirect and remote considerations, which will rarely prevail over the immediate interest which one party may find in disregarding the rights of another, or the good of the whole.

The inference to which we are brought, is, that the *causes* of faction cannot be removed; and that relief is only to be sought in the means of controlling its *effects*.

If a faction consists of less than a majority, relief is supplied by the republican principle, which enables the majority to defeat its sinister views by regular vote: It may clog the administration, it may convulse the society; but it will be unable to execute and mask its violence under the forms of the Constitution. When a majority is included in a faction, the form of popular government on the other hand enables it to sacrifice to its ruling passion or interest, both the public good and the rights of other citizens. To secure the public good, and private rights, against the danger of such a faction, and at the same time to preserve the spirit and the form of popular government, is then the great object to which our enquiries are directed: Let me add that it is the great desideratum, by which alone this form of government can be rescued from the opprobrium under which it has so long labored, and be recommended to the esteem and adoption of mankind.

By what means is this object attainable? Evidently by one of two only. Either the existence of the same passion or interest in a majority at the same time, must be prevented; or the majority, having such co-existent passion or interest, must be rendered, by their number and local situation, unable to concert and carry into effect schemes of oppression. If the impulse and the opportunity be suffered to coincide, we well know that neither moral nor religious motives can be relied on as an adequate control. They are not found to be such on the injustice and violence of individuals, and lose their efficacy in proportion to the number combined together; that is, in proportion as their efficacy becomes needful.

From this view of the subject, it may be concluded, that a pure Democracy, by which I mean, a Society, consisting of a small number of citizens, who assemble and administer the Government in person, can admit of no cure for the mischiefs of faction. A common passion or interest will, in almost every case, be felt by a majority of the whole; a communication and concert results from the form of Government itself; and there is nothing to check the inducements to sacrifice the weaker party, or an obnoxious individual. Hence it is, that such Democracies have ever been spectacles of turbulence and contention; have ever been found incompatible with personal security, or the rights of property; and have in general been as short in their lives, as they have been violent in their deaths. Theoretic politicians, who have patronized this species of Government, have erroneously supposed, that by reducing mankind to a perfect equality in their political rights, they would, at the same time, be perfectly equalized and assimilated in their possessions, their opinions, and their passions.

A republic, by which I mean a government in which the scheme of representation takes place, opens a different prospect, and promises the cure for which we are seeking. Let us examine the points in which it varies from pure democracy, and we shall comprehend both the nature of the cure and the efficacy which it must derive from the union.

The two great points of difference, between a democracy and a republic, are, first, the delegation of the government, in the latter, to a small number of citizens, elected by the rest; secondly, the greater number of citizens, and greater sphere of country, over which the latter may be extended.

The effect of the first difference is, on the one hand, to refine and enlarge the public views, by passing them through the medium of a chosen body of citizens, whose wisdom may best discern the true interest of their country, and whose patriotism and love of justice, will be least likely to sacrifice it to temporary or partial considerations. Under such a regulation, it may well happen, that the public voice, pronounced by the representatives of the people, will be more consonant to the public good, than if pronounced by the people themselves, convened for the purpose. On the other hand the effect may be inverted. Men of factious tempers, of local prejudices, or of sinister designs, may by intrigue, by corruption, or by other means, first obtain the suffrages, and then betray the interest of the people. The question resulting is, whether small or extensive republics are most favorable to the election of proper guardians of the public weal; and it is clearly decided in favor of the latter by two obvious considerations.

In the first place, it is to be remarked that, however small the republic may be, the representatives must be raised to a certain number, in order to guard against the cabals of a few; and that however large it may be, they must be limited to a certain number, in order to guard against the confusion of a multitude. Hence, the number of representatives in the two cases not being in proportion to that of the constituents, and being proportionally greatest in the small republic, it follows, that if the proportion of fit characters be not less in the large than in the small republic, the former will present a greater option, and consequently a greater probability of a fit choice.

In the next place, as each Representative will be chosen by a greater number of citizens in the large than in the small Republic, it will be more difficult for unworthy candidates to practise with success the vicious arts, by which elections are too often carried; and the suffrages of the people being more free, will be more likely to center on men who possess the most attractive merit, and the most diffusive and established characters.

It must be confessed, that in this, as in most other cases, there is a mean, on both sides of which inconveniences will be found to lie. By enlarging too much the number of electors, you render the representative too little acquainted with all their local circumstances and lesser interests; as by reducing it too much, you render him unduly attached to these, and too little fit to comprehend and pursue great and national objects. The Federal Constitution forms a happy combination in this respect; the great and aggregate interests being referred to the national, the local and particular, to the state legislatures.

The other point of difference is, the greater number of citizens and extent of territory which may be brought within the compass of Republican, than of Democratic Government; and it is this circumstance principally which renders factious combinations less to be dreaded in the former, than in the latter. The smaller the society, the fewer probably will be the distinct parties and interests composing it; the fewer the distinct parties and interests, the more frequently will a majority be found of the same party; and the smaller the number of individuals composing a majority, and the smaller the compass within which they are placed, the more easily will they concert and execute their plans of oppression. Extend the sphere, and you take in a greater variety of parties and interests; you make it less probable that a majority of the whole will have a common motive to invade the rights of other citizens; or if such a common motive exists, it will be more difficult for all who feel it to discover their own strength, and to act in unison with each other. Besides other impediments, it may be remarked, that where there is a consciousness of unjust or dishonorable purpose, communication is always checked by distrust, in proportion to the number whose concurrence is necessary.

Hence it clearly appears, that the same advantage, which a Republic has over a Democracy, in controlling the effects of faction, is enjoyed by a large over a small Republic — is enjoyed by the Union over the States composing it. Does this advantage consist in the substitution of Representatives, whose enlightened views and virtuous sentiments render them superior to local prejudices, and to schemes of injustice? It will not be denied, that the Representation of the Union will be most likely to possess these requisite endowments. Does it consist in the greater security afforded by a greater variety of parties, against the event of any one party being able to outnumber and oppress the rest? In an equal degree does the increased variety of parties, comprised within the Union, increase this security? Does it, in fine, consist in the greater obstacles opposed to the concert and accomplishment of the secret wishes of an unjust and interested majority? Here, again, the extent of the Union gives it the most palpable advantage.

The influence of factious leaders may kindle a flame within their particular States, but will be unable to spread a general conflagration through the other States: a religious sect, may degenerate into a political faction in a part of the Confederacy but the variety of sects dispersed over the entire face of it, must secure the national Councils against any danger from that source: a rage for paper money, for an abolition of debts, for an equal division of property, or for any other improper or wicked project, will be less apt to pervade the whole body of the Union, than a particular member of it; in the same proportion as such a malady is more likely to taint a particular county or district, than an entire State.

In the extent and proper structure of the Union, therefore, we behold a Republican remedy for the diseases most incident to Republican Government. And according to the degree of pleasure and pride, we feel in being Republicans, ought to be our zeal in cherishing the spirit, and supporting the character of Federalists.

PUBLIUS

The Federalist No. 51
James Madison

February 6, 1788

To what expedient then shall we finally resort for maintaining in practice the necessary partition of power among the several departments, as laid down in the constitution? The only answer that can be given is, that as all these exterior provisions are found to be inadequate, the defect must be supplied, by so contriving the interior structure of the government, as that its several constituent parts may, by their mutual relations, be the means of keeping each other in their proper places. Without presuming to undertake a full development of this important idea, I will hazard a few general observations, which may perhaps place it in a clearer light, and enable us to form a more correct judgment of the principles and structure of the government planned by the convention.

In order to lay a due foundation for that separate and distinct exercise of the different powers of government, which to a certain extent, is admitted on all hands to be essential to the preservation of liberty, it is evident that each department should have a will of its own; and consequently should be so constituted, that the members of each should have as little agency as possible in the appointment of the members of the others. Were this principle rigorously adhered to, it would require that all the appointments for the supreme executive, legislative, and judiciary magistracies, should be drawn from the same fountain of authority, the people, through channels, having no communication whatever with one another. Perhaps such a plan of constructing the several departments would be less difficult in practice than it may in contemplation appear. Some difficulties however, and some additional expense, would attend the execution of it. Some deviations therefore from the principle must be admitted. In the constitution of the judiciary department in particular, it might be inexpedient to insist rigorously on the principle; first, because peculiar qualifications being essential in the members, the primary consideration ought to be to select that mode of choice, which best secures these qualifications; secondly, because the permanent tenure by which the appointments are held in that department, must soon destroy all sense of dependence on the authority conferring them.

It is equally evident that the members of each department should be as little dependent as possible on those of the others, for the emoluments annexed to their offices. Were the executive magistrate, or the judges, not independent of the legislature in this particular, their independence in every other would be merely nominal.

But the great security against a gradual concentration of the several powers in the same department, consists in giving to those who administer each department, the necessary constitutional means, and personal motives, to resist encroachments of the others. The provision for defense must in this, as in all other cases, be made commensurate to the danger of attack. Ambition must be made to counteract ambition. The interest of the man must be connected with the constitutional rights of the place. It may be a reflection on human nature, that such devices should be necessary to control the abuses of government. But what is government itself but the greatest of all reflections on human nature? If men were angels, no government would be necessary. If angels were to govern men, neither external nor internal controls on government would be necessary. In framing a government which is to be administered by men over men, the great difficulty lies in this: You must first enable the government to control the governed; and in the next place, oblige it to control itself. A dependence on the people is no doubt the primary control on the government; but experience has taught mankind the necessity of auxiliary precautions.

This policy of supplying by opposite and rival interests, the defect of better motives, might be traced through the whole system of human affairs, private as well as public. We see it particularly displayed in all the subordinate distributions of power; where the constant aim is to divide and arrange the several offices in such a manner as that each may be a check on the other; that the private interest of every individual, may be a sentinel over the public rights. These inventions of prudence cannot be less requisite in the distribution of the supreme powers of the state.

But it is not possible to give to each department an equal power of self defense. In republican government the legislative authority, necessarily, predominates. The remedy for this inconveniency is, to divide the legislature into different branches; and to render them by different modes of election, and different principles of action, as little connected with each other, as the nature of their common functions, and their common dependence on the society, will admit. It may even be necessary to guard against dangerous encroachments by still further precautions. As the weight of the legislative authority requires that it should be thus divided, the weakness of the executive may require, on the other hand, that it should be fortified. An absolute negative, on the legislature, appears at first view to be the natural defense with which the executive magistrate should be armed. But perhaps it would be neither altogether safe, nor alone sufficient. On ordinary occasions, it might not be exerted with the requisite firmness; and on extraordinary occasions, it might be perfidiously abused. May not this defect of an absolute negative be supplied, by some qualified connection between this weaker department, and the weaker branch of the stronger department, by which the latter may be led to support the constitutional rights of the former, without being too much detached from the rights of its own department?

If the principles on which these observations are founded be just, as I persuade myself they are, and they be applied as a criterion, to the several state constitutions, and to the federal constitution, it will be found, that if the latter does not perfectly correspond with them, the former are infinitely less able to bear such a test.

There are moreover two considerations particularly applicable to the federal system of America, which place that system in a very interesting point of view.

First. In a single republic, all the power surrendered by the people, is submitted to the administration of a single government; and usurpations are guarded against by a division of the government into distinct and separate departments. In the compound republic of America, the power surrendered by the people, is first divided between two distinct governments, and then the portion allotted to each, subdivided among distinct and separate departments. Hence a double security arises to the rights of the people. The different governments will control each other; at the same time that each will be controlled by itself.

Second. It is of great importance in a republic, not only to guard the society against the oppression of its rulers; but to guard one part of the society against the injustice of the other part. Different interests necessarily exist in different classes of citizens. If a majority be united by a common interest, the rights of the minority will be insecure. There are but two methods of providing against this evil: The one by creating a will in the community independent of the majority, that is, of the society itself; the other by comprehending in the society so many separate descriptions of citizens, as will render an unjust combination of a majority of the whole, very improbable, if not impracticable. The first method prevails in all governments possessing an hereditary or self appointed authority. This at best is but a precarious security; because a power independent of the society may as well espouse the unjust views of the major, as the rightful interests, of the minor party, and may possibly be turned against both parties. The second method will be exemplified in the federal republic of the United States. While all authority in it will be derived from and dependent on the society, the society itself will be broken into so many parts, interests and classes of citizens, that the rights of individuals or of the minority, will be in little danger from interested combinations of the majority. In a free government, the security for civil rights must be the same as for religious rights. It consists in the one case in the multiplicity of interests, and in the other, in the multiplicity of sects. The degree of security in both cases will depend on the number of interests and sects; and this may be presumed to depend on the extent of country and number of people comprehended under the same government. This view of the subject must particularly recommend a proper federal system to all the sincere and considerate friends of republican government: Since it shows that in exact proportion as the territory of the union may be formed into more circumscribed confederacies or states, oppressive combinations of a majority will be facilitated, the best security under the republican form, for the rights of every class of citizens, will be diminished; and consequently, the stability and independence of some member of the government, the only other security, must be proportionally increased. Justice is the end of government. It is the end of civil society. It ever has been, and ever will be pursued, until it be obtained, or until liberty be lost in the pursuit. In a society under the forms of which the stronger faction can readily unite and oppress the weaker, anarchy may as truly be said to reign, as in a state of nature where the weaker individual is not secured against the violence of the stronger: And as in the latter state even the stronger individuals are prompted by the uncertainty of their condition, to submit to a government which may protect the weak as well as themselves: So in the former state, will the more powerful factions or parties be gradually induced by a like motive, to wish for a government which will protect all parties, the weaker as well as the more powerful. It can be little doubted, that if the state of Rhode Island was separated from the confederacy, and left to itself, the insecurity of rights under the popular form of government within such narrow limits, would be displayed by such reiterated oppressions of factious majorities, that some power altogether independent of the people would soon be called for by the voice of the very factions whose misrule had proved the necessity of it. In the extended republic of the United States, and among the great variety of interests, parties and sects which it embraces, a coalition of a majority of the whole society could seldom take place on any other principles than those of justice and the general good; and there being thus less danger to a minor from the will of the major party, there must be less pretext also, to provide for the security of the former, by introducing into the government a will not dependent on the latter; or in other words, a will independent of the society itself. It is no less certain than it is important, notwithstanding the contrary opinions which have been entertained, that the larger the society, provided it lie within a practicable sphere, the more duly capable it will be of self government. And happily for the *republican cause,* the practicable sphere may be carried to a very great extent, by a judicious modification and mixture of the *federal principle.*

PUBLIUS

Presidents, 1789 – 1993

Year	President and Vice President	Party of President	Congress
1789 – 1797	**George Washington** John Adams	None	1st 2d 3d 4th
1797 – 1801	**John Adams** Thomas Jefferson	Federalist	5th 6th
1801 – 1809	**Thomas Jefferson** Aaron Burr (to 1805) George Clinton (to 1809)	Democratic-Republican	7th 8th 9th 10th
1809 – 1817	**James Madison** George Clinton (to 1813) Elbridge Gerry (to 1817)	Democratic-Republican	11th 12th 13th 14th
1817 – 1825	**James Monroe** Daniel D. Tompkins	Democratic-Republican	15th 16th 17th 18th
1825 – 1829	**John Quincy Adams** John C. Calhoun	National-Republican	19th 20th
1829 – 1837	**Andrew Jackson** John C. Calhoun (to 1833) Martin Van Buren (to 1837)	Democrat	21st 22d 23d 24th
1837 – 1841	**Martin Van Buren** Richard M. Johnson	Democrat	25th 26th
1841	**William H. Harrison*** John Tyler	Whig	
1841 – 1845	**John Tyler** (VP vacant)	Whig	27th 28th
1845 – 1849	**James K. Polk** George M. Dallas	Democrat	29th 30th
1849 – 1850	**Zachary Taylor*** Millard Fillmore	Whig	31st

* Died in office.

Year	President and Vice President	Party of President	Congress
1850 – 1853	**Millard Fillmore** (VP vacant)	Whig	32d
1853 – 1857	**Franklin Pierce** William R. King	Democrat	33d 34th
1857 – 1861	**James Buchanan** John C. Breckinridge	Democrat	35th 36th
1861 – 1865	**Abraham Lincoln*** Hannibal Hamlin (to 1865) Andrew Johnson (1865)	Republican	37th 38th
1865 – 1869	**Andrew Johnson** (VP vacant)	Republican	39th 40th
1869 – 1877	**Ulysses S. Grant** Schuyler Colfax (to 1873) Henry Wilson (to 1877)	Republican	41st 42d 43d 44th
1877 – 1881	**Rutherford B. Hayes** William A. Wheeler	Republican	45th 46th
1881	**James A. Garfield*** Chester A. Arthur	Republican	47th
1881 – 1885	**Chester A. Arthur** (VP vacant)	Republican	48th
1885 – 1889	**Grover Cleveland** Thomas A. Hendricks	Democrat	49th 50th
1889 – 1893	**Benjamin Harrison** Levi P. Morton	Republican	51st 52d
1893 – 1897	**Grover Cleveland** Adlai E. Stevenson	Democrat	53d 54th
1897 – 1901	**William McKinley*** Garret A. Hobart (to 1901) Theodore Roosevelt (1901)	Republican	55th 56th
1901 – 1909	**Theodore Roosevelt** (VP vacant, 1901 – 1905) Charles W. Fairbanks (1905 – 1909)	Republican	57th 58th 59th 60th

* Died in office.

Year	President and Vice President	Party of President	Congress
1909 – 1913	**William Howard Taft** James S. Sherman	Republican	61st 62d
1913 – 1921	**Woodrow Wilson** Thomas R. Marshall	Democrat	63d 64th 65th 66th
1921 – 1923	**Warren G. Harding*** Calvin Coolidge	Republican	67th
1923 – 1929	**Calvin Coolidge** (VP vacant, 1923 – 1925) Charles G. Dawes (1925 – 1929)	Republican	68th 69th 70th
1929 – 1933	**Herbert Hoover** Charles Curtis	Republican	71st 72d
1933 – 1945	**Franklin D. Roosevelt*** John N. Garner (1933 – 1941) Henry A. Wallace (1941 – 1945) Harry S Truman (1945)	Democrat	73d 74th 75th 76th 77th 78th
1945 – 1953	**Harry S Truman** (VP vacant, 1945 – 1949) Alben W. Barkley (1949 – 1953)	Democrat	79th 80th 81st 82d
1953 – 1961	**Dwight D. Eisenhower** Richard M. Nixon	Republican	83d 84th 85th 86th
1961 – 1963	**John F. Kennedy*** Lyndon B. Johnson	Democrat	87th
1963 – 1969	**Lyndon B. Johnson** (VP vacant, 1963 – 1965) Hubert H. Humphrey (1965 – 1969)	Democrat	88th 89th 90th
1969 – 1974	**Richard M. Nixon†** Spiro T. Agnew (1969 – 1974) Gerald R. Ford†† (1974)	Republican	91st 92d

* Died in office.
† Resigned from the presidency.
†† Appointed vice president.

Year	President and Vice President	Party of President	Congress
1974 – 1977	**Gerald R. Ford** Nelson A. Rockefeller††	Republican	93d 94th
1977 – 1981	**Jimmy Carter** Walter Mondale	Democrat	95th 96th
1981 – 1989	**Ronald Reagan** George Bush	Republican	97th 98th 99th 100th
1989 – 1993	**George Bush** Dan Quayle	Republican	101st 102d
1993 –	**Bill Clinton** Albert Gore, Jr.	Democrat	103d

†† Appointed vice president.

References

CHAPTER 2   THE CONSTITUTION

1. *Federalist No. 51*
2. *Ibid.*
3. Gordon S. Wood, *The Creation of the American Republic* (Chapel Hill: University of North Carolina Press, 1969). See also *Federalist No. 49.*
4. Letters of Thomas Jefferson to James Madison (January 30, 1787) and to Colonel William S. Smith (November 13, 1787). In Bernard Mayo, ed., *Jefferson Himself* (Boston: Houghton Mifflin, 1942), p. 145.
5. Letter of George Washington to Henry Lee, October 31, 1787. In John C. Fitzpatrick, ed., *Writings of George Washington* (Washington, D.C.: Government Printing Office, 1939), Vol. 29, p. 34.
6. See, for example, John Hope Franklin, *Racial Equality in America* (Chicago: University of Chicago Press, 1976), Ch. 1, esp. pp. 12–20.

CHAPTER 3   FEDERALISM

1. William H. Riker, "Federalism," in Fred I. Greenstein and Nelson W. Polsby, eds., *Handbook of Political Science* (Reading, Mass.: Addison-Wesley, 1975), Vol. 5, p. 101.
2. Harold J. Laski, "The Obsolescence of Federalism," *New Republic* (May 3, 1939), pp. 367–369, and Riker, *op. cit.,* p. 154.
3. Daniel J. Elazar, *American Federalism: A View from the States* (New York: Crowell, 1966), p. 216.
4. United States v. Sprague, 282 U.S. 716 (1931); Garcia v. San Antonio Metropolitan Transit Authority, 105 S. Ct. 1005 (1985).
5. Article I, Section 8, paragraph 18.
6. McCulloch v. Maryland, 4 Wheat. 316 (1819).
7. Collector v. Day, 11 Wall. 113 (1870), overruled in part in Graves v. New York, 306 U.S. 466 (1939); Pollock v. Farmers' Loan and Trust Co., 157 U.S. 429 (1895), overruled in South Carolina v. Baker, No. 94 (1988).
8. Texas v. White, 7 Wall. 700 (1869).

9. Wickard v. Filburn, 317 U.S. 111 (1942); NLRB v. Jones & Laughlin Steel Corp., 301 U.S. 58 (1937).

10. Kirschbaum Co. v. Walling, 316 U.S. 517 (1942).

11. Neal R. Pierce, "Partnership for City Aid," *Boston Globe,* March 30, 1978.

12. Samuel H. Beer, "The Modernization of American Federalism," *Publius,* Vol. 3 (Fall, 1973), esp. pp. 74–79, and Beer, "Federalism, Nationalism, and Democracy in America," *American Political Science Review,* Vol. 72 (March 1978), pp. 18–19.

13. *National Journal,* October 11, 1986, p. 2430.

14. Catherine H. Lovell et al., *Federal and State Mandating on Local Governments* (Riverside, Calif.: University of California at Riverside Graduate School of Public Administration, 1979), p. 71.

15. *Congressional Record,* Vol. 126 (Feb. 5, 1980), pp. S1009–S1013.

16. R. Douglas Arnold, "The Local Roots of Domestic Policy," in Thomas E. Mann and Norman J. Ornstein, eds., *The New Congress* (Washington, D.C.: American Enterprise Institute, 1981), p. 268.

17. Morton Grodzins, "Why Decentralization Won't Work," in Edward C. Banfield, ed., *Urban Government* (Glencoe, Ill.: Free Press, 1961), p. 122.

CHAPTER 4 PUBLIC OPINION AND THE MEDIA

1. R. L. Lowenstein, *World Press Freedom, 1966* (Columbia, Mo.: Freedom of Information Center, 1967). Publication No. 11; D. E. Butler, "Why American Political Reporting Is Better Than England's," *Harper's* (May 1963), pp. 15–25.

2. *New York Times,* March 15, 1975.

3. M. Kent Jennings and Richard G. Niemi, "The Transmission of Political Values from Parent to Child," *American Political Science Review,* Vol. 62 (March 1968), p. 173; Robert D. Hess and Judith V. Torney, *The Development of Political Attitudes in Children* (Chicago, Aldine, 1967), p. 90.

4. Several studies of child-parent agreement on party preference are summarized in David O. Sears, "Political Behavior," in Gardner Lindzey and Elliot Aronson, eds., *The Handbook of Social Psychology,* 2d ed. (Reading, Mass.: Addison-Wesley, 1969), Vol. 5, p. 376.

5. Norman H. Nie, Sidney Verba, and John R. Petrocik, *The Changing American Voter* (Cambridge, Mass.: Harvard University Press, 1976), Ch. 4.

6. Jennings and Niemi, *op. cit.*

7. Robert S. Erikson and Norman R. Luttbeg, *American Public Opinion: Its Origins, Content, and Impact* (New York: John Wiley, 1973), p. 197; and Seymour Martin Lipset, *Revolution and Counterrevolution,* rev. ed. (Garden City, N.Y.: Doubleday Anchor Books, 1970), pp. 338–342.

8. Erikson and Luttbeg, *op. cit.,* p. 194.

9. Seymour Martin Lipset and Earl Raab, "The Election and the Evangelicals," *Commentary* (March 1981), pp. 25–31.

10. *The Baron Report,* June 18, 1984.

11. Polls by Gallup, ABC News/*Washington Post,* and *Time*/Yankelovich, Skelly, and White, as summarized in *Public Opinion* (April/May 1982), pp. 30–32.

12. Alexander M. Astin, *Four Critical Years: Effects of College on Beliefs, Attitudes, and Knowledge* (San Francisco: Joddey-Bass, 1978), p. 38; J. L. Spaeth and Andrew M. Greeley, *Recent Alumni and Higher Education* (New York: McGraw-Hill, 1970), pp. 100–110; Erland Nelson, "Persistence of Attitudes of College Students Fourteen Years Later," *Psychological Monographs,* Vol. 68 (1954), pp. 1–13; Kenneth A. Feldman and Theodore M. Newcomb, *The Impact of College on Students* (San Francisco: Jossey-Bass, 1969), Vol. 1, pp. 99–100, 312–320.

13. Everett Carll Ladd, Jr., and Seymour Martin Lipset, *The Divided Academy: Professors and Politics* (New York: McGraw-Hill, 1975), pp. 26–27, 55–67, 184–190.

14. *Statistical Abstract of the United States, 1986,* p. 133.

15. Kay Lehman Schlozman and Sidney Verba, *Insult to Injury: Unemployment, Class, and Political Response* (Cambridge, Mass.: Harvard University Press, 1979), pp. 115–118.

16. David Butler and Donald Stokes, *Political Change in Great Britain* (New York: St. Martin's, 1969), pp. 70, 77; Erikson and Luttbeg, *op. cit.,* p. 184; *National Journal,* November 8, 1980, p. 1878.

17. V. O. Key, Jr., *Public Opinion and American Democracy* (New York: Knopf, 1961), pp. 122–138; Richard E. Dawson, *Public Opinion and Contemporary Disarray* (New York: Harper & Row, 1973), Ch. 4.

18. *Public Opinion* (April/May 1981), pp. 32–40, citing polls by Gallup, NORC, and ABC News/*Washington Post;* Philip E. Converse *et al., American Social Attitudes, 1947–1978* (Cambridge, Mass.: Harvard University Press, 1980), p. 109; and Robert S. Erikson, Norman E. Luttbeg, and Kent L. Tedin, *American Public Opinion,* 2d ed. (New York: Wiley, 1980), p. 169, citing polls by University of Michigan and Gallup.

19. Nie et al., *op. cit.,* pp. 253–256.

20. Schlozman and Verba, *op. cit.,* p. 172.

21. *Ibid.,* pp. 168, 170; *Public Opinion* (April/May 1981), p. 26, citing polls by Dresner, Morris, and Tortorello Research.

22. Everett Carll Ladd, Jr., *Transformations of the American Party System,* 2d ed. (New York: Norton, 1978), pp. 147–150.

23. Center for Political Studies, University of Michigan, 1976 survey, as reported in Erikson and Luttbeg, *op. cit.*

24. Nie, Verba, and Petrocik, *op. cit.,* pp. 247–250.

25. *Ibid.,* p. 218.

26. Ladd, *Transformations of the American Party System,* p. 280.

27. Philip E. Converse, "The Nature of Belief Systems in Mass Publics," in David Apter, ed., *Ideology and Discontent* (New York: Free Press of Glencoe, 1964), pp. 206–261.

28. Christopher H. Achen, "Mass Political Attitudes and the Survey Proposal," *American Political Science Review,* Vol. 69 (December 1975), pp. 1218–1231.

29. Nie, Verba, and Petrocik, *op. cit.,* pp. 115, 129, 142.

30. John L. Sullivan et al., "Ideological Constraint in the Mass Public: A Methodological Critique and Some New Findings," *American Journal of Political Science,* Vol. 22 (May 1978), pp. 233–249; and George F. Bishop et al., "Change in the Structure of American Political Attitudes: The Nagging Question of Question Wording," *American Journal of Political Science,* Vol. 22 (May 1978), pp. 250–269.

31. Converse, *op. cit.*

32. Seymour Martin Lipset and Earl Raab, *The Politics of Unreason* (New York: Harper & Row, 1970), Ch. 11; and James A. Stimson, "Belief Systems: Constraint, Complexity, and the 1972 Election," *American Journal of Political Science,* Vol. 19 (1975), pp. 393–417.

33. Stimson, *op. cit.* See also Allen H. Barton and R. Wayne Parsons, "Measuring Belief System Structure," *Public Opinion Quarterly,* Vol. 41 (Summer 1977), pp. 159–180.

34. Everett Carll Ladd, Jr., "The Unmaking of the Republican Party," *Fortune* (September 1977), p. 95.

35. Ladd, *Transformations of the American Party System,* pp. 287, 289; Nie, Verba, and Petrocik, *op. cit.,* pp. 262–263.

36. John McAdams, "Testing the Theory of the New Class," unpub. paper, Department of Political Science, Marquette University.

37. Data from various *New York Times*/CBS polls as reported in the *New York Times,* March 1 and April 5, 1984, and *Congressional Quarterly Weekly Report,* May 19, 1984, pp. 1179–1182.

38. Edward Jay Epstein, *News from Nowhere: Television and the News* (New York: Random House, 1974), p. 37.

39. Allen H. Barton, "Consensus and Conflict Among American Leaders," *Public Opinion Quarterly,* Vol. 38 (Winter 1974–1975), pp. 507–530.

40. Paul H. Weaver, "The New Journalism and the Old—Thoughts After Watergate," *The Public Interest* (Spring 1974), pp. 67–88.

41. Near v. Minnesota, 283 U.S. 697 (1931); New York Times v. United States, 403 U.S. 713 (1971).

42. New York Times v. Sullivan, 376 U.S. 254 (1964); Miami Herald Publishing Co. v. Tornillo, 418 U.S. 241 (1974); Yates v. United States, 354 U.S. 298 (1957).

43. Henry Fairlie, "The Rise of the Press Secretary," *The New Republic* (March 18, 1978), pp. 20 – 23; George Juergens, "Theodore Roosevelt and the Press," *Daedalus* (Fall 1982), pp. 113–133.

44. Michael J. Robinson, "A Twentieth-Century Medium in a Nineteenth-Century Legislature: The Effects of Television on the American Congress," in Norman J. Ornstein, ed., *Congress in Change* (New York: Praeger, 1975), pp. 240–261.

45. Survey of 240 journalists and broadcasters employed by the national news media, reported in S. Robert Lichter and Stanley Rothman, "Media and Business Elites," *Public Opinion* (October/November 1981), p. 44

46. Michael J. Robinson, "Just How Liberal Is the News? 1980 Revisited," *Public Opinion* (February/March 1983), pp. 55–60.

47. Peter Braestrup: *Big Story: How the American Press and Television Reported and Interpreted the Crises of Tet 1968 in Vietnam and Washington* (Boulder, Col.: Westview, 1977), 2 vols.

CHAPTER 5   POLITICAL PARTIES AND INTEREST GROUPS

1. Leon D. Epstein, "Political Parties," in Fred I. Greenstein and Nelson W. Polsby, eds., *Handbook of Political Science* (Reading, Mass.: Addison-Wesley, 1975), Vol. 4, p. 230.

2. Byron E. Shafer, *Quiet Revolution: The Struggle for the Democratic Party and the Shaping of Post-Reform Politics* (New York: Russell Sage Foundation, 1983), p. 230.

3. Martin Shefter, "Parties, Bureaucracy, and Political Change in the United States," in Louis Maisel and Joseph Cooper, eds., The Development of Political Parties, Sage Electoral Studies Yearbook, Vol. 4 (Beverly Hills, Calif.: Sage, 1978).

4. James Q. Wilson, *The Amateur Democrat: Club Politics in Three Cities* (Chicago: University of Chicago Press, 1962).

5. Dwaine Marvick and Charles R. Nixon, "Recruitment Contrasts in Rival Campaign Groups," in Dwaine Marvick, ed., *Political Decision-Makers* (New York: The Free Press, 1961), pp. 212–213; and David Nexon, "Asymmetry in the Political System," *American Political Science Review,* Vol. 65 (September 1971), pp. 716–730.

6. Samuel J. Eldersveld, *Political Parties: A Behavioral Analysis* (Chicago: Rand McNally, 1964), pp. 278, 287; and Robert H. Salisbury, "The Urban Political Organization Member," *Public Opinion Quarterly,* Vol. 29 (Winter 1965–1966), pp. 550–564.

7. Salisbury, *op. cit.,* pp. 557, 559.

8. Eldersveld, *op. cit.;* and J. David Greenstone, *Labor in American Politics* (New York: Knopf, 1969), p. 187.

9. Seymour Martin Lipset, "The Congressional Candidate," *Journal of Contemporary Studies,* Vol. 6 (Summer 1983), p. 102; Mondale delegate count in *Boston Globe,* July 9, 1984, p. 1.

10. William Nisbet Chambers and Walter Dean Burnham, eds., *The American Party System: Stages of Political Development,* 2d ed. (New York: Oxford University Press, 1975), p. 6.

11. James Q. Wilson, *Political Organizations* (New York: Basic Books, 1973), Ch. 12.

12. On 1972 and 1976, see Jeane Kirkpatrick, *The New Presidential Elite* (New York: Russell Sage Foundation and Twentieth Century Fund, 1976), pp. 297–315; on 1980, see *New York Times,* August 13, 1980.

13. Nelson W. Polsby, *Consequences of Party Reform* (New York: Oxford University Press, 1983), pp. 9–11, 64.

14. *Ibid,* p. 158.

15. Michael J. Malbin, "Democratic Party Rules Are Made to Be Broken," *National Journal,* August 23, 1980; and Kirkpatrick, *op. cit.,* Ch. 4.

16. Gallup Poll, various dates in 1980.

17. Norman H. Nie, Sidney Verba, and John R. Petrocik, *The Changing American Voter* (Cambridge, Mass.: Harvard University Press, 1976), p. 203; Barry Sussman, "Elites in America," *Washington Post,* September 26–30, 1976; and Kirkpatrick, *op. cit.,* Tables 10–1, 10–2, 10–3, 10–7.

18. Nie et al., *op. cit.,* p. 203.

19. L. Harmon Zeigler and Hendrik van Dalen, "Interest Groups in the States," in Herbert Jacob and Kenneth N. Vines, eds., *Politics in the American States,* 2d ed. (Boston: Little, Brown, 1974), pp. 122–160; and Edward C. Banfield and James Q. Wilson, *City Politics* (Cambridge, Mass.: Harvard University Press, 1963); Chs. 18, 19.

20. Joseph LaPalombara, *Interest Groups in Italian Politics* (Princeton, N.J.: Princeton University Press, 1964).

21. Kay Lehman Schlozman and John T. Tierney, "More of the Same: Washington Pressure Group Activity in a Decade of Change," *Journal of Politics,* Vol. 45 (1983), p. 356.

22. The use of injunctions in labor disputes was restricted by the Norris-La Guardia Act of 1932; the rights to collective bargaining and to the union shop were guaranteed by the Wagner Act of 1935.

23. Schlozman and Tierney, *op. cit.,* p. 355.

24. The distinction is drawn by Kay Lehman Schlozman and John T. Tierney, *The Mischiefs of Faction: Organized Interests in American Politics* (New York: Harper & Row, 1985).

25. Jeffrey M. Berry, *The Interest Group Society* (Boston: Little, Brown, 1984), pp. 20–21, 24, 130.

26. Gabriel A. Almond and Sidney Verba, *The Civic Culture* (Princeton, N.J.: Princeton University Press, 1963), p. 302; Derek C. Bok and John T. Dunlop, *Labor and the American Community* (New York: Simon & Schuster, 1970), p. 49; *Statistical Abstract of the United States, 1975,* p. 373.

27. Almond and Verba, *op. cit.,* p. 194.

28. *Ibid.,* p. 134.

29. Bok and Dunlop, *op. cit.,* p. 134.

30. Henry J. Pratt, *The Liberalization of American Protestantism* (Detroit, Mich.: Wayne State University Press, 1972), Ch. 12; Gerhard Lenski, *The Religious Factor* (Garden City, N.Y.: Doubleday, 1961), Ch. 4.

31. Jeffrey M. Berry, *Lobbying for the People* (Princeton, N.J.: Princeton University Press, 1977), p. 71–76.

32. Berry, *The Interest Group Society, op. cit.,* p. 88.

33. *National Journal,* August 6, 1983, p. 1632.

34. Schlozman and Tierney, *The Mischiefs of Faction, op. cit.*

35. *Ibid.,* Table 5–4.

36. *New York Times,* Dec. 8, 1983, p. 1.

37. Raymond A. Bauer, Ithiel de Sola Pool, and Lewis Anthony Dexter, *American Business and Public Policy* (New York: Atherton, 1963), Ch. 30.

38. Michael J. Malbin, ed., *Money and Politics in the United States* (Chatham, N.J.: Chatham House, 1984), Tables A.14 and A.15, pp. 298–299.

39. Margaret Ann Latus, "Assessing Ideological PACs: From Outrage to Understanding," in Malbin, *op, cit.,* p. 143.

40. *Ibid.,* p. 144; and Berry, *The Interest Group Society, op. cit.,* p. 163.

41. Theodore J. Eismeier and Philip H. Pollock, "Political Action Committees: Varieties of Organization Strategy," in Malbin, *op. cit.,* p. 132.

42. Malbin, *op. cit.,* Table A.8, pp. 290–291.

43. Michael J. Malbin, "Looking Back at the Future of Campaign Finance Reform: Interest Groups and American Election," in Malbin, *Money and Politics, op. cit.,* p. 248; James B. Kau and Paul H. Rubin, *Congressmen, Constituents, and Contributions* (Boston: Martinus Nijhoff, 1982); Henry W. Chappell, Jr., "Campaign Contributions and Voting on the Cargo Preference Bill: A Comparison of Simultaneous Models," *Public Choice,* Vol. 36 (1981), pp. 301–312; W. P. Welch, "Campaign Contributions and Voting: Milk Money and Dairy Price Supports," *Western Political Quarterly,* Vol. 35 (1982), pp. 478–495.

44. *National Journal,* November 19, 1977, p. 1800, quoting a study by the staff of Senator William Proxmire.

45. William T. Gormley, "A Test of the Revolving Door Hypothesis at the FCC," *American Journal of Political Science,* Vol. 23 (1979), pp. 665–683; Paul J. Quirk, *Industry Influence in Federal Regulatory Agencies* (Princeton, N.J.: Princeton University Press, 1981); Suzanne Weaver, *Decision to Prosecute* (Cambridge, Mass.: MIT Press, 1977), pp. 154–163.

46. United States v. Harriss, 347 U.S. 612 (1954).

47. Hope Eastman, *Lobbying: A Constitutionally Protected Right* (Washington, D.C.: American Enterprise Institute, 1977), p. 30.

48. One such bill was S. 1785, 95th Congress. See Eastman, *op. cit.,* p. 10.

49. Eastman, *op. cit.,* pp. 20–21.

50. *United States Code,* Title 26, Sec. 501(c)(3).

51. Wilson, *Political Organizations, op. cit.,* p. 321.

CHAPTER 6　CAMPAIGNS AND ELECTIONS

1. G. Bingham Powell, Jr., "Voting Turnout in Thirty Democracies," in Richard Rose, ed., *Electoral Participation: A Comparative Analysis* (London and Beverly Hills: Sage, 1980), p. 6.

2. Sidney Verba and Norman H. Nie, *Participation in America* (New York: Harper & Row, 1972), pp. 118–119.

3. Norman H. Nie and Sidney Verba, "Political Participation," in Fred I. Greenstein and Nelson W. Polsby, eds., *Handbook of Political Science* (Reading, Mass.: Addison-Wesley, 1975), Vol. 4, pp. 24–25.

4. Lester W. Milbrath and M. L. Goel, *Political Participation,* 2d ed. (Chicago: Rand McNally, 1977), pp. 98–116; Raymond E. Wolfinger and Steven J. Rosenstone, *Who Votes?* (New Haven, Conn.: Yale University Press, 1980).

5. Nie and Verba, *op. cit.,* pp. 151–157; Milbrath and Goel, *op. cit.,* p. 120.

6. Verba and Nie, *op. cit.,* pp. 160–164.

7. Richard A. Brody, "The Puzzle of Political Participation in America," in Anthony King, ed., *The New American Political System* (Washington, D.C.: American Enterprise Institute, 1978), pp. 315–323; and Charles Lewis Taylor and Michael C. Hudson, *World Handbook of Political and Social Indicators,* 2d ed. (New Haven, Conn.: Yale University Press, 1972), Table 3.1.

8. Verba and Nie, *op. cit.,* Ch. 18.

9. Voter Education Project, Inc., of Atlanta, Georgia, as reported in *Statistical Abstract of the United States, 1984,* p. 261.

10. Congressional Quarterly, *Congress and the Nation,* Vol. 3: 1969–1972 (Washington, D.C.: Congressional Quarterly, Inc., 1973), p. 1006; and *Statistical Abstract of the United States, 1975,* p. 450.

11. Walter Dean Burnham, "The Changing Shape of the American Political Universe," *American Political Science Review,* Vol. 59 (March 1965); E. E. Schattschneider, *The Semisovereign People* (New York: Holt, Rinehart, and Winston, 1960), Chs. 5, 6.

12. Morton Keller, *Affairs of State* (Cambridge, Mass.: Harvard University Press, 1977), pp. 523–524.

13. Jerrold D. Rusk, "The Effect of the Australian Ballot Reforms on Split-Ticket Voting, 1876–1908," *American Political Science Review,* Vol. 64 (December 1970), pp. 1220–1238.

14. Richard G. Smolka, *Election Day Registration: The Minnesota and Wisconsin Experience in 1976* (Washington, D.C.: American Enterprise Institute, 1977).

15. Wolfinger and Rosenstone, *op. cit.*

16. Thomas E. Patterson and Robert D. McClure, *The Unseeing Eye: The Myth of Television Power in National Elections* (New York: Putnam, 1976).

17. Gerald M. Pomper et al., *The Election of 1980* (Chatham, N.J.: Chatham House, 1981), pp. 75, 105–106.

18. Angus Campbell, Philip E. Converse, Warren E. Miller, and Donald E. Stokes, *The American Voter* (New York: Wiley, 1960), p. 757.

19. Richard Wirthlin, Vincent Breglio, and Richard Beal, "Campaign Chronicle," *Public Opinion* (February/March 1981), pp. 43–49 (written by Reagan pollsters).

20. Seymour Martin Lipset and Earl Raab, "The Election and the Evangelicals," *Commentary* (March 1981), p. 29.

21. Norman H. Nie, Sidney Verba, and John R. Petrocik, *The Changing American Voter* (Cambridge, Mass.: Harvard University Press, 1976).

22. Campbell et al., *op. cit.,* Ch. 8.

23. V. O. Key, Jr., *The Responsible Electorate* (Cambridge, Mass.: Harvard University Press, 1966).

24. David RePass, "Issue Salience and Party Choice," *American Political Science Review,* Vol. 65 (June 1971), pp. 389–400.

25. Gerald M. Pomper, "From Confusion to Clarity: Issues and American Voters, 1956–1968," *American Political Science Review,* Vol. 66 (June 1972), pp. 415–428; and Arthur H. Miller et al., "A Majority Party in Disarray: Policy Polarization in the 1972 Election," *American Political Science Review,* Vol. 70 (September 1976).

26. Morris P. Fiorina, *Retrospective Voting in American Elections* (New Haven, Conn.: Yale University Press, 1981).

27. Walter Dean Burnham, *Critical Elections and the Mainsprings of American Politics* (New York: Norton, 1970), p. 10.

28. James L. Sundquist, *Dynamics of the Party System* (Washington, D.C.: Brookings Institution, 1973), Ch. 7.

29. Edward G. Carmines and James A. Stimson, "Issue Evolution, Population Replacement, and Normal Partisan Change," *American Political Science Review,* Vol. 75 (March 1981), pp. 107–118; and Gregory B. Markus, "Political Attitudes in an Election Year," *American Political Science Review,* Vol. 76 (September 1982), pp. 538–560.

30. Rusk, *op. cit.,* pp. 1220–1238.

31. Robert Axelrod, "Where the Votes Come From: An Analysis of Electoral Coalition, 1952–1968," *American Political Science Review,* Vol. 66 (March 1972), pp. 11–20; and Axelrod, "Communication," *American Political Science Review,* Vol. 68 (June 1974), pp. 718–719.

32. Herbert Asher, *Presidential Elections and American Politics* (Homewood, Ill.: Dorsey Press, 1976), pp. 239–240 (and studies cited therein).

33. David O. Sears and Richard E. Whitney, "Political Persuasion," in Ithiel de Sola Pool, Wilbur Schramm, et al., *Handbook of Communication* (Chicago: Rand McNally, 1973), pp. 253–289.

34. Patterson and McClure, *op. cit.;* and Xandra Kayden, *Campaign Organization* (Lexington, Mass.: Heath, 1978), Ch. 6.

35. Robert S. Erikson, "The Influence of Newspaper Endorsements in Presidential Elections: The Case of 1964," *American Journal of Political Science,* Vol. 20 (May 1976), pp. 207–233.

36. Maxwell E. McCombs and Donald R. Shaw, "The Agenda Setting Function of the Mass Media," *Public Opinion Quarterly,* Vol. 36 (Summer 1972), p. 176–187.

37. G. Ray Funkhouser, "The Issues of the Sixties," *Public Opinion Quarterly,* Vol. 37 (Spring 1973), pp. 62–75.

38. Gary C. Jacobson, *Money in Congressional Elections* (New Haven, Conn.: Yale University Press, 1980).

39. Buckley v. Valeo, 424 U.S. 1 (1976).

40. *Ibid.*

41. Congressional Quarterly, *Dollar Politics* (Washington, D.C.: Congressional Quarterly, Inc., 1974), pp. 66–69.

42. William J. Crotty, *Political Reform and the American Experiment* (New York: Crowell, 1977), p. 121.

43. *Ibid.,* p. 114, reporting data from Common Cause.

44. Gerald M. Pomper, *Elections in America* (New York: Dodd, Mead, 1971), p. 178.

CHAPTER 7 CONGRESS

1. Wesberry v. Sanders, 376 U.S. 1 (1964).

2. H. Douglas Price, "Careers and Committees in the American Congress," in William O. Aydelotte, ed., *The History of Parliamentary Behavior* (Princeton, N.J.: Princeton University Press, 1977), pp. 28–62; John F. Bibby, Thomas E. Mann, and Norman J. Ornstein, *Vital Statistics on Congress, 1980* (Washington, D.C.: American Enterprise Institute, 1980), pp. 53–54; Thomas E. Cavanagh, "The Dispersion of Authority in the House of Representatives," *Political Science Quarterly,* Vol. 97 (1982–1983), pp. 625–626.

3. David R. Mayhew, *Congress: The Electoral Connection* (New Haven, Conn.: Yale University Press, 1974); Bibby, Mann, and Ornstein, *op. cit.,* pp. 14–15.

4. Mayhew, *op. cit.;* Morris P. Fiorina, *Congress: Keystone of the Washington Establishment* (New Haven, Conn.: Yale University Press, 1977).

5. Richard F. Fenno, Jr., "U.S. House Members and Their Constituencies: An Exploration," *American Political Science Review,* Vol. 71 (September 1977), pp. 883–917, esp. p. 914.

6. Richard F. Fenno, Jr., *Congressmen in Committees* (Boston: Little, Brown, 1973).

7. Bibby, Mann, and Ornstein, *op. cit.,* pp. 65–74.

8. Fiorina, *op. cit.*

9. Bibby, Mann, and Ornstein, *op. cit.,* p. 60.

10. Michael J. Malbin, "Delegation, Deliberation, and the New Role of Congressional Staff," in Thomas E. Mann and Norman J. Ornstein, eds., *The New Congress* (Washington, D.C.: American Enterprise Institute, 1981), pp. 134–177, esp. pp. 170–171.

11. Malcolm E. Jewell and Samuel C. Patterson, *The Legislative Process in the United States,* 3d ed. (New York: Random House, 1977), p. 439.

12. Warren E. Miller and Donald E. Stokes, "Constituency Influence in Congress," in Angus Campbell et al., eds. *Elections and the Political Order* (New York: Wiley, 1966), p. 359.

13. *Congressional Quarterly Weekly Report,* Feb. 9, 1980, pp. 323–342.

CHAPTER 8 THE PRESIDENCY

1. Jean Blondel, *An Introduction to Comparative Government* (New York: Praeger, 1969), as cited in Nelson W. Polsby, "Legislatures," in Fred I. Greenstein and Nelson W. Polsby, eds., *Handbook of Political Science* (Reading, Mass.: Addison-Wesley, 1975), Vol. 5, p. 275.

2. Woodrow Wilson, *Congressional Government* (New York: Meridian, 1956), pp. 167–168, 170 (first published in 1885).

3. Stephen Hess, *Organizing the Presidency* (Washington, D.C.: Brookings Institution, 1976), p. 3.

4. Walter D. Burnham, "Insulation and Responsiveness in Congressional Elections," *Political Science Quarterly,* Vol. 90 (Fall 1975), pp. 412–413; George C. Edwards III, *Presidential Influence in Congress* (San Francisco, Calif.: Freeman, 1980), pp. 70–78; Warren E. Miller, "Presidential Coattails: A Study in Political Myth and Methodology," *Public Opinion Quarterly,* Vol. 19 (Winter 1955–1956), p. 368; and Miller, "The Motivational Basis for Straight and Split Ticket Voting," *American Political Science Review,* Vol. 51 (June 1957), pp. 293–312.

5. Edwards, *op. cit.,* pp. 86–100; Douglas Rivers and Nancy L. Rose, "Passing the President's Program: Public Opinion and Presidential Influence in Congress," paper delivered at the 1981 annual meeting of the Midwestern Political Science Association.

6. United States v. Nixon, 418 U.S. 683 (1974).

CHAPTER 9   THE BUREAUCRACY

1. Charles E. Lindblom, *Politics and Markets* (New York: Basic Books, 1977), p. 114.

2. Article II, Section 2, paragraph 2.

3. Article II, Section 3.

4. Calculated from data in *Historical Statistics of the United States: Colonial Times to 1970* (Washington, D.C.: Government Printing Office, 1975), Vol. 2, pp. 1102–1103.

5. Panama Refining Co. v. Ryan, 293 U.S. 388 (1935); Hampton Jr. & Co. v. United States, 276 U.S. 394 (1928).

6. Edward S. Corwin, *The Constitution and What It Means Today,* 13th ed. (Princeton, N.J.: Princeton University Press, 1973), p. 151.

7. Bruce D. Porter, "Parkinson's Law Revisited: War and the Growth of American Government," *Public Interest* (Summer 1980), pp. 50–68.

8. See the cases cited in Corwin, *op. cit.,* p. 8.

9. *Historical Statistics of the United States,* Vol. 2, p. 1107.

10. *Statistical Abstract of the United States, 1975* (Washington, D.C.: Government Printing Office, 1975), p. 242.

11. *National Journal,* July 18, 1981, pp. 1296–1299.

12. J. Donald Kingsley, *Representative Bureaucracy* (Yellow Springs, Ohio: Antioch Press, 1944); Richard P. Nathan, *The Plot That Failed: Nixon and the Administrative Presidency* (New York: Wiley, 1975).

13. Stanley Rothman and S. Robert Lichter, "How Liberal Are Bureaucrats?" *Regulation* (November–December 1983), pp. 17–18.

14. Kenneth Meier and Lloyd Nigro, "Representative Bureaucracy and Policy Preferences: A Study of the Attitudes of Federal Executives," *Public Administration Review,* Vol. 36 (July–August 1976), pp. 458–467; Bernard Mennis, *American Foreign Policy Officials* (Columbus, Ohio: Ohio State University Press, 1971); Joel D. Aberbach and Bert A. Rockman, "Clashing Beliefs Within the Executive

Branch: The Nixon Administration Bureaucracy," *American Political Science Review,* Vol. 70 (June 1976), pp. 456–468.

15. James Q. Wilson, *The Investigators* (New York: Basic Books, 1978).

16. Graham K. Wilson, "Are Department Secretaries Really a President's Natural Enemies?" *British Journal of Political Science,* Vol. 7 (1977), pp. 273–299.

17. Richard F. Fenno, Jr., *The Power of the Purse* (Boston: Little, Brown, 1966), pp. 450, 597.

18. John E. Schwartz and L. Earl Shaw, *The United States Congress in Comparative Perspective* (Hinsdale, Ill.: Dryden, 1976), pp. 262–263; *National Journal,* July 4, 1981, pp. 1211–1214.

19. Immigration and Naturalization Service v. Chadha, 103 S. Ct. 2764 (1983).

20. See cases cited in Corwin, *op. cit.,* p. 22.

21. Daniel Katz et al., *Bureaucratic Encounters* (Ann Arbor: Survey Research Center of the University of Michigan, 1975), pp. 63–69, 118–120, 184–188.

CHAPTER 10   THE JUDICIARY

1. Henry J. Abraham, *The Judicial Process,* 3d ed. (New York: Oxford University Press, 1975), pp. 279–280.

2. Robert G. McCloskey, *The American Supreme Court* (Chicago: University of Chicago Press, 1960), p. 27.

3. Marbury v. Madison, 1 Cranch 137 (1803); McCulloch v. Maryland, 4 Wheaton 316 (1819).

4. Martin v. Hunter's Lessee, 1 Wheaton 304 (1816); Cohens v. Virginia, 6 Wheaton 264 (1821); and Gibbons v. Ogden, 9 Wheaton 1 (1824).

5. Quoted in Albert J. Beveridge, *The Life of John Marshall* (Boston: Houghton Mifflin, 1919), Vol. 4, p. 551.

6. Dred Scott v. Sandford, 19 Howard 393 (1857).

7. Quoted in Henry J. Abraham, *Justices and Presidents* (New York: Oxford University Press, 1974), p. 74.

8. *Ibid.,* p. 75.

9. Gideon v. Wainwright, 372 U.S. 335 (1963). The story is told in Anthony Lewis, *Gideon's Trumpet* (New York: Random House, 1964).

10. Erwin Griswold, "Rationing Justice: The Supreme Court's Case Load and What the Court Does Not Do," *Cornell Law Review,* Vol. 60 (1975), pp. 335–354.

11. Paul A. Freund, *Report of the Study Group on the Caseload of the Supreme Court* (Washington, D.C.: Federal Judiciary Center, 1972).

12. Alyeska Pipeline Service Co. v. Wilderness Society, 421 U.S. 240; Maine v. Thiboutot, 100 S. Ct. 2502 (1980).

13. Flast v. Cohen, 392 U.S. 83 (1968), which modified the earlier Frothingham v. Mellon, 262 U.S. 447 (1923); United States v. Richardson, 418 U.S. 166 (1947).

14. Brown v. Board of Education of Topeka, 347 U.S. 483 (1954).

15. Baker v. Carr, 369 U.S. 186 (1962).

16. See Louise Weinberg, "A New Judicial Federalism?" *Daedalus* (Winter 1978), pp. 129–141.

17. *Harvard Law Review,* Vol. 100 (1986), p. 305.

18. A. P. Blaustein and A. H. Field, "Overruling Opinions in the Supreme Court," *Michigan Law Review,* Vol. 47 (1958), p. 151; Henry J. Abraham, *The Judicial Process,* 4th ed. (New York: Oxford University Press, 1980), p. 349.

19. The Court abandoned the "political question" doctrine in Baker v. Carr, 369 U.S. 186 (1962), and began to change congressional district apportionment in Wesberry v. Sanders, 376 U.S. 1 (1964).

20. Donald J. Horowitz, *The Courts and Social Policy* (Washington, D.C.: Brookings Inst., 1977), p. 6.

21. Gates v. Collier, 349 F. Supp. 881 (1972); and Lau v. Nichols, 414 U.S. 563 (1974).

22. *International Directory of Bar Associations,* 3d ed. (Chicago: American Bar Foundation, 1973).

23. Annual Reports of the Director of the Administrative Office of the United States Courts, 1975 (Table 17), and 1983 (Table 16).

24. Warner W. Gardner, "Federal Courts and Agencies: An Audit of the Partnership Books," *Columbia Law Review,* Vol. 75 (1975), pp. 800–822.

25. Anthony Partridge and William B. Eldridge, *The Second Circuit Sentencing Study* (Washington, D.C.: Federal Judicial Center, 1974).

26. Abraham, *The Judicial Process,* p. 332.

27. *Ex Parte* McCardle, 7 Wallace 506 (1869).

28. Walter J. Murphy, *Congress and the Court* (Chicago: University of Chicago Press, 1962); and C. Herman Prichett, *Congress Versus the Supreme Court* (Minneapolis: University of Minnesota Press, 1961).

29. Joseph T. Tanenhaus and Walter F. Murphy, "Patterns of Public Support for the Supreme Court: A Panel Study," *Journal of Politics,* Vol. 43 (1981), pp. 24–39, and Gregory A. Caldeira, "Neither the Purse Nor the Sword: Dynamics of Public Confidence in the Supreme Court," *American Political Science Review,* Vol. 80 (1988), p. 1213.

CHAPTER 11 CIVIL LIBERTIES AND CIVIL RIGHTS

1. Barron v. Baltimore, 7 Peters 243 (1833).

2. Gitlow v. New York, 268 U.S. 652 (1925); Palko v. Connecticut, 302 U.S. 319 (1937).

3. Schad v. Borough of Mt. Ephraim, 452 U.S. 61 (1981).

4. United States v. Carolene Products, 304 U.S. 144 (1938).

5. Near v. Minnesota, 283 U.S. 697 (1931).

6. Brandenburg v. Ohio, 395 U.S. 765 (1978).

7. Kunz v. New York, 340 U.S. 290 (1951).

8. Hynes v. Mayor and Council of Oradell, 425 U.S. 610 (1976).

9. Nebraska Press Association v. Stuart, 427 U.S. 539 (1976).

10. *New York Times* v. Sullivan, 376 U.S. 254 (1964). But compare Time, Inc. v. Firestone, 424 U.S. 448 (1976).

11. United States v. O'Brien, 391 U.S. 367 (1968).

12. Texas v. Johnson, 109 S. Ct. 2533 (1989); Tinker v. Des Moines Community School District, 393 U.S. 503 (1969).

13. Chaplinsky v. New Hampshire, 315 U.S. 568 (1942). But compare Gooding v. Wilson, 405 U.S. 518 (1972) and Rosenfeld v. New Jersey, 408 U.S. 901 (1972).

14. Village of Skokie v. National Socialist Party, 97 S. Ct. 2205 (1977); 366 N.E. 2d 349 (1977); 373 N.E. 2d 21 (1978).

15. Henry J. Abraham, *Freedom and the Court: Civil Rights and Civil Liberties in the United States,* 3d ed. (New York: Oxford University Press, 1977), pp. 214–215, fn. 178.

16. Concurring opinion in Jacobellis v. Ohio, 378 U.S. 184 (1964), at p. 197.

17. Miller v. California, 413 U.S. 15 (1973).

18. Renton v. Playtime Theaters, 475 U.S. 41 (1986); Young v. American Mini-Theaters, Inc., 427 U.S. 50 (1976).

19. First National Bank of Boston v. Bellotti, 435 U.S. 765 (1978); Pacific Gas and Electric Co. v. Public Utilities Commissioners, 475 U.S. 1 (1986).

20. Federal Election Commission v. Massachusetts Citizens for Life, Inc., 107 S. Ct. 616 (1986).

21. Hazelwood School District v. Kuhlmeier, et al., 56 Law Week 4079 (1988).

22. Murdock v. Pennsylvania, 319 U.S. 105 (1943).

23. Reynolds v. United States, 98 U.S. 145 (1878).

24. Jacobson v. Massachusetts, 197 U.S. 11 (1905).

25. Faith Baptist Church v. Douglas, 454 U.S. 803 (1981).

26. Welsh v. United States, 398 U.S. 333 (1970).

27. Sherbert v. Verner, 374 U.S. 398 (1963); Wisconsin v. Yoder, 406 U.S. 207 (1972).

28. Walter Berns, *The First Amendment and the Future of American Democracy* (New York: Basic Books, 1976).

29. C. Herman Pritchett, *Constitutional Civil Liberties* (Englewood Cliffs, N.J.: Prentice-Hall, 1984), pp. 145–147.

30. Everson v. Board of Education, 330 U.S. 1 (1947).

31. Engel v. Vitale, 370 U.S. 107 (1962).

32. Lubbock Independent School District v. Lubbock Civil Liberties Union, 103 S. Ct. 800 (1983).

33. School District of Abington Township v. Schempp, 374 U.S. 203 (1963).

34. Epperson v. Arkansas, 393 U.S. 97 (1968); McLean v. Arkansas Board of Education, 529 F. Supp. 1255 (1982).

35. McCollum v. Board of Education, 333 U.S. 203 (1948); Zorach v. Clauson, 343 U.S. 306 (1952).

36. Tilton v. Richardson, 403 U.S. 672 (1971).

37. Board of Education v. Allen, 392 U.S. 236 (1968).

38. Walz v. Tax Commission, 397 U.S. 664 (1970).

39. Mueller v. Allen, 103 S. Ct. 3062 (1983).

40. Lemon v. Kurtzman, 403 U.S. 602 (1971).

41. Committee for Public Education v. Nyquist, 413 U.S. 756 (1973).

42. Meek v. Pittenger, 421 U.S. 349 (1975).

43. Wolman v. Walter, 433 U.S. 299 (1977).

44. Lemon v. Kurtzman, 403 U.S. 602 (1971).

45. Lynch v. Donnelly, 104 S. Ct. 1355 (1984); County of Allegheny v. ACLU, 109 S. Ct. 3086 (1989).

46. Marsh v. Chambers, 103 S. Ct. 3330 (1983).

47. Stephen R. Schlesinger, *Exclusionary Injustice: The Problem of Illegally Obtained Evidence* (New York: Dekker, 1975).

48. Yale Kamisar, "Does (Did) (Should) the Exclusionary Rule Rest on a 'Principled Basis' Rather Than an 'Empirical Proposition'?" *Creighton Law Review,* Vol. 16 (1982–1983), pp. 565–667.

49. Wolf v. Colorado, 338 U.S. 25 (1949).

50. Mapp v. Ohio, 367 U.S. 643 (1961).

51. Chimel v. California, 395 U.S. 752 (1969).

52. Washington v. Chrisman, 455 U.S. 1 (1982).

53. Oliver v. United States, 104 S. Ct. 1735 (1984).

54. Arkansas v. Sanders, 422 U.S. 753 (1979); Robbins v. California, 453 U.S. 420 (1981).

55. United States v. Ross, 456 U.S. 798 (1982).

56. Winston v. Lee, 470 U.S. 753 (1985).

57. South Dakota v. Neville, 103 S. Ct. 916 (1983); Schmerber v. California, 384 U.S. 757 (1966).

58. United States v. Dunn, 107 S. Ct. 1134 (1987); California v. Ciraolo, 106 S. Ct. 1809 (1986); California v. Carney, 471 U.S. 386 (1985).

59. O'Connor v. Ortega, 107 S. Ct. 1492 (1987).

60. New Jersey v. T.L.O., 105 S. Ct. 733 (1985).

61. Skinner v. Railway Labor Executives Association, 109 S. Ct. 1402 (1989), and National Treasury Employees Union v. von Raab, 109 S. Ct. 1384 (1989).

62. Escobedo v. Illinois, 378 U.S. 478 (1964); Miranda v. Arizona, 384 U.S. 436 (1966).

63 Malloy v. Hogan, 378 U.S. 1 (1964).

64. Miranda v. Arizona, 384 U.S. 436 (1966).

65. Gilbert v. California, 388 U.S. 263 (1967).

66. Estelle v. Smith, 451 U.S. 454 (1981).

67. Brewer v. Williams, 430 U.S. 387 (1977).

68. Fare v. Michael C., 442 U.S. 707 (1979).

69. United States v. Leon, 104 S. Ct. 3405 (1984).

70. New York v. Quarles, 104 S. Ct. 2626 (1984).

71. Nix v. Williams, 104 S. Ct. 2501 (1984).

72. Brown v. Board of Education of Topeka, 347 U.S. 483 (1955).

73. Fullilove v. Klutznick, 448 U.S. 448 (1980); Swann v. Charlotte-Mecklenburg Board of Education, 402 U.S. 1 (1971); Regents of the University of California v. Bakke, 438 U.S. 265 (1979).

74. Green v. School Board of New Kent County, 391 U.S. 430 (1968); Swann v. Charlotte-Mecklenburg Board of Education, 402 U.S. 1 (1971).

75. Milliken v. Bradley, 418 U.S. 717 (1974); Keyes v. School District No. 1 of Denver, 423 U.S. 189 (1973); Delaware State Board v. Evans, 446 U.S. 923 (1980); Armour v. Nix, 446 U.S. 930 (1980); Crawford v. Board of Education, 102 S. Ct. 3211 (1982).

76. Regents of the University of California v. Bakke, 438 U.S. 265 (1978).

77. Fullilove v. Klutznick, 448 U.S. 448 (1980); Local 28 of the Sheet Metal Workers v. EEOC, 106 S. Ct. 3019 (1986); U.S. v. Paradise, 107 S. Ct. 1053 (1987); Local 93, International Association of Firefighters v. Cleveland, 106 S. Ct. 3063 (1986); United Steelworkers v. Weber, 443 U.S. 197 (1979).

78. Wygant v. Jackson Board of Education, 106 S. Ct. 1842 (1984).

79. Johnson v. Santa Clara County Transportation Agency, 107 S. Ct. 1442 (1987).

80. Mueller v. Oregon, 208 U.S. 412 (1908).

81. Reed v. Reed, 404 U.S. 71 (1971).

82. Frontiero v. Richardson, 411 U.S. 677 (1973).

83. Stanton v. Stanton, 421 U.S. 7 (1975).

84. Craig v. Boren, 429 U.S. 191 (1976).

85. Dothard v. Rawlinson, 433 U.S. 321 (1977).

86. Cleveland Board of Education v. LaFleur, 414 U.S. 632 (1974).

87. Fortin v. Darlington Little League, 514 F. 2d 344 (1975).

88. Roberts v. United States Jaycees, 104 S. Ct. 3244 (1984); Board of Directors of Rotary International v. Rotary Club of Duarte, 95 L. E. 2d 474 (1987).

89. Arizona Governing Committee for Tax Deferred Annuity and Tax Deferred Compensation Plans v. Norris, 103 S. Ct. 3492 (1983).

90. E.E.O.C. v. Madison Community School District No. 12, 55 U.S.L.W. 2644 (7th Circuit, May 15, 1987).

91. Michael M. v. Superior Court, 450 U.S. 464 (1981).

92. Vorchheimer v. School District of Philadelphia, 430 U.S. 703 (1977).

93. Kahn v. Shevin, 416 U.S. 351 (1974).

94. Schlesinger v. Ballard, 419 U.S. 498 (1975).

95. Rostker v. Goldberg, 453 U.S. 57 (1981).

96. Roe v. Wade, 410 U.S. 113 (1973).

97. Harris v. McRae, 448 U.S. 297 (1980); Beal v. Doe, 432 U.S. 438 (1977); Maher v. Roe, 432 U.S. 464 (1977).

98. Planned Parenthood Federation of Central Missouri v. Danforth, 428 U.S. 52 (1976); Bellotti v. Baird, 443 U.S. 622 (1979); Akron v. Akron Center for Reproductive Health, 103 S. Ct. 2481 (1983).

99. Planned Parenthood v. Casey, 112 S. Ct. 2791 (1992).

PHOTO CREDITS

Glossary

NOTE: Several of the definitions in this glossary are taken from *The American Political Dictionary,* 5th ed. (New York: Holt, Rinehart and Winston, Inc., 1979). Reprinted by permission of the publisher.

Acquittal The formal determination by a court that the accused is not guilty of the offense as charged.

Activist An individual who is extensively and vigorously involved in political activity, either within or outside the party system.

Administrative oversight The attempt by Congress to ensure that the executive-branch bureaucracy is doing what Congress has told it to do and is doing it efficiently.

Affirmative action The requirement, imposed by law or administrative regulation, that an organization (business firm, government agency, labor union, school, or college) take positive steps to increase the number or proportion of women, blacks, or other minorities in its membership.

Agenda A list of specific items of business to be considered at a legislative session, conference, or meeting. *See also* Calendar

Amendment   (constitutional) Changes in, or additions to, a constitution. Proposed by a two-thirds vote of both houses of Congress or by a convention called by Congress at the request of two-thirds of the state legislatures. Ratified by approval of three-fourths of the states.

Amicus curiae A legal term meaning "friend of the court." As amicus curiae, individuals or groups not parties to a lawsuit may file a brief (or written argument) with a court.

Appellate jurisdiction Authority of a court to review decisions of a lower court. *See also* Jurisdiction

Apportionment The determination of the number of congressional representatives that each state shall elect. The Constitution requires that the apportionment be adjusted every ten years based upon the national census.

Appropriation A legislative grant of money to finance a government program. *See also* Authorization

Australian ballot A secret ballot, first used in the United States in 1888, that is prepared, distributed, and tabulated by government officials. Oral voting or voting on party-supplied ballots, often of different colors, was employed before the Australian ballot, thus allowing errors or fraud.

Authorization Legislative permission to begin or continue a government program. An authorization bill may grant permission to spend a certain sum of

427

money, but that money does not ordinarily become available unless it is also appropriated. *See also* Appropriation

Bicameral legislature A lawmaking body made up of two chambers, or parts. The United States Congress, composed of a House of Representatives and a Senate, is a bicameral legislature.

Bill of attainder A law that declares a person, without a trial, to be guilty of a crime. The state legislatures and Congress are forbidden to pass such acts by Article I, sections 9 and 10, of the Constitution.

Bill of Rights The first ten amendments to the United States Constitution. Contains a list of individual rights and liberties, such as freedom of speech, religion, and the press.

Block grants Grants of money from the federal government to states for programs in certain general areas rather than for specific kinds of programs. *See also* Grant-in-aid

Boycott An organized refusal to deal with a person, organization, or nation. Designed to bring about policy changes by exerting economic or social pressures. The term originated from the ostracizing of a land agent, Captain Boycott, by his neighbors during the Land League troubles in Ireland in 1880.

Bureaucracy A large, complex organization composed of appointed officials. The departments and agencies of the United States government make up its bureaucracy.

Cabinet An advisory group selected by the president to aid him in making decisions. Traditionally members include the vice president and the heads of the major departments.

Calendar A legislative schedule that contains the names of all bills to be considered before committees or in either legislative chamber. When a House committee reports out a bill, it is placed on one of five calendars: *Consent* (noncontroversial bills), *Discharge* (discharge petitions), *House* (nonfiscal public bills), *Private* (private bills), or *Union* (revenue and appropriations bills). In the Senate all bills go on a single calendar; nonlegislative matters, however, are placed on the *Executive* Calendar.

Calendar Wednesday A procedure of the House of Representatives whereby Wednesdays may be used to call the roll of the standing committees for the purpose of bringing up any of their bills for consideration from the House or Union Calendars.

Capitalism An economic system based on private ownership of the means of production and on a market economy. *See also* Laissez-faire

Caucus (legislative) A meeting of all the members of one party in a particular house of Congress for the purpose of selecting party leaders and deciding on legislative business. The Democrats use the term *caucus*; the Republicans use the term *conference*. *See also* Caucus (nominating)

Caucus (nominating) A closed meeting of party leaders to select party candidates. The term *to caucus* is also used to describe any private meeting of politicians seeking to reach agreement on a course of political action. The term was originally an Indian word meaning "counselor." *See also* Caucus (legislative)

Censorship Broadly, any government restrictions on speech or writing. More precisely, government restrictions on forms of expression before they are disseminated. Except in time of war or national emergency, prior restraint upon freedom of speech or the press is ordinarily forbidden.

Certiorari, writ of An order issued by a higher court to a lower court to send up the record of a case for review. Most cases reach the Supreme Court through the writ of certiorari, issued when at least four of the nine justices feel that the case should be reviewed. *Certiorari* is a Latin term that means "made more certain."

Civil case A court case involving a dispute between private persons or between the government and individuals over noncriminal matters. *See also* Criminal case

Civil liberties The freedoms of speech, press, religion, and petition, together with freedom from arbitrary arrest or prosecution.

Civil rights The rights of citizens to vote, to receive equal treatment before the law, and to share equally with other citizens the benefits of public facilities (such as schools).

Civil service Those persons employed by government (excluding the military) who are appointed or promoted under the merit system as distinguished from those appointed for political or policy reasons.

Class-action suit A case brought into court by a person on behalf, not only of himself or herself, but of all other persons in the country under similar circumstances. For example, in *Brown v. Board of Education of Topeka, Kansas,* the Court decided that not only Linda Brown but all others similarly situated had the right to attend an unsegregated school.

Clear-and-present-danger rule A test formulated by Justice Oliver Wendell Holmes in *Schenck* v. *United States* to measure the permissible bounds of free speech: "The question in every case is whether the words are used in circumstances and are of such a nature as to create a clear and present danger that they will bring about substantive evils that Congress has a right to prevent."

Clientele agency A federal agency having a clearly defined constituency that maintains a close relationship with the agency. Example: Veterans Administration.

Client politics The politics of policy-making in which some small group receives the benefits of the policy and the public at large bears the costs. Because those who benefit find it easier to organize, they will strongly influence the making of policy.

Closed primary The selection of a party's candidates in an election limited to registered party members. Prevents members of other parties from "crossing over" to influence the nomination of an opposing party's candidate. *See also* Open primary; Primary election

Closed rule An order, from the House Rules Committee, that sets a time limit on debate and forbids a particular bill from being amended on the legislative floor. *See also* Open rule; Rule

Closed shop A workplace that hires only union members. Outlawed by the Taft-Hartley Act of 1947. *See also* Union shop

Cloture A parliamentary technique (Rule 22 in the Senate) used by a legislative body to end or limit debate. Designed to prevent "talking a bill to death" by filibuster. *See also* Filibuster

Coalition A combination of two or more factions or parties for the purpose of achieving some political goal. An example is the coalition sometimes formed in Congress between southern Democrats and conservative Republicans.

Coattail effect The tendency of lesser-known or weaker candidates to profit in an election by the presence on the ticket of a more popular candidate. The phrase derives from a speech by President Lincoln in which he accused certain unpopular candidates of hiding under the coattails of a popular politician in their party.

Commerce clause A clause in Article I of the Constitution that grants to Congress the authority to regulate commerce with foreign nations and among the states.

Committee of the Whole The members of the House of Representatives organized into a committee for the consideration of bills and other matters. Most House business is transacted in the Committee of the Whole so that the formal requirements of its regular sessions, such as having a quorum of one-half the membership, can be avoided.

Committee on Committees Party committees in Congress that determine assignments to standing committees.

Common law Judge-made law that originated in England from decisions shaped by prevailing custom and precedents.

Concurrent powers Authority shared by both the state and national governments. Examples include the power to tax, to maintain courts, and to charter banks. *See also* Delegated powers; Implied powers

Concurrent resolution An expression of congressional opinion without the force of law that requires the approval of both the House and Senate but not of the president. Often used to set the time of final adjournment. *See also* Joint resolution; Resolution

Concurring opinion A written opinion of one or more judges that supports the conclusions of a majority of the court but offers different reasons for reaching those conclusions. *See also* Dissenting opinion

Confederation A political system in which states or regional governments retain ultimate authority except for those powers that they expressly delegate to a central government. The United States was a confederation from 1776 to 1787 under the Articles of Confederation. *See also* Federalism; Unitary state

Conference committee A special joint committee of the House and Senate that reconciles differences when a bill passes the two houses of Congress in different forms.

Conflict of interest A situation in which an official's public actions are or may be affected by his or her private interests.

Congressional Record The daily printed account of proceedings, debates, and statements in both the House and Senate. Members may edit and revise remarks made on the floor and have additional remarks printed in an appendix.

Consent Calendar The legislative schedule for the consideration of non-controversial items in the House of Representatives.

Constant dollars The value of something expressed in dollars adjusted for inflation, obtained by dividing the value in current dollars by a price index. Permits one to compare something purchased today with something purchased in a previous year, as if inflation had not occurred.

Constituent A resident of a legislator's district. The district itself is referred to as the legislator's constituency.

Constitution The set of fundamental laws and principles that prescribe the nature, functions, offices, and limits of a government. A constitution may be written (as in the United States) or unwritten (as in Great Britain).

Constitutional court A federal court established under the provisions of Article III of the Constitution, as distinguished from a "legislative court" created by Congress. The major constitutional courts are the district courts, courts of appeals, and Supreme Court. *See also* Legislative court

Containment policy A policy adopted in 1947 by the Truman administration to build "situations of strength" around the globe in order to contain Soviet power.

Cooperative federalism Arrangements permitting local, state, and national governments to share the responsibility for providing services to the citizens. Examples: grant-in-aid programs and interstate highway systems. *See also* Grant-in-aid

Criminal case A court case involving an alleged violation of criminal laws; that is, an offense against the state. There are three categories of criminal cases: felonies, misdemeanors, and petty offenses. *See also* Civil case

Critical election *See* Realigning election

De facto segregation Racial segregation in schools that occurs, not because of laws or administrative decisions, but as a result of patterns of residential settlement. To the extent that blacks and

whites live in separate neighborhoods, neighborhood schools will often be segregated "de facto." *See also* De jure segregation

Deficit financing What happens when the government spends more than it takes in from taxes; accomplished by borrowing or printing money.

De jure segregation Racial segregation that occurs because of laws or administrative decisions by public agencies. When state laws, for example, required blacks and whites to attend separate schools or sit in separate sections of a bus, "de jure" segregation resulted. It may also occur because of administrative decisions about the site of a new school building or the residential boundaries for neighborhood schools that make it impossible for blacks and whites to attend the same school. *See also* De facto segregation

Delegated powers Powers expressly granted to the national government by the Constitution. These powers, found in Article I, section 8, include the authority to provide for the common defense, to coin money, and to regulate commerce.

Depression A serious economic slump characterized by very high unemployment.

Direct primary *See* Primary election

Discharge Calendar The legislative schedule for bills brought out of committee by discharge petitions. *See also* Discharge petition

Discharge petition A device by which any member of the House, after a committee has had a bill for thirty days, may petition to have it brought to the floor. If a majority of the members agree, the bill is discharged from the committee. Designed to prevent a committee from killing a bill by holding it for too long. *See also* Discharge Calendar

Discount rate The interest rate that a bank pays when it borrows from a Federal Reserve Bank; one of the tools of monetary policy.

Dissenting opinion A written opinion of one or more judges that disagrees with the decision reached by a majority of the court. *See also* Concurring opinion

District court The federal court of "original jurisdiction," where most federal cases begin. It is the only federal court where trials are held, juries are used, and witnesses are called; there are ninety-four district courts in the United States and its territories.

Division vote A method of voting used in a legislative body in which members voting for or against the motion alternately rise and are counted by the presiding officer. Under this procedure a total vote count is secured, but it is difficult to know who voted for or against a measure. Often referred to as a "standing vote."

Double jeopardy The guarantee in the Fifth Amendment to the Constitution that one may not be tried twice for the same crime. For example, an individual declared not guilty of murdering a neighbor cannot be tried again for that murder. The person is not, however, exempt from being tried for the murder of another individual.

Due process of law Protection against arbitrary deprivation of life, liberty, or property as guaranteed in the Fifth and Fourteenth Amendments.

Elastic clause *See* Necessary-and-proper clause

Electoral college A group of persons called "electors," selected by the voters in each state, that officially elects the president and vice president. The number of electors in each state is equal to its number of representatives in both houses of Congress.

Elite Persons who possess a disproportionate share of some valued resource (money, power, beauty, intelligence, strength), *or* who exercise disproportionate influence on the making of public policy, or both.

Eminent domain The constitutional power to take private property, provided that it is taken for a public purpose and that just compensation is awarded.

Entitlement A law that requires the paying of monetary benefits to some person who meets the eligibility requirements established by the law; a binding obligation of the government (for example, Social Security payments).

Entrepreneurial politics The politics of policy-making in which some small group bears the costs of a policy that allegedly will benefit everyone. For the policy to be adopted, a "policy entrepreneur" must arise who will find ways of pulling together a legislative majority on behalf of unorganized interests over the objections of organized ones.

Enumerated power *See* Delegated powers

Equal-time provision A regulation that requires that all candidates for a public office be given equal access to the use of television and radio. Thus if a radio or television station provides time for one candidate or party, it must offer equal time to the opposition candidates or parties.

Establishment clause First Amendment clause that forbids the passage of any law "respecting an establishment of religion."

Executive agreement An international agreement made between the president and foreign nations that, unlike a treaty, does not require Senate consent (though it is usually made pursuant to some congressional authorization).

Executive Calendar The Senate schedule for all nonlegislative matters, such as treaties and appointments.

Executive privilege The claimed right of executive officials to refuse to appear before, or to withhold information from, the legislature or courts on the grounds that the information is confidential and would damage the national interest. For example, President Nixon refused, unsuccessfully, to surrender his subpoenaed White House tapes by claiming executive privilege.

Ex post facto law A law that makes criminal an act that was legal when it was committed, or that increases the penalty for a crime after it has been committed, or that changes the rules of evidence to make conviction easier; a retroactive criminal law. A Latin term meaning "after the fact." The state legislatures and Congress are forbidden to pass such laws by Article I, sections 9 and 10, of the Constitution.

Extradition Provision of Article IV of the Constitution that an individual charged in any state with treason, felony, or other crimes, who has fled from justice and is found in another state, shall be returned to the state having jurisdiction over the crime.

Favorite son A presidential nominee whose support is exclusively or largely from his or her home state's delegation. Usually a favorite son is not a serious candidate and such a nomination is merely a means of honoring him or her or of delaying commitment of the state delegation's vote.

Federalism (or federation) A political system in which ultimate authority is shared between a central government and state or regional governments. *See also* Confederation; Unitary state

Federalist papers A series of eighty-five essays written by Alexander Hamilton, James Madison, and John Jay (all using the name "Publius"), which were published in New York newspapers in 1787–1788 to convince New Yorkers to adopt the newly proposed Constitution.

Fee shifting Situation in which the losing party pays the legal costs of the winning party in a court case.

Filibuster An attempt to defeat a bill in the Senate by talking indefinitely, thus preventing the Senate from doing any other work. From the Spanish *filibustero,* which means a "freebooter," a military adventurer.

Fiscal policy Efforts to manage the economy by altering the level of government spending and taxation. Ordinarily the government will endeavor to run a surplus (take in more by taxation that it spends) when there is inflation and to run a deficit (spend more than it takes in by taxation) during a recession. *See also* Monetary policy

Fiscal year A yearly accounting period; for the federal government the fiscal year runs from October 1 to September 30. A fiscal year is designated by the year in which it ends (for example, "fiscal 1994" or "FY 1994").

Franking privilege A policy that enables members of Congress to send material through the mail free of charge by substituting their facsimile signature (frank) for postage. From the Latin *francus,* meaning "free."

Free rider An individual who benefits from the success of an organization or project without having helped to bring about that success. For example, a free rider benefits from, but does not participate in, an ecology group's clean-air efforts.

Full faith and credit   Provision of Article IV, section 1, of the Constitution, that requires states to honor the civil rulings of other states: "Full faith and credit shall be given in each state to the public acts, records, and judicial proceedings of every other state."

Gag rule   A legislative rule that limits the time available for debate or consideration of a measure.

General election   An election to fill public offices. *See also* Primary election

Gerrymander   The drawing of legislative-district boundaries in such a way as to give special advantage to one party or special-interest group. The term arose when a political artist in 1812 drew a picture of a sprawling Massachusetts district that resembled a salamander. An editor changed the title to "Gerrymander" because the governor at that time was Elbridge Gerry.

Grandfather clause   Originally a legal provision granting the franchise to persons otherwise ineligible to vote whose ancestors ("grandfathers") had voted prior to the passage of the Fifteenth Amendment. The clause was intended to keep blacks from voting. Refers today to any legal provision protecting persons having some right or benefit from changes in that right or benefit.

Grant-in-aid   Funds made available by Congress to state and local governments for expenditure in accordance with prescribed standards and conditions. Major functions financed through grants-in-aid include highways, airports, education, welfare, and health. *See also* Block grants

Gross national product (GNP)   The total value of all the goods and services produced by a nation during a specified period. The GNP is the most common measure of economic activity and growth.

Habeas corpus   A court order directing a police officer, sheriff, or warden who has a person in custody to bring the prisoner before a judge and show sufficient cause for his or her detention. Designed to prevent illegal arrests and unlawful imprisonment. A Latin term meaning "you shall have the body."

Hearing   A public or private session of a legislative body in which witnesses present testimony on matters under consideration by the committee. The objective is to gather information that will help determine whether new legislation should be passed or to build political support for a policy already preferred by the committee.

House Calendar   The legislative schedule in the House for the consideration of nonfiscal public bills.

Ideology   A comprehensive set of political, economic, and social views or ideas, concerned with the form and role of government. Thus we speak of a "liberal," "conservative," or "Marxist" ideology.

Impeachment   A formal accusation against a public official by the lower house of a legislative body. Impeachment is merely an accusation and not a conviction. Only one president, Andrew Johnson in 1868, was ever impeached. He was not, however, convicted, for the Senate failed by one vote to obtain the necessary two-thirds vote required for conviction.

Implied powers Authority possessed by the national government by inference from those powers expressly delegated to it in the Constitution. For example, the national government's power to draft persons into the armed forces is deduced from its delegated power to raise armies and navies. Based on the national government's constitutional authority to do all things "necessary and proper" to carry out its delegated powers. *See also* Concurrent, Delegated, and Reserved powers

Impoundment A refusal by the president to spend money appropriated by Congress, usually because he opposes the program being financed.

Incumbent The person currently in office.

Independent regulatory commission An agency, partially independent of the executive branch, designed to regulate some important aspect of the economy. Examples include the Federal Communications Commission, the Interstate Commerce Commission, and the Federal Reserve Board.

Indiana ballot *See* Party-column ballot

Inflation Generally rising prices for goods and services.

In forma pauperis A procedure whereby an indigent can file and be heard in court as a pauper, free of charge.

Initiative An electoral procedure whereby citizens can propose legislation or constitutional amendments and refer the decision to a popular vote by obtaining the required number of signatures on a petition.

Injunction A court order requiring some specified action or preventing some anticipated action.

Interest group An organization of persons that seeks to influence the making of public policy.

Interest-group politics The politics of policy-making in which one small group bears the costs of the policy and another small group receives the benefits. Each group has an incentive to organize and to press its interests.

Interstate compact An agreement between two or more states for the solution of common problems. According to Article I, section 10, of the Constitution, such compacts are forbidden without the consent of Congress. Compacts cover such issues as flood control and the management of ports.

Interstate rendition *See* Extradition

Item veto The power (exercised by governors in all but a few states) to veto sections or items of an appropriation bill while signing the remainder of the bill into law. The president does not have an item veto. *See also* Pocket veto; Veto

Jawboning Efforts by the president to persuade businesses and labor unions to avoid or minimize increases in prices and wages.

Jim Crow laws Laws or governmental practices designed to segregate blacks or otherwise keep them in a subordinate or politically powerless position.

Joint committee A legislative committee composed of members of both houses.

Joint resolution A formal expression of congressional opinion, in the form of a bill, that must be approved by both houses of Congress and by the president. Joint resolutions proposing a constitutional amendment need not be signed by the president. *See also* Concurrent resolution; Resolution

Judicial activism The tendency of courts, or of individual judges, to enlarge the scope of their authority or to decide cases on the basis of their beliefs as to what public policy ought to be. *See also* Judicial self-restraint

Judicial review The power of the courts to declare acts of the legislature and of the executive to be unconstitutional and hence null and void.

Judicial self-restraint The tendency of judges to decide cases in such a way as to defer to the enactments of the legislature except where such an enactment plainly contradicts the Constitution or is otherwise patently unreasonable. *See also* Judicial activism

Jurisdiction Authority vested in a court to hear and decide certain types of cases. The term literally means "to say the law."

Laissez-faire An economic doctrine emphasizing little or no government intervention in the economy; a "hands-off" policy, based on the assumption that if everyone competes in pursuit of his or her own self-interest, all will benefit. From a French phrase meaning "let do" or "let alone."

Lame duck A person, legislature, or administration that has been defeated in an election but still holds office for a period of time. For example, after Bill Clinton defeated George Bush, Bush was a lame-duck president from November until January, when Clinton was inaugurated.

Legislative court A court, not mentioned in the Constitution, set up by Congress for some specialized purpose. Legislative courts include the Court of Military Appeals and the Tax Court. *See also* Constitutional court

Legislative veto The rejection of a presidential or administrative-agency action by a vote of one or both houses of Congress without the consent of the president. In 1983 the Supreme Court declared the legislative veto to be unconstitutional.

Legitimacy The acceptance by citizens of a political system or governmental order as proper, lawful, and entitled to obedience.

Libel To defame or injure a person's reputation by a published writing; often punishable under criminal law.

Libertarianism The political doctrine or ideology holding that personal liberty is the supreme value that society ought to protect and that the powers of government should be kept to a minimum.

Line-item veto *See* Item veto

Lobbyist A person, usually acting as an agent for a group, who seeks to bring about the passage or defeat of legislative bills, to influence their content, or to influence administrative actions. The term originates from the practice of persons' meeting legislators in the lobbies of the Capitol to express their views or to influence officeholders.

Logrolling Trading votes on different bills; for example, a rural member of Congress supports a mass-transit bill and in return gets a vote for a farm bill from an urban representative. The term originates from the practice of backwoodsmen who would join together to roll large timber logs to an area for burning them. "You help me roll my logs, and I'll help you roll yours."

Machine A hierarchically organized, centrally led state or local party organization that rewards members with material benefits (patronage).

Majoritarian politics The politics of policy-making in which all or most citizens receive some benefits and pay the costs.

Majority leader (floor leader) The chief spokesperson and strategist of the majority party in a legislative body. *See also* Minority leader

Mandamus, writ of A court order issued to an individual, corporation, or public official to compel performance of a specified act of public, official, or ministerial duty. Thus a contract must be fulfilled as agreed upon or a writ of mandamus will be issued to order its enforcement. *Mandamus* is a Latin term meaning "we command."

Markup The act of revising a legislative proposal in a committee.

Marxism Economic, political, and philosophical theories, developed by Karl Marx, that maintain that economic factors determine the structure of society and its politics and that society is controlled by those who own the means of production.

Massachusetts ballot *See* Office-bloc ballot

Merit system The selection or promotion of government employees on the basis of demonstrated merit rather than on the basis of political patronage. *See also* Civil service

Military-industrial complex An alleged alliance among key military, governmental, and corporate decision makers involved in weapons procurement and military-support systems. The phrase was coined by Dwight D. Eisenhower.

Minority leader (floor leader) The chief spokesperson and strategist of the minority party in a legislative body. *See also* Majority leader

Monetary policy Government policy that alters the money supply and the availability of credit in order to manage the economy. For example, the Federal Reserve Board uses "tight-money" policies to fight inflation and "loose-money" policies to fight recession.

Multimember district An area represented in the legislature by two or more persons. *See also* Single-member district

National supremacy *See* Supremacy clause

Necessary-and-proper clause (elastic clause) The final paragraph of Article I, section 8, of the Constitution, which authorizes Congress to pass all laws "necessary and proper" to carry out the enumerated powers. Sometimes called the "elastic clause" because of the flexibility that it provides to Congress.

North Atlantic Treaty Organization (NATO) The alliance of certain North American and European nations, established under the North Atlantic Treaty of 1949, to create a single unified defense force to safeguard the security of the North Atlantic area.

Office-bloc ballot A ballot listing all candidates for a given office under the name of that office; also called a "Massachusetts" ballot. *See also* Party-column ballot

Oligarchy A system of government in which political power is exercised by a small group of people, usually self-selected.

Open primary An election that permits voters to choose on election day the party primary in which they wish to vote. They may vote for candidates of only one party. *See also* Closed primary; Primary election

Open rule An order, from the House Rules Committee, that permits a bill to be amended on the legislative floor. *See also* Closed rule; Rule

Opinion (of the court) A written statement giving the reasons for the decision in a particular case. When agreed to by a majority of the judges, it becomes the opinion of the court. *See also* Concurring opinion; Dissenting opinion

Original jurisdiction The authority of a court to hear a case at its inception. Generally courts of original jurisdiction are trial courts. Courts of appellate jurisdiction hear cases on appeal from courts of original jurisdiction. *See also* Appellate jurisdiction

Pardon The granting, by a president or governor, of a release from the punishment or legal consequences of a crime before or after conviction. An "absolute pardon" restores the individual to the position enjoyed prior to conviction; a "conditional pardon" requires that certain obligations be met before the pardon becomes effective.

Parliamentary government A political system in which the legislature selects the executive head of the government (usually called the prime minister).

Participatory democracy A system of governance in which all or most citizens participate directly by either holding office or helping to make policy. The town meeting, in which citizens vote on major issues, is an example of participatory democracy.

Party boss A political leader who controls a strong party organization or machine. Richard Daley of Chicago was a well-known party boss.

Party-column ballot A ballot listing all candidates of a given party together under the name of that party; also called an "Indiana" ballot. *See also* Office-bloc ballot

Party identification The feeling of individuals that a particular party is their party and deserves their support because it represents their point of view.

Party-line vote A vote in a legislature in which a majority of one party votes together against a majority of the other party or parties.

Party platform The principles, policies, and promises adopted by a party.

Patronage Material rewards — jobs, contracts, favors — given by political leaders and organizations to supporters and friends. *See also* Spoils system

Pentagon The headquarters of the Department of Defense, which includes the departments of the navy, army, and air force. The name comes from the shape of the five-sided building.

Plaintiff In civil law the person who initiates the lawsuit or brings an action to court.

Pluralism A concept describing a society in which all affected interests vie through the political process to achieve their objectives, as opposed to one in which one interest or group dominates the process to the exclusion of others.

Plurality A number of votes received by a candidate that is greater than that received by any other candidate, but less than a majority of the total vote.

Pocket veto A special veto power exercised when the legislative body adjourns, whereby bills not signed by the chief executive die after a specified time. The president puts the bill "in his pocket" and therefore kills it. *See also* Item veto; Veto

Political-action committee (PAC) A committee set up by and representing a corporation, labor union, or special-interest group that raises and spends campaign contributions on behalf of one or more candidates or causes.

Political culture A broadly shared way of thinking about how politics and governing ought to be carried out.

Political efficacy The belief of citizens that they can affect the workings of government or that government takes citizen opinions into account in making its decisions.

Political power The ability to affect in accordance with one's intentions the selection of persons who will hold government office or the decisions made by them.

Political question A doctrine enunciated by the Supreme Court holding that certain constitutional issues cannot be decided by the courts, but are to be decided by the executive or legislative branches. Examples: presidential power to recognize foreign governments and congressional power to determine whether constitutional amendments have been ratified within a reasonable time.

Poll tax A tax that must be paid before one can vote; it is now unconstitutional.

Pork barrel Legislation that gives tangible benefits (such as highways, dams, and post offices) to the constituents of a member of Congress. Ori-

gin: members of Congress, in their eagerness to get appropriations for local projects, behaved like hungry slaves in the South who rushed to the pork barrel to get their meager rations.

Preferred-position doctrine The judicial doctrine, not fully accepted, that the rights guaranteed by the First Amendment to the Constitution are more important than other parts of the Bill of Rights and thus occupy a "preferred position." *See also* Civil liberties.

President pro tempore The temporary presiding officer of the Senate in the absence of the vice president; usually the most senior senator. *Pro tempore* is a Latin term that means "for the time being," "temporarily."

Primary election (direct primary) An election prior to the general election in which voters select the candidates who will run on each party's ticket. Primaries are also used to choose convention delegates and party leaders, and may be open or closed. *See also* Closed primary; Open primary

Private bill A bill that deals only with specific private, personal, or local matters rather than with general legislative affairs. The main kinds include immigration and naturalization bills (referring to particular individuals) and personal-claim bills. *See also* Public bill

Private Calendar The legislative schedule for private bills to be considered by the House.

"Privileged" bills Bills that go directly to the floor of the House after being in committee, rather than through the Rules Committee.

Progressive tax Any tax in which the tax *rate* increases as the amount to be taxed increases. For example, those in high-income brackets might pay income taxes of 28 percent while those in lower brackets might pay only 15 percent. *See also* Regressive tax

Proletariat The working class as distinguished from the propertied class, the bourgeoisie, or the nobility.

Proportional representation A system of allocating seats in a legislature so that each political party is given a percentage of seats roughly equivalent to its percentage of the popular vote. For example, a minority party that receives 5 percent of the total vote will win 5 percent of the legislature seats. Not used in American elections for national offices.

Public bill A legislative bill that deals with matters of general concern. A bill involving defense expenditures is a public bill; a bill pertaining to an individual's becoming a naturalized citizen is not. *See also* Private bill

Quorum The minimum number of members of a legislative chamber who must be present in order to transact business. Fewer than a quorum may be present if no votes on legislation are to be taken. The Constitution specifies that "a majority of each house shall constitute a quorum to do business" (Article I, section 5). This means 218 representatives and 51 senators.

Ranking member The member of a legislative committee with the greatest seniority on that committee of any member of the same political party. The ranking member of the majority party ordinarily becomes chairman of the committee; the most senior member of the minority party is often called the "ranking member."

Realigning election An election in which a new lasting coalition of voters is formed that identifies with one or both of the major parties; also called a "critical election."

Reconciliation A concurrent resolution, passed by both houses of Congress, that reconciles the specific amounts to be spent in the coming fiscal year with the overall budget ceiling.

Referendum An electoral device available in half the states by which voters can approve or disapprove a state constitutional amendment or legislative act. The legislature "refers" its proposal to the electorate.

Regressive tax Any tax in which the burden falls relatively more heavily upon low-income persons than upon more affluent ones. Opposite of progressive tax, in which tax rates increase as ability to pay increases. *See also* Progressive tax

Representative democracy A principle of governance in which leaders and representatives acquire political power by means of a competitive struggle for the people's vote.

Reserved powers Powers that are not delegated to the national government nor prohibited to the states by the Constitution and that are reserved for the states under the Tenth Amendment to the Constitution. *See also* Delegated powers

Resolution A formal expression of the opinion or will of one house of Congress, adopted by vote and in the form of a bill, but unlike a bill in having no enforcement clause. *See also* Concurrent resolution; Joint resolution

Revenue sharing A law providing that the federal government will automatically return to the states and localities some fixed amount or share of federal tax revenues.

Rider A provision, unlikely to pass on its own merits, added to an important bill so that it will "ride" through the legislative process. A farm-price provision added to a defense bill is an example of a rider.

Roll-call vote (or record vote) A vote taken in a legislative body in which each member votes yes or no, either by answering a roll call or by electronic voting.

Rule The procedure, determined by the Rules Committee, by which a bill is considered on the House floor. For example a rule might set a time limit on debate or forbid the introduction of amendments. *See also* Closed rule; Open rule

Sampling A method by which the characteristics or responses of a population are estimated by choosing at random individuals from that population. A public-opinion poll is based upon a sample of a local or national population.

Sampling error The difference between the results of two surveys or samples. For example, if one random sample showed that 60 percent of all Americans like cats and another random sample taken at the same time showed that 65 percent do, the sampling error is 5 percent. *See also* Sampling

Secondary boycott A boycott by workers of a firm other than the one against which they are striking — for example, an organized refusal to purchase products from a competitor.

Sedition Actions that incite rebellion or discontent against a duly established government. Espionage, sabotage, or attempts to overthrow the government constitute sedition.

Select committee A legislative committee established for a limited time period and for a special purpose. An

example in the House is the Select Committee on Aging.

Senatorial courtesy The tradition of referring the names of candidates for appointive office to the senators of the states in which they reside and withdrawing any nominee deemed objectionable by a senator of the president's party.

Seniority A tradition widely observed in Congress of assigning positions of authority, especially committee chairmanships, on the basis of length of service in a legislative chamber or on the committee.

Separate-but-equal doctrine The doctrine, established in *Plessy* v. *Ferguson* (1896), in which the Supreme Court ruled that a state could provide "separate but equal" facilities for blacks.

Separation of powers A principle of American government whereby constitutional authority is distributed among three branches of government — the legislative, the executive, and the judicial.

Single-member district An electoral district from which a single legislator is chosen, usually by a plurality vote. This system of representation is used in the United States Congress and in most (but not all) state legislatures. *See also* Multimember district

Split-ticket voting Voting for candidates of different parties for various offices in the same election. For example, voting for a Republican for senator and a Democrat for president. *See also* Straight-ticket voting

Spoils system The award of government jobs to political supporters and friends. The term derives from Senator William Marcy's 1832 statement, "To the victors belong the spoils." *See also* Patronage

Standing A legal concept referring to who is entitled to bring a lawsuit to court. For example, an individual must ordinarily show personal harm in order to acquire standing and be heard in court.

Standing committee A permanently established legislative committee that considers and is responsible for legislation within a certain subject area. Examples: the House Ways and Means Committee, the Appropriations Committee, the Judiciary Committee.

Stare decisis The practice of basing judicial decisions on similar cases decided in the past. A Latin phrase meaning "let the decision stand."

States' rights Technically those rights which, under the Tenth Amendment to the Constitution, are reserved to the states. More broadly the term is used to connote opposition to increasing the national government's power at the expense of state power or authority.

Steering committee (or policy committee) A committee, composed of leaders of the same party in a legislative body, that coordinates the party's legislative program and attempts to secure its adoption.

Straight-ticket voting Voting for candidates who are all of the same party. For example, voting for Republican candidates for senator, representative, and president. *See also* Split-ticket voting

Subpoena An order of a court, grand jury, or any authorized administrative agency or congressional committee that commands a witness to appear and give testimony. A Latin term meaning "under penalty."

Subsidy A payment or benefit, supplied by the government to an individual or corporation, for which there is no charge. A subsidy may take the form of a cash grant, a tax deduction, or the provision of a loan at below-market interest rates.

Supremacy clause A clause in Article VI of the Constitution providing that the Constitution, laws passed by the national government under its constitutional powers, and all treaties are the supreme law of the land.

Symbolic speech The claim that an otherwise illegal act, such as burning a draft card, is constitutionally protected if the act is meant to convey a political message.

Teller vote A vote taken in a legislative body in which members are counted as they file past designated tellers, who count first those who are in favor of an action and then those who are opposed.

Third party Any political party other than the two major parties; a minor party. Examples: Socialist party, Bull Moose party, Libertarian party.

Ticket splitting *See* Split-ticket voting

Unicameral legislature A legislature with only one legislative body, as contrasted with a two-house legislature, such as that of the United States Congress. Nebraska has the only unicameral state legislature. *See also* Bicameral legislature

Union Calendar (Calendar of the Whole House on the State of the Union) The legislative schedule in the House for all revenue and appropriations bills.

Union shop An establishment that hires nonunion employees on the condition that they join the union within a given number of days. *See also* Closed shop

Unitary state A centralized government in which local or state governments exercise only those powers given to them by the central government. It differs from a federal system (such as that of the United States), in which power is constitutionally divided between the central government and state governments.

Unit rule A rule once applicable in Democratic national conventions providing that a state delegation may cast its total vote in a block for the presidential candidate preferred by a majority of that state's delegation.

Veto The power of a president, governor, or mayor to kill a piece of legislation by refusing to sign the act. *Veto* is a Latin term meaning "I forbid."

Whip An assistant to the majority or minority party leader whose duties include organizing the party members and inducing them to vote with the leadership. The term originates from the English fox-hunting term *whipper:* the one who keeps the hounds from wandering by whipping them into their line of chase.

White primary A primary election in which blacks and other nonwhites were systematically excluded from voting. In *Smith* v. *Allwright* (1944) the Supreme Court ruled that the white primary violated the Fifteenth Amendment.

Index

Italic page numbers indicate boxes, illustrations, or tables.